Intercultural Communication in Japan

Japan is heterogeneous and culturally diverse, both historically through ancient waves of immigration and in recent years due to its foreign relations and internationalization. However, Japan has socially, culturally, politically, and intellectually constructed a distinct and homogeneous identity. More recently, this identity construction has been rightfully questioned and challenged by Japan's culturally diverse groups.

This book explores the discursive systems of cultural identities that regenerate the illusion of Japan as a homogeneous nation. Contributors from a variety of disciplines and methodological approaches investigate the ways in which Japan's homogenizing discourses are challenged and modified by counter-homogeneous message systems. They examine the discursive push-and-pull between homogenizing and heterogenizing vectors, found in domestic and transnational contexts and mobilized by various identity politics, such as gender, sexuality, ethnicity, foreign status, nationality, multiculturalism, and internationalization. After offering a careful and critical analysis, the book calls for a complicating of Japan's homogenizing discourses in nuanced and contextual ways, with an explicit goal of working towards a culturally diverse Japan.

Taking a critical intercultural communication perspective, this book will be of interest to students and scholars of Japanese Studies, Japanese Culture and Japanese Society.

Satoshi Toyosaki is an associate professor in the Department of Communication Studies at Southern Illinois University, Carbondale, USA.

Shinsuke Eguchi is an assistant professor of intercultural communication in the Department of Communication and Journalism at the University of New Mexico, USA.

Routledge Contemporary Japan Series

53 **Heritage Conservation and Japan's Cultural Diplomacy**
Heritage, National Identity and National Interest
Natsuko Akagawa

54 **Religion and Psychotherapy in Modern Japan**
Edited by Christopher Harding, Iwata Fumiaki and Yoshinaga Shin'ichi

55 **Party Politics in Japan**
Political Chaos and Stalemate in the 21st Century
Edited by Ronald J. Hrebenar and Akira Nakamura

56 **Career Women in Contemporary Japan**
Pursuing Identities, Fashioning Lives
Anne Stefanie Aronsson

57 **Visions of Precarity in Japanese Popular Culture and Literature**
Edited by Kristina Iwata-Weickgenannt and Roman Rosenbaum

58 **Decision-Making Reform in Japan**
The DPJ's Failed Attempt at a Politician-led Government
Karol Zakowski

59 **Examining Japan's Lost Decades**
Edited by Yoichi Funabashi and Barak Kushner

60 **Japanese Women in Science and Engineering**
History and Policy Change
Naonori Kodate and Kashiko Kodate

61 **Japan's Border Issues**
Pitfalls and Prospects
Akihiro Iwashita

62 **Japan, Russia and Territorial Dispute**
The Northern Delusion
James D.J. Brown

63 **Fukushima and the Arts in Japan**
Negotiating Disaster
Edited by Barbara Geilhorn and Kristina Iwata-Weickgenannt

64 **Social Inequality in Post-Growth Japan**
Transformation during Economic and Demographic Stagnation
Edited by David Chiavacci and Carola Hommerich

65 **The End of Cool Japan**
Ethical, Legal, and Cultural Challenges to Japanese Popular Culture
Edited by Mark McLelland

66 **Regional Administration in Japan**
Departure from Uniformity
Shunsuke Kimura

67 **Japanese Media at the Beginning of the 21st Century**
Consuming the Past
Katsuyuki Hidaka

68 **Intercultural Communication in Japan**
Theorizing Homogenizing Discourse
Edited by Satoshi Toyosaki and Shinsuke Eguchi

Intercultural Communication in Japan
Theorizing Homogenizing Discourse

Edited by Satoshi Toyosaki and
Shinsuke Eguchi

LONDON AND NEW YORK

First published 2017
by Routledge
2 Park Square, Milton Park, Abingdon, Oxon OX14 4RN

and by Routledge
711 Third Avenue, New York, NY 10017

Routledge is an imprint of the Taylor & Francis Group, an informa business

© 2017 selection and editorial matter, Satoshi Toyosaki and Shinsuke
Eguchi; individual chapters, the contributors

The right of the editors to be identified as the authors of the editorial
matter, and of the authors for their individual chapters, has been asserted
in accordance with sections 77 and 78 of the Copyright, Designs and
Patents Act 1988.

All rights reserved. No part of this book may be reprinted or reproduced or
utilized in any form or by any electronic, mechanical, or other means, now
known or hereafter invented, including photocopying and recording, or in
any information storage or retrieval system, without permission in writing
from the publishers.

Trademark notice: Product or corporate names may be trademarks or
registered trademarks, and are used only for identification and explanation
without intent to infringe.

British Library Cataloguing in Publication Data
A catalogue record for this book is available from the British Library

Library of Congress Cataloging in Publication Data
Names: Toyosaki, Satoshi, editor. | Eguchi, Shinsuke, editor.
Title: Intercultural communication in Japan : theorizing homogenizing
discourse / edited by Satoshi Toyosaki and Shinsuke Eguchi.
Description: Abingdon, Oxon ; New York, NY : Routledge, 2017. |
Series: Routledge contemporary japan series ; 68 | Includes bibliographical
references and index.
Identifiers: LCCN 2016043187 | ISBN 9781138699373 (hardback) |
ISBN 9781315516936 (ebook)
Subjects: LCSH: Mass media–Social aspects–Japan. | Intercultural
communication–Japan. | Multiculturalism–Japan. | National characteristics,
Japanese. | Japan–Civilization–21st century.
Classification: LCC HN730.Z9 M3337 2017 | DDC 302.230952–dc23
LC record available at https://lccn.loc.gov/2016043187

ISBN: 978-1-138-69937-3 (hbk)
ISBN: 978-1-315-51693-6 (ebk)

Typeset in Times New Roman
by Wearset Ltd, Boldon, Tyne and Wear

Contents

Notes on contributors	viii
Acknowledgments	xii

Introduction: intercultural communication in Japan:
theorizing homogenized discourse 1
SATOSHI TOYOSAKI AND SHINSUKE EGUCHI

PART I
Gender, sexuality, and the body 25

1 **The affective politics of the feminine: an interpassive**
analysis of Japanese female comedians 27
SACHI SEKIMOTO AND YUSAKU YAJIMA

2 **"It's a wonderful single life": constructions and**
representations of female singleness in Japan's
contemporary *josei dorama* 41
EMI KANEMOTO AND KRISTIE COLLINS

3 **The shifting gender landscape of Japanese society** 55
JUSTIN CHARLEBOIS

PART II
Performance and queerness 71

4 **Japanese male-queer femininity: an autoethnographic**
reflection on *Matsuko Deluxe* **as an** *onē-kei* **talent** 73
SHINSUKE EGUCHI

vi *Contents*

5 Bleach in color: unpacking gendered, queered, and raced performances in anime   86

RESLIE CORTÉS

PART III
Inclusiveness and Otherness   99

6 The discursive pushes and pulls of J-pop and K-pop in Taiwan: cultural homogenization and identity co-optation   101

HSUN-YU (SHARON) CHUANG

7 "Hating Korea" (*kenkan*) in postcolonial Japan   114

ANDRE HAAG

8 Japan's internationalization: dialectics of Orientalism and hybridism   129

SATOSHI TOYOSAKI AND ERIC FORBUSH

PART IV
Media and framing   143

9 Ishihara Shintaro's manga moral panic: the homogenizing rhetoric of Japanese nationalism   145

LUCY J. MILLER

10 mixi and an imagined boundary of Japan   159

RYUTA KOMAKI

PART V
Environment and movement   175

11 Historicization of cherry blossoms: a study of Japan's homogenizing discourses   177

TAKUYA SAKURAI

12 Alternative vs. conventional: dialectic relations of the organic agriculture discourse   190

SAKI ICHIHARA FOMSGAARD

Contents vii

PART VI
Education and internationalization 205

13 **A dialectic between nationalism and multiculturalism: an analysis of the internationalization discourse in Japan** 207
AKO INUZUKA

14 **"I never wanted to be famous": pushes and pulls of Whiteness through the eyes of foreign English language teachers in Japan** 224
NATHANIEL SIMMONS AND YEA-WEN CHEN

Index 238

Contributors

Editors

Satoshi Toyosaki (Ph.D., Southern Illinois University, Carbondale) is an associate professor in the Department of Communication Studies at Southern Illinois University, Carbondale. He teaches and researches international and intercultural communication, relational communication, communication pedagogy, and qualitative/critical methodologies. His essays can be found in *Journal of International and Intercultural Communication, Journal of Intercultural Communication Research, Cultural Studies↔Critical Methodologies, Journal of Multicultural Discourses, International Review of Qualitative Research*, and *Qualitative Communication Research* (now known as *Departures in Critical Qualitative Research*).

Shinsuke Eguchi (Ph.D., Howard University) is an assistant professor of intercultural communication in the Department of Communication and Journalism at the University of New Mexico (UNM). Prior to joining UNM in 2012, Dr. Eguchi was a post-doctoral fellow on transnationalism, diaspora, and migration in the communication studies department at University of Denver. His research interests focus on international and intercultural communication, queer (of color) studies, critical race studies, Asian/American studies, and performance studies. His work has appeared for publication in various journals such as *Communication Theory, Communication, Culture, & Critique, Text and Performance Quarterly, Journal of International and Intercultural Communication, Journal of Communication Inquiry*, and *Howard Journal of Communication*.

Authors

Justin Charlebois (Ph.D., Lancaster University) is an associate professor at the University of Tsukuba in Tsukuba, Japan. His areas of scholarly interest include discourse analysis, gender, and intercultural communication. He is the author of *Japanese Femininities* and a number of articles and book chapters. Charlebois is a native of upstate New York but has resided in Japan for several years.

Contributors ix

Yea-Wen Chen (Ph.D., University of New Mexico) is an assistant professor in the School of Communication at San Diego State University. She is a certified diversity educator, a trained mediator, and a teacher–scholar of intercultural communication and praxis. Taken as a whole, her scholarship aims to raise awareness of the particular ways in which communication—including silence—about cultural identities impacts diversity, inclusion, and social justice across varying contexts. Dr. Chen has published over 35 works, including an edited book, book chapters, and peer-reviewed articles in national and international journals such as *Communication Monographs, Journal of International and Intercultural Communication,* and *International Journal of Diversity in Organizations, Communities, and Nations: Annual Review.*

Hsun-Yu (Sharon) Chuang (M.A., Southern Illinois University, Carbondale) is a Ph.D. candidate in the Department of Communication Studies (formerly Speech Communication) at Southern Illinois University, Carbondale (SIUC). She joined the Department of Communication at Denison University as Assistant Professor in fall 2016. Her research and teaching interests include (critical) intercultural/international communication, interpersonal communication, and topics that relate to culture, identity, language, pedagogy, East Asian Studies, and Taiwan Studies. Her most recent and main research project is her doctoral dissertation, titled "Interpretive and Critical Examinations of English Education in Taiwan: Implications of Identity Management Theory." Her scholarly works also appear in *The International Journal of Qualitative Methods* (2015) and *Kaleidoscope: A Graduate Journal of Qualitative Communication Research* (co-authored, 2014).

Kristie Collins (Ph.D., University of Tsukuba) is an associate professor in the Faculty of Humanities and Social Sciences at the University of Tsukuba, Japan. Kristie's research draws from media and gender studies, life course approaches, and narrative analysis. In particular, she studies media representations and lived experiences of female singleness. Her first monograph, *The Marginalized Majority: Media Representation and Lived Experiences of Single Women* (Bern: Peter Lang), was published in 2013.

Reslie Cortés (M.A., University of New Mexico) is a Ph.D. student at the Hugh Downs School of Human Communication at Arizona State University. Her research focuses on intersectional identity performances and representations in popular media.

Saki Ichihara Fomsgaard (Ph.D., Aalborg University) has been a lecturer in Asian studies and comparative politics in the Department of Culture and Global Studies at Aalborg University and in the Department of Culture and Society at Aarhus University. Until 2014 Dr. Fomsgaard was a Ph.D. fellow at Aalborg University's Doctoral Programme in Culture and Global Studies. She is a member of a research unit (Global Development Studies) at Aalborg University, having conducted various research projects such as those focusing

x *Contributors*

on strategies on climate change in South Asia and post-Fukushima energy and environmental policy-making in Japan. Her field of interest is environmental politics, collective action/social movement studies, and sustainable food systems. Since November 2016 she has been affiliated to an enterprise for project management in Tokyo as an analyst and developer for educational programs.

Eric Forbush (B.A., Northeastern University) is a doctoral student at the Annenberg School for Communication at the University of Pennsylvania. He specializes in intercultural communication and ethnicity and race in communication. In particular, he uses a computational lens to study issues related to cross-cultural adaptation, segregation, and team composition/performance. His work has an interdisciplinary focus, utilizing a range of analytical techniques developed across a variety of backgrounds such as computer science, communication, engineering, sociology, and psychology.

Andre Haag (Ph.D., Stanford University) is Assistant Professor of Japanese literature and culture in the Department of East Asian Languages and Literatures at the University of Hawaii in Mānoa. Haag's research explores the interplay between nationalism, colonialism, and violence in the language and culture of the Japanese colonial empire. His most recent project investigates how Japanese fear of Korean crime and "terrorism" inflected colonial vocabularies, representations, and narratives of imperial identities in the decades following the Korean annexation.

Ako Inuzuka (Ph.D., Bowling Green State University) is an associate professor in the Department of Communication at the University of Pittsburgh in Johnstown. Her areas of research include international and intercultural communication and collective memory studies. Her recent essays have been published in *Howard Journal of Communications, Journal of International Communication, Communication Quarterly*, and *Journal of Multicultural Discourses*.

Emi Kanemoto (M.A., Texas State University) is a doctoral student in the School of Media and Communication at Bowling Green State University. She is currently serving as secretary for Japan–US Communication Association which is affiliated to the National Communication Association. Her research interests center on Japanese political rhetoric and intercultural aspects of Japanese popular culture. Her most recent research examines the role of peace discourse in post-WWII Japan.

Ryuta Komaki (Ph.D., University of Illinois at Urbana-Champaign) is currently a Japanese and Korean studies librarian at Washington University in St. Louis. His dissertation research looked at the use of digital media, mobile media, and traditional media by Japanese–Brazilian return migrants in Japan. His ongoing research focuses on media, literature, and reading and writing in the early and contemporary Japanese diaspora. Ryuta has presented papers at annual meetings of the International Communication Association, National

Communication Association, Association for Asian Studies, Association for Asian American Studies, and Society for Social Studies of Science. He has also co-authored (and is co-authoring) book chapters on game studies and librarianship.

Lucy J. Miller (Ph.D., Texas A&M University) is a lecturer in the Department of Communication at Texas A&M University. She is co-editor with Amanda R. Martinez of *Gender in a Transitional Era: Changes and Challenges* (Lanham, MD: Lexington Books, 2015). Her work also appears in *Transgender Communication Studies: Histories, Trends, and Trajectories* edited by Leland G. Spencer and Jamie C. Capuzza (Lanham, MD: Lexington Books, 2015).

Takuya Sakurai (Ph.D., University of Oklahoma) is an assistant professor in the Department of English at Tokyo Denki University. His research interests are intercultural communication, language and social interaction, ethnography of communication, and religious communication. His work has appeared in *Journal of Communication and Religion, Intercultural Communication Studies*, and *Waseda Review*.

Sachi Sekimoto (Ph.D., University of New Mexico) is an associate professor in the Department of Communication Studies at Minnesota State University, Mankato. Her research interests focus on the sensory and affective politics of culture, identity, language, and embodiment. She is a co-editor of *Globalizing Intercultural Communication: A Reader* (Thousand Oaks, CA: Sage, 2016). Her work has appeared in *Journal of International and Intercultural Communication, Communication Quarterly*, and *Departures in Critical Qualitative Research*.

Nathaniel Simmons (Ph.D., Ohio University) is a faculty member and communication course mentor within the General Education Department at Western Governors University. He specializes in critical intercultural communication, critical pedagogy, and health communication. In particular, he studies privacy negotiations and intercultural communication pedagogy from an interpretive–critical perspective using qualitative methodology. His recent publications (single- and co-authored) can be found in *Intercultural Communication Studies, Health Communication, Sexuality & Culture*, and *Journal of International and Intercultural Communication*.

Yusaku Yajima (M.A., Minnesota State University, Mankato) is a graduate assistant and Ph.D. student in the Department of Communication Studies at Southern Illinois University, Carbondale. He teaches introduction to communication studies and intercultural communication. His research interests are critical (communication) pedagogy, critical intercultural communication, phenomenology, and post-colonialism.

Acknowledgments

This edited collection is by a group of scholars from various disciplines who engage in innovative research centralizing issues of communication and discourse of and about Japan's homogenization and cultural politics. We wish to thank the chapter contributors for their essays and their continuous labor promoting cultural diversity and internationalization in and for Japan. Their rigorous and intellectual work made this collection possible and valuable. We could not have completed this collection without their hard and collaborative work. We would also like to thank the blind reviewers whose comments and suggestions have enriched this project. Finally, we thank Rebecca Lawrence at Routledge for her continuous support throughout the process. We would like to extend our appreciation to Routledge's editing and production teams.

Introduction

Intercultural communication in Japan: theorizing homogenized discourse

Satoshi Toyosaki and Shinsuke Eguchi

Japan is heterogeneous. This has been the underlying theme of recent and emerging research on Japanese society, culture, and identity (see Befu, 2006; Denoon, Hudson, McCormack, & Morris-Suzuki, 2001; Eguchi, 2015; Lee, Murphy-Shigematsu, & Befu, 2006; McCormack, 2001; Macdonald & Maher, 1995; Okano & Tsuchiya, 1999; Suganuma, 2012). Japan originally became populated through "several ancient and distinct waves of immigration" from South-East Asia and South China to North-East Asia through the Korean peninsula (McCormack, 2001, p. 4). However, through its long histories and intellectual, political, cultural, and social activities, Japan as a concept has been constructed as homogenous; in some cases, scholars, politicians, and other stakeholders throughout Japan's histories have insisted on its distinct and homogeneous identity. Such an identity construction has been rightfully questioned and challenged by Japan's culturally diverse groups, for example, *Okinawans*, the *Ainu* people, *Burakumin, zainichi*-Koreans, women, LGBTQ (lesbian-gay-bisexual-transgender-queer) people, and foreign laborers. Throughout its history, Japan has, indeed, been culturally heterogeneous. Yet, "the dominant theme underlying most of the discourse is familiar: 'Japan' is a homogeneous entity, sharply-defined and yet-to-be-understood" (Macdonald & Maher, 1995, p. 3).

In this edited collection, chapter authors from various disciplines and through various methodological approaches investigate mysterious and homogenizing discursive systems of cultural identities in and about Japan. Japan's homogeneities have been emerging out of, and have come to exist from, the complex long histories of their makings. Such makings are moving into the future while simultaneously being challenged by Japan's rapidly shifting demographics and political/global landscapings. Japan's homogenizing discourses are regenerative between discursive pushes and pulls of their regenerative and deconstructive forces. Always being in the liminal and postmodern space, Japan is made and remade dialectically and conceptually. We find powerful opportunities in this liminal and postmodern space—the moments of and potentialities for cultural shifting and future-makings to procure Japan's renewed sense of national identity, internationalization, cultural diversity, and global presence in today's world.

Homogeneity

In scholarly circles, homogeneity, in general, has a bad reputation, often being viewed as the opposite of cultural diversity. In this section, we critically examine such a notion of homogeneity. Put simply, homogeneity is understood as "similarity" and heterogeneity as "difference(s) in a group, culture, or population" (Martin & Nakayama, 2010, p. 8). Similarity and difference as the opposites of each other—our epistemological habit—renders the image of the static dichotomy between homogeneity and heterogeneity. Martin and Nakayama issue a warning about the static and dichotomous theorization of homogeneity. It is not productive to understand homogeneity as simply oppositional to heterogeneity or cultural diversity (see Macdonald & Maher, 1995). Here, we characterize a more complex and nuanced theorization of homogeneity, which we hope will help us understand and possibly critique the ways in which homogeneity works.

First, homogeneity is constantly renewed and changing. Martin and Nakayama (2010) suggest the plasticity of culture by discouraging us from understanding it in terms of the dichotomy between homogeneity and heterogeneity: "Cultures can change over time and become more or less homogeneous" (p. 8). Thus, homogeneity and heterogeneity are not timeless, dichotomous monoliths: they are a degree toward which one may describe a group, culture, or population to be oriented toward a singular mode of existing or thinking.

Second, homogeneity and heterogeneity are relational co-constructs. Take whiteness as an example. Whiteness is a historically informed homogenizing effect on racial construction, a central ideology and a force that has constructed and perpetuated the hierarchy of difference (Nakayama & Krizek, 1995). On this point, Yep (2007) explains that whiteness is a relational construct—"parasitic on 'blackness'" (West in Yep, p. 89) or non-whiteness. Suspending in the relational liminality, homogeneity—the centering force of power politics derived from cultural similarity—"simultaneously is stable (creating shared, relatively fixed, discourse) and unstable (continually articulating the possibilities for its own transformation)" (Mumby, 1997, p. 16). Homogeneity and heterogeneity are relational co-constructs, functioning as centrifugal and centripetal discursive forces (Bakhtin, 1981; Holquist, 1981) while constructing the collective identity of a group, a culture, or a population. Ontologically speaking, homogeneity does not exist as an objective and static reality. Pure homogeneity and heterogeneity are both, in an ontological sense, artificial, relational, and discursive constructs that translate and materialize power politics among people whose selfhoods discursively come to exist somewhere on the spectrum of the power relation between homogeneous and heterogeneous cultural "orientations." When the spectrum becomes institutionalized, the hierarchy of difference comes to exist with real materialistic consequences (both advantages and disadvantages) to people who are stratified by it.

Third, homogeneity and heterogeneity are, thus, to be studied dialectically. By focusing on understanding culture through the lens of dialectics, Martin and Nakayama (2010) instruct us that "emphasizing only differences can lead to stereotyping and prejudice...; emphasizing only similarities can lead us to

Introduction   3

ignore the important cultural variations that exist" (p. 74). We are both similar to and different from others; we are neither homogeneous nor heterogeneous. We are always both homogenizing and heterogenizing ourselves and others. Thus, studying homogeneity "and" heterogeneity requires self-reflexive navigation of our own educational training and Western epistemological habits. Studying homogenizing discourses in a complex and nuanced manner involves complicating the ways in which we researchers approach the notion of homogeneity.

Fourth, homogeneity is a historically informed series of performative accomplishments. Butler's (1990) phenomenological theory of acts explains that gender, for example, "is an identity tenuously constituted in time—an identity instituted through a styled repetition of acts" (p. 270). Warren extends Butler's theory of gender as follows:

> [It] understands the subject to be essentially unstable, never natural and thus constructed through embodied actions. Performativity denies ... the stability of identity, moving toward a notion of repetition as a way of understanding that those markers used to describe one's identity ... get constructed through the continual performance of those markers.
>
> (Warren, 2001, p. 95)

Homogeneity is a historical stream of discursive institutionalizations of cultural markers and performative acts; it is of our own doing for/to ourselves and to others. The ways in which we use, mark, and perform homogeneity in a culturally blind and power-driven manner are often malicious; we instrumentalize and mobilize homogeneity as a rhetorical strategy (see Nakayama & Krizek, 1995), as a mode of dominating, silencing, and marginalizing *Others*.

Similarly, we need homogeneous orientations to make sense of our own selfhoods, to exist intersubjectively (Schrag, 1986), and to narrate them into existence. Thus, the fifth characteristic of complex and nuanced theorization is the constructive nature of homogenous orientations for our identity development. What does it mean to be, for example, Japanese? Our identities are communicative and discursive ontologies (Anderson & Baym, 2004) that are predicated on namings and markings of similarities and differences. Furthermore, the discursive materiality of homogeneity is, ironically, a necessary condition against which cultural diversity can be imagined, promoted, and labored. Cultural diversity labor is probable within the dialectics betwixt and between similarities and differences (Martin & Nakayama, 1999, 2010). We argue that homogeneity as a logic of unquestioned standards and a form of domination ought to be examined, critiqued, and possibly remedied; however, homogeneity is a mundane part of our sense-making and the narrating of our identities.

Overall, homogeneity is not simply bad all the time; however, a simplistic theorization of homogeneity as a simple opposite of heterogeneity may lead to a simple critique. This anthology meaningfully makes more complex and nuances homogeneity. We call for careful examination of homogeneity as we locate the embodied carefulness in our analyses within a "heuristically rich paradox" of

4   *S. Toyosaki and S. Eguchi*

"both/and, yes/but, instead of either/or" (Conquergood, 1985, p. 9). Chapter contributors in this anthology engage in complex and nuanced analyses of the push-and-pull between homogenizing and heterogenizing discursive forces to meaningfully complicate "Japan" and "Japanese" as homogenizing conceptual categories.

Methodological approaches: critical intercultural communication

Critical intercultural communication is a recently recognized and expanded sub-discipline of intercultural communication studies (see Halualani, Mendoza, & Drzewiecka, 2009; Martin & Nakayama, 2010; Nakayama & Halualani, 2010), although there have always been scholars (e.g., Collier, Hegde, Lee, Nakayama, & Yep, 2001; Drzewiecka & Halualani, 2002; Lee, Chung, Wang, & Hertel, 1995; Moon, 1996; Ono, 1998; Shome & Hegde, 2002). Adhering to the tenets of critical theory, critical intercultural communication research, instead of aiming at the predictability of human interaction while understanding "culture" as a variable, engages a complex and context-oriented interrogation of power that (re)produces and is (re)produced through our intercultural encounters. "Critical theory suggests that rigorous and insightful research is only made possible by its being grounded in the realities of the social world, including the power relationships, the distortions and the pathologies that affect how we live" (McArthur, 2013, p. 10). Hence, our focus is located on "communication" as constitutive of social realities. We understand communication as a primary means of rearticulation to explore how meanings, practices, structures, and discourses are developed and negotiated.

A historical analysis: Japan's homogeneity and cultural diversity

Examining literature pertaining to Japan's cultural diversity and internationalization, we can discern four general phases marked by historical events while hinting at the fifth phase later in this chapter. Our discernment relies on Sugita's three developmental phases of Japan's multiculturalism (cited in Graburn & Ertl, 2008) while diverging slightly from it. In this chapter, we propose five stages to capturing and outlining key movements and characteristics in modern Japan's multiculturalism: (1) pre-1868 (pre-*Meiji*); (2) from 1868 to the end of WWII; (3) post-WWII to around 1980; (4) "New Japan" (Graburn, Ertl, & Tierney, 2008); and (5) post-New Japan. Although we recognize that these phases are not entirely exclusive, we argue that they are instructive in understanding how Japan has constructed, characterized, treated, and/or responded to its cultural diversity. We use "cultural diversity" in an inclusive manner to mean multiculturalism, internationalization, heterogenizing movements, and other cultural phenomena that insist upon and/or celebrate cultural differences and visibilities among Japanese people, residents, and sojourners in Japan.

Introduction 5

Pre-1868 (pre-Meiji)

Throughout most of the *Edo* period (1603–1868), Japan was under the *Sakoku* policy (1663–1853). *Sakoku* literally means "chained nation." Under this policy, Japan outlawed most foreign contacts (Donahue, 1998); however, it was not a complete outlaw. *Edo* authorities placed strict restrictions and practiced control on international trade and exchange (McCormack, 2001). That is, Japan kept its international relations with certain nations but at a minimum. Later in the *Edo* period, after 1793, "a true *sakoku* policy … emerged" (McCormack, 2001, p. 9). This very minimum extent of international relations gave Japan an opportunity to develop the cultural borrowing that took place prior to and sporadically during *sakoku* into its culturally distinctive customs, which rationalized the authorities' decision to stay closed and restrict even more its international relations with other nations (Donahue, 1998). In the eighteenth century with Japan's *sakoku* in the background, *kokugaku* scholarship ["National Learning"] gained impetus and emphasized "a pure and untrimmed (that is, non-Chinese) Japanese essence" (McCormack, 2001, p. 1). The *kokugaku* movement built the scholarly foundation that portrayed the view that "Japan [was] a homogeneous 'natural' community" (McCormack, 2001, p. 1).

The historically limited and selective exposure to international trade allowed Japanese people to control the comfortable interpolation of "foreign" objects into existing Japanese culture and the culturally specific adaptation of "foreign" concepts and languages into their lives. The "foreign" back then was constructed as visible and exotic difference that did not threaten Japan's homogeneity and its everyday practices. Such minimum and unthreatening importation of the "foreign" also helped Japanese intellectuals form the *kokugaku* scholarship and theorize the "pure" and homogeneous essence of Japanese, although there were multiple regional cultures in Japan.

From 1868 to the end of WWII: modern Japan

Japan used to be decentralized with many governments, regions, and cultures, often competing and sometimes coordinated. However, Japan became centralized (around 1860), which, in turn, resulted in the development of a somewhat unified image of Japan as homogeneous. This hegemonic reorganization consequently eradicated regional and cultural diversity within its image construction. The new and emerging Japanese government built a more stabilized network structure and system that centralized power and unified Japan's homogenizing discourses in rendering a "grand" narrative of Japaneseness. This inward and controlled homogenization was influenced by Japan's formal acknowledgment of its international relations and its official step toward Westernization. Japanese identity was somewhere between the pull toward the center—the pure Japanese essence—and the pull toward Westernization.

The year 1868 marks the beginning of Japan's *Meiji* era. The *Meiji* restoration led to a new Japanese government that was more centralized than ever

6 S. Toyosaki and S. Eguchi

before in the country's history. Moving out of its *sakoku* condition, Japan looked outwardly while it held a strong interest in continuing the trajectory of the *kokugaku* movement inwardly. Three major policies/ideological stances characterize Japan's navigation through the *Meiji* restoration and the consequential period before Japan's defeat in WWII. These are: *datsu-A nyū-O, fukoku kyōhei*, and *kokutai*, all contested terms. We provide brief, oversimplified explanations of these below.

Datsu-A nyū-O literally means "leave Asia, and enter the West." The major figure in this political and intellectual movement was Yukichi Fukuzawa (1835–1901), the intellectual father of modern Japan. His work *Leaving Asia* promoted various strategies at different locations, which helped Japan "emulate … the advanced nations of the West and leave Asia by dissociating itself from its backward neighbors" (Onishi, 2005, pp. A1–A6). *Datsu-A nyū-O* influenced "modern" Japanese people's nationalistic identity construction (see Fujimoto, 2001; Toyosaki, 2011). Westernization, back then, did not permeate Japanese people's everyday lives; however, it remained ideological—a model for national reformation. Japan's Westernization became an ideological platform for the country's new homogenizing discourse. This kind of intellectual thinking prompted Japan, after the *Meiji* restoration, to put in place government policy that transformed the country "into an industrialised, military powerful nation with its own colonial empire to rival those" among the Western great powers (McCormack, 2001, p. 9).

Japan's emulation of those Western powers was manifested in *fukoku kyōhei* ["wealthy nation and strong military"] (see, Graburn & Ertl, 2008). During this time, Japan strengthened itself structurally (i.e., industrially, institutionally, militaristically, and educationally); its militaristic advancements/invasions were notoriously noteworthy for about three decades thereafter, exemplified by cases such as China in 1895 and Russia in 1905 (Graburn & Ertl, 2008). Navigating the liminal space between the West and Asia, at various locations, Japan's inward homogenizing movement, described as *kokutai* ["national policy"] (McCormick, 2001, p. 12), emerged in order to resist Japan's Westernization. The *kokutai* ideology—a highly debated concept among Japan studies scholars—helped construct Japan's homogeneity against the powerful West and its superiority against Asia. Through *kokutai* discourse, Japan became embossed as "a unique family state united around the emperor" (McCormick, 2001, pp. 1–2). Thus, Japan's rapid militaristic Westernization and its *kokutai* movement both became competing homogenizing discourses for Japanese identity. Amid these competing homogenizations, cultural minorities in Japan—for example, foreign laborers/resident Koreans—continued to be discriminated against. The massacre of Koreans was reported after the great Kanto earthquake in 1923 (see Ryang, 2003). The challenge to Japan's homogeneous conception from within did not gain any momentum.

Japan transformed itself from a self-chained nation and forged itself on the international stage against the West and the surrounding Asian region. Japan's *Meiji* restoration revolutionalized the educational system that schooled its

Introduction 7

citizens to meet and realize the government's political and ideological agendas—nationalism and militarism (Okano & Tsuchiya, 1999). Japan continued engaging in militaristic ventures at multiple sites during this period; however, "such ventures eventually led the nation to a series of resounding defeats and tragedies … and the abandonment of militarism" (Okano & Tsuchiya, 1999, p. 2), marked by the atomic bombs in Hiroshima and Nagasaki in 1945. Most of Japan's cultural exchanges and movements during this period were outward-oriented, such as toward the powerful West and Asia. The competing homogenizing discourses of Japanese identity emerged as Japan's Westernization and the *kokutai* movement; Japanese identity became polarized. What is noteworthy here is that, during this period, there were some critical movements that questioned Japan's homogenous identity/ideology. For example, "the *Suiheisha* (Levelers Association) was established in 1922 as the first stable Buraku rights organization" (Graburn & Ertl, 2008, p. 6).

From 1945 to around 1980: Japan's post-WWII reconstruction

With much of Japan physically destroyed following its defeat in the Pacific war, the country then had a great task of rebuilding to do. Japanese people "demonstrated a dynamic ability to erupt and renew themselves" in the post-WWII recovery (Haglund, 1988, p. 84). Instead of the militaristic strength which it had sought in the *Meiji* era, Japan was now forbidden to accommodate its military and encouraged to rebuild itself with democracy as the political and ideological platform. Japan, once again, utilized its education system in order to transform itself "into a democratic society" (Okano & Tsuchiya, 1999, p. xii). In the post-WWII period of the political and ideological shift, Japan focused on its industrial production (Graburn & Ertl, 2008). "Starting small and gaining market shares in industry after industry" (Graburn & Ertl, 2008, p. 2), Japan revitalized and remade itself as a renowned industrial and technological nation. However, there were some problems: "Japan's newfound international self-confidence led to ever-widening export markets and to increasing numbers of affluent tourists exploring the world" (Graburn & Ertl, 2008, p. 2). This time, Westernization did not simply remain ideological; it permeated Japanese people's everyday lives. Japanese people started hearing expressions such as *kokusai kōryū* [international exchange]. *kokusai kōryū* introduced international and intercultural "cooperative" practices, such as sister-city relations, ethnic education (interaction among immigrants from Vietnam and Korea), international exchange programs, and international tourism (see Graburn & Ertl, 2008, p. 7). The Japanese concept, *kokusai kōryū*, was undeveloped in practice and invited both pragmatic and critical questions. As the movement swept through Japan, the reconstruction of Japaneseness took place. Japan's post-WWII period is characterized by various image reconstructions.

The Western world had become reimagined during this period through Japan's informal and governmental initiatives known as *kokusaika* [internationalization], which Graburn and Ertl (2008) refer to as Japan's "second great

8   S. Toyosaki and S. Eguchi

encounter with the Western world" (p. 6). This time, the West did not function as an ideological model for Japan to emulate, compete with, and conquer; the West became reconstructed as a target of desire that Japan could not reach. The gaze toward the West produced a homogenizing effect among Japanese people's national identity construction.

After WWII and the Occupation, opportunities for Japanese people to interact with foreigners, mainly Westerners, increased at a tremendous speed (Suganuma, 2012). While the Occupation had brought foreigners to Japan, during this period many Japanese people traveled to foreigners' home countries (Graburn & Ertl, 2008). They learned foreign—Western—languages in order to communicate effectively and to be functional at the sojourn destinations. "Informal and governmental initiatives of internationalization … were implemented in many forms" (Graburn & Ertl, 2008, p. 6). Many others who did not travel to foreign counties experienced internationalization through the media. In the 1960s, Japanese television networks developed and an enormous demand to fill their airtime emerged from the booming television/media industry. The "demand [was] satisfied by U.S. imports. Shows like *Laramie, Ben Casey, Combat*, and *Bewitched* found large, appreciative audiences" in Japan (Schilling, 1997, p. 10). The West, through these USAmerican media programs, became reimagined by Japanese viewers.

Coinciding with the construction of the West, *nihonjinron* emerged as a postwar literature that prompted homogenizing effects. *Nihonjinron* is translated and/or understood in various ways, ranging from "Japanese Character Studies" (Graburn & Ertl, 2008, p. 3) and "theories of the Japanese" (Hambleton, 2011, p. 31) to Japanese people's "phallocentric obsession" (Macdonald & Maher, 1995, p. 5). Japanese character studies, back then, often used the United States of America as Japan's counterpart in constructing the "Japanese" character and "perpetuated the most basic of assumptions that the study of Japan was the study of 'the Japanese people' " (Graburn & Ertl, 2008, p. 4). The authors continue:

> This bias reinforced the illusion of homogeneity as studies largely ignored the legacy of Japan's recent colonial endeavors, expansion to its frontier territories, and historical interactions with the outside world, favoring analyses that stressed enduring and native cultural traits (Ryang, 2004).
>
> (Graburn & Ertl, 2008, p. 4)

In this way, *nihonjinron* helped construct and spread "the 'myth' of Japanese homogeneity" (Graburn & Ertl, 2008, p. 3).

In the 1960s, Japan (or its image) transformed from "a defeated, divided country without a first rate economy" to a nation of "greater prosperity and confidence" (Wilson, 2011, p. 159). Wilson describes the 1960s as follows: "In this decade … while poverty, division and the lingering effects of war remained important parts of the social, cultural, political and economic landscape, new collective images were beginning to emerge" (p. 160). Both the Tokyo Olympics (1964) and the Osaka Expo (1970) functioned as thresholds for such image

Introduction   9

rebuilding (Wilson, 2011, p. 160). These large events, the first Olympics and World Exposition in Asia, revitalized Japan "as a bridge between the East and the West ... and ... as a representative of Asia or more broadly of the non-Western world" (p. 169). During the events, Japan reconstructed its image as "a modern Westernized country" (Wilson, 2011, p. 169) and exhibited "an enormous sense of confidence in the powers of science and technology" (p. 167). However, the image construction that took place was of "the representative Westernized nation in Asia," not a Western nation; the West remained the target of desire that Japan would never reach. The West was an ideological apparatus that homogenized "new" post-WWII Japanese, while *nihonjinron* produced the counter-homogeneous effects.

Through Japan's *kokusaika*, *nihonjinron* discourse, and foci on science and technology, little attention was paid to non-Western foreigners—mainly Koreans, Chinese, and South-East Asians—and their wellbeing in Japan. Such neglect derived from the image of "pure" Japanese homogeneity. That is, "pure" Japanese who Westernized while retaining their Japanese cultural essence—the post-WWII adaptation of *Datsu-A nyū-O*. In the 1960s and 1970s, foreigners were mainly of Korean and Chinese descent while a smaller number of them were from South-East Asia (Befu, 2006). According to Graburn and Ertl (2008), cultural minorities in Japan, such as Ainu, Okinawans, and Buraku, as well as *Zainichi* (Japan-dwelling) Chinese and Koreans, did not gain recognition until the 1980s. One social apparatus that is worth mentioning here is Japan's postwar schooling. As argued above, Japan had strategically utilized its education system in order to reflect its political ideology when teaching citizens during and after the *Meiji* restoration. The Japanese education system after the WWII defeat advanced the country's agenda to maintain its monocultural hegemony. Postwar schooling "assume[d] that all students [were] from a single ethnic group (Japanese) ... and [this meant] that state-sponsored schools cater[d] almost exclusively for their needs" (Okano & Tsuchiya, 1999, p. xiii).

New Japan: the 1980s and 1990s

Graburn et al., (2008) coin the term "new Japan" to describe Japan's situation after its recovery from the WWII defeat. During this period, Japan remained powerful in both economic and political terms, sustained its high standard of living, and continued to open "its borders and economic markets to the international community" (Graburn & Ertl, 2008, p. 2). Japan experienced the intense economic development known as the "bubble." "The end of this cycle came rather suddenly at the end of the 1980s following [damaging] economic consequences stemming largely from property speculation at home and abroad" (Graburn & Ertl, 2008, p. 2). This was the period when Japan's homogeneity was challenged while the right-wing public policy makers insisted that Japan remain homogeneous (Graburn & Ertl, 2008, p. 7).

In the 1980s, the word *kokusaika* became part of Japanese everyday lexicons. More foreigners came to Japan, and more Japanese went to foreign countries,

10   S. Toyosaki and S. Eguchi

mainly the Western world (Graburn & Ertl, 2008, p. 6). International mobility became less difficult as Japan's bubble economy (Befu, 2006) and technology flourished in the 1980s. Japanese people's desire for international travel as a leisure activity was practically attainable, and international travel became a "status" symbol of Japan's unique middle-class construction that was predicated on an interesting paradoxical merger between Japanese populism and Japanese elite cosmopolitanism, often understood as dichotomous opposites (Satsuka, 2009). Satsuka explains Japanese populist cosmopolitanism as middle-class fascination for overseas, which grew out of the bubble and the reconstructed image of the West.

Due to the economic boom between the mid-1980s and the early-1990s, Japan's enormous middle-class population grew. This flourishing middle-class challenged and deconstructed the boundary between middle and upper class cultures (Martinez, 1998a, 1998b). "Practices which we might label elite and high culture [became] more and more the domain of the huge middle class" (Martinez, 1998a, p. 5). Put simply, it was the "rich" middle-class that possessed both populist character and cosmopolitan/elitist desires and means. The middle-class consisted of the post-WWII generation who

> observed, as children, how many adults suddenly reversed their values at the end of the war. The emperor who they considered a god turned out to be a mere human being; teachers who had taught that Americans were demon enemies suddenly started admiring them, as if Americans had replaced the emperor in terms of determining the destiny of the Japanese; the English tongue that had been prohibited as an enemy language became a tool of survival, used for panhandling or as a means of bringing oneself closer to the Americans (cf. Dower 1999; Oguma 2002).
>
> (Satsuka, 2009, p. 74)

Satsuka (2009) explains Sakai's notion of transferential desire, "the Japanese desire to see oneself from another position"—mainly the West that was "constructed as a normative interlocutor in the Japanese imagination. The particularity of Japan [was] always thought out in reference to the generality or universality of the West" (Satsuka, 2009, p. 71). In this way, the West, particularly USAmerica, became internalized very deeply in Japan in general as well as in its citizens' everyday lives (Eguchi, 2015; Sekimoto, 2014; Suganuma, 2012; Toyosaki, 2011; Yoshimi, cited in Satsuka, 2009).

However, Japanese people's transferential desire toward the U.S. faded as it had been too "internalized in Japanese everyday life" (Yoshimi cited in Satsuka, 2009, p. 78). USAmerica—the cultural concept—slowly lost its symbolic significance in new Japan's identity construction, and Japanese people started to critically question their subjective construction that desired "to catch up with America and to obtain the American lifestyle" (Satsuka, 2009, p. 78). Thus, Satsuka (2009) argues: "The internalized America had lost its significance as a transcendental referee for Japanese behavior" (p. 78). As the Japanese

Introduction 11

middle-class increased in number and its transferential desire for USAmerica was fading, terms such as "world," "international," and "foreign" came to mean many different things—concepts, regions, and nations— while its residual effects continued to be evident (Fujimoto, 2001; Toyosaki, 2011).

In this era, Japan had commenced its ideological heterogenization and cultural diversification. Thus far, Japan had been polarized between two competing homogenizing discourses—going back/retaining its "pure essence" and becoming Westernized—while denying its cultural diversity. However, such homogenizations could not sustain their legitimacy any longer. Even though there had always been foreigners in Japan, the 1980s marked a shift in Japan's immigration landscape (Befu, 2006)—both legal and illegal (see Graburn & Ertl, 2008). For two decades, Japan experienced a tremendous increase in immigrants/migrants, particularly unskilled laborers (Befu, 2006; Graburn & Ertl, 2008). Befu (2006) describes three factors that led to the increase: first, sustaining the economic bubble necessitated more laborers; second, the birth rate declined; and third, more Japanese people went into higher education. These three factors, combined, shrank the younger population that had traditionally entered the labor market prior to the 1980s. Finally, an increasing number of Japanese youth were capable of being selective about their job choices, supported by the bubble economy and their acquired higher education. They avoided low-paying work characterized as 3K—*kitanai* [dirty], *kitsui* [physically hard labor], and *kiken* [dangerous] (see Befu, 2006; Graburn & Ertl, 2008).

Graburn and Ertl (2008) state that: "Awareness of these minorities arose only when visibly non-Japanese arrived in numbers, such as Vietnamese refugees, and immigrant workers, especially Filipinos, South East Asians, and South Asians including Singhalese and Nepalis, and Middle Easterners" (p. 7). For example, in 1990, Japan revisited and revised its immigration law—"more accurately, the 'Immigration Control and Refuge Certification Act'" (Befu, 2006, p. 1). The revision "allow[ed] those of Japanese descent, up to the third generation, to establish legal residence in Japan and to work" (Befu, 2006, p. 1). Many non-governmental organizations (NGOs) were established to support and protect legal and illegal immigrants from abuse and discrimination and help them navigate their social, cultural, and linguistic adaptation to Japan. "Most of these NGOs [spoke] of *kyōsei*, which [was] translated most literally as 'living together' or 'co-existence,' but sometimes also as 'symbiosis,' as a major goal of their support activities. But the meaning of this term is ill-defined" (Befu, 2006, p. 2). Often, *cultural Others* were subsumed and mainstreamed into Japan's culture and cultural differences were eradicated.

Multiculturalism functioned as a mystified mechanism of homogeneity while encouraging its unthreatening and comfortable heterogenization. Multiculturalism became "an ideal for public policy" (Graburn & Ertl, 2008, p. 3). Japan's internationalization effort was manifested in the various ways in which the government tried to assist foreigners to transit from their home country to Japan, to promote more interactions between Japanese people and foreigners in Japan and abroad, and to ameliorate Japan's general image globally (Graburn & Ertl,

12　S. Toyosaki and S. Eguchi

2008). McCormack (2001) makes an important note of population mobility internally in Japan and explains that recently Japan (1980s onward) entered "a new stage of hybridisation of culture" (McCormack, 2001, p. 12). This stage was prompted by Japan's urban metropolitanization populated by Japanese leaving rural areas and by foreigners attracted by Japan's prosperity associated with the bubble. Even in depopulated rural areas, young famers welcomed "brides from China, Korea, the Philippines, Thailand and Sri Lanka" (McCormack, 2001, p. 12). Japan's relations with its neighboring countries became visible around the textbook (Brender, 2005) and apology issues surrounding Japan's advancement/invasion during the war period (i.e., the mystifying ways in which Japan's past advancements were represented in textbooks in Japanese education and why, and how, Japan needed to apologize for its advancements). The textbook and apology issues encouraged some Japanese to reflect upon their history while others ignored these issues.

New Japan transformed itself from the speedy "recovery" from WWII defeat to a relatively wealthy and internationalizing/ed nation. Japan attracted many researchers to study its *kokusaika*/internationalization. In the 1990s, Donahue (1998) observed: "the field of Japanese studies [was] growing at an unprecedented rate.... This attention [was] a direct result of Japan's increased importance in world affairs" (p. 4). Similarly, McCormack (2001) noted that research on Japan's *kokusaika* had proliferated. Macdonald and Maher (1995) claimed that: "books about its culture, business practices, history and lifestyle ... proliferated in [the 1990s]. However, the dominant theme underlying most of the discourse [was] familiar: 'Japan' [was] a homogeneous entity, sharply-defined and yet-to-be understood" (p. 3).

External characterization: theorizing Japan as homogeneous

The North American conception of Japan is the epitome of the Far East, reports Donahue (1998). Studies about and of Japan—Japanese cultural orientations, pop culture, films, business practices, and new and emerging lifestyles—have proliferated. However, mainstream portrayal of Japan reflects the historically constructed image of homogeneity.

Japan has been constructed as *cultural Other* in many different contexts, particularly in studies of culture. "All too often, literature about Japan focuses on what is different about it, how it can be compared or contrasted with other, particularly 'western,' nations" (Macdonald & Maher, 1995, p. 4). The famous and significant work of Edward T. Hall (1976; 1983) comes to mind. In his work, Japanese people and their "cultural" orientations are compared and contrasted to his understandings and perceptions of "USAmerican" people and their cultural orientations. From his studies, Hall discusses time orientations, for example. Too often, Japanese people or college students have been used as samples for statistical analyses in various social scientific intercultural communication research projects. Macdonald and Maher (1995) explain that research activities have a tendency to depict Japan as homogeneous. Macdonald and Maher (1995) and

Introduction   13

Iwabuchi (2010) point to a historical tendency in research and warn how Eurocentric theories and perspectives, utilized in studying Japan, orientalize and exoticize it as the homogeneous *cultural Other*. Thus, recent work on Japan challenges the chronic orientalization, exoticization, and othering of Japan and proposes to dismantle the West as the center of "gazing."

The fifth phase: post-New Japan, space and time of uncertainty

The "new" in New Japan highlights the fact that Japan grew out of "in recovery" mode. Japan grew, economically and industrially, out of this phase. New Japan is characterized by its internationalization and immigration/migration. Japan continues to be more culturally diverse than ever before. There are "1.91 million officially registered foreigners, consisting nearly 2 percent of the total population (Nakamura, 2005), with an additional unknown number of non-registered immigrants and ethnically unclear Japanese nationals" (Graburn & Ertl, 2008, p. 1). Japan's internal diversity issues—ethnic minorities, *zaichini*, gender/sex, sexuality, disability, inter-racial citizens, etc.—were, generally speaking, put on the back burner. While this trend has remained constant throughout history with the primary attention put on its *kokusaika*, Japan has entered a new phase of uncertainty. Its economy has been slowly declining. *Shōshika*, or a low birth rate, is the major concern of many politicians, economists, researchers, and many Japanese people. Japan is aging. The population over the age of 65 provides a marker for understanding a nation's population and aging trend. It is reported that 7.1 percent of Japan's population were over the age of 65 in 1970, 14.5 percent in 1995, and 23 percent in 2010, when it was finally categorized as a hyper-aged society (Statistics Bureau, Ministry of Internal Affairs and Communications, 2013). According to the National Institute of Population and Social Security Research (2012), this trend continues: Japan's population over the age of 65 is anticipated to reach 33.4 percent in 2035 and nearly 40 percent in 2060. Japan's population is expected to decrease from 127.74 million in 2006 to 86.78 million in 2060 (National Institute of Population and Social Security Research, 2012). Meanwhile, Hambleton (2011) reports that the foreign population residing in Japan has been increasing—there was a 45 percent increase between 1997 and 2007. In 2007, foreigners comprised 1.69 percent of the population in Japan (Hambleton, 2011). Japan has entered the post-New Japan phase. It is a phase of uncertainty and future possibilities. The questions are: What now? Where do we want to go from here? How will we get there?

Recent Japan studies and its efforts for cultural diversification

Contrary to the constructed image of Japan as homogeneous (Macdonald & Maher, 1995), many recent researchers (see Befu, 2006; Denoon et al., 2001; Lee et al., 2006; McCormack, 2001; Macdonald & Maher, 1995; McLelland,

14   S. Toyosaki and S. Eguchi

2000; Okano & Tsuchiya, 1999; Trent, 1999) understand and study Japan as heterogeneous while paying significant attention to its complexity (Donahue, 1998; Macdonald & Maher, 1995). Donahue (1998) describes the scholarly attention to Japan's complexity as "a paradigmatic shift" (p. 4). In this section, we introduce some trends and approaches that are utilized in studying Japan's cultural diversity and complexity and that challenge Japan's homogenizing discourses.

McCormack (2001) insists that the foundations upon which Japan's homogeneity has been established have been challenged and, in some cases, disbanded in recent years. Denoon et al.'s (2001) anthology "challenges the conventional approach by arguing that Japan has long been 'multicultural', and that what is distinctive is the success with which that diversity has been cloaked by the ideology of 'uniqueness' and 'monoculturalism' " (McCormack, 2001, p. 3) or homogeneity. Graburn and Ertl (2008) suggest that studying the "new" Japan with its unique historical backdrop is of academic importance. They write: "We find that multiculturalism has become a key concept used to describe areas where old hegemonies are giving way to new social forms, while simultaneously providing a model and a method for achieving a new Japanese state" (Graburn & Ertl, 2008, p. 3).

Graburn and Ertl (2008) chronicle recent research on Japanese cultural diversity and minorities. Three representative cultural groups that have been studied are: (1) "Japan's 'indigenous' people, the Ainu, Okinawan, and Buraku," (2) "Koreans and Chinese brought to Japan during the Pacific War and their [descendants]," and (3) "resent migrant workers from Latin America and Asia" (Graburn & Ertl, 2008, p. 4). They further identify the research approaches. First, such research relies on the concept of difference (peripheries), consequently tarnishing and challenging the homogeneous core (center). Second, much research understands Japanese minority populations as "invisible," subsumed by the monolithic homogeneity of Japanese culture. Third, research reports that Japan's minorities are vanishing—an ultimate form of homogeneous assimilation. Graburn and Ertl (2008) conclude that "much of the early research on minorities inadvertently reinforced the image of Japanese homogeneity" (p. 4).

Additionally, there is an emerging field of Japanese gender and sexuality studies. These collections of scholarship unpack the marginalization of women and LGBTQ people. More precisely, single women who are over 30 years old are characterized as "loser dogs" because they do not conform to the heteronormative duty of marriage and reproduction (Maeda & Hecht, 2012)—Japan's homogeneous gender performance. While there was localized practice of same-sex sexual desire in pre-modern Japan, non-heteronormative sexualities have been stigmatized (McLelland, 2000; Trent, 1999). If there is representation of male same-sex lovers, they are hyper-feminized (Maree, 2008; McLelland, 2000) and ab/normalized as cross-dressing sex industry workers (Mitsuhashi, 2006), sustaining and forcing cultural interpretations consistent with Japan's homogeneous gender expectations. Critical attention paid to these

Introduction 15

non-homogeneous, non-heteronormative gender performances and sexualities help elucidate hidden normative/homogeneous cultural assumptions. In this context, Japanese queer/non-heteronormative sexual men gravitate toward the western/USAmerican ways of gay life by desiring white men (Suganuma, 2012) and/or black/African American men (Eguchi, 2015). However, issues related to women and LGBTQ people remain largely understudied and require further attention.

Another trend focuses on the bi-civilized (Donahue, 1998) nature of Japanese culture. Donahue understands Japan as a hybrid culture between the East and the West. Japan has been characterized by its "massive cultural borrowing" (Reischauer, cited in Donahue, 1998, p. 2). Historically speaking, Japan regulated its cultural borrowing from the West by becoming bi-civilized in unique ways while sustaining its identity and autonomy. Japan's culturally and historically specific glocalization (Endo, 2013, p. 86) of the West has gained researchers' interest. On this topic, some researchers (see Darling-Wolf, 2004; Iwabuchi, 2010) take an explicitly critical approach. Iwabuchi (in Darling-Wolf, 2004) writes: "No matter how strong its economy becomes, Japan is culturally and psychologically dominated by the West" (p. 326). Historically, Japan has been understood through "its relation to powerful others" (Ohnuki-Tierney, cited in Graburn & Ertl, 2008, p. 6). Darling-Wolf (2004) develops Yoshioka's concept of internalized colonization in explaining Japan's voluntary Westernization. This concept explains the dual and simultaneous function of Japan as the colonizer and as colonized by the West. Japan colonizes itself by learning how to gaze at itself from a Western perspective, evaluate itself from that perspective, and impose Western ideologies on itself. Resistant to everyday Westernization, cultural nationalism has emerged in Japan and has been studied by researchers. Cultural nationalism aims at "regenerat[ing] the national community by creating, preserving or strengthening a people's cultural identity when it is felt to be lacking, inadequate or threatened" (Yoshino, cited in Hambleton, 2011, p. 31). Some local communities in Japan try to preserve their authentic cultural traits and events against Japan's internalized Westernization and *kokusaika*.

Japan and its media, in relation to other nations and their media, has been a focus in media studies of the East Asian region. Iwabuchi (2010) explains, from a scholarly media perspective, that East Asia is such an important region. First, in East Asia, media productions exhibit a high level of cultural mixing and collaboration. Second, the high volume of intra-regional media exchanges (consumption) is evident.

> In recent years, a great deal of research has examined the dynamics of the production, circulation and consumption of media cultures in East Asia under the process of globalization, much of it expressly aiming to theorize the socio-historically specific experiences that characterize East Asia as a region.
>
> (Iwabuchi, 2010, p. 403)

16   S. Toyosaki and S. Eguchi

Implications for future research

Hambleton (2011) observes the relational nature of Japan's homogeneity. Japan's Westernization has been challenged by movements that revitalize and preserve Japan (i.e., its people's cultural identity) and which have been threatened by its Westernization (see Yoshino in Hambleton, 2011). Ethnographic and historical studies have helped explain the ways in which Japanese indigenous minorities had and have become secluded as the marginalized *Others* in relation to the "dominant" Japanese (see Graburn & Ertl, 2008). Of course, this relational co-construction between homogeneity and heterogeneity is not culturally neutral: it is power driven. Hence, it is imperative to study the political nature of the co-construction. On this point, Iwabuchi (2010) writes about a constructive way of analyzing issues related to culture and globalization. Such analysis

> must locate these transnationally shared structural forces and their interactions—which often operate contradictorily but inter-constitutively—in terms of both homogenization/heterogenization and decentering/recentering. Rigorous examination is also required of the ways in which they are articulated in specific socio-historical local contexts in order to elucidate the latter's distinctiveness.
>
> (Iwabuchi, 2010, p. 404)

Thus, studies of Japan's homogeneity must examine the discursive push-and-pull between the homogenizing and heterogenizing vectors, found in various domestic and transnational contexts and mobilized by diverse power politics—such as gender, sexuality, marginalized cultural groups, nationality, multiculturalism, and internationalization.

Responding to Conquergood's (1985) characterization of a "heuristically rich paradox" as a moral act, we discuss a few methodological focal points in studying Japan's homogenizing discourses. First, we ought to resituate the relationship between Westernized/ing and Asianized/ing theorization mechanisms. Through orientalism (Said, 1979), Japan, along with many other "oriental" nations, has been constructed through the Western capitalistic heteropatriarchal gaze. Research on Japan's homogeneity needs to challenge such a uni-directional gaze. However, Iwabuchi (2010) cautions that "de-Westernization should not be regarded as a blunt denial of Western theory" (p. 403). He explains that such a denial only leads us to "a well-demarcated East–West dichotomy" (p. 404) that certainly fails to understand Japan which has been enormously influenced by the West. Thus, we need a more complex deployment and amalgam of various Western, Eastern, and other (indigenous, etc.) theories in rendering the "heuristically rich paradox" from which our complex analysis emerges.

Second, we see cultural diversity and plurality as the concepts situated within the "heuristically rich paradox" between homogeneity and heterogeneity. We certainly regard it as intolerable when homogeneity is used and embodied as a

Introduction 17

performative means to deny, silence, and marginalize cultural diversity and plurality. The value we place on laboring toward Japan's cultural diversity coincides with Macdonald and Maher's (1995) understanding of diversity.

> Diversity and consequent social and linguistic plurality are essential for our social and intellectual survival. It is as important to maintain diversity in the world, and to encourage its interaction through social plurality as it is to maintain it within the biological world. The exchanges are vital. Without species diversity and interaction, plants will die; without social diversity our social life will die; without a diversity of ideas, there are no ideas.
> (Macdonald & Maher, 1995, p. 8)

It is essential for people to work toward cultural diversity. The critical question here is: Will we achieve cultural diversity if we eliminate homogeneity? For the purposes of this anthology, we would like to entertain a notion and practice of cultural diversity that helps situate our ontologically paradoxical and dialectical being/becoming within *both* homogeneity and heterogeneity simultaneously in a given temporal and spacial context.

Third, within our analysis a "heuristically rich paradox" can be envisioned, found, and possibly enacted which focuses on both consensual and conflictual theorizations at once (Fiske, 1991; Okano & Tsuchiya, 1999; Toyosaki, 2011). Consensual theory assumes culturally shared meanings while conflictual theory emphasizes the political nature of the production of meaning. Okano and Tsuchiya (1999) explain that consensus theory helps us understand "the relatively stable and harmonious" (p. 6) characteristics of a group, culture, or population. The stable and harmonious consensus can function as a cynical mechanism that constructs and oppresses *Others* as "deviant" (Okano & Tsuchiya, 1999, p. 7). Conflict theory rigorously interrogates the crafty machinery of consensus and "how such a consensus is maintained despite the fact that it brings little benefit to the majority" (Okano & Tsuchiya, 1999, p. 8). Thus, simultaneous consensual and conflictual theorization renders a "heuristically rich paradox"—an analytic space—where researchers can interrogate the power politics found in the push-and-pull between homogeneity and heterogeneity.

Organization of the book

The sensible and critical approach to homogeneity we suggest will, we hope, engage with the research implications we have discussed above by envisioning cultural diversity as a new social order, inclusive of many cultural voices, and practicing both confrontational and self-reflexive tactics in challenging ourselves and our readers to think of and (re)imagine Japan's homogenizing discourses and cultural diversity. There are six parts to this volume: Gender, sexuality, and the body; Performance and queerness; Inclusiveness and Otherness; Media and framing; Environment and movement; and Education and internationalization.

18   S. Toyosaki and S. Eguchi

Part I Gender, sexuality, and the body

The first part, *Gender, sexuality, and the body*, examines complex and shifting landscapes of contemporary gender relations in Japan. In "The affective politics of the feminine: An interpassive analysis of Japanese female comedians," Sachi Sekimoto and Yusaku Yajima look at female comedians' (un)desirable performance of femininity. Their critique is that the gender politics of desirability is always already produced and constituted according to heterosexist and patriarchal social norms. In "The shifting gender landscape of Japanese society," Justin Charlebois explores non-hegemonic masculinities and non-emphasized femininities to identify the ways in which heteronormative gender roles are shifting due to the gradual increase in women in a workforce that has been historically available only to men. To further explicate this line of gender shifting, Emi Kanemoto and Kristie Collins analyze four Japanese TV drama series in "'It's a wonderful single life': Construction and representations of female singleness in Japan's contemporary *josei dorama*." They identify and critique media representations of singlehood in a patriarchal society that stigmatizes unmarried women.

Part II Performance and queerness

The authors in this part examine the emerging visibility of performance that disrupts hetero/normative constructions of gender, sexuality, and the body. In "Japanese male-queer femininity: An autoethnographic reflection on *Matsuko Deluxe* as an *onē-kei* talent," Shinsuke Eguchi locates his body as a central site of knowledge to read the performative rhetoric of Matsuko Deluxe (マ ツ コ デ ラ ッ ク ス) as an *onē-kei* talent. More specifically, he utilizes his embodied memories of experience to call into question the Japanese cultural and communicative practices of male-queer femininity. In "Bleach in color: Unpacking gendered, queered, and raced performances in anime," Reslie Cortés utilizes a queer of color critique to examine textual representations of Japaneseness in the popular anime *Bleach*. She rearticulates the anime's ambiguous representations of gender, sexuality, and the body as a site of possibility for change for Japanese cultural tradition, authenticity, and identity.

Part III Inclusiveness and Otherness

In this part, the authors investigate how communicative practices of "Othering" become a social apparatus for constructing, reconstructing, and sustaining Japan's homogeneities and political cultural boundaries. The complexity and nuanced mechanisms of the "Othering" that perpetuate Japan's homogenizing boundary setting is performed and challenged by Japanese, "Otherized" Japanese, and non-Japanese people globally. In "The discursive pushes and pulls of J-pop and K-pop in Taiwan: Cultural homogenization and identity co-optation," Hsun-Yu (Sharon) Chuang carefully analyzes how perceived Japanese culture in J-pop in Taiwan becomes homogenized in comparison to and contrast with K-pop and the ways in which such a cultural perception becomes co-opted to

Introduction 19

Taiwanese pop-culture consumers' national identity constructions. In "'Hating Korea' (*Kenkan*) in postcolonial Japan," Andre Haag engages readers in a difficult yet necessary topic—Korea–Japan relationships. Haag constructs a sharp cultural analysis of the relationality between *kenkan* (hating Korea) and *hannichi* (anti-Japan) discourses. In Chapter 8, Toyosaki and Forbush, through their duoethnography, trace the intricate nature of the ways USAmerican orientalism and Japan's hybridism paint a complex picture of Japan's *kokusaika* (internationalization) performed at the micro-communicative level. These three chapters carefully theorize and critique the boundary setting and policing of Japan's inclusiveness and Otherness.

Part IV Media and framing

The fourth part of this book, *Media and framing*, analyzes the ways in which the media facilitates an on-going interplay of cultural tension between Japan's heterogeneity and homogeneity. In "Ishihara Shintaro's manga moral panic: The homogenizing rhetoric of Japanese nationalism," Lucy Miller analyzes a previous Tokyo governor's nationalistic rhetoric around moral panic over Bill 156, which gave the government the power to restrict the sale of manga, anime, and video games based on their perceived harmful effects on children. Her critique is that the need for excluded others is the rhetorical method of nationalism in order to maintain a homogenous construction of Japaneseness. Ryuta Komaki examines a Japanese social networking site to identify the ways in which the boundary of Japan is imagined in "mixi and an imagined boundary of Japan." By discussing how mixi affects the actions and experiences of users who belong to minority identity groups, Komaki examines the politics and discourses of inclusion and exclusion within and around mixi's interface.

Part V Environment and movement

The authors in this part take up a new and emerging subject area of environment, social movement, and communication. *Environment and movement* unfolds intricate discursive networks of Japan's national identity and homogeneity embedded in cultural understandings of human relationships with nature, natural symbols, and the effects of industry on nature. In "Historicization of cherry blossoms: A study of Japan's homogenizing discourses," Takuya Sakurai analyzes cherry blossom as a cultural symbol closely tied to the historical construction of Japan's homogeneity and its dialectical co-emergents, cultural Others. In Chapter 12, Saki Ichihara Fomsgaard discusses Japan's homogenization in recent discourses surrounding the debate over alternative and conventional agriculture. Through her critical discourse analysis, she unfolds the intricate dance of the persuasive messages of the debate in "Alternative vs. conventional: Dialectic relations of the organic agriculture discourse."

20   S. Toyosaki and S. Eguchi

Part VI Education and internationalization

The final part is titled *Education and internationalization*. In this section, the authors study and discuss governmental and educational movements and programs that have been designed to "internationalize" Japan's education. In their examinations of Japan's internationalization education, they raise critical issues regarding Westernization, English hegemony, whiteness, and cultural commodification. In "A dialectic between nationalism and multiculturalism: An analysis of the internationalization discourse in Japan," Ako Inuzuka examines "super global universities" by identifying and critiquing themes associated with schools' internationalization initiatives and programs. Her careful analysis points out that Japan's internationalization education privileges the West and the English language. The final chapter is entitled "'I never wanted to be famous': Pushes and pulls of whiteness through the eyes of foreign English language teachers in Japan." Nathaniel Simmons and Yea-Wen Chen investigate (white) English language teachers' identity management and negotiations in Japan's educational contexts.

In this edited collection, we call for a complex understanding of Japan's homogenizing discourses in a nuanced and contextual manner with the explicit goal of working toward a culturally diverse Japan. Japan faces many difficult questions regarding its future, such as its low birth rate, foreign labor politics, the human rights of various minority residents, and so on. The country's uncertain future can be scary; however, it is filled with many opportunities and possibilities. We hope this collection will help us and its readers examine current cultural politics and Japan's homogenizing discourses and envision such opportunities and possibilities. In so doing, this collection emphasizes "intercultural" and "communication" by facilitating further "cross-border dialogue across various divides" (Iwabuchi, 2010, p. 416). It is our hope that this collection provides such critical work for the future of Japan's cultural diversity.

References

Anderson, J. A., & Baym, G. (2004). Philosophies and philosophic issues in communication, 1995–2004. *Journal of Communication, 54*(4), 589–615.

Bakhtin, M. M. (1981). *The dialogic imagination: Four essays* (M. Holquist, Ed., C. Emerson & M. Holquist, Trans.). Austin, TX: University of Texas Press.

Befu, H. (2006). Conditions of living together (kyōsei). In S. I. Lee, S. Murphy-Shigematsu, & H. Befu (Eds.), *Japan's diverse dilemmas: Ethnicity, citizenship, and education* (pp. 1–10). New York: iUniverse.

Brender, A. (2005). Two professors confront Japan's disputed past with a textbook. *Chronicle of Higher Education, 51*(38). Retrieved from http://chronicle.com/article/2-Professors-Confront-Japans/11476.

Butler, J. (1990). *Gender trouble: Feminism and the subversion of identity*. New York: Routledge.

Collier, M. J., Hegde, R. S., Lee, W. S., Nakayama, T. K., & Yep, G. A. (2001). Dialogue on the edges: Ferment in communication and culture. In M. J. Collier (Ed.), *International and intercultural communication annual 24: Transforming communication about culture: Critical new directions* (pp. 219–280). Thousand Oaks, CA: Sage.

Introduction 21

Conquergood, D. (1985). Performing as a moral act: Ethical dimensions of the ethnography of performance. *Literature in Performance, 5*(2), 1–13.

Darling-Wolf, F. (2004). Sites of attractiveness: Japanese women and westernized representations of feminine beauty. *Critical Studies in Media Communication, 21*(4), 325–345. doi: 10.1080/0739318042000245354

Denoon, D., Hudson, M., McCormack, G., & Morris-Suzuki, T. (Eds.). (2001). *Multicultural Japan: Palaeolithic to postmodern.* Cambridge, UK: Cambridge University Press.

Drzewiecka, J. A., & Halualani, R. T. (2002). The structural-cultural dialectics of diasporic politics. *Communication Theory, 12*(3), 340–366.

Donahue, R. T. (1998). *Japanese culture and communication: Critical cultural analysis.* Lanham, MD: University Press of America.

Dower, J. W. (1999). *Embracing defeat: Japan in the wake of World War II.* New York: Norton.

Eguchi, S. (2015). Queer intercultural relationality: An autoethnography of Asian-Black (dis)connections in White gay America. *Journal of International and Intercultural Communication, 8*(1), 27–43. doi: 10.1080/17513057.2015.991077

Endo, K. (2013). Overview of media sociology in Japan. *International Journal of Japanese Sociology, 22*, 80–93. doi: 10.1111/ijjs.12005

Fiske, J. (1991). Writing ethnographies: Contribution to a dialogue. *Quarterly Journal of Speech, 77*, 330–335. doi: 10.1080?00335639109383964

Fujimoto, E. (2001). Japanese-ness, whiteness, and the "other" in Japan's internationalization. In M. J. Collier (Ed.), *Transforming communication about culture: Critical new directions* (pp. 1–24). Thousand Oaks, CA: Sage.

Graburn, N., & Ertl, J. (2008). Introduction: Internal boundaries and models of multiculturalism in contemporary Japan. In N. H. H. Graburn, J. Ertl, & R. K. Tierney (Eds.), *Multiculturalism in the new Japan: Crossing the boundaries within* (pp. 1–31). New York: Berghahn Books.

Graburn, N. H. H., Ertl, J., & Tierney, R. K. (Eds.). (2008). *Multiculturalism in the new Japan: Crossing the boundaries within.* New York: Berghahn Books.

Haglund, E. (1988). Japan: Cultural considerations. In L. A. Samovar & R. E. Porter (Eds.), *Intercultural communication: A reader* (pp. 84–94). Belmont, CA: Wadsworth.

Hambleton, A. (2011). Reinforcing identities? Non-Japanese residents, television and cultural nationalism in Japan. *Contemporary Japan, 23*, 27–47. doi: 10.1515/cj.2011.003

Hall, E. T. (1976). *Beyond culture.* Garden City, NY: Anchor Press.

Hall, E. T. (1983). *The dance of life: The other dimension of time.* Garden City, NY: Anchor Books.

Halualani, R. T., & Nakayama, T. (2010). Critical intercultural communication studies: At a cross roads. In T. K. Nakayama & R. T. Halualani (Eds.), *The handbook of critical intercultural communication* (pp. 1–16). Malden, MA: Wiley-Blackwell.

Halualani, R. T., Mendoza, L., & Drzewiecka, J. A. (2009). "Critical" junctures in intercultural communication studies: A review. *The Review of Communication, 9*(1), 17–35.

Holquist, M. (1981). Introduction. In M. Holquist (Ed.), *The dialogic imagination: Four essays* (pp. xv–xxxiii). Austin, TX: University of Texas Press.

Iwabuchi, K. (2010). De-Westernization and the governance of global cultural connectivity: A dialogic approach to East Asian media cultures. *Postcolonial Studies, 13*(4), 403–419. doi: 10.1080/13688790.2010.518349

Lee, S-i., Murphy-Shigematsu, S., & Befu, H. (2006). *Japan's diverse dilemmas: Ethnicity, citizenship, and education.* New York: iUniverse.

Lee, W. S., Chung, J., Wang, J., & Hertel, E. (1995). A sociohistorical approach to intercultural communication. *Howard Journal of Communications, 6*, 262–291.

Macdonald, G., & Maher, J. C. (1995). Culture and diversity in Japan. In J. C. Maher & G. Macdonald (Eds.), *Diversity in Japanese culture and language* (pp. 3–23). London: Kegan Paul International.

Maeda, E., & Hecht, M. L. (2012). Identity search: Interpersonal relationships and relational identities of always-single Japanese women over time. *Western Journal of Communication, 76*(1), 44–64. doi: 10.1080/10570314.2012.637539

Maree, C. (2008). Grrrl-queens: One-kotoba and the negotiation of heterosexist gender language norms and lesbo(homo)phobic stereotypes in Japan. In F. Martin, P. A. Jackson, M. McLelland, & A. Yue (Eds.), *Asiapacific queer: Rethinking genders and sexualities* (pp. 67–84). Urbana and Chicago, IL: University of Illinois Press.

Martin, J. N., & Nakayama, T. K. (1999). Thinking dialectically about culture and communication. *Communication Theory, 9*(1), 1–25. doi: 10.1111/j.1468-28815.1999.tb00160.x

Martin, J. N., & Nakayama, T. K. (2010). Intercultural communication in contexts (4th ed.). Boston, MA: McGraw Hill.

Martinez, D. P. (1998a). Gender, shifting boundaries and global cultures. In D. P. Martinez (Ed.), *The worlds of Japanese popular culture: Gender, shifting boundaries and global cultures* (pp. 1–18). Cambridge, UK: Cambridge University Press.

Martinez, D. P. (Ed.). (1998b). *The worlds of Japanese popular culture: Gender, shifting boundaries and global cultures.* Cambridge, UK: Cambridge University Press.

McArthur, J. (2013). *Rethinking knowledge within higher education: Adorno and social justice.* London: Bloomsbury Academic.

McCormack, G. (2001). Introduction. In D. Denoon, M. Hudson, G. McCormack, & T. Morris-Suzuki (Eds.), *Multicultural Japan: Palaeolithic to postmodern* (pp. 1–15). Cambridge, UK: Cambridge University Press.

McLelland, M. J. (2000). *Male homosexuality in modern Japan: Cultural myths and social realities.* New York: Routledge.

Mitsuhashi, J. (2006). The transgender world in contemporary Japan: The male to female cross-dressers' community in Shinjuku. *Inter-Asia Cultural Studies, 7*(2), 202–227. doi: 10.1080/14649370600673847

Moon, D. G. (1996). Concepts of "culture": Implications for intercultural communication research. *Communication Quarterly, 44*(1), 70–84.

Mumby, D. K. (1997). Modernism, postmodernism, and communication studies: A rereading of an ongoing debate. *Communication Theory, 7*(1), 1–28. doi: 10.1111/j.1468-2885.1997.tb00140x

Nakamura, A. (2005, February 12). Migration expert makes case for helping foreign workers. *Japan Times.*

Nakayama, T. K., & Halualani, R. T. (Eds.). (2010). *The handbook of critical intercultural communication.* Malden, MA: Wiley-Blackwell.

Nakayama, T. K., & Krizek, R. L. (1995). Whiteness: A strategic rhetoric. *Quarterly Journal of Speech, 81*, 291–309. doi: 10.1088/00335639509384117

National Institute of Population and Social Security Research. (2012). *Summary of the Japanese population projection* [Nihonno shoraisuikeijinkou (Heisei24nen1gatsusuikei)]. Retrieved from www.ipss.go.jp/site-ad/index_english/esuikei/ppfj2012.pdf.

Oguma, E. (2002). *Democracy and patriotism: Nationalism and public space in the Post-WWII Japan* [「民主」と「愛国」 — 戦後日本のナショナリズムと公共性]. Tokyo: Shinyosha.

Introduction 23

Okano, K., & Tsuchiya, M. (1999). *Education in contemporary Japan.* Cambridge, UK: Cambridge University Press.

Onishi, N. (2005, November 19). Ugly images of Asian rivals become best sellers in Japan. *New York Times*, pp. A1–A6.

Ono, K. A. (1998). Problematizing "nation" in intercultural communication research. In D. Tanno & A. Gonzalez (Eds.), *Communication and identity across cultures* (pp. 34–55). Thousand Oaks, CA: Sage.

Ryang, S. (2003). The great Kanto earthquake and the massacre of Koreans in 1923: Notes on Japan's modern national sovereignty. *Anthropological Quarterly, 76*(4), 731–748.

Ryang, S. (2004). Chrysanthemum's strange life: Ruth Benedict in postwar Japan. *Japan Policy Research Institute, Occasional Papers, 32.* Retrieved from www.jpri.org/publications/occasionalpapers/op32.html.

Said, E. W. (1979). *Orientalism.* New York: Vintage Books.

Satsuka, S. (2009). Populist cosmopolitanism: The predicament of subjectivity and the Japanese fascination with overseas. *Inter-Asia Cultural Studies, 10*, 67–82. doi: 10.1080/14649370802605241

Schrag, C. O. (1986). *Communicative praxis and the space of subjectivity.* Bloomington, IN: Indiana University Press.

Sekimoto, S. (2014). Transnational Asia: Dis/orienting identity in the globalized world. *Communication Quarterly, 62*(4), 381–398. doi: 10.1080/01463373.2014.922485

Schilling, M. (1997). *The encyclopedia of Japanese pop culture.* New York: Weatherhill.

Shome, R., & Hegde, R. S. (2002). Postcolonial approaches to communication: Charting the terrain, engaging the intersections. *Communication Theory, 12*(3), 249–270. doi: 10.1111/j.1468-2885.2002.tb00269.x

Soh, C. S. (2004). Aspiring to craft modern gendered selves: "Comfort women" and Chŏngsindae in late colonial Korea. *Critical Asian Studies, 36*(2), 175–198. doi: 10.1080/14672710410001676025

Statistics Bureau, Ministry of Internal Affairs and Communications. (2013). The population of elderly people [Kōreishano jinkou]. Retrieved from www.stat.go.jp/data/topics/topi721.htm.

Suganuma, K. (2012). *Contact moments: The politics of intercultural desire in Japanese male-queer cultures.* Hong Kong: Hong Kong University Press.

Toyosaki, S. (2011). Critical complete-member ethnography: Theorizing dialectics of consensus and conflict intercultural communication. *Journal of International and Intercultural Communication, 4*(1), 62–80. doi: 10.1080/17513057.2010.533786

Trent, J. W. (1999). *Great mirrors shattered: Homosexuality, orientalism, and Japan.* New York: Oxford University Press.

Warren, J. T. (2001). Absence from whom? An autoethnography of White subjectivity. *Cultural Studies ↔ Critical Methodologies, 1*(1), 36–49. doi: 10.1177/153270860100100104

Wilson, S. (2011). Exhibiting a new Japan: The Tokyo Olympics of 1964 and Expo '70 in Osaka. *Historical Research, 85*, 159–178. doi: 10.1111/j.1468-2281.2010.00568.x

Yep, G. A. (2007). Pedagogy of the opaque: The subject of whiteness in communication and diversity courses. In L. M. Cooks & J. S. Simpson (Eds.), *Dis/placing race: Whiteness, pedagogy, performance* (pp. 87–110). Lanham, MD: Lexington Books.

Part I

Gender, sexuality, and the body

1 The affective politics of the feminine

An interpassive analysis of Japanese female comedians

Sachi Sekimoto and Yusaku Yajima

In January 2007, Health, Labor and Welfare Minister Hakuo Yanagisawa made the infamous remark that women are "birth-giving machines" (McCurry, 2007). He apologized immediately after he made the remark; yet public outrage, especially of women in Japan, was expressed. Behind this remark lies not only the history of patriarchal and nationalist ideologies concerning women's bodies and their reproductive rights, but also a decline in birthrates that has become one of the most troubling and urgent issues. The underlying ideologies concerning the relationship between women and the nation resurfaced publicly again in 2014 when a 35-year-old assemblywoman, Ayaka Shiomura, endured sexist heckling during her speech demanding improvements in childbirth and childcare for women in Tokyo. Several male legislators interrupted her saying, "You should hurry up and get married" and "Can't you even bear a child?" followed by laughter from several other individuals. In the context of a shrinking population and hyper-aging society, the declining birthrate is often simplistically framed as a women's issue, invoking hetero/normative gender roles deeply rooted in the construction of Japanese national identity.

Japan's population is aging due to increased longevity and decreasing due to the declining birthrate. Japan has the highest ratio of the population aged 65 or above and is the only country in the world categorized as a hyper-aged society (Cabinet Office, 2013). Population decline is one of the most significant concerns faced by the Japanese government and its people. Japan's population reached a peak of 127.74 million in 2006, and is expected to drop to 86.78 million by 2060 (National Institute of Population and Social Security Research, 2012). In 2005 the birthrate was the lowest on record with an average of 1.26 babies per woman during her lifetime, and it will stay around 1.35 in the future, which means that Japan is aging and population decline will not stop unless there is a viable solution (National Institute of Population and Social Security Research, 2012). Among the reasons for the low birthrate is economic instability which has resulted in a tendency to marry later and have fewer children (National Institute of Population and Social Security Research, 2010).

The escalated process of population decline and a hyper-aging society presents a gloomy prospect for the nation, deeply unsettling the historical imagination of nationhood and Japaneseness (Anderson, 1991; Oguma, 2002). Humor

28   *S. Sekimoto and Y. Yajima*

and comedy both reflect and shape the affective climate of the nation. The entertainment industry plays a key role in reflecting, mediating, and/or alleviating the psychological and affective experiences of viewers. Informed by Zillmann and Bryant's (1985) mood management theory on the relation between individual stress and television viewing, Anderson, Collins, Schmitt, and Jacobvitz (1996) report that people under stress tend to watch TV programs that serve "to replace anxious thoughts and that will replace negative moods with positive moods" (p. 255). In postindustrial society, consumers seek immaterial services as sources of healing and relaxation (Plourde, 2014). Comedy also plays a significant role in helping people question and challenge taken-for-granted norms, realities, and social structures (e.g., power inequalities, hegemony, marginalized subjectivities, stereotypes) (Greenbaum, 1999). Rossing (2010) states that comedy has the capacity to unmask social inequalities and realities in society, claiming: "Because comedy exaggerates features of our everyday life it reveals overlooked tensions and contradictions" (p. 15).

In this chapter, we explore (un)desirable performance of femininity as ideological and affective labor, paying particular attention to how the performances of female comedians make visible, humorously challenge, and/or reinforce the social stigma of being an unmarried, childless, or childfree woman in Japan. Through the analysis of selected TV episodes and other media sources, we reveal the affective politics of female desire embedded in heterosexist and patriarchal Japanese society. Using the notions of *interpassivity* (Žižek, 1998) and *affective labor* (Hardt & Negri, 2004), we problematize what we call *the affective labor of the feminine* in which an array of women's emotions—shame, guilt, jealousy, aspirations, hope, and happiness—are used to intensify or redirect the emotional involvement with, and ideological anchoring on, the gendered politics of reproducing Japan as a nation. Our goal is not to provide an overarching analysis of Japanese female comedians, but rather to propose an interpretive framework for revealing the tension between homogenizing and heterogenizing forces that shape the shifting ideological and affective landscape of femininity, heteropatriarchy, and humor.

As researchers, we engage in the critique of the cultural politics of femininity as sojourners/immigrants from Japan in the United States. Having lived away from Japan for many years, we situate ourselves as cultural "insider–outsider" whose cultural and gender identities are shaped by and implicated in the system of Japanese heteropatriarchy. Our analytical perspectives are informed and shaped by transnational cultural belonging and identity negotiation (Eguchi, 2014a). Born in the 1980s, we grew up fantasizing about the West, particularly the U.S., and have been in U.S. higher education/academia since the 2000s (first author) and the 2010s (second author) where we have been Americanized/racialized into an Other (Eguchi, 2014b; Toyosaki, 2007) and have trained ourselves to survive English hegemony (Tsuda, 2008a, 2008b, 2010) while simultaneously challenging it. Our analysis and theorizing, therefore, are critical observations from the other side of the Pacific; we attempt to make sense of the seemingly familiar, yet constantly renewed, cultural maneuvering in Japanese comedy that

The affective politics of the feminine   29

simultaneously upholds traditional norms while making room for more heterogeneous and counterhegemonic gender identities and ways of living.

Multiplicity in discourses of gender in Japan

The homogeneous image of Japanese society has been destabilized and collapsed in the late 1980s. The late 1980s and early 1990s witnessed a surge in the popularity of several unique trends in Japanese popular culture, such as anime, manga, video games, and cosplay. During this period, various interesting popular culture movements began including, but not limited to, the appearance of boys' love (BL) manga (Martin, 2012), visual kei music (McLeod, 2013), the "feminization of masculinity" (Iida, 2005, p. 57), herbivorous men, or *sōshoku-kei danshi*, that reject conventional Japanese masculinity, and carnivorous women (Nihei, 2013), and TV dramas and movies about gender identities and politics (Min, 2011). These trends embody nuanced, contested, or non-normative representations/performances of gender, potentially encouraging people in Japan to criticize, question, negotiate, or transform traditional gender hierarchy as well as conventional binary gender norms and roles that are pervasive in Japanese society, "including the binaries of male/female, heterosexual/homosexual, 'normal'/GID, homosexual/transsexual" (Min, 2011, p. 395).[1] Popular culture provides a space for people in Japan to explore—and commodify—alternative forms of gender performance outside of heteronormative femininity and masculinity.

Theoretical perspectives: interpassivity and affective labor

In analyzing the affective politics of humor and comedy in the context of population decline, we interweave two theoretical perspectives: interpassivity and affective labor. Žižek (1998) advances the notion of interpassivity as a form of commodity fetishism in which we entrust our enjoyment and suffering to something or someone else, particularly through the consumption of popular media. He distinguishes the notion of interpassivity from interactivity. The consumer is interactive when mediated signifiers seek his or her active participation—that is, the consumer experiences a spectacle with and through the signifier/Other.

Interpassivity, on the other hand, occurs when the object itself takes over the consumer's role of enjoying, feeling, or suffering. Mediated signifiers take on the consumer's responsibility and labor to be an active, independent, thinking subject. Examples of interpassivity include so-called "weepers" who are hired to cry at funerals, "canned laughter" on TV shows, and avatars in cyberspace. Žižek (1998) contends that interpassivity is a "relationship of substitution" in which the consumer decenters the work of subjectivity and delegates the labor of emotional life to the Other. He writes:

> By way of surrendering my innermost content, including my dreams and anxieties, to the Other, a space opens up in which I am free to breathe: when

30 *S. Sekimoto and Y. Yajima*

the Other laughs for me, I am free to take a rest; when the Other is sacrificed instead of me, I am free to go on living with the awareness that I have paid for my guilt, and so on.

(Žižek 1998, para. 10)

The relevance of interpassivity as an analytical concept is evident in various studies on popular culture in late capitalist contexts. Muhr and Pedersen (2010) elaborate on how Facebook functions as an interpassive medium in which our Facebook personas and profiles can feel and believe for us, socialize and enjoy friendships, and support a social cause by pressing the "like" button. This "[relieves our] own real bodily self of all these sometimes unbearable duties and injunctions of being a decent human being" (Muhr & Pedersen, 2010, p. 267).

The notion of interpassivity illuminates the "outsourcing" of emotional engagement and affective labor that otherwise requires a considerable amount of energy and attention in one's everyday life. The notion of affective labor speaks to the mode of production and consumption that sustains the interpassive relationship between the consumer and the consumed. Hardt and Negri (2004) use the term "affective labor" to refer to a form of immaterial labor that produces immaterial products such as "knowledge, information, communication, a relationship or an emotional response" (p. 108). Affect refers to the intensity of our emotional and physiological involvement, commitment, or anchoring that directs and regulates social formation and social relations (Gregg & Seigworth, 2010). In contrast with emotions that are felt mentally and individually, affect involves both qualitative bodily experiences (joy, sadness, satisfaction, etc.) and a collective mode of thinking, feeling, and organizing social reality (Ahmed, 2004).

Comedians are affective laborers in the sense that their job is to induce laughter—something immaterial yet bodily felt and socially cultivated. Shouse (2007) focuses on the affective dimension of stand-up comedy performance, arguing that humor is *"transmitted between bodies"* (p. 39, emphasis in original) and not simply conveyed by cognitive understanding of humorous words. As affective laborers, comedians produce or manipulate affects such as "a feeling of ease, well-being, satisfaction, excitement, or passion" (Hardt & Negri, 2004, p. 108). In analyzing selected media representations of two female Japanese comedians, Mitsuura Yasuko and Okubo Kayoko, we examine how their comedic personas engage in affective labor and enable interpassive engagement—viewers delegate and outsource their gendered obligations and negotiations with what it means to desire and feel like a woman in contemporary sociopolitical and cultural contexts of Japan.

Gender, affective labor, and female comedians

Japanese comedy has historically been dominated by male comedians, making it difficult for female performers to break into the industry. There are pervasive stereotypes that women cannot be funny and female comedians are not physically attractive (De Haven, 2013). Greenbaum (1999) argues that female

The affective politics of the feminine   31

comedians need to work harder than male comedians to establish and perform a comic persona (e.g., verbal roughhousing) in the male dominated arena of comedy. Even with a humorous script, their performances are not perceived as funny if they fail to create such a persona. Female comedians are required to violate the cultural expectations of femininity (e.g., not using passive voice and being "aggressive"). It is more common for female comedians to use their "less than attractive" physical appearance as a source of humor, thus playing into the existing sexist cultural framework in which Japanese women's worth is measured by their physical attractiveness. Japanese female comedians are often found to be funny based on their self-deprecating and apologetic attitude about their unattractiveness. The gender dynamic in Japanese comedy may be considered as in stark contrast to U.S. comedy in which critics find subversive and oppositional possibility in female comedic performance (Gilbert, 1997).

We focus on two popular and influential female comedians: Mitsuura Yasuko and Okubo Kayoko. They began their careers as a duo in 1992, gradually increasing their popularity over the next two decades. Mitsuura Yasuko is one of the pioneers who established their popularity as female comedians in Japan. Mitsuura's comedic character plays into the stereotypical framing of female comedian in that she claims her identity as the so-called *busu-kyara* (ugly character) and her humor is based on her tragic experiences of male rejection and unfulfilled female desire. If Mitsuura's *busu-kyara* is more nerdy and introverted, Okubo's comedic character plays on her performances of oversexualized femininity. Okubo plays into her "ugly" appearance, yet exaggerates her erotic appeal. As a woman in her forties, she has established her comedic persona by playing on the gap between her *busu-kyara* and her "expertise" in seducing men.

We propose an interpassive reading of Mitsuura and Okubo's comedic presence and performance that illuminates the underlying tension behind the shifting gender relations in the context of population decline and hyper-aging society in Japan. We propose that Mitsuura and Okubo's humor is not simply about perpetuating gender stereotypes of unattractive women, but rather functions as a medium through which the audience engages in an interpassive consumption of desire, purity, normative happiness, and emphasized femininity. Through overexaggerated comedic and emotional performance, Mitsuura and Okubo allow the audience to interpassively consume the traditional gender norms that are increasingly eroding and contested in Japan.

Interpassive consumption of desire and purity

In various TV episodes, male comedians ridicule Mitsuura for being unattractive and undesirable. In Japanese comedic TV shows, the canned laughter behind the scene is typically male voice, reinforcing a male-dominated environment and humor. Mitsuura accepts the ridicule and expresses her misery about not being wanted by men. She expresses her anger at the unfairness of beauty standards, but she does not contest the social judgment about (her lack of) beauty. Despite her status as *busu-kyara* (and her economic success as such), Mitsuura continues

32   S. Sekimoto and Y. Yajima

to proclaim that she dreams about marriage and is ready to abandon her career if she finds the right person.

In an episode of *mecha-mecha iketeru* (Mecha Mecha Iketeru, 2014, August 10), a popular prime time variety show, the group of comedians take Mitsuura on a "marriage-hunting (*konkatsu*) tour" and rally around her despair at not having had any physical contact with men. Under the banner of "Mitsuura's desperate marriage-hunting tour," they are all "worried" about Mitsuura's lack of romantic experience and that she will never be able to find happiness as a woman. In a series of visits to various male celebrities, the tour is intended to teach Mitsuura how to have physical contact with men, forcing her to touch them in subtle and not so subtle ways. In this episode, Mitsuura is portrayed as a desperate woman who is clumsy, naïve, and shy, yet driven by her sexual desire for the male body. Well into her forties, she is inexperienced and awkward around men; yet, she brings laughter to the audience when her shy and clumsy attitude is taken over by her sexual desire for physical contact, as she forces male celebrities to the ground as if she is a professional wrestler. She brings laughter to the audience by juxtaposing the shy and timid girl with the wild, unruly woman overtaken by her animalistic instinct.

Mitsuura Yasuko enables an interpassive consumption of desire and purity through her performances of a woman in her forties who desires and dreams about finding a male partner and getting married—despite the seeming impossibility of being found "attractive" by men. She has established a very successful and visible career based on her "miserable" and "tragic" life as an "ugly" woman. There is an interesting paradox in which her comedic humor and success are sustained by the fact that she portrays herself as "unmarriageable" and "undesirable." That is, her professional success is predicated on her being single without the presence of a romantic partner in her life.

Mitsuura's comedic character as "old maid" or "spinster" may perpetuate and stigmatize single women of a certain age who do not have children. It can be argued that the comedic relief the audience receives from Mitsuura's tragic humor may implicitly reinforce the idea that population decline and declining marriage rates are women's fault. If a woman wants to get married and yet cannot, there must be something wrong with her. Mitsuura's character confirms this sexist rhetorical strategy of blaming female undesirability as the reason for the decline of social institutions such as marriage and the family. Her comedic persona reinforces the traditional gender ideology that women believe marriage to be their life goal and the ultimate source of happiness. Gilbert (1997) points out that humor tends to be stereotypic/objectifying when employed by a marginal group in a way that challenges social inequalities, including marginal positionalities, by exposing them to cultural scrutiny. Furthermore, Gilbert argues that female comedians tend to employ self-deprecatory humor to potentially challenge the unequal status quo (e.g., hegemonic values) because doing so might overturn their positionality as a marginalized group by "educating" the audience in a safe way. She insists that self-deprecation is a safe yet "effective means of entertainment and social control" (Gilbert, 1997, pp. 326–327), as it

The affective politics of the feminine 33

does not blame the audience but criticizes the status quo without risk of punishment. Yet, this means, in the context of public performance, that comedians hardly make any substantial or immediate difference because they are "protected/being watched" by the status quo. That is, the status quo "has institutionally 'allowed' a potentially subversive discourse to be voiced" (p. 327). The use of marginal humor by female comedians may bring about some critical reflection by exposing inequalities, while perpetuating the status quo by operating under the sanction of the hegemonic ideologies.

What is interesting, however, is that from the perspective of interpassivity, there might be something more than a mere perpetuation of patriarchal and misogynistic attitudes toward unmarried and childless/childfree women. In the context of Japanese society which is undergoing a gradual yet tangible change in terms of gender relations and economic conditions, Mitsuura's comedic performance of a tragically unmarriageable woman who dreams and fantasizes about marriage enables the audience to "outsource" and delegate their duty to desire and uphold the institution of marriage and traditional family life. Through the consumption of Mitsuura's over-exaggerated performance of self-deprecation, childlike dreams of the purity of marriage and love, and crude sexual humor combined with her unwanted sexual advances, the audience can relieve themselves of the duty to desire—affective desire for marriage, desire for reproduction, or even the desire for normative forms of happiness.

The Japanese economy has long faced a sluggish recovery since the burst of the economic bubble in the 1990s and, with a hyper-aging society, the younger generations are increasingly resembling minorities. The government focuses on the welfare and benefits of older voters, while systematically neglecting the need to improve the availability of childcare, paid parental leave, and secure employment with reasonable working hours for young families. Raising children in Japan, particularly in the metropolitan areas, is often unrealistic for many working adults. In a context where the traditional ways of life—marriage, children, stable employment, a home—are increasingly difficult to attain for younger generations, Mitsuura provides a space for interpassive consumption of desire for an "ideal, happy life." As long as Mitsuura—well into her forties and without any prospect of marriage or romance—continues to strongly and naively desire traditional forms of happiness, audiences can delegate or delay their duty to desire these goals. Thus, Mitsuura's comedic presence both perpetuates old-fashioned gender stereotypes, while subtly displacing our affective labor and civic duty to abide by the traditional gender norms. Viewers do not interact with Mitsuura's emotional roller-coaster and empathize with her despair. Rather, they passively bypass the affective investment surrounding the decline of the nation and patriarchy, while laughing at the tragedy of an undesirable, unmarriageable woman. Such interpassive consumption both humorously displaces and ironically reproduces the patriarchal institution of marriage and gender norms.

Interpassive consumption of normative femininity

Mitsuura's comedic persona as *busu-kyara* entails her paradoxical portrayal as a woman who is unattractive, who admits to her unattractiveness, yet is concerned about her femininity and driven by her maternal instinct and affection. In an episode of *mecha-mecha iketeru* (June 7, 2014), the group of comedians discuss a number of Mitsuura's personal traits and behaviors that they deem unacceptable. Through a series of humorous anecdotes, they accuse Mitsuura of taking advantage of her popularity, acting selfishly, being pessimistic, and being inconsiderate to others. During the entire episode, Mitsuura is reprimanded not only for violating the collective harmony of the show, but also for exhibiting arrogant, unladylike behavior. For example, when one cast member points out that Mitsuura gets in a bad mood when male staff members call on her before a recording of the TV show, she answers: "You don't want anyone to see your face when you don't have your makeup on, do you?" This invites a male comedian to reply, "You know it doesn't make any difference [even if Mitsuura puts on makeup]." In response, she appears confused and clumsy as if she were saying, "I really have no idea why you are all saying such a thing to me and laughing at me." Acting in such a way brings laughter to all the comedians and the audience. Then another comedian points out that when men ask Mitsuura out for lunch or dinner she first questions their motive, asking, "What is your purpose?" To clarify why she reacts in this way, she remarks: "I want to know if they want to have sex with me, or protect me, or take some money from me, you know." Other male comedians respond, saying, "No man wants to have sex with you [because you are not attractive as a woman]," making everyone burst into laughter. It is through this gap between her unwomanly, crude behavior and her exaggerated female self-consciousness that Mitsuura succeeds in her self-deprecating humor.

Through her comedic persona, Mitsuura also embodies another normative femininity when she talks about her "overflowing" maternal instinct (*bosei*). In an episode of the prime-time TV show *Akan Keisatsu* (2014) in which celebrities are exposed for their "crimes," Mitsuura is spotted among other parents in a picture of an admission ceremony at a kindergarten. In keeping with the aims of the show, she is put on trial for posing as a parent. Mitsuura explains that she accompanied her friend to his daughter's special day, only to be invited to be photographed with the rest of the parents and the children. This incident is framed as Mitsuura's desperate desire, as a woman who is single and without children of her own, to be a caregiver for small children. As a self-acclaimed *busu-kyara*, Mitsuura decries that she cannot find the object of her maternal affection, only to be seen as pathetic and sad by others. In addition to TV appearances, Mitsuura cultivated another area of expertise in arts and crafts, publishing a few books. On one of her book covers, she wrote: "I have a heart to love someone. I have maternal affection. I have to make craftwork." In this statement she implies that without someone to love or take care of (romantic partner or children), she has to redirect her maternal affection toward her creative work in crafts.

The affective politics of the feminine 35

Mitsuura's comedic performance as a spinster perpetuates the stigma attached to women who are unmarried and without children. From the perspective of interpassivity, it can be argued that the audience is able to passively consume normative femininity when Mitsuura worries about her appearance or male sexual advances and is troubled by her overflowing maternal affection. That is, despite her undesirability as a woman, she nonetheless exhibits strong tendencies toward normative feminine behaviors. In a social context where normative gender roles are disrupted, Mitsuura's comedic performance assures viewers that "women will be women no matter what." Mitsuura's humor reassures the audience that women's desire for marriage and children are innate and essential, just as she continues to hope and dream about her fulfillment as a woman/mother. Viewers passively deflect the tension surrounding the crisis of normative femininity/motherhood and entrust in Mitsuura their duty to enact normative femininity.

Affective labor of *ara-fō*, or women around 40

Gaining greater popularity in recent years when in her forties, Okubo Kayoko presents a different type of humor than Mitsuura. Over the past two decades, her comedic persona has evolved into what is called *nikushoku-kei joshi* (carnivorous women) who aggressively pursue and "eat" men, in contrast with *shōshoku-kei danshi* (herbivorous men) who fail to exhibit hegemonic masculine behaviors (Nihei, 2013). Okubo is positioned as an "expert" in seduction and sexuality and makes the audience laugh by playing on the gap between her not-so-attractive appearance and her overly seductive and sexualized demeanors. In various TV appearances, she offers advice to young women on how to attract and seduce men. In an episode of one television show, Okubo is invited as a guest to share her techniques on how to be popular with men (Okubo Kayoko no Moteru Tekunikku, 2015, February 1). With a serious demeanor, she offers advice on how to become an attractive woman to a group of twenty-something female idols by demonstrating, for example, how to drink a glass of wine or eat a slice of pizza seductively. Her humor plays on the performance of excess and emphasized femininity juxtaposed with more "pure" and "natural" femininity embodied in "inexperienced" and "naïve" Japanese female idols.

A similar juxtaposition can be found in a TV program hosted by Okubo, *iionna no joken* (criteria for attractive women), in which she invites actresses or female models as guests and interviews them on their lifestyle and beauty secrets. Again, her comedic persona is juxtaposed with the more "authentic" beauty and femininity of Japanese actresses and models, while Okubo still assumes a position of authority on ideal femininity. Okubo ironically juxtaposes her comedic persona with normative and idealized femininity embodied in actresses, idols, and models, making it look as though these women are clueless and naïve about their womanhood, femininity, and sexuality. By mocking idealized femininity and desirable female sexuality, Okubo's parodic performance reveals the fiction of idealized Japanese femininity. Based on Butler's (1990)

36 S. Sekimoto and Y. Yajima

discussion on the subversive potential of parody, Warren and Heuman (2007) argue that parody, as a repetitive variation of normative identity performance, can reveal, resist, and transform the constructedness of hegemonic identity performance. Okubo's parodic humor presents the potential to be subversive of normative femininity in Japanese society that glorifies young, innocent, and inexperienced women as desirable.

Through her exaggerated performance as an expert in mature single womanhood, Okubo attracts fans of various ages, particularly women around 40 years of age. In contrast with Mitsuura's self-deprecating humor that emphasizes her "deficiency" (lack of marriage, children, or attractiveness), Okubo breaks the taboo of (unattractive, older, and/or single) women by honestly and openly talking about and wanting sex. Her comedic persona is no longer just humorous; she is seen as an experienced woman respected by other women. On many occasions, she has talked about her conservative lifestyle, saving money and having worked part-time as an office worker until she was in her late thirties. She is an "ordinary" woman in her forties who spent years slowly gaining popularity, who remains financially responsible and independent, is honest about her needs and desires, and is unafraid to voice her opinions. If the audience interpassively consumed Mitsuura's self-deprecating performance of normative femininity, Okubo facilitates a more direct identification and connection with viewers. Her comedic career began with Mitsuura and they shared the same *busu-kyara* approach to humor. Okubo's increasing (and greater) popularity over Mitsuura, however, indicates the impact of her affective labor in humorously and ironically exposing the feelings of despair and desire shared by many women in Japan. Okubo's humor seems to represent a subtle yet meaningful revolt against traditional gender roles and normative femininity.

Conclusion

Reading Mitsuura Yasuko and Okubo Kayoko's comedic performance of (un) desirable femininity in the context of population decline and a hyper-aging society reveals the significance of affective labor that makes visible, humorously challenges, and/or reinforces the social stigma placed on unmarried, childless, or childfree Japanese women. Using the framework of interpassivity, our analysis examined how Mitsuura's comedic persona enables the viewer to delegate and outsource the duty to enact or believe in normative femininity. Mitsuura embodies a woman who continues to desire, hope, and aspire for heteronormative happiness within the patriarchal institution of marriage and the family with a hint of irony and self-deprecation. From the perspective of interpassivity, when a woman such as Mitsuura—someone who is labeled as highly unlikely to get married and have children—continues to dream about her happy ending, the viewer is released from the duty to either endorse or question the normative definition of happiness. In a social context where the traditional definitions of marriage and the family are increasingly unstable and contested, Mitsuura takes over our duty to believe in these normative values. Mitsuura must forever remain

The affective politics of the feminine 37

single, miserable, yet hopeful, while releasing social tensions and attending to gender inequalities by expressing the grievances of being a single woman in her forties in the sexist and patriarchal culture of Japan. Driven by her maternal affection, Mitsuura must continue to dream and hope for normative happiness defined by hegemonic Japanese gender relations so that we—the viewers and citizens—are less burdened by such affective labor.

Mitsuura's comedic persona accompanies the dominant discourse surrounding population decline and declining marriage rates that young people *do* want to get married but *cannot*, largely for economic reasons. It is in fact true that personal income is strongly correlated with marital status. The general political solution to population decline primarily concerns the rhetoric of "we want to get married and have kids, but cannot." Rather than simply perpetuating the stigma against unmarried women, Mitsuura represents the growing public sentiment that the desire for the normative lifestyle is increasingly difficult to fulfill. In this sense, Mitsuura's comedic performance can be viewed as *the affective labor of the feminine* in which her emotions are used to intensify or redirect viewers' emotional involvement with and ideological anchoring on the gendered politics of reproducing Japan as a nation. Insofar as women desire marriage and children (but cannot attain them for personal or social reasons), we can redirect our energy into *helping* women to achieve *their* happiness. Population decline becomes a women's issue, a matter of *their happiness*. Women's happiness becomes a target of national policy; to want to be happy means to want to reproduce (the nation).

The popularity of Okubo Kayoko, on the other hand, indicates a slight shift in the affective politics of the feminine from that which Mitsuura established. Okubo does not agonize over the lack of male partner or marriage; she does not play on her "deficiency" but rather on her excess of femininity and sexuality. In the comedic appeal to her erotic hyper-femininity, she perpetuates stereotypical and heteropatriarchal gender relations in that her focus is still on attracting and pleasing men. However, Okubo also plays on her female undesirability and turns it against itself. That is, because it is presumed that men are not sexually interested in her and because she is a successful, independent woman, *she does not have to be desirable*. This is in stark contrast with other young Japanese idols and actresses whose career depends on their attractive appearance and acceptance by men. Okubo's humor displaces, in a subtle yet ironic way, the traditional gender hierarchy that regards normative femininity as a prerequisite for social acceptance and success. As a woman in her forties with a successful career, she frames her sexual humor as connected to her own pleasure and desire, not to the institution of marriage or the family. Okubo's affective labor redirects viewers' emotional investment in feminized forms of happiness and carves out a discursive space that many women of her age can and want to identify with.

Insofar as Japanese citizens continue to desire happiness within the heteropatriarchal framework of marriage and children, the government can rely on this affective energy to frame its policies on population decline. Without a viable and immediate political solution to population decline and a hyper-aging society,

38 S. Sekimoto and Y. Yajima

political intervention in the shifting demographics hinges on citizens' desire to produce offspring within the heteronormative institution of marriage. But what if young people stopped wanting these things? What if we let go of this affective politics of desiring the normative lifestyle and gender performance? What would the government do? The heteronormative hope for Japan's future seems to rest, at this point, on the affective labor of the feminine in which women bear the burden of carrying on the desire for marriage, family, and children, driven by their "maternal affection." As shown in the incident involving assemblywoman Ayaka Shiomura at the start of this chapter, women who cannot—or do not want to—exhibit such a desire may be viewed as unpatriotic or selfish. Female comedians such as Mitsuura and Okubo present both the limitations and the possibilities of the politics of affective labor that directs, mediates, and transforms the shifting ideological and affective landscape of gender identity and national subjectivity. Gilbert (1997) argues that although our social realities, or prevailing hegemony, do not change dramatically or immediately through a comedy, female comedians can provide powerful narratives that may help transform social inequalities using "the inherently subversive power of humor" (p. 328). Mitsuura and Okubo's (un)desirable performance of femininity presents one such potential to humorously and ironically subvert the burden of desiring female subjects.

Note

1 GID is an abbreviation for gender identity disorder.

References

Ahmed, S. (2004). *The cultural politics of emotion.* New York: Routledge.

Akan Keisatsu. (2014, August 15). 光浦靖子の子どもの入園式に勝手に出席しちゃっている事件 [Video file]. Retrieved from www.youtube.com/watch?v=Er61Na-.

Anderson, B. (1991). *Imagined communities: Reflections on the origins and spread of nationalism* (Rev. ed.). London: Verso.

Anderson, D. R., Collins, P. A., Schmitt, K. L., & Jacobvitz, R. S. (1996). Stressful life events and television viewing. *Communication Research, 23*(3), 243–260.

Butler, J. (1990). *Gender trouble: Feminism and subversion of identity.* New York: Routledge.

Cabinet Office. (2013). *Report on the population aging of Japan.* 平成25年度高齢化の状況及 び高齢社会対策の実施状況. Retrieved from www8.cao.go.jp/kourei/whitepaper/w-2014/gaiyou/pdf/1s1s.pdf.

Cabinet Office. (2014). *Report on the population aging of Japan.* 平成26年度高齢社会対策. Retrieved from www8.cao.go.jp/kourei/whitepaper/w-2014/gaiyou/pdf/t1.pdf.

Coulmas, F. (2007). *Population decline and ageing in Japan: The social consequences.* London: Routledge.

De Haven, S. (2013). Japanese manzai and gender: Personal perspectives from young female performers. *Japan Studies: The Frontier,* 41–52.

Eguchi, S. (2014a). Ongoing cross-national identity transformation: Living on the queer Japan–U.S. transnational borderland. *Sexuality & Culture 18,* 977–993. doi: 10.1007/s12119-014-9234-5

The affective politics of the feminine   39

Eguchi, S. (2014b). Disidentifications from the West(ern): An autoethnography of becoming an Other. *Cultural Studies ↔ Critical Methodologies, 14*(3), 279–285.

Gilbert, J. R. (1997). Performing marginality: Comedy, identity, and cultural critique. *Text & Performance Quarterly, 17*(4), 317–330.

Greenbaum, A. (1999). Stand-up comedy as rhetorical argument: An investigation of comic culture. *HUMOR: International Journal of Humor Research, 12*(1), 33–46.

Gregg, M., & Seigworth, G. J. (Eds.). (2010). *The affect theory reader.* Durham, NC: Duke University.

Harada, Y. (2003). Is there reason to be pessimistic about Japan's declining population? *Japanese Institute of Global Communication.* Retrieved from www.glocom.org/opinions/essays/20030916_harada_is/index.html.

Hardt, M., & Negri, A. (2004). *Multitude: War and democracy in the age of empire.* New York: Penguin Books.

Iida, Y. (2005). Beyond the "feminization of masculinity": Transforming patriarchy with the "feminine" in contemporary Japanese youth culture. *Inter-Asia Cultural Studies, 6*(1), 56–74.

Japan remains near bottom of gender gap ranking. (2014, October 29). *The Japan Times.* Retrieved from www.japantimes.co.jp/news/2014/10/29/national/japan-remains-near-bottom-of-gender-gap-ranking/#.VGUpgUsSFg3.

Katayama, H. (2009). A cross-cultural analysis of humor in stand-up comedy in the United States and Japan. *The Journal of Linguistic and Intercultural Education, 2,* 124–142.

Levine, L. (1977). *Black culture and black consciousness: Afro-American folk thought from slavery to freedom.* New York: Oxford University Press.

Martin, F. (2012). Girls who love boys' love: Japanese homoerotic manga as transnational Taiwan culture. *Inter-Asia Cultural Studies, 13*(3), 365–383.

McCurry, J. (2007, January 28). Japanese minister wants "birth-giving machines," aka women, to have more babies. *Guardian.* Retrieved from www.theguardian.com/world/2007/jan/29/japan.justinmccurry.

McLeod, K. (2013). Visual Kei: Hybridity and Gender in Japanese Popular Culture. *Young, 21*(4), 309–325.

Mecha Iketeru. (2014, June 7). めちゃイケ　光浦必死の婚活ツアー P1 [Video file]. Retrieved from https://m.youtube.com/watch?v=p3xgAziqeHY.

Mecha Mecha Iketeru. (2014, August 10). めちゃイケ「ダメトーーク 光浦靖子ダメ芸人」 P1 [Video file]. Retrieved from www.youtube.com/watch?v=_TOMi0FnwpQ.

Min, Y. S. (2011). Last Friends, beyond friends – articulating non-normative gender and sexuality on mainstream Japanese television. *Inter-Asia Cultural Studies, 12*(3), 383–400.

Ministry of Internal Affairs and Communications. (2013). *Report on information technology.* 第1部特集「スマートICT」の戦略的活用でいかに日本に元気と成長をもたらすか Retrieved from www.soumu.go.jp/johotsusintokei/whitepaper/ja/h25/html/nc123000.html.

Muhr, S. L., & Pedersen, M. (2010). Faking it on Facebook. In D. E. Wittkower (Ed.), *Facebook and philosophy: What's on your mind?* (pp. 265–275). Chicago, IL: Open Court.

National Institute of Population and Social Security Research. (2010). *Survey on marriage and childbirth.* 平成２２年度出生動向基本調査 (結婚と出産に関する全国調査) Retrieved from www.ipss.go.jp/ps-doukou/j/doukou14/doukou14.pdf.

National Institute of Population and Social Security Research. (2012). *Summary of the*

Japanese population projection. 日本の将来推計人口 (平成 24 年1月推計). Retrieved from www.ipss.go.jp/ps-doukou/j/doukou14/doukou14.asp.

Nihei, C. (2013). Resistance and negotiation: "Herbivorous men" and Murakami Haruki's gender and political ambiguity. *Asian Studies Review, 37*(1), 62–79.

Oguma, E. (2002). *A genealogy of "Japanese" self-images.* (D. Askew, Trans.). Melbourne: Trans Pacific.

Okubo Kayoko no Moteru Tekunikku. (2015, February 1). 大久保佳代子のモテるテクニック [Video file]. Retrieved from www.youtube.com/watch?v=CreD7uIZ9QY.

Plourde, L. (2014). Cat cafés, affective labor, and the healing boom in Japan. *Japanese Studies, 34*(2), 115–133. doi: 10.1080/10371397.2014.928183

Rossing, J. P. (2010). Critical intersections and comic possibilities: Extending racialized critical rhetorical scholarship. *Communication Law Review, 10*(1), 10–27.

Rossing, J. P. (2012). Deconstructing postracialism: Humor as a critical, cultural project. *Journal of Communication Inquiry, 36*(1), 44–61.

Shouse, E. (2007). The role of affect in the performance of stand-up comedy: Theorizing the mind–body connection in humor studies. *Journal of the Northwest Communication Association, 36*, 34–49.

Statistics Bureau, Ministry of Internal Affairs and Communications. (2013). *The population of elderly people.* 高齢者の人口. Retrieved from www.stat.go.jp/data/topics/topi721.htm.

Toyosaki, S. (2007). Communication *sensei*'s storytelling: Projecting identity into critical pedagogy. *Cultural Studies ↔ Critical Methodologies, 7*(1), 48–73.

Tsuda, Y. (2008a). English hegemony and English divide. *China Media Research, 4*(1), 47–55.

Tsuda, Y. (2008b). The hegemony of English and strategies for linguistic pluralism: Proposing the ecology of language paradigm. In M. K. Asante, Y. Miike, & J. Yin (Eds.), *The global intercultural communication reader* (pp. 167–177). New York: Routledge.

Tsuda, Y. (2010). Speaking against hegemony of English: Problems, ideologies, and solutions. In T. K. Nakayama & R. T. Halualani (Eds.), *The handbook of critical intercultural communication* (pp. 248–269). Chichester, UK: Wiley-Blackwell.

Warren, J. T., & Fassett, D. L. (2011). *Communication: A critical/cultural introduction.* Thousand Oaks, CA: Sage Publications.

Warren, J. T., & Heuman, A. N. (2007). Performing parody: Toward a politics of variation in whiteness. In L. M. Cooks & J. Simpson (Eds.), *Whiteness, pedagogy, performance: Dis/placing race* (pp. 215–232). Lanham, MD: Lexington.

Zillmann, D., & Bryant, J. (1985). Affect, mood, and emotion as determinants of selective exposure. In D. Zillmann & J. Bryant (Eds.), *Selective exposure to communication* (pp. 157–190). Hillsdale, NJ: Lawrence Erlbaum Associates.

Žižek, S. (1998). The interpassive subject. Centre Georges Pompidou Traverses. Retrieved from www.lacan.com/zizek-pompidou.htm.

2 "It's a wonderful single life"

Constructions and representations of female singleness in Japan's contemporary *josei dorama*

Emi Kanemoto and Kristie Collins

Social and media discourses in Japan have long upheld a view about the best time for women to marry. In the 1980s, the metaphor for single and never been married women was "Christmas cakes," meaning they had better marry before their twenty-fifth birthday. In the new millennium, the notion of "New Year's noodles" came about, meaning they had better marry before their thirty-first birthday. This indicates a gradual acceptance of women remaining unmarried throughout their twenties. Though being single or choosing to remain single either temporarily or permanently is becoming acceptable as marriage traditions are changing, female life in Japanese society remains inextricably linked to marriage, motherhood, and the *ryōsai kenbo* (良妻賢母) (good wife/wise mother) ideology. As evidenced worldwide by the *Bridget Jones's Diary* and *Sex and the City* franchises, the storylines surrounding women who have remained single have found receptive audiences in Japan in recent years; they have overwhelmingly presented single-never-married females in Japan as simply being in a holding pattern before inevitable (heteronormative) marriage.

And yet, Japan is experiencing a boom in female singleness; the average age of first marriage for both men and women currently hovers around the age of thirty (Ministry of Health, Labour and Welfare, 2015a). The messages to women (and to men) regarding society's hopes for—and expectations of—them are uneven and often contradictory. On the one hand, Japanese women are being encouraged by the current Abe government to participate in the labor force and re-energize the nation's long-stagnant economy; on the other hand, there is pressure to adhere to traditional scripts of femininity and devote themselves to halting the country's plummeting birthrate and tending to overworked husbands (Dalton, 2015).

If the very notion of womanhood in Japan is tied so tightly to the marital relationship and to motherhood, how is social identity among never-married Japanese women embedded in Japanese society? This question flags up the significant role the media plays in creating representations of problematic or marginalized identities. To be sure, media texts can equally serve to normalize or stigmatize traits, ideas, and groups of people, and the simple invisibility of positive representation can be pejorative because when "social representations do not exist, or only have a negative meaning, then presentation and construction

42 E. Kanemoto and K. Collins

of the self becomes more problematic" (Zajicek & Koski, 2003, p. 382). As such, it is essential to unpack single female representations in the media because Japan has been experiencing a dilemma in navigating traditional and non-traditional conceptions of womanhood related to marital status, motherhood, and career trajectories. A close examination of four contemporary *josei dorama* (female dramas) may offer us a lens through which we can observe female, single-centered media representations with regard to larger social discourses on shifting gender roles in Japan. Although these dramas are composed of multiple aspects of womanhood such as sisterhood, friendship, and familyhood, we focus here on the main single female characters' dilemma between marriage/romantic relationships and their pursuit of a successful career.

In this chapter, we first discuss the historical construction of female single-hood in Japanese society. Second, we briefly introduce the artifacts—four single-centered *josei dorama* from 2006–2016. Then, we move on to unpack how the female singlehood of the lead female characters is framed in the dialogs, particu-larly when they experience internal and external dilemmas in relation to making a decision regarding marriage/romance or career path. Although multiple com-ponents such as age and class (re)construct female singlehood in Japan, we put our central focus on the navigation of female singlehood in the dramas, which emerges from the contradiction experienced in choosing between marriage/romance and career path.

Traditional construction of the single female in Japanese society

Here we briefly discuss historical female gender construction and look specifi-cally at the discourse around the single female regarding marriage status and career path. We consider that *ryōsai kenbo* (良妻賢母) (good wife/wise mother) and *danson johi* (男尊女卑) (male superiority/female inferiority) ideologies are constructed, and are fundamental to the traditional construction of female single-ness in Japanese society. To unpack how these ideologies are socially con-structed, we first explain how single females who do not fit into *ryōsai kenbo* ideology are labeled in Japanese society.

To begin with, if a woman is unmarried and over thirty years old, she is fre-quently portrayed as *makeinu* (underdog) in comparison to the "winners" who married and had children before reaching the age of thirty (Sakai, 2003). *Mikon* is the common description of never-married women; *mi* in the Chinese character means "not yet," and *kon* means marriage (Maeda & Hecht, 2012). *Urenokori* (leftover or unsold) is another common term used to describe unmarried women. This leads to the analogy of Japanese women as "Christmas cakes," which implies that the best time to marry is/used to be before the age of twenty-five. At the same time, it is socially acceptable for unmarried women in Japan to engage in self-exploration in the workplace, through travel, and during interaction with peers until their late twenties or early thirties; however, they start to be seen as immature and self-centered if they remain single in their late thirties and early

"It's a wonderful single life" 43

forties (Rosenberger, 2007). Ultimately, maturity for Japanese women is more likely to be measured through their roles as wife, mother and daughter-in-law, as upheld by *ryōsai kenbo* ideology.

Those single females who devote time to self-exploration are often constructed as being selfish in circumnavigating marriage and childrearing, and consequently blamed for the nation's precarious welfare as social demographics dramatically shift—observed in contemporary Japan's rapidly aging society, falling birthrate, and in the growing numbers of individuals who delay or opt out of marriage altogether (Rosenberger, 2001). This alludes to their sense of obligation/responsibility to marry and have children for the sake of the country. Accordingly, single females who do not fulfill (or have not fulfilled) their obligation/responsibility feel their identities as immature individuals. Females who do not marry are largely seen as deficient and inferior to those who have followed *ryōsai kenbo* as a social norm by taking on the role of loyal, caring helpmates to their salaryman husbands (Dalton, 2015). Thus, both *ryōsai kenbo* and *danson johi* ideologies require "superior" males to join the labor force and females to be housewives that assist their male husbands.

We propose that the *ryōsai kenbo* and *danson johi* ideologies are historically and politically constructed and are influential components of a discussion of female singleness in Japan. Following these ideologies, womanhood is inextricably linked to marriage and unlinked to working careers. As such, we consider that the pursuit of happiness among females has been traditionally tied to the pursuit of *kekkon* (marriage) while female singleness, invariably linked to the pursuit of career success, has been viewed less favorably. However, the Japanese government has recently been attempting to increase the number of women in the workforce, mainly due to a projected decrease in the (male) labor force resulting both from the rapidly aging society and the falling birthrate (Ministry of Health, Labour and Welfare, 2015b; Rosenberger, 2001). Thus, women are encouraged to both marry and work in current Japanese society. While being aware that there are countless components that comprise female singlehood, given the current social, political, and economic situation in Japan we consider the following as the central—and often conflicting—concerns of this chapter: (1) the feminine pursuit of happiness entangled with marriage; and (2) female singleness and its relation to a career path.

Artifacts: four *josei dorama* (female dramas)

To explore the discourse on female singleness in contemporary Japan, we focus on the way in which single working women are presented in a small selection of Japanese *josei dorama* from 2006–2016. These artifacts were chosen because they featured unmarried central female characters around, or past, the average age of first marriage, and because they dealt explicitly with the conflicts faced by single women, especially those who actively and enthusiastically work in contemporary Japanese society. Below, we briefly introduce the storylines of four Japanese television dramas in chronological order from

44 *E. Kanemoto and K. Collins*

the time of airing, so that we can then discuss how female singleness is framed in these drama series.

Hataraki Man *(Working Man)*

Hataraki Man is a series about a single, hard-working, twenty-eight-year-old magazine editor named Hiroko Matsukata—commonly referred to as "Hiro" by her friends and co-workers. Adapted from Moyoco Anno's long-running manga series (since March 2004), *Hataraki Man* was aired as an eleven episode drama series on Nippon Television (NTV) from October to December 2007 (Yoshida, 2007). The storyline centers on Hiro's efforts to uncover and report the best news items for her magazine, and delves into her struggles with balancing her work life and her private life. On the one hand, Hiro is depicted as being largely fulfilled by her career and her work relationships; on the other hand, we see the mounting social (and self-imposed) pressure that she must negotiate in sustaining a faltering relationship with her over-worked boyfriend of four years, Shinji Yamashiro. Although Hiro attracts romantic suitors, those around her position her as "masculine" because of her commitment to and passion for her work.

Around 40

Around 40 aired on Tokyo Broadcasting System (TBS) as an eleven episode dramatic series from April to June 2008 (Hashibe, 2008). The series depicts the professional and personal life of a never-married thirty-nine-year-old psychiatrist, named Satoko, as she contemplates the way her future is unfolding. The storyline focuses on Satoko's life as she is fast-approaching her fortieth birthday. By all accounts—including her own—she is very satisfied with her (single) lifestyle. At the same time, her friends, Nao and Mizue, are shown to be questioning their own life choices. As Satoko counsels Nao through a rocky marriage and painful fertility issues and lends support to Mizue in dealing with an ungrateful husband and son, Satoko's single life seems all the richer in contrast. However, when Keitaro, an eccentric male care worker, arrives in Satoko's ward her previous certainty about the completeness of her life is called into question, and she is compelled to consider the desirability of romantic partnership and even parenthood.

Ohitorisama *(Ms. One Person)*

Ohitorisama aired on Tokyo Broadcasting System (TBS) from October to December 2009 (Ozaki & Seki, 2009). The series features a thirty-three-year-old private high school teacher named Satomi who, due to her serious work ethic and perfectionist tendencies, is viewed by her colleagues as being resolutely "*ohitorisama*" ("Ms. One Person"). Early portrayals of Satomi's singleness are empowering for viewers; for example, in asides to the camera, she discusses the pleasure she takes in dining out alone and in joining classes for self-development—opportunities she credits with having because of her single status.

"It's a wonderful single life" 45

She is also passionate and determined in her teaching and encourages students at the all-girls high school to aim to reach their full potential, too. Satomi is, however, faced with a decision that requires her to choose between work and love, and although she chose her teaching career over an earlier marriage proposal, she finds herself reconsidering when she falls for a part-time teacher, ten years her junior, named Shinichi Kamisaka.

Kekkon Shinai *(not marrying—English title: Wonderful Single Life)*

Kekkon Shinai aired on Fuji Television from October to December 2012 (Yamazaki & Sakaguchi, 2012). The storyline is evenly split between soon-to-be thirty-five-year-old Chiharu and forty-four-year-old Haruko. The two women first meet in a Tokyo park, which viewers soon learn is Haruko's first garden design project as well as discovering that Chiharu's ex-boyfriend has recently become engaged. While Haruko begins the series as a resolute single, self-identifying as married to her design work and years into an affair with her older married boss, she later severs the tie to her lover and eventually moves in with her new romantic partner, Professor Tanigawa, a regular customer at Haruko's flower shop. Chiharu also finds love through the flower shop with Junpei Kudo. Although Chiharu begins the series at a loose end in terms of both love and work, not knowing what she desires, she later learns the value of self-reliance from Haruko. The new relationship with Junpei does not derail her from pursuing her training qualifications to become a licensed travel agent.

We next explore how female singleness is constructed in these four drama series: *Hataraki Man, Around 40, Ohitorisama*, and *Kekkon Shinai*.

Female singleness in Japanese contemporary *josei dorama*

In unpacking the thematic patterns of each drama, we argue that the dilemma between achieving *kekkon* (marriage) and career success is the most dominant theme in terms of the media representations of single females. Single female characters tend to start questioning themselves—especially about focusing their lifestyles on careers—even though at the beginning of these drama series they were presented as happy and proud of their single lives. Here, through examining the main female characters' emotions and capacity for decision-making, as well as their interactions with others, we carefully explore how these dramas repeatedly frame the dilemma among single females regarding their unmarried status and career success. Under this dominant theme, two significant themes emerge from the media discourse to (re)construct the "expression of gender" wherein the lead single female characters experience a dilemma between choosing a career path and/or a privileged marital status. These are: what it means to be a "man" at work and single women's choices between romance and a career.

46 *E. Kanemoto and K. Collins*

Theme 1 To be a "man" at work

As previously stated, males are traditionally associated with work as breadwinners while females are associated with motherhood/wifehood. The first theme relating to the lead single females is being a man at work, specifically by demonstrating their willingness to overwork and sacrifice their lives for their career/work, as males do, so that these (single) females can become "one of 'the boys' " (Nemoto, 2013, p. 161).

Examples of being a "man" at work

Hiro—a twenty-eight-year-old magazine editor from *Hataraki Man*—is a good example. She cancels her anniversary date with Shinji—her boyfriend of four years—and chooses to prioritize her work. Later, when Shinji breaks up with her largely because of this decision to prioritize her work, Hiro immediately returns to work and stays up all night to finish editing an article while she is crying. She successfully finishes her work and receives high praise from her colleagues for her efforts. Here, she is sacrificing her romantic/private life and committing herself to her work. As another example, Satoko—the soon-to-be-forty-year-old well-respected psychiatrist from *Around 40*—is faced with a situation in which her father falls unconscious. Even in these circumstances, she still leaves the hospital room to go to her job. As a side note, immediately after leaving the room, Keitaro (Satoko's romantic partner) arrives and offers to cover her shift, so she actually ends up staying with her family. However, the salient point remains that Satoko still attempts to go to work even in such a dire situation—and her family does not stop her.

And yet, interestingly enough, while they are choosing their work over everything else, these single females still question their choice in doing so. In Satoko's case, she expresses her regrets when her father suddenly falls ill. Crying in front of her younger brother, his wife and child, she says: "I have not done anything for [family/father] with filial piety [*oyakoukou*] ... I should have married ... I should have had children.... Why didn't I marry previously so that so that [my Dad] did not have to worry about me?" Here, Satoko implicitly regrets that she has always prioritized work instead of being a good daughter (and a married one in this context). In Hiro's case, when Shinji breaks up with her, she actually cries and works at the same time. Even though her boyfriend broke up with her because she always prioritizes work, she continues to work even while heartbroken.

Responses to the choice to be a "man"

Even though these single females experience conflicted feelings, their colleagues, including their bosses and subordinates, praise and admire them when they make "male-like" choices at work. As a clear example of this, Hiro's colleagues constantly express how impressive she is as a *Hataraki Man* (working man) when she concentrates intently on her work and/or when she does a great

"It's a wonderful single life" 47

job as a journalist/editor of their magazine. Based on these reactions, a single female who is a *Hataraki Man* is treated in a positive manner in her workplace. Hiro also frames her choice of prioritizing her work in a positive way. When she is successful after the breakup of her relationship, her inner monologue says: *"there is a thing I lost because of my work. There is a night I cried because of thinking of it. But there is a morning—the work saves me."* It becomes clear how strong the connection is between Hiro and her career, and she will be fine without a romantic partner because she is saved by her work. In a similar fashion, when Satoko prioritizes her career over potential marriages, her friends become supportive of her decision to sacrifice her private life just as men do (Benson, Yuasa, & Debroux, 2007). Thus, these females' "male-like" choices in their work lives are praised by the people around them and even by themselves.

We argue that the lead characters are both perpetuating and shifting traditional social norms related to female singleness. In particular, the lead single females, including Hiro and Satomi, have been represented as responsible, successful single women at work, instead of being positioned within traditional typologies of single females as self-centered and immature (Rosenberger, 2007). In this way, these dramas offer non-traditional representations of female singleness in Japanese society. At the same time, the lead single females are regarded as "males" who are willing to overwork and prioritize their work over everything else (Benson et al., 2007). Like the example Nemoto (2013) provides to demonstrate how occasionally a woman works long hours and can effectively become one of the "guys," this representation of workaholic women such as Hiro and Satoko invites females to act like "males" in pursuing their careers so that they can be "one of the boys" at work.

We now want to pay attention to Hiro's nickname, *Hataraki Man* ("working man"), in critically discussing the single female as male at work. The term "man" is commonly used in Japanese media and society to signify male individuals rather than human beings in the wider sense. Like U.S. popular cultural products such as Superman and Spiderman, there are multiple Japanese popular cultural products/programs whose title ends with "man"—such as Ultra Man, Kinniku Man, and Anpan Man. The lead characters, identified as "something something man," are most likely males who immediately run to save others no matter what. While associating with the term "man," as discussed above, Hiro is a *"Hataraki Man"* (Working Man) who immediately runs to work no matter what the risk may be. Hiro and single female characters in other dramas share this behavioral pattern; they choose their work over everything just as strong heroic "men," such as Superman and Ultraman, choose to save others enduring any kind of hardship. The nickname *"Hataraki Man"* is explained as a process Hiro undergoes when focusing intently on her work. To all intents and purposes, she becomes a man for the purposes of her career. As a successful, passionate journalist/editor, Hiro is never called a *"Hataraki Woman."* Thus, *Hataraki Man* along with other dramas is (re)constructing the idea that intensive work attitudes are ideologically associated with "heroic" male figures (and females who act like males).

48 *E. Kanemoto and K. Collins*

As a comparison to Hiro as "*Hataraki Man*," Yumi is another female single character in the series. She is a hardworking sports writer who is known for her feminine power (*Joshi ryoku*) and openly states that her work motto is to act like a woman because she is a woman. In the end, when she resigns to prepare for her upcoming marriage, Hiro asks the reason for her resignation. Yumi answers that she has found something more important than work (implying marriage). These two types illustrate that the single female as "*Hataraki Man*" continues to stay at her work, while the single female who claims herself as a woman leaves work for marriage. These two representations are perpetuating the social norm that males (and male-like females) keep working while females express their desire to act as females by becoming wives to support working males.

All in all, while the dramas present lead single females in non-traditional ways as responsible, well-respected and admired workers, they push them into a male-oriented workplace ideology. By following the aforementioned media representations, the workplace is socially constructed for males or females who are prepared to behave like traditional working men—sacrificing their private lives and marriages. *Danson johi* (male superiority/female inferiority) ideology in Japan is perpetuated in these dramas through the presentation of single females who act like males by choosing work rather than behaving like females by choosing marriage.

Theme 2 Single women's choices regarding the dilemma between romance and career

The second theme is the "choices" available to single females when they are faced with the dilemma between romance and career. In these four TV dramas, all lead single females are somehow put in situations where they must choose a path between pursuing a romantic relationship and pursuing a career. (Single) females in Japanese society are currently under pressure from society, their families, and government to marry as well as to work (Maeda & Hecht, 2012; Ministry of Health, Labour and Welfare, 2015b; Rosenberger, 2007). The lead characters in the dramas often face situations in which their parents specifically express their wishes for them to marry or where they are aware of their parents' desires for them to marry. This kind of expression emerges from *ryōsai kenbo* (good wife/wise mother) ideology as well as from the sense of social obligation to marry and have children for the sake of the country (Rosenberger, 2001). While the single female lead characters in these shows experience such pressure, the majority of their romantic partners relocate themselves to other cities, mainly because of a new job and their careers. The lead females then have to decide what to do. In the following section, we show how three dramas (*Ohitorisama*, *Hataraki Man*, and *Around 40*) present the choices offered to single females, and then we go on to reveal how *Kekkon Shinai* differs from the others. Finally, we suggest how the choices made by single females are negotiated around *ryōsai kenbo* ideology.

"It's a wonderful single life" 49

Examples from the first three dramas

The first three dramas repeatedly construct a situation where the single female has to prioritize either traditional female happiness with her romantic partner or non-traditional female happiness through her career. In the case of these artifacts, Satomi from *Ohitorisama* chooses romance/potential marriage over her career, while Satoko from *Around 40* and Hiro from *Hataraki Man* choose their careers over romance/potential marriage. Satomi—a thirty-three-year-old private high school teacher in *Ohitorisama*—chooses a romantic relationship to gain traditional happiness linked with the *ryōsai kenbo* ideology. This happens when she and Shinichi—her romantic partner and a teacher at the same school—are faced with the view that romantic relationships between teachers may cause confusion and have negative influences on their students. Only two options are presented for Satomi by her colleagues at the school. They either break up and continue as teachers, or one of them quits teaching and they continue as a couple. Accordingly, she announces her resignation in front of the entire student body and her colleagues. She argues that she would not be a good teacher anymore if she broke up with Shinichi because she would be lying to herself about her romantic feelings. The student body is impressed by her speech and expresses a supportive attitude. In the end, though, Shinichi relocates to another school in a different prefecture. He does this for reasons of "self-improvement," while Satomi was willing to sacrifice her career for the romantic relationship.

Satoko and Hiro, on the other hand, choose different paths when in a similar situation to that which Satomi faced. In Satoko's case, she is suddenly faced with the choice of either staying in Tokyo to continue her calling as a psychiatrist (and to restructure her hospital as the new director) or going to Hokkaido with her fiancé, Keitaro, to pursue the traditional route to happiness for females—achieving the "accomplishment" of marriage. In Hiro's case in *Hataraki Man*, Shinji (Hiro's ex-partner) contacts Hiro and tells her he is leaving for Fukuoka—a city in Kyushu, far-removed from Tokyo. This provides an opportunity for Hiro to get back with Shinji (potentially marry) and go to Fukuoka together—which would require Hiro to quit her job in Tokyo. Both Satoko and Hiro are told by their best friends that these opportunities are their "last chance" to achieve happiness as females. However, both choose to pursue their careers instead. Interestingly, both Keitaro and Shinji encourage Satoko and Hiro to do good work when they choose their careers over potential marriage. Keitaro even apologizes to Satoko; he knew that she would want to stay at the hospital as the new director, but he selfishly remained silent about this because he still hoped she would go with him. As a result, they cancel their engagement. Therefore, Satoko loses her engagement when she chooses her career.

Together, the lead single female characters, their (ex)romantic partners, and their friends are repeatedly constructing situations where the single females have to prioritize between their careers and their last chance to gain traditional female happiness with romantic partners. These artifacts create an "either-or-binary"

50 E. Kanemoto and K. Collins

between marriage and career path which is only resolved when the male leads are physically removed to somewhere far away.

Examples from Kekkon Shinai

Moving on to *Kekkon Shinai*, the lead characters—Haruko and Chiharu—approach a similar situation differently. They do not choose their path from an "either-or-binary" between career and marriage. Rather, both Haruko and Chiharu pursue happiness by choosing their career path with their romantic partners (Professor Tanigawa and Junpei, respectively) without the bind of marriage. In the case of Chiharu, a thirty-three-year-old single female, Junpei relocates because of his job as a painter in a similar manner to the other men in the dramas. Chiharu falls into the traditional single female role in the earlier episodes, devastated at not having married and feeling the social pressure to do so. Yet, she ends up believing that it is enough to follow her career as a licensed travel agent and to simply stay connected with the one she loves without marrying. Junpei agrees, and they seem destined for a long, happy, unmarried future together even after his relocation. In other words, Chiharu chooses her working career and non-traditional love, but not legal marriage.

With regard to the other couple in the drama series, Haruko moves in with Professor Tanigawa, who earlier proposed marriage but was gently declined. In the very last episode, Haruko again suggests to Professor Tanigawa that they do not need a marriage certificate to define their relationship status. Rather, she seemingly implies that they have *jijitsukon* (practical marriage) in which unmarried couples live in a similar manner to married couples—long term, committed relationships—although she does not use the term *jijitsukon* explicitly. In any case, Haruko chooses to be happy with her partner without formally legalizing their relationship, while continuing on the career path. We note that *Kekkon Shinai* was aired in 2012 while other three dramas were aired in 2007, 2008, and 2009. The chronology may suggest that *Kekkon Shinai* would offer a different narrative about single working women than the earlier dramas.

Choices around ryōsai kenbo *ideology*

The single females in all four dramas face situations in which they must make a choice about the direction they wish their lives to take. We argue that although Satomi in *Ohitorisama*, Satoko in *Around 40*, and Hiro in *Hataraki Man* respond differently to the relocation of their romantic partners, all three of them are compelled to choose between either career success or a romantic relationship (and potential marriage). *Kekkon Shinai*, on the other hand, presents an alternative, which varies from the "either-or-binary" ending. Overall, we suggest that the traditional happiness embraced by *ryōsai kenbo* (good wife/wise mother) ideology is still the central focus among the representations of the lead single females. At the same time, the portrayals of paths to happiness among the single females in

"It's a wonderful single life" 51

these four dramas present multiple frames through which we may consider happiness and agency in relation to (single) women in Japanese society.

More specifically, the repeated pattern of "either-or-binary" in the first three dramas calls into question the utility of the *ryōsai kenbo* ideology. The "either-or-binary" means that women are forced to either follow the ideology, as Satomi in *Ohitorisama* does, or stray away from it—as Satoko in *Around 40* and Hiro in *Hataraki Man* do. We suggest that although some lead single female characters in the end prioritize their career goals ahead of potential marriages and *ryōsai kenbo* ideology, they do not simply say, "I am happy with my choice." Instead, Satoko in *Around 40* states that she will regret it if she does not stay in Tokyo to restructure her hospital as the new director. The lead single female characters often say that they choose professional goals over marriage in order *not to regret*, instead of simply *choosing to be happy*. Those who choose marriage, on the other hand, do so to be happy.

In the end, female singlehood in Japanese society at large can be appraised by tracking the repeated presentation of female singleness in media discourses. This representation of choosing career over marriage may be enacted by (single) females in Japanese society when they select a path based on not wanting to regret leaving work, rather than simply selecting a surer path to happiness through marriage. Thus, following the path of ideology does not lead all women to a happy ending. Rather, the binary pattern of "either following or not following ryōsai kenbo" still ideologically reinforces getting married as the only route to Japanese women's happiness. Thus, the single females in the first three dramas experience a dialectical tension between choosing work or traditional happiness tied in with *ryōsai kenbo* ideology. This represents the binary option available to single females: getting married or not marrying.

Yet, this binary option is problematic. The main reason for this is that, in contemporary Japan, single females are blamed for the falling birthrate and are still expected to marry and have children while (single) women are also encouraged by the Japanese government and its precarious socio-economic situation to remain at work and contribute to the lagging economy instead of leaving after marriage (Ministry of Health, Labour and Welfare, 2015b; Rosenberger, 2001). Thus, if the single female chooses to work and not to marry—like Hiro and Satoko—they are not meeting the social expectation to marry and have children. If the single female chooses to marry over pursuing a career—as Satomi almost does—they are not meeting the expectation of contributing to the labor force. Put differently, if the expression of female singleness in Japanese society follows the repeated patterns of the "either-or-binary" in media discourse, then (single) women will always be the object of blame.

Kekkon Shinai, on the other hand, negotiates a way to construct female singlehood in Japanese society by presenting a path that is still connected, but veers away from the conventional path of *ryōsai kenbo* ideology. Breaking this argument down, by portraying how both Haruko and Chiharu are satisfied with their unmarried long-term romantic relationships and their career paths, the representation of *jijitsukon* (practical marriage) is constructing another choice for

52   E. Kanemoto and K. Collins

single females other than the dichotomous choice between marriage and non-marriage/work. By showing *jijitsukon* as a potential option for single females, the drama is not privileging Japanese institutionalized marriage. Thus, at first glance, this drama challenges *ryōsai kenbo* ideology which is established within the institutionalized marriage system.

However, we must point out that this drama still portrays the idea that a single female cannot have both marriage and a career at the same time. Rather, the lead characters can find a happy medium—not quite *ryōsai kenbo* ideology embedded in the legal marriage system nor a successful salaryman ideology embedded in the workplace. We argue that there is a possibility that the representation of *jijitsukon* is constructing a new social space afforded to adult single females in current Japanese society—which still pressurizes females to marry and work and blames them for not being married or for not working. *Kekkon Shinai* could be constructing "happy-for-now" endings so that single females can leave the options of marriage or career open for the future. Although *Kekkon Shinai*, being the last of the four dramas—chronologically speaking—offers a different narrative for single working women in Japan, it is still navigating around *ryōsai kenbo* ideology, which sustains the notion of female singles as "have-nots" and as "inferior" to those with (heterosexual) married status (Maeda & Hecht, 2012; Rosenberger, 2007; Sakai, 2003).

Conclusions

In this chapter, our central focus was on how media discourse constructs the "expression of gender" regarding female singlehood in Japanese society with respect to the double-edged sword presented between the choices of career and preferred marital relationship. Female singlehood in society at large can be "an act which has been rehearsed" by following the repetitions presented in media discourse (Butler, 1990b. p. 272). While exploring two central themes—being a "man" at work and single females' choice of paths to happiness—using the dilemma of choosing between marriage and career, the representations of single females in these four *josei doramas* perpetuate, challenge, and together shift historical female gender construction(s) in Japan.

Regarding the first theme—being a "man" at work—as argued above, the represented expression of the single female as acting like a "man" willing to overwork and sacrifice her life for career/work allows these females to become one of the (male) team (Benson et al., 2007; Nemoto, 2013). The depiction of female singlehood in the workplace offers non-traditional representations of strong, successful, career-focused single women, rather than immature and selfish single females as homogeneous, traditional narratives portray (Rosenberger, 2007). At the same time, such depictions of the workplace reinforce the traditional representation of social norms in which men work and women, as wives, support their husbands—because these single females act like men at work and their work attitudes are thus portrayed positively. These social norms sustain the traditional ideology of *danson johi* (male superiority/female

"It's a wonderful single life" 53

inferiority). Regarding the second theme, the dilemma between romance and career, the central focus of the "either-or-binary" is on traditional *ryōsai kenbo* ideology (good wife/wise mother). Yet, while *Kekkon Shinai* offers an option of "a happy for now" ending through the practice of *jijitsukon* (practical marriage), the single female can postpone choosing between either marriage or career.

Contemporary Japanese society puts different kinds of pressure on single females to marry and have children and/or to work after marriage (Ministry of Health, Labour and Welfare, 2015b; Rosenberger, 2001). Furthermore, we should be aware that married women who remain in Japan's labor force still do not receive sufficient support from their employers, families, and even some husbands who may originally have shown supportive attutudes (Hinz, 2004). When single women are making choices in such a societal situation, valuing only traditional ideologies—such as *ryōsai kenbo* and *danson johi*—limits (single) females' happiness and potential in Japanese society both at the workplace and at home. As we found in this chapter, these ideologies are both perpetuatated and challenged to a certan extent in media discourses. As the Japanese workforce continues to require increased and diverse participation, the TV representations of gender roles across many professions will become increasingly important and worthy of additional study. This chapter is intended to contribute to the exploration of the negotiation process around these homogeneous ideologies with respect to single females in Japanese society.

References

Benson, J., Yuasa, M., & Debroux, P. (2007). The prospect for gender diversity in Japanese employment. *International Journal of Human Resource Management, 18*(5), 890–907. doi: 10.1080/09585190701249495

Butler, J. (1990a). *Gender trouble: Feminism and the subversion of identity.* New York: Routledge.

Butler, J. (1990b). Performative acts and gender constitution: An essay in phenomenology and feminist theory. In S. E. Case (Ed.), *Performing feminisms: Feminist critical theory and theatre* (pp. 270–282). Baltimore, MD: Johns Hopkins University Press.

Conquergood, D. (1985). Performing as a moral act: Ethical demensions of the ethnography of performance. *Text and Performance Quarterly, 5*(2), 1–13. doi: 10.1080/10462938509391578

Dalton, E. (2015). *Women and politics in contemporary Japan.* Abingdon, UK: Routledge.

Darlington, T. (2013). Josei drama and Japanese television's "new woman." *Journal of Popular Television, 1*(1), 25–37. doi: 10.1386/jptv.1.1.25_1

Gill, R. (2007). *Gender and the media.* Cambridge, UK: Polity Press.

Harden, B. (2008, August 28). Japanese women shy from dual mommy role. *Washington Post*, p. A8.

Hashibe, A. (Writer). (2008). *Around 40.* [Television series]. Japan: Tokyo Broadcasting System (TBS).

Hinz, C. (2004). Women beyond the pale: Marital "misfits and outcasts" among Japanese women entrepreneurs. *Women's Studies, 33*(4), 453–479. doi: 10.1080/00497870490444965

54 E. Kanemoto and K. Collins

Maeda, E., & Hecht, M. (2012). Identity search: Interpersonal relationships and relational identities of always-single Japanese women over time. *Western Journal of Communication, 76*(1), 44–64. doi: 10.1080/10570314.2012.637539

Ministry of Health, Labour and Welfare. (2015a). *Heisei 27 nen jinkoudoutai toikei geppounennkei (gaisuu) no gaiyou* [2015: Summary of vital statistics monthly report, year meter]. Tokyo: Ministry of Foreign Affairs. Retrieved from www.mhlw.go.jp/toukei/saikin/hw/jinkou/geppo/nengai15/dl/gaikyou27.pdf.

Ministry of Health, Labour and Welfare. (2015b). *Chiiki de torikumu jyosei no katuyaku suishin* [Engaging in the local area – promotion of female employees]. Tokyo: Ministry of Foreign Affairs. Retrieved from www.mhlw.go.jp/file/06-Seisakujouhou-11900000-Koyoukintoujidoukateikyoku/img-415210428.pdf.

National Institute of Population and Social Security Research. (2009). *Jinkou Toukei Shiryousyuu 2015* [Population statistics]. Retrieved from www.ipss.go.jp/syoushika/tohkei/Popular/Popular2015.asp?chap=0.

Nemoto, K. (2013). When culture resists progress: Masculine organizational culture and its impacts on the vertical segregation of women in Japanese companies. *Work, Employment and Society, 27*(1), 153–169. doi: 10.1177/0950017012460324

Osborne, P. (1994). Gender as performance: An interview with Judith Butler. *Radical Philosophy, 67*, 32–39.

Ozaki, M., & Seki, E. (Writers). (2009). *Ohitorisama.* [Television series]. Japan: Tokyo Broadcasting System (TBS).

Rosenberger, N. (2001). Gambling with virtue: Japanese women and the search for self in a changing nation. Honolulu: University of Hawaii Press.

Rosenberger, N. (2007). Rethinking emerging adulthood in Japan: Perspectives from long-term single women. *Child Development Perspectives, 1*, 92–95. doi: 10.1111=j.1750-8606.2007.00021.x

Sakai, J. (2003). *Makeinu no touboe* [Howl of underdogs]. Tokyo: Koudansya.

Salih, S. (2002). *Judith Butler*. London: Routledge.

Yamazaki, T., & Sakaguchi, R. (Writers). (2012). *Kekkon Shinai.* [Television series]. Japan: Fuji Television.

Yoshida, T. (Writer). (2007). *Hataraki Man.* [Television series]. Japan: Nippon Television (NTV).

Zajicek, A., & Koski, P. (2003). Strategies of resistance to stigmatization among White middle-class singles. *Sociological Spectrum, 23*, 377–403. doi: 10.1080/02732170309203

3   The shifting gender landscape of Japanese society

Justin Charlebois

Traditional gender discourses position adult men as family breadwinners and women as family caregivers. Regardless of the seemingly hegemonic status of these homogenizing discourses, they exist alongside alternate discourses that evidence tensions, contradictions, and inconsistencies in the social landscape of Japan. Sociocultural changes have provided space for and partially catalyzed the emergence of alternate forms of masculinity and femininity that depart from the mainstream and expose the culturally diverse and heterogeneous nature of Japan.

In this chapter, I discuss masculinities and femininities that diverge from and therefore challenge the powerful discourses of the male breadwinner and female caregiver. The chapter specifically investigates *ikumen* (caregiving fathers), white-collar professional women, and single women, and argues that they can be considered alternative masculinities and femininities. The results of the analysis indicate that while long-established archetypes may be in a state of upheaval and reconfiguration, it is necessary to exercise caution before drawing the conclusion that gender relations are necessarily becoming more equal in Japan. The chapter will discuss how these oppositional masculinities and femininities simultaneously reaffirm, disaffirm, and reconfigure archetypical forms of masculinity and femininity.

Salaryman hegemonic masculinity and housewife emphasized femininity

The culturally iconic corporate salaryman (*sarariiman*) and full-time housewife (*sengyô shufu*) represent archetypes of hegemonic masculinity and emphasized femininity in post-World War II Japan (Dasgupta, 2013; Hidaka, 2011). Hegemonic masculinity is defined as "those masculinities that *legitimate* an unequal *relationship* between men and women, between masculinity and femininity, and among masculinities" (Messerschmidt, 2016, p. 50). "Hegemony" references a state of gender inequality that is achieved, not through the use of brute force and coercion, but by processes of cultural ascendancy and persuasion so that an existing social arrangement is viewed as natural and inevitable.

Hegemonic masculinities incur intelligibility through their relationship with subaltern masculinities and *emphasized femininity*—"those femininities

56   *J. Charlebois*

practiced in a complementary, compliant, and accommodating subordinate relationship with hegemonic masculinity" (Messerschmidt, 2012, p. 35). At the same time, it is crucial to emphasize that discourses of masculinity and femininity are not ahistorical and monolithic, but also intersect with and thus vary by class, race/ethnicity, and sociocultural context (Collins, 2010; Skeggs, 1997). Although the relationship between hegemonic masculinity and emphasized femininity is fundamentally unequal, it is important to recognize that gender relations are not static and inevitable but dynamic and complex. Furthermore, the exercise of power is not unidirectional and absolute but multidirectional and fluid, so individuals shift between occupying positions with various degrees of powerfulness and powerlessness (Weedon, 1996).

In their reformulation of *hegemonic masculinity*, Connell and Messerschmidt (2005) propose a tripartite framework that provides a precise methodological tool to empirically investigate the construction of hegemonic masculinities, emphasized femininities, and other masculinities and femininities (Connell & Messerschmidt, 2005; Messerschmidt, 2016). Masculinities and femininities are *locally* constructed through face-to-face interaction within major social institutions such as families, schools, and workplace organizations. They are also *regionally* construed at a society-wide level through film actors, politicians, and business executives. Finally, masculinities and femininities are *globally* constructed in the arenas of international politics, business, and media. Discourses exist at the regional level, but in our increasingly interconnected, globalized world these discourses potentially penetrate the global level and vice versa.

Dasgupta (2010) chronicles how a discourse of a white-collar executive *transnational business masculinity*, which encourages bodily consciousness, has infiltrated discourses of contemporary salaryman masculinity. Dasgupta adopts the more precise term *glocally hegemonic* discourses of transitional corporate masculinity to capture how global discourses do not monolithically permeate the regional and local levels but interact with these levels in complex and multifarious ways. *Transnational business masculinity* originated in Anglophone contexts (Connell & Wood, 2005); however, the Japanese glocal variant of the discourse is observable in men's magazines that depict contemporary salarymen as well-groomed, stylish, and attuned to maintaining their physique. This depiction sharply contrasts with the sober image of the overweight, disheveled, and unstylish salaryman of the past. This example demonstrates how discourses from these different levels intersect and thus infiltrate other levels. Naturally, various facets of Western configurations of the discourse such as competitive individualism have not been transported to the Japanese glocal version.

The discourse of the salaryman is associated with a corporate employee who spends the duration of his career employed by a single organization (Dasgupta, 2013; Hidaka, 2011). Salarymen were core workers, hired for life (*shushin koyosei*), and thus recipients of calibrated salary increases (*nenkō joretsu*). Those who exhibited organizational loyalty received the corporate *total embrace* (*marugakae*), which includes lifetime employment, financial security, and social status (Dasgupta, 2013). The *kigyō senshi* (corporate warrior) or *kaisha ningen*

Shifting gender landscape of Japanese society 57

(corporate person) metaphors are frequently applied to salarymen because they were expected to sacrifice their time, autonomy, family life, and even their health in order to successfully perform their role in the public sphere. A section of the middle class could access a stable lifestyle by enacting the complementary roles of salaryman hegemonic masculinity and full-time housewife emphasized femininity. Therefore, stable employment, marriage and fatherhood were crucial rites of passage for men, while marriage and motherhood were critical life milestones for women.

The *sengyô shufu* (professional full-time housewife) discourse complements salaryman masculinity, and together they form the relational dynamic that constitutes hegemonic masculinity and emphasized femininity. In this discourse, a wife's altruistic domestic support enables a salaryman to prioritize his career and the corporation's demands. The classification of *sengyô shufu* as a profession is significant because it indicates that motherhood is a full-time endeavor, so wives are expected to prioritize their domestic role over other roles or professional ambitions (Kawano, Roberts, & Long, 2014). In reality, however, many housewives engage in part-time or temporary work and thus balance two sometimes conflicting roles (Nemoto, 2010; Tachibanaki, 2010). It is necessary to emphasize, however, that the central purpose of the wife's earned income is often to supplement the household income, which is a further reflection of the centrality of the domestic role. *Kengyô shufu* (working housewife) more accurately represents the heterogeneous and sometimes conflictual roles that many wives perform. As role perfectionism is a cherished sociocultural value, individuals are not only expected to conform to socially legitimated roles but also exert effort to excel in these roles (Holloway, 2010).

Before continuing with the discussion, it is crucial to emphasize that any attempt to identify and name particular discourses is a fundamentally subjective and interpretive process (Sunderland, 2004). While we can identify and name discourses of salaryman hegemonic masculinity and professional housewife emphasized femininity, these discourses are provisional and contingent. To capture this nuanced conceptualization of discourses, it is more accurate to conceptualize discourses of salaryman masculinities and emphasized femininities. This chapter focuses on hegemonic and non-hegemonic gender discourses but also recognizes that other discourses exist alongside and intersect with those discussed here.

Post-lost decade salaryman masculinity

The 1990s and ensuing decades have witnessed a prolonged period of economic stagnation and social upheaval (Dasgupta, 2013). Japan experienced a period of low economic growth and rising unemployment rates and a resulting sense of apprehension and uncertainty that is commonly referred to as the nation's *ushinawareta jûnen* (lost decade) (Dasgupta, 2009). A significant and enduring consequence of this period is that the salaryman lifestyle is increasingly inaccessible to subsequent generations. Compared to more economically prosperous times,

58   J. Charlebois

masculinity cannot always be constructed through the social resources of stable employment, professional status, and financial wealth.

Against a backdrop of this era, defined by social ambivalence and uncertainty, the emergence and social legitimation of alternant discourses of masculinity can be viewed as a positive consequence. Non-hegemonic masculinities are emerging which significantly diverge from and potentially undermine the force of the salaryman discourse (Dasgupta, 2009). Non-hegemonic masculinities reference those forms of masculinity that do not legitimate and sustain an unequal relationship between men and women, between masculinity and femininity, and among masculinities. In Japan, non-hegemonic forms of masculinity have emerged such as *otaku* (geeks) associated with animation and computer technology (Dasgupta, 2009; Napier, 2011), *furītā* (freelance workers) associated with unstable employment and the avoidance of social responsibility (Kosugi, 2008; Yuji, 2005), and the passive *sôshokukei danshi* (herbivorous men) who are apathetic toward professional success and romance (Charlebois, 2013). The passage of gender-neutral childcare leave legislation contributed to the emergence of more domestically involved fathers (*ikumen*). Regrettably, however, the number of fathers who take childcare leave is exceedingly small; yet the fact that *ikumen* receive a degree of social recognition by the media and larger society reflects the dispersion of shifting discourses of masculinity. While these non-hegemonic forms of masculinity are not associated with economic or social power, their emergence not only demonstrates the agency of subordinated groups but also that the ascendant position of hegemonic masculinity is tenuous and subject to challenge.

Discourses of salaryman masculinity have also experienced various shifts in the wake of the lost decade. While pre-1990s salarymen strengthened collegial bonds through after-work socialization, *shinjinrui* (new breed) salarymen are more frugal both with their time and their money (Allison, 1994; Dasgupta, 2010). This generation possesses significantly less disposable income and is accordingly less inclined to invest a considerable amount of time and money in after work *nommunication* sessions. Traditionally, alcohol functioned as a social lubricant that facilitated more direct communication among salarymen about work-related issues in the informal venue of a bar or restaurant (Allison, 1994). Today, however, many men dutifully attend the obligatory end of year (*bônenkai*) and New Year parties (*shinnenkai*) and also participate in some informal socialization, but the time invested is considerably less than that spent by their predecessors. Simultaneously, Japanese corporate values are seemingly shifting from the prioritization of hard work (*kinben*) and group harmony (*kyōchōsei*) to self-responsibility (*jikosekinin*), individual ability, and the formation of a competitive society (*kyōsō shakai*) (Dasgupta, 2010; Takeyama, 2010). Salarymen are less focused on using informal socialization opportunities to solidify group harmony and strengthen interpersonal relationships.

Concomitantly, *involved father* discourses are emerging that position salarymen in a more involved parental role (Nakatani, 2006). Considering the resilience of the *daikokubashira* (family breadwinner) discourse, it is unsurprising

Shifting gender landscape of Japanese society 59

that wives perform most of the domestic labor, regardless of their employment status (Dasgupta, 2013; Hidaka, 2011). Furthermore, the nature of the domestic contribution is also gender-segregated. Mothers perform the more instrumental, mundane aspects of caregiving such as cooking, cleaning, and feeding the children, while husbands do the less demanding and arguably more interesting tasks such as shopping and playing with children (Dasgupta, 2013). At the same time, however, contemporary wives expect their husbands to be not only family breadwinners but also compatible and communicative (Mathews, 2014). Although alternative discourses that challenge the entrenched *daikokubashira* ideology circulate in contemporary Japanese society, they have failed to catalyze a significant redistribution of gendered labor.

Regardless of these discursive shifts, participation in the labor force and the ability to perform the role of family breadwinner are interwoven into the fabric of contemporary salaryman masculinity (Dasgupta, 2013; Hidaka, 2011). The replacement of a seniority-based advancement system with performance- based assessment necessitates that employees work long hours to secure corporate advancement (Dasgupta, 2013; Higashino, 2011). Therefore, the precarious nature of permanent employment and emphasis on employees' productivity or performance reaffirms the cultural practice of working long hours. For these reasons, the lost decade period has not triggered a complete realignment of the work–production–masculinity nexus.

In an unstable economic environment, the discourse of the salaryman represents hegemonic masculinity precisely because it continues to exercise ideological force and therein diminish other discourses. Like hegemonic masculinities in other sociocultural contexts, salaryman masculinity is not the most mainstream or common form of masculinity in Japan, but it nevertheless exercises discursive power over other masculinities (Connell & Messerschmidt, 2005; Dasgupta, 2013; Messerschmidt, 2016). In a stagnant economy, increasing numbers of younger men are unable to secure permanent employment and thus must accept non-permanent forms of employment (Dasgupta, 2009, 2010). As a result, the aforementioned alternative masculinities that diverge from the hegemonic salaryman may be embodied by greater numbers of men.

Alternative masculinities and femininities

The above discussion has demonstrated that the position of hegemonic masculinity is not always permanent and secure; rather, it is tenuous and can be disrupted by sociocultural changes and the emergence of alternative or competing forms of masculinity and femininity. Thus, this discussion remains incomplete without acknowledging the agency of subordinated groups. *Subordinate* masculinities and femininities reference "those masculinities and femininities situationally constructed as lesser than or aberrant and deviant to hegemonic masculinity or emphasized femininity" (Messerschmidt, 2016, p. 55). Subordination can occur on the basis of race, class, age, sexualities, or body display/behavior (Messerschmidt, 2016, p. 55). Furthermore, subordinate femininities "often

60   J. Charlebois

simultaneously are 'oppositional' in the sense that their embodied practice—either intentionally or unintentionally—refuses to complement hegemonic masculinity in a relation of subordination" (Messerschmidt, 2011, p. 206). The emergence and legitimation of masculinities and femininities that depart from the status quo threaten the dominance of hegemonic masculinity.

Ikumen

Ikumen is a term that refers to men who are actively involved in childrearing. *Ikumen* was initially coined by an advertising company and received recognition as one of the most popular buzzwords in 2010 (Mizukoshi, Kohlbacher, & Schimkowsky, 2015, p. 2), coinciding with the launch of the Japanese government's "Ikumen Project" campaign. The prefix *iku* means "raise" and men is an English loanword. *Ikumen* thus encompasses stay-at-home dads and working fathers who actively participate in the domestic realm. *Ikumen* represents a significant departure from fathering in previous eras, where fathers' involvement was minimal and viewed as an obligation (Ishii-Kuntz, 2003). In contrast, *ikumen*'s phonetic resemblance to *ikemen* (handsome men) and *iketeru* (cool) indicates that fathering is considered a cool activity in contemporary Japan (Ishii-Kuntz, 2015; Mizukoshi et al., 2015). Nevertheless, coining a specific term for involved fathers is significant because it indicates that parenting is gendered feminine and involved fathers represent an anomaly. While actively involved fathers may be regarded as voguish or cool, an unequal division of household labor still constitutes the norm in many households (Dasgupta, 2009; Tachibanaki, 2010). Mothers are almost exclusively responsible for the more instrumental aspects of caregiving and housework, while fathers' involvement consists of bonding with their children through playing, giving a bath, and general socializing (Dasgupta, 2013; Nakatani, 2006). Thus, it is necessary to exercise vigilance and caution before concluding that the emergence of *ikumen* has prompted a significant redistribution of household labor.

As discussed, the discourse of salaryman masculinity delineates that a man's corporate role takes precedence over any domestic involvement. Accordingly, Japanese families are described as "fatherless" and their work-centered lifestyle ensures they are "healthy and out of the house" (Ishii-Kuntz, 2003, p. 199). Since the 1970s, the term *kazoku sābisu* (family service) has been used as a descriptor for spending time with one's family. The term conveys the nuance that family time is an unavoidable duty or obligation that interferes with the pursuit of personal leisure activities. *Sābisu* is used by restaurant and store employees to indicate that the customer is being given a discounted or free product and thus has positive connotations. In contrast, *sābisu zangyo* (free overtime) refers to uncompensated overtime labor in the workplace and carries negative connotations. Likewise, *kazoku sābisu* connotes that the father is sacrificing his personal leisure time to dutifully engage in family-oriented activities.

In recent years, however, discourses of active paternal involvement that significantly depart from the *kazoku sābisu* discourse have been circulating. In a

Shifting gender landscape of Japanese society 61

survey of newspaper articles, Mizukoshi et al. (2015) found that *ikumen* is gradually replacing *kazoku sābisu* to depict modern fatherhood. Therefore, the media is disseminating an *ikumen* discourse, which constitutes fatherhood as enjoyable rather than as an unavoidable duty. Nevertheless, a direct correlation does not necessarily exist between the circulation of the voguish term in the media and popular culture and fathers' greater domestic involvement. Rather, individuals' identification with this *ikumen* discourse is diverse and multifarious.

Data generated from interviews with soon-to-be parents provides an insight into how men and women interact with the *ikumen* discourse and reveals the complexities and contradictions associated with *ikumen* and fatherhood in contemporary Japan (Mizukoshi et al., 2015). Regardless of the dissemination and prominence of *ikumen* in the media, none of the male interviewees invoked the term during the interview. In response to interviewer-generated explicit prompts about *ikumen*, interviewees drew a distinction between a strong (*tsuyoi*) and weak (*futsû no*) *ikumen* image. The strong image was defined as taking parental leave and becoming a stay-at-home father, while the weak image was associated with active involvement in childcare and domestic labor. The interviewees characterized the weak image as natural behavior and the strong image as unrealistic. For these interviewees, a limited degree of involvement in the household is regarded as normal, but the husband's/father's main role is to serve as the family breadwinner. It is necessary to emphasize that since the interviewees were first-time expectant parents, men's actual involvement in the household remains uncertain.

The female participants' interview data provides additional insights into how individuals engage with the *ikumen* discourse. Like their husbands, the women did not explicitly reference the term *ikumen*, but they did express a desire that their husbands cooperate with household chores and parenting activities. Moreover, they specifically stated that uninvolved fathers are considered anomalies. Regardless of these seemingly progressive viewpoints, female interviewees expressed support for their husbands' domestic involvement to the extent that it did not negatively impact their careers. Both male and female interviewees conveyed disapproval toward the strong *ikumen* image. Their opposition may stem from practical reasons, such as the necessity of the father's income or concern that leave-taking would impact future career advancement opportunities. In any case, their narratives are built on the presupposition of a male primary breadwinner and female caregiver and do not advocate the revision of traditional gender roles.

We can draw a couple of conclusions from the fact that none of the interviewees specifically invoked the term *ikumen* in the interviews. First, the individuals may associate the term with the strong version of a stay-at-home-father, and they may either disapprove of this unorthodox gender division of labor or feel that it is unrealistic. In this traditional view, masculinity is associated with serving as the *daikokubashira* and full-time caregiving with femininity and a role revision is considered transgressive and unappealing. This interpretation is supported by the fact that none of the male interviewees expressed a desire to take paternal

62   J. Charlebois

leave. Therefore, men and women consciously or unconsciously avoid or reject the term in order to distance themselves from what they view as a radical role reversal. Relatedly, *ikumen* may be a media buzzword and not a term that individuals actually use to describe modern fathers. In any case, there is a gap between media-generated *ikumen* discourse and individuals' actual identification with the term.

Men who take childcare leave or exercise flexitime options can be seen as appropriating the strong version of the *ikumen* discourse and more directly resisting hegemonic masculinity. Ishii-Kuntz (2003) interviewed a sample of corporate salarymen and civil servants who either took childcare leave or used flexible working hours. Participants were members of the *Ikujiren* association which aims to increase parental involvement in childcare. Their membership of this organization indicates resistance to the discourse of *daikokubashira* and hegemonic masculinity.

These men drew on alternate practices and discursive strategies to construct masculinities that depart from the hegemonic salaryman. Some study participants said that caring for their children rather than breadwinning was their primary family responsibility. In doing so, they directly challenged traditional gender ideologies and configured an alternate or oppositional masculinity. Other interviewees stated that their presence in the home provided their offspring with a diverse environment that benefitted their development. By assuming the role of primary caregiver, these men discursively challenged the well-established "myth of three year olds" (*sansaiji shinwa*) (see Kawano, 2014), which posits that a full-time mother's presence is critical to an infant's development. Significantly, however, their accounts rest on an assumption that the act of parenting varies by gender. By constructing parenting as gender specific, they were able to construct a form of masculinity that is not constituted from a breadwinner role but is clearly distinct from femininity.

Working-class (blue-collar) *ikumen* fathers further depart from the white-collar hegemonic salaryman masculinity discourse. Unlike "elite" salarymen or civil servants, their class position locates them in a subordinate position vis-à-vis hegemonic masculinity. As these men are involved in more unstable waged labor, childcare leave or flexible working hours arrangements are unavailable to them. In some cases, the family's financial situation necessitates that both parents work, so these *ikumen* balance the demands of a physically exhausting job with a caregiving role.

Consequently, working-class men interact with the *ikumen* discourse differently from their middle-class counterparts. Ishii-Kuntz's (2009) study of working-class *ikumen* sheds light on how they interact with the discourse. One interviewee described how he managed to make time to bathe with his children on weekdays and allocate additional time for childcare on weekends. It is worth noting that he did not characterize this involvement as a form of family service but expressed a desire to spend more time with his children. The articulation of this view indicates that this man was engaging with emergent involved father discourses rather than the long established *kazoku sābisu* discourse. Ishii-Kuntz also found that the nature of involvement between working-class and middle-class men differed. While white-collar *ikumen* reported carrying out the more instrumental physical care of their children, working-class fathers' involvement materialized as engaging in fun activities such as playing with their children. Although working-class men challenged the notion that fathers remain uninvolved in caregiving, they legitimated the norm that women are primary caregivers. We see then how individuals can simultaneously resist and preserve elements of hegemonic masculinity.

The focus of the next section shifts to non-emphasized femininities. In a culture where marriage and full-time motherhood constitute the *sine qua non* of middle-class femininity, women who create identities outside of these social parameters can be viewed as oppositional femininities. The next section will discuss how white-collar working mothers engaged in continuous full-time employment and single women can be seen as non-emphasized femininities.

Post-millennial salarywomen femininity

This section presents the results of some qualitative interview data with women who combine marriage and family with a career. These women are following a salaryman-type career trajectory without the support provided by a full-time homemaker. Significantly, their refusal to choose between either raising a family or pursuing a career challenges the hierarchical and complementary relationship definitive of hegemonic masculinity and emphasized femininity.

Roberts (2011) conducted a study of urban salarywomen working at a large manufacturing firm. The company provides employees with permanent lifetime employment and other benefits in an implicit understanding that they will dedicate long hours to the organization. The company has instituted progressive family-friendly policies that materialize in the form of flexible working arrangements, generous leave packages, and an in-house daycare center.

The research participants indicated that an orthodox division of labor was common in most of the families, so the women faced the *second shift* (Hochschild & Machung, 2012) of domestic labor at the end of a long working day. These women assumed the bulk of the burden of preparing dinner, getting their children ready for bed, and doing the dishes and laundry. While a housekeeper could perform many of the household chores, participants hesitated to outsource the labor because this decision would give others the impression that they were neglecting their duties as a mother and thus potentially damaging the family's reputation.

The primary strategy women used to manage the demands posed by their careers and the domestic realm was to request their husbands' and extended family members' support, place their children in daycare centers, and make use of flexible scheduling. The assistance of extended family members is particularly indispensable when daycare centers are closed or school is out of session. Consequently, some participants relocated to reside in closer proximity to their parents or in-laws.

In addition to the various difficulties involved in securing a career-track position, a residual stigma still exists toward full-time working mothers because motherhood is regarded as a full-time endeavor in contemporary Japan (Kawano et al., 2014). The *seken* or "imagined community that has the normative power of approving or disapproving of and sanctioning individual behavior" (Sugimoto, 2014, p. 301) is a continual presence that encourages individuals to conform to social norms or face sanction. The *seken* would thus encourage adherence to traditional gender roles. Consequently, although some of Robert's participants possessed the financial resources and desire to employ a babysitter, they expressed concern that this decision would signify maternal negligence and result in the decline of their social standing in the local community. These professional women face the arduous task of balancing the sometimes conflicting demands posed by their careers, their families, and traditional social norms. In the process, while they contested the *sengyô shufu* discourse, they nevertheless still faced the gendered challenge of balancing work with family.

Single women

Just as employment, marriage and fatherhood are non-negotiable components of salaryman hegemonic masculinity, marriage and motherhood are critical rites of passage necessary for the embodiment of emphasized femininity. In a strongly marriage-oriented social climate, permanently single women contest the ideology underpinning the frequently repeated phrase "marriage is women's happiness" (Nemoto, 2008, p. 230). At the same time, however, alternate discourses are emerging that define marriage and parenthood as a matter of personal choice rather than as a social mandate (Nemoto, Fuwa, & Ishiguro, 2012; Rosenberger, 2013). In any case, the lifestyle of (financially independent) single women represents a noticeable departure from the traditional life course; thus they refuse to occupy a complementary, compliant, and accommodating subordinate position with regard to hegemonic masculinity and therein challenge unequal gender relations.

Women with a high level of education and career ambitions may find limited marriage options in a culture that idolizes youth, docility, beauty, and the willingness to manage domestic work, childcare, and eldercare (Nakano, 2014). In the marriage market, men express a preference to marry young, passive women who are willing to manage the household. Accordingly, highly educated women with career ambitions face a declining marriage market and decide to opt out of marriage. Indeed, highly educated single women cite losing their autonomy, men's unwillingness to share domestic labor, and being viewed as unfeminine and thus undesirable by men as factors contributing to their decision to remain single (Nemoto, 2008). This finding echoes Kimmel's (2008) point that success confirms masculinity but disconfirms femininity. Remaining single is one available option for contemporary women who wish to chart an alternate life course that departs from and contests emphasized femininity.

Permanently single women challenge unequal gender relations precisely because they must achieve a certain level of financial independence and are thus not dependent on a male breadwinner. Some white-collar single women even view their financial independence and autonomy as a way of resisting traditional femininity (Nemoto, 2008). Single women reject what some women consider to be their *gendered privilege* of exiting the workforce after marriage or childbirth (Nemoto, 2013, p. 522). Women who decide to leave the workforce and depend on a male breadwinner reinforce the ideology of separate spheres and sustain their unequal position in Japanese society.

Single woman is a non-monolithic category that encompasses women of different social classes. An income disparity exists between white-collar and pink- or blue-collar single women (Nemoto, 2008). Therefore, unmarried women engaged in unstable forms of employment face the concern of sustaining their financial independence for the duration of their working lives. As age discrimination toward women is particularly acute, they face the challenge of securing uninterrupted employment (Nakano, 2014). In some cases, unmarried adult daughters also serve as their parents' primary caregivers, which can involve additional stress and financial strain. The stress can be particularly acute for women in non-regular forms of employment, who do not have the corporate benefits packages and job security associated with regular employment. While the creation of a long-term public care insurance program (*kaigo hoken*) has reduced the burden of family caregivers by increasing access to professional care, the system has not made family caregiving completely obsolete (Kawano et al., 2014). For these and other reasons, single women in non-regular forms of employment face additional challenges compared to their middle-class counterparts, who have more financial security.

Discussion

This chapter has demonstrated how the social practices of both men and women perform a critical role in creating and sustaining gender hegemony. As gender hegemony emerges from the legitimation of an unequal relationship between men and women, the agency and social practices of women also contribute to the *cultivation* of hegemonic masculinity (Messerschmidt, 2016). The chapter will next consider how the social practices of women sustain hegemonic masculinity.

The *ikumens'* wives can be seen as contributing to the cultivation of hegemonic masculinity. While they voiced support for a degree of domestic involvement by their husbands, they discursively sustained a *part-time father/mother as main parent* discourse (Sunderland, 2000). The women expressed a desire for a degree of cooperation or assistance from their husbands, but their narratives presuppose that the mother assumes the role of main caregiver and the father accepts a part-time assistant role. Rather than problematizing the long hours that corporations demand of their employees or men's resistance to assuming a more active domestic role, they legitimated the necessity of a male breadwinner and therein cultivated hegemonic masculinity.

66   J. Charlebois

The single women that cite the lack of "masculine" marriage prospects as contributing to their single status also cultivate hegemonic masculinity (Nemoto, 2008). A man with adequate financial resources to serve as the sole family breadwinner and support a full-time housewife is their central criterion for selecting a marriage partner. Their accounts are underpinned by a traditional discourse of male breadwinner and female caregiver, and the rearticulation of this discourse also contributes to the cultivation of hegemonic masculinity.

The non-hegemonic masculinities and non-emphasized femininities discussed in this chapter demonstrate how masculinities and femininities can both contribute to gender inequality and also equalize gender relations. *Positive masculinities* and *femininities* are "those that actually may help legitimate an egalitarian relationship between men and women, between masculinity and femininity, and among masculinities and femininities, and therefore are constructed exterior to gender hegemonic relational and discursive structures in any particular setting" (Messerschmidt, 2016, p. 56). This section will next consider how such positive masculinities and femininities contribute to gender equality.

Strong and weak *ikumen* are built on gender practices that contest a domestically uninvolved male breadwinner ideology. Yet we must distinguish weak *ikumen* who contribute to a more equal redistribution of household labor from those who limit their domestic involvement to the more peripheral role of playmate. Needless to say, the long working hours that many corporations demand of their employees make it increasingly challenging to combine a full-time career with active domestic participation. Nevertheless, the white-collar salarywomen in Roberts' (2011) study demonstrate that the challenges that accompany combining the twin pursuits of career and family are not insurmountable. Likewise, weak *ikumen* fathers who are committed to reducing their work hours and increasing their domestic involvement can be viewed as positive masculinities because they contribute to the dissemination of *shared parenting* and *hands-on father* discourses (Sunderland, 2004). This hands-on involvement includes both the instrumental aspects of childcare and playing with their children. *Ikumen* who limit their domestic involvement to playing with their children sustain an ideology that the mother is the primary caregiver while the father is the family breadwinner and part-time parent or mother's assistant (Sunderland, 2000).

Married professional women simultaneously contest and sustain unequal gender relations. Women who equally divide domestic labor with their spouses delegitimize the ideology of separate spheres and can be viewed as positive femininities. At the same time, while married professional women who perform the lion's share of domestic work challenge the unequal gender relations, they cultivate hegemonic masculinity by not redefining working and parenting as equally shared endeavors.

Single women also contribute to democratizing the relationship between hegemonic masculinity and emphasized femininity, but not all single women can be viewed as positive femininities. Single women who choose to remain single because of their career ambitions or desire for autonomy are financially and emotionally independent and can thus be viewed as positive femininities.

Nonetheless, single women who are involved in more precarious, non-permanent forms of employment cannot be viewed as positive femininities due to their class position. Rather, they are *subordinate oppositional femininities* (Messerschmidt, 2016) because while they exist outside the hegemonic masculinity-emphasized femininity dynamic, their class position inhibits them from securing the necessary income to access a secure lifestyle. Their class position becomes increasingly insecure in non-permanent forms of employment that valorize women's youth, docility, and ability to assist male career workers (Kawano et al., 2014, p. 6; Nakano, 2014). Regrettably, these individuals occupy a subordinate position in relation to hegemonic masculinity and other forms of femininity.

Conclusion

This analysis of non-hegemonic masculinities and non-emphasized femininities provides an insight into the increasingly heterogeneous and diverse nature of the genderscape in contemporary Japanese society. The present state of social upheaval and uncertainty has contributed to the emergence of alternative masculinities and femininities that sustain, undermine, and reformulate the male breadwinner and female homemaker ideology. While *ikumen* discourses may circulate in society, individuals express ambivalence and uncertainty toward a more equal distribution of household labor.

We also saw some men construct parenting as variable by gender. The act of distinguishing between fatherhood and motherhood is significant because it can be viewed as a discursive strategy to justify men's involvement in the feminine realm of the home. This interpretation suggests that men still face difficulties in discursively embracing a fatherhood role without threatening their masculinity.

More optimistically, the positive masculinities and femininities discussed in this chapter are underpinned by discourses that problematize the ideology of separate spheres and women's financial dependence on a male breadwinner. Although hegemonic masculinity can be challenged and undermined by alternative masculinities, it also reformulates over time as a strategy to maintain ascendancy (Connell & Messerschmidt, 2005). The significant discursive shifts discussed in this chapter may catalyze a realignment of more egalitarian gender relations or the reformulation of hegemonic masculinity. Therefore, we must exercise analytical vigilance and distinguish positive masculinities and femininities from reconfigured or hybrid forms of masculinity or femininity that legitimate gender inequality.

References

Allison, A. (1994). *Nightwork: Sexuality, pleasure, and corporate masculinity in a Tokyo hostess club*. Chicago, IL: University of Chicago Press.
Charlebois, J. (2013). Herbivore masculinity as an oppositional form of masculinity. *Culture, Society & Masculinities, 5*(1), 89–104. doi: 10.3149/CSM.0501.89

68   *J. Charlebois*

Collins, P. H. (2010). Toward a new vision: Race, class, and gender as categories of analysis and connection. In R. Plante & L. Maurer (Eds.), *Doing gender diversity: Readings in theory and real-world experience* (pp. 20–32). Boulder, CO: Westview Press.

Connell, R. W., & Messerschmidt, J.W. (2005). Hegemonic masculinity: Rethinking the concept. *Gender & Society, 19*(6), 829–859. doi: 10.1177/0891243205278639.

Connell, R.W., & Wood, J. (2005). Gobalization and business masculinities. *Men & Masculinities, 7*(4), 347–364. doi: 10.1177/1097184X03260969

Dasgupta, R. (2009). The "lost decade" of the 1990s and shifting masculinities in Japan. *Culture, Society, & Masculinity, 1*(1), 79–95. doi: 10.3149_CSM0101.79

Dasgupta, R. (2010). Globalization and the bodily performance of "cool" and "un-cool" masculinities in corporate Japan. *Intersections: Gender and Sexuality in Asia and the Pacific 23*. Retrieved from http://intersections.anu.edu.au/issue23/dasgupta.htm.

Dasgupta, R. (2013). *Re-reading the salaryman in Japan: Crafting masculinities*. London: Routledge.

Hidaka, T. (2011). Masculinity and the family system: The ideology of the "salaryman" across three generations. In R. Ronald & A. Alexy (Eds.), *Home and family in Japan: Continuity and transformation* (pp. 112–130). New York: Routledge.

Higashino, M. (2011). Changing work patterns. In F. Taga (Ed.), *Yuragu sarariiman seikatsu* [Uncertain salaryman life] (pp. 35–63). Tokyo: Minervashobo.

Hochschild, A., & Machung, A. (2012). *The second shift: Working families and the revolution at home*. New York: Penguin Books.

Holloway, S. (2010). *Women and family in contemporary Japan*. New York: Cambridge University Press.

Ishii-Kuntz, M. (2003). Balancing fatherhood and work: Emergence of diverse masculinities in contemporary Japan. In J. E. Roberson & N. Suzuki (Eds.), *Men and masculinities in contemporary Japan: Dislocating the salaryman doxa* (pp. 198–216). New York: Routledge.

Ishii-Kuntz, M. (2009). Working-class fatherhood and masculinities in contemporary Japan. In S. Lloyd, A. Few, & K. Allen (Eds.), *Handbook of feminist family studies* (pp. 192–204). Thousand Oaks, CA: Sage.

Ishii-Kuntz, M. (2015). Fatherhood in Asian contexts. In S. Quah (Ed.), *Handbook of Families in Asia* (pp. 161–173). New York: Routledge.

Kawano, S. (2014). A sociocultural analysis of childrearing support for mothers with preschoolers living in Tokyo. *Japan Forum, 26*(1), 46–64.

Kawano, S., Roberts, G., & Long, S. (2014). Introduction. In S. Kawano, G. Roberts, & S. Long (Eds.), *Capturing contemporary Japan: Differentiation and uncertainty* (pp. 1–24). Honolulu: University of Hawaii Press.

Kimmel, M. (2008). *Guyland: The perilous world where boys become men*. New York: HarperCollins.

Kosugi, R. (2008). *Escape from work: Freelancing youth and the challenge to corporate Japan*. Sydney: Trans Pacific Press.

Mathews, G. (2014). Being a man in a straightened Japan: The view from twenty years later. In S. Kawano, G. Roberts, & S. Long (Eds.), *Capturing contemporary Japan: Differentiation and uncertainty* (pp. 60–80). Honolulu: University of Hawaii Press.

Messerschmidt, J. W. (2011). The struggle for heterofeminine recognition: Bullying, embodiment, and reactive sexual offending by adolescent girls. *Feminist Criminology, 6*(3), 203–233. doi: 10.1177/1557085111408062

Messerschmidt, J. W. (2012). *Gender, heterosexuality, and youth violence*. Lanham, MD: Rowman & Littlefield.

Messerschmidt, J. W. (2016). *Masculinities in the making: From the local to the global.* Lanham, MD: Rowman & Littlefield.

Mizukoshi, K., Kohlbacher, F., & Schimkowsky, C. (2015). Japan's *ikumen* discourse: Macro and micro perspectives on modern fatherhood. *Japan Forum, 28.* doi: 10.108009555803.2015.1099558

Nakano, L. Y. (2014). Single women in marriage and employment markets in Japan. In S. Kawano, G. Roberts, & S. Long (Eds.), *Capturing contemporary Japan: Differentiation and uncertainty* (pp. 163–182). Honolulu: University of Hawaii Press.

Nakatani, A. (2006). The emergence of "nurturing fathers": Discourses and practices of fatherhood in contemporary Japan. In M. Rebick & A. Tanaka (Eds.), *The changing Japanese family* (pp. 94–108). New York: Routledge.

Napier, S. (2011). Where have all of the salarymen gone? In S. Fruhstuck & W. Walthall (Eds.), *Recreating Japanese men* (pp. 154–176). Berkeley, CA: University of California Press.

Nemoto, K. (2008). Postponed marriage: Exploring women's views of matrimony and work in Japan. *Gender & Society, 22*(2), 219–237. doi: 10.1177/0891243208315868

Nemoto, K. (2010). Sexual harassment and gendered organizational culture in Japanese Firms. In C. Williams & K. Dellinger (Eds.), *Gender and sexuality in the workplace: Research in the Sociology of Work* (Vol. 20, pp. 203–225). Bingley, UK: Emerald Group Publishing.

Nemoto, K. (2013). Long working hours and the corporate gender divide in Japan. *Gender, Work and Organization, 20*(5), 512–527. doi:10.1111/j.1468-0432.2012.00599.x

Nemoto, K., Fuwa, M., & Ishiguro, K. (2012). Never-married employed men's gender beliefs and ambivalence toward matrimony in Japan. *Journal of Family Issues, 34*(12), 1673–1695. doi: 10.1177/0192513X12462573

Roberts, G. (2011). Salary women and family well-being in urban Japan. *Marriage & Family Review, 47,* 571–589.

Rosenberger, N. (2013). *Dilemmas of adulthood: Japanese women and the nuances of long-term resistance.* Honolulu: University of Hawaii Press.

Skeggs, B. (1997). *Formations of class & gender: Becoming respectable.* Thousand Oaks, CA: Sage.

Sugimoto, Y. (2014). *An introduction to Japanese society.* New York: Cambridge University Press.

Sunderland, J. (2000). Baby entertainer, bumbling assistant and line manager: Discourses of fatherhood in parentcraft texts. *Discourse & Society, 11*(2), 249–274.

Sunderland, J. (2004). *Gendered discourses.* New York: Palgrave Macmillan.

Tachibanaki, T. (2010). *The new paradox for Japanese women: Greater choice, greater Inequality.* Tokyo: International House of Japan.

Takeyama, A. (2010). Intimacy for sale: Masculinity, entrepreneurship, and commodity self in Japan's neoliberal situation. *Japanese Studies, 30*(2), 231–246. doi: 10.1080/10371397.2010.497579

Weedon, C. (1996). *Feminist practice and poststructuralist theory.* Hoboken, NJ: Wiley-Blackwell.

Yuji, G. (2005). *A nagging sense of job insecurity: The new reality facing Japanese youth.* Tokyo: International House of Japan.

Part II
Performance and queerness

4 Japanese male-queer femininity

An autoethnographic reflection on *Matsuko Deluxe* as an *onē-kei* talent

Shinsuke Eguchi

> Autoethnographers look in (at themselves) and out (at the world) connecting the personal to the cultural. Autoethnographic research combines the impulses of self-consciousness with cultural awareness reflecting the larger world against personal lived experiences oftentimes blurring the lines between them.
>
> (Boylorn, 2008, p. 413)

> Critical autoethnographic reflection, in its affects and effects, is always a social endeavor – in the equipment we use in applying the method, the larger cultural terrain on which the examination is done, as well as the manner or venue in which we share our findings and processes of knowing.
>
> (Alexander, 2012, p. 141)

I have been visiting frequently Japan for summer and/or winter breaks since I voluntarily relocated to the U.S. in 2001. In recent years, when I have returned to Japan I have observed that the queer visibility of *onē-kei talento* (オネエ系タレント) [queeny or sisterly talents/entertainers] is sensationally circulated through Japanese mainstream media and popular culture. These entertainers engage in the trans/gendered aesthetic of a camp speech style known as *onē-kotoba* (オネエ言葉)—that is, queeny or sisterly language. Maree (2008) asserts that *onē-kotoba* is "a parody of stereotypical women's language that is generally used by gay (gei) men in a performance of (hyper)femininity" (p. 67). I recognize that this *onē-kei* genre has been present in the post-second world war development of Japanese media and popular culture (McLelland, 2000).

In this chapter, I engage in critical autoethnographic reflection on the performative rhetoric of an *onē-kei* talent, Matsuko Deluxe (マツコデラックス). I use "zie," a gender-neutral, gender-inclusive pronoun for he/she, and "zir" (his/her) when referring to Matsuko Deluxe. The reason why I have chosen Matsuko is that zie is extremely popular in today's Japanese entertainment business. In October 2015, zie was appearing in ten talk shows per week, aired across various major Japanese TV networks. Zie is largely positioned as a good life adviser who "scolds" guests with zir tough love. Matsuko has also been appearing in various commercials. The large number of magazine and newspaper articles featuring Matsuko has reinforced zir sensational popularity. Here, zie has openly

74   *S. Eguchi*

challenged Japanese political figures such as the prime minister, Abe Shinzou (安倍晋三), and the previous governor of Tokyo, Ishihara Shintarou (石原慎太郎). Furthermore, Matsuko discusses the promotion of equal rights for lesbian, gay, bisexual and transgender (LGBT) people in Japan. Thus, I consider Matsuko Deluxe to be an important public figure and *onē-kei* talent in contemporary Japanese media and popular culture. By locating my "body as a site of knowledge" for this critical intercultural communication research (Calafell & Moreman, 2010, p. 414), I carefully reveal my responses to Matsuko Deluxe as a *performative* action of research.

I am particularly interested in politicizing and historicizing my embodied memories of experience to call into question the Japanese cultural and communicative practices of sex/gender and sexuality as I focus on my embodied performance of queerness as "not simply a being but doing for and toward the future" (Muñoz, 2009, p. 1). To do so, I draw upon a recently emerging field of queer intercultural communication as my theoretical framework. Chávez (2013) asserts that a large body of critical communication scholarship does not explicitly explicate issues of sex/gender and sexuality when examining the fluid and complex intersections and interplays between culture, power, and communication. Still, it has mostly addressed the needs and concerns of White U.S.American middle-class genders and sexualities (e.g., Chávez, 2013; Lee, 2003; Yep, 2013). The complex and contested multiplicity of racialized, gendered, sexualized, and classed knowledge(s) related to practices and processes of sex/gender and sexuality across cultures remains understudied (e.g., Eguchi, Calafell, & Files-Thompson, 2014; Johnson, 2001; McCune, 2008; Moreman & McIntosh, 2010).

At the same time, constructions of LGBT identities, performances, and politics, emerging from Western/U.S.American thinking, are increasingly becoming, and functioning as, a default in the contemporary context of globalization (e.g., Eguchi, 2015; Eng, 2010; Lim, 2014; Suganuma, 2012). The localized nuances of sex/gender and sexuality are often marginalized, erased, and/or replaced by Western/U.S.American narratives about LGBT identities and cultures. Darling-Wolf (2004) reinforces this point: "Because Japan exhibits many of the characteristics of a postcolonial nation, even though it was never actually colonized, issues of gender and race are particularly significant to this country's negotiation of its position vis-à-vis the West" (p. 366). Thus, my larger commitment in writing this chapter is to create a path to visualize currently unspecified maps of Japanese male-queerness.

Methodology: queer autoethnography

I perform my embodied translation of Matsuko Deluxe as an *onē-kei* talent "to speak as subjects rather than objects of knowledge" (Yep, 2013, p. 124). Chávez (2009) suggests that "the question of translation should ... not be whether the translation is correct, but for whom is it correct" (p. 23). To accomplish this task, I adapt, perform, and advance Stacy Holman Jones and Tony Adams' (2010) call for *queer autoethnography*. A conceptual intersection of queer theory and

Japanese male-queer femininity 75

autoethnography reveals a similar intellectual and political space. Queer theory reinforces a theoretical idealism of individual agency and sexual freedom that ignores communal ties and structural constraints (e.g., Johnson, 2001; Lee, 2003). Seemingly, however, it remains impractical. At the same time, autoethnography tends to focus on the personal without making a clear connection to the social, cultural, and political (Boylorn, 2008). Consequently, its writing becomes narcissistic and self-indulgent. I embrace these contradictions of queer theory and autoethnography that mirror a marginalized space of knowing, being, and acting. I argue that my embodied performance of intersectionality—"the interlocking nature of identity and power" (Chávez, 2012, p. 21)—takes place outside of the center in the context of globalization, which always re/centers the simultaneous functions of Whiteness, U.S.American/Western, able-bodied, cis-gendered male, heterosexuality, and/or the affluent as normative identities, discourses, ideologies, and structures. I am not perfectly situated within the center. So others already stigmatize, chastise, and correct the ways in which I perform, write, and speak about memories of my experiences. Still, this becomes and is my way of performing *a politics of disruption*.

Moraga and Anzaldúa's (1983) notion of *theories in the flesh* guides my methodology. Theories in the flesh pay careful attention to privileged marginalized people whose voices are often unheard, ignored, and erased. By paying attention to the state of marginality, E. P. Johnson (2001) asserts, "[t]heories in the flesh emphasize the diversity within and among LGBT people of color while simultaneously accounting for how racism and classism affect how we experience and theorize the world" (p. 3.). Theories in the flesh reveal the complex and particular nuances of racialized, gendered, sexualized, classed, and (trans)nationalized knowledge embedded in the material realities of LGBT people of color. Theories in the flesh account for ways in which the macro-structural productions and constitutions of difference affect who we are, where we come from, and how we talk about experience (Madison, 1993). Storytelling, which is a central component of queer autoethnography, illuminates socio-historical imbalanced power relations.

Storytelling also enables queer sexual minoritarians to produce counternarratives that interrupt master narratives. The queer praxis of storytelling from the margin requires an act of remapping. Buckland (2002) contends that "many queers are worldless, cut off in many instances from family, church, and other institutions of community-building. They have to fashion their worlds from their own bodies out" (p. 38). Due to the heteronormalization of institutional lives, non-heteronormative sexual minoritarians must utilize their bodily knowing, being, and acting in relation to the social, cultural, political, economic, and historical to change their worldlessness in a way that is appropriate for them. As Muñoz (1999) maintains, "the minoritarian subject employs disidentifications as a crucial practice of contesting social subordination through the project of world-making" (p. 200). In this intellectual process, the body is a key site of knowledge production as it holds memories of affect, such as desire, attraction, love, pain, and tension (Calafell, 2012). Therefore, I believe that the queer performative

76 *S. Eguchi*

mechanism of autoethnography is a tool that can reset the mapping of socio-historical imbalanced power relations.

With this line of argument, I advocate that queer autoethnography is a critical qualitative method of knowledge production. Muñoz (1999) reminds us that: "Autoethnography is a strategy that seeks to disrupt the hierarchal economy of colonial images and representations by making visible the presence of subaltern energies and urgencies in metropolitan culture" (p. 82). It represents a methodological commitment to identify with, critique, and shift the discursive and material effects of existing power relations to one specific location. Accordingly, Holman Jones and Adams suggest that,

> by hinging autoethnography and queer theory, we work to be out and queer in autoethnography and work to use autoethnography to be out and queer. Being out and queer in autoethnography means making ourselves vulnerable to critique, by risking living – in language and in life – the terms we keep in question by embodying possibilities.
>
> (Holman Jones & Adams, 2010, p. 142)

Thus, I approach queer autoethnography as a *refreshing* methodology to articulate possibilities for the future. I will now enter the world of Japanese media and popular culture to read the performative rhetoric of an *onē-kei* talent, Matsuko Deluxe (マツコデラックス).

Reflecting the performative rhetoric of *Matsuko Deluxe*

It is 5 pm on December 14, 2015. I am visiting my parents' home in Yokohama, Japan for my winter break. I am watching Matsuko's appearance in a talk show titled *Gojinimuchuu* (5時に夢中) ["Crazy for 5 pm"] aired by a Tokyo City-based local network, Tokyo MX Television. Matsuko sits around the table along with a male comedian/emcee, Fukawa Ryo (ふかわりょう), a female announcer, Naitou Satoko (内藤聡子), and a female commentator, Wakabayashi Fumie (若林史江). Matsuko's big, tall body covered in drag/cross-dressing attire stands out. Five minutes later, following the introduction, Fukawa Ryo (ふかわりょう) begins the talk show by introducing some news featured in the evening editions of the newspapers. Both Matsuko and Wakabayashi offer their perspectives on a number of news items. When they discuss an issue relating to the recent approval of an increase in consumption tax for take-away and fast food beef bowl restaurants, Matsuko suddenly becomes very outspoken. Zie critiques this change by questioning why the government tries to increase the tax, little by little, on an everyday item of necessity. Zie uses a phrase of Japanese slang "*cho-ko-ma-ka cho-ko-maka*" (ちょこまかちょこまか) to describe "little by little." Then, Matsuko discloses that zie is a smoker. With the bitter and spiteful tone of *onē-kei kotoba* (オネエ言葉) [literally the queeny language], Matsuko says: "I am ready for a tax increase on cigarettes. A box of cigarettes should be about 1,000 yen [US$10 at the time of writing] because it is actually

Japanese male-queer femininity 77

not a necessary everyday item." Wakabayashi immediately laughs at Matsuko's valid point. At this moment, I am wondering if Wakabayashi would have laughed if an *ordinary* looking male commentator had said this.

Still, I am reminded that the performative rhetoric of Matsuko as an *onē-kei* talent serves as a contested and contradictory site of cultural fiction in which the audience laughs at, teases, and/or jokes about. As Butler (2006) suggests, "the performance of drag plays upon the distinction between the anatomy of the performer and the gender that is being performed" (p. 187). According to Japanese ethnocentric heteropatriarchal imaginary, Matsuko's drag/cross-dressing body presentation with *onē-kei kotoba* constructs Matsuko as an (*unserious*) *Other*. As an *onē-kei* talent, Matsuko is automatically framed to have a unique, showy, and effeminate personality. This embodied text of Matsuko explicates, elucidates, and elaborates ways in which the unchallenged and taken-for-granted media and popular cultural representations of queer men are always as drag queens/cross-dressers.

This popular cultural genre of male-to-female (MTF) cross-dressing transgender performance has been historically known as "new-half" [Mr. Lady] in Japan. As Mitsuhashi (2006) writes, "the new-half community is usually situated within commercial businesses like entertainment (as hostess of bars and clubs), show business (as dancers and performers), and sex services (as sex workers)" (p. 204). What this means is that performances of male-queer femininity are only socially and culturally acceptable for the purposes of commercial business on the continuum of Japanese elitist, ethnocentric heteropatriarchy. New-halfs have interchangeably been called okama (オ カ マ) [slang for anus that started in the Edo (1603–1868) period]. McLelland (2000) asserts: "Okama are represented as humorous but ultimately sad and pathetic women manqué who try to act like or perform as women, but ultimately fail" (p. 59). Still, the commercial popularity of new-halfs easily overshadows complex and multiple differences among male-queers. The Japanese cultural tradition of family registry called *koseki* (戸籍) is a major source of ideological struggle that materializes in such a gendered and sexualized homogenization.

More precisely, I argue that *koseki* functions as a culturally specific paradox to otherize non-normative members of groups, such as LGBT people, who do not conform to the underlying normative assumptions about family and kinship. Transgender people especially struggle to change their registered gender/sex under *koseki* because the government often denies their requests (Mitsuhashi, 2006). Instead, differences among male-queers are both ignorantly and simply homogenized as *okama* in opposition to the hegemony of heteronormative Japanese masculinity. The discursive and ideological operations of singular, stable, and fixed imaginary binaries (i.e., heterosexuality–homosexuality, masculinity–femininity, and men–women) homogenize the heterogeneous practices of Japanese male-queer femininity. For example, several Japanese acquaintances sometimes ask me why I am not interested in doing drag and/or becoming a (trans)woman. As McLelland (2000) maintains: "The prominence of cross-dressed individuals featured in the media means that cross-dressing is the main

78 *S. Eguchi*

paradigm Japanese people have for understanding non-normative sexualities" (p. 8). In responding to their questions, I always become uncomfortable. I sense my inner resistive feelings toward their cultural interpretations of my queerness because my gender/sex and sexuality are simply coded as *okama*.

As I read the performative rhetoric of Matsuko Deluxe in that talk show, I simultaneously re-recognize that my internalization of cissexism has impacted how I resist the label *okama* imposed on my body. As Serano (2007) defines it, cissexism is "the belief that transsexuals' identified genders are inferior to, or less authentic than, those of cissexuals" (p. 138). My peers used to characterize my embodied performance of queerness as *okama* when I was a high school student. They saw me as "*like* a girl." However, I did not struggle to make sense of whether my sex/gender identity aligned with my morphology. More precisely, I did not question my male sex/gender body even when I was repeatedly categorized as effeminate. This is because I am the only cis-sexual male child in a middle-class Japanese heteropatriarchal household. Since I am culturally expected to carry on my family's name to the next generation, family members have treated me in a privileged way. This is not unique to me: male offspring's succession has been socio-historically embraced in the heteropatriarchal system of Japan. Johnson (2013) contends that "cispersons receive unearned privileges for the way bodies and identities align" (p. 138). Thus, I reflect that exploring my potential for doing drag and/or becoming (trans)gender is in fact contested and contradictory for me as I must challenge my own embodiment of the Japanese elitist, ethnocentric heteropatriarchy.

At the same time, my embodied aspiration for male same-sex sexual desire, intimacy, and relationality signifies the master narrative of shame that protects the Japanese elitist, ethnocentric, and patriarchal tradition of blood-based kinship. At this point, I do not perform my cultural conformity and belonging to the heteropatriarchal duty of reproduction that transcends a family's legacy to the next generation. However, conforming to and harmonizing with Others is a normative beauty of Japanese morality and communication. Gannon (2001) suggests that: "To the Japanese, social conformity is not a sign of weakness but of strong inner self-control" (p. 42). And Toyosaki (2011) maintains that "incapability of belonging is coded oftentimes as a sign of weak inner self-control" (p. 68). In other words, *everyone is supposed to be the same*. This mediocre rhetoric implies everyone must be normal—by normal, I mean heteronormative. The heterogeneous constructions of sexual differences are discursively homogenized for the systemic sustainability of heteropatriarchy. In this cultural environment, I could be culturally read as *weak* because I *choose not to* control my same-sex sexual desire. Thus, I must acknowledge the highly possible reading of my body as an abnormal, unordinary and troubling *okama*.

As I think of my cissexual privilege and same-sex sexual desire, I continue my viewing of Matsuko's live show appearance. An emcee, Fukawa Ryo, reveals news about a Japanese hammer thrower and Olympic athlete, Murofushi Koji (室伏広治), who has criticized the lack of self-management skills among athletes in Japan who fully depend on their personal trainers for health

Japanese male-queer femininity 79

maintenance. Fukawa asks Matsuko for zir opinion. Matsuko replies, "This is not unique to athletes." Zie reveals how zie actively collaborates in order to create TV programs in which zie mainly appears. Zie continues that zie enjoys more behind-the-scenes preparations than actual appearances in the industry. Then, zie stops and says, bluntly, "Actually people working on this TV show refuse to work with me behind-the-scenes." Fukawa laughs and says, "Are you sure?" Wakabayashi supports Matsuko by suggesting that zie really enjoys discussing the behind-the-scenes politics. Then, Matsuko continues: "Well, this [local] TV network [compared to major national TV networks] does not even really have any politics. So, I rarely talk about this network." Fukawa immediately cuts Matsuko off saying, "*Arigatougozaimashita*" [thank you very much]. At the same time, other members of the cast and staff members start laughing. With a serious face, Matsuko says, "Why did you cut in now?" Fukawa repeats, "*Arigatougozaimashita*," and moves on to the next news.

At this moment, I burst into laughter. The culture-specific and text-specific ambiguity of the rhetoric performed by Matsuko is something I always miss while in the U.S. Matsuko's rhetorical performance explicates zir tough love for this TV talk show in which zie appears weekly. As an insider of Japan's male-queer cultures, I have read that Matsuko demonstrates zir care for this show while zie jokes about the people zie is working with. However, I question whether some viewers read Matsuko's *onē-kei* performative rhetoric as rude and mean because they might have internalized normative ideas and social relations embedded in the material realities of Japanese elitist, ethnocentric heteropatriarchy. As I argued earlier, a cultural performance of social conformity is always already embraced as a normative script of Japaneseness (e.g., Gannon, 2001; Toyosaki, 2011). I contend that, influenced by Japan's homogenizing discursive forces, some viewers may feel the need to discipline Matsuko's frankness. Zie violates the unwritten norms of Japanese cultural communication rules as zie talks "negatively" about the people zie is working with. For other viewers, at the same time, I am certain that zie is automatically *excusable* because zie is an *onē-kei* talent who says what people normally would not say for the purposes of entertainment. An *onē-kei* talent is abnormally and unordinarily framed in Japan's mainstream cultural paradigm. Here, I argue that the push-and-pull between the homogenizing and heterogenizing discursive forces of Japanese cultural tradition, authenticity, and identity ironically both recenters the center and decenters queerness in the historical continuum of Japan's national, ethnic, and cultural particularization.

Accordingly, I recall that my grandmother (who was born in 1931 and died in 2011) used to describe an *onē-kei* singer and TV personality, Mikawa Kenichi (美川憲一), by saying "*ki-mo-chi-wa-rui*" (気持ち悪い) [literally, "looking strange"]. Since the mid-1960's Mikawa has been a well-known, gender-ambiguous, queer male talent in Japan. Since the late 1980s Mikawa has established zir positionality as an *onē-kei* celebrity, frequently featuring in gossip-based TV programs because of zir open and frank critiques of other talents. When I was a high school student, I used to fantasize about Mikawa's

80   S. Eguchi

queer performance of a bitter, bitchy, and spiteful personality because people around me were not openly sassy and frank as Mikawa was. I wanted to be like Mikawa. Simultaneously, I understood that my grandmother's reaction to Mikawa exposed the wider social, cultural, and political sustainability of Japanese elitist, ethnocentric heteropatriarchy. The gendered and (homo)sexualized nuances of *onē*'s bitter, bitchy, and spiteful style of speech disrupt viewers' heteronormative comforts. The expression "*kimochiwarui*" explicitly explicates how (in)visible discriminations and prejudices against queerness take place.

Japan has never historically prohibited and criminalized same-sex practices through its legal and institutional system (McLelland, 2000). Male same-sex sexual practice, labeled as *nanshoku* (男色) [literally, "male color"], was common in pre-modern Japan. Buddhist practitioners and samurai warriors were especially known for engaging in the male same-sex practice of *nanshoku*. This cultural tradition "contained a wide variety of terms for describing the partners involved in homosexual acts depending upon such factors as age (their junior or senior role), status, and the context in which the acts took place" (during the Tokugawa period, 1600–1867) (McLelland, 2000, p. 7). This homoerotism gradually disappeared, especially after Japan's modernization and industrialization that started from the mid-1800s. Since then, however, there has been some evidence of literature pointing to ambiguous and subtle practices of same-sex sexual desire, intimacy, and relationality (Treat, 1996). Yet, the *actual* penalty for same-sex sexual practices in Japan has been an unspoken and unwritten social alienation. Queers and transgenders are *silently* forced to disidentify with "unordinary" acts, behaviors, and practices. Thus, they do not evidently disrupt the normative and "business-as-usual" structure of Japanese elitist, ethnocentric heteropatriarchy.

As I think of the historical context in Japan that supports the constructions of male same-sex desire, I begin to read differently the performative rhetoric of Matsuko presented on the TV screen in front of me. Based on one of the evening news articles, Wakabayashi and Matsuko are now debating whether men can get sexually aroused by playing with their own nipples. At the same time, this scene strategically visualizes the framing of Matsuko as a representative voice of Japanese male-queer cultures in mainstream media streaming. Maree (2008) maintains: "The *onē* or *okama* character continues to reappear on commercial television, and the use of so called women's language by male personalities is said to index homosexuality" (p. 80). There is nearly no alternative representation of queer male talents outside of drag, cross-dressing and/or effeminacy in Japanese mainstream media. McLelland (2000) notes that: "Representations of 'ordinary looking' men [with same-sex sexual desire] doing ordinary things and living ordinary lives are conspicuously absent in Japanese media" (p. 58). Thus, I begin to see that Matsuko is actually a commercial and marketable product of queer illusion for the Japanese elitist, ethnocentric, heteropatriarchal gaze.

Watching Matsuko on the screen forces me to question my queerness again. *Why haven't I become an onē like Matsuko?* To answer this question, I first acknowledge that how I speak Japanese has been greatly influenced by the mainstream representations of *onē-kotoba* performed by a number of male TV

Japanese male-queer femininity 81

personalities. Growing up, I was (un)consciously subjected to *onē-kotoba* since it was one of the few symbols of queer performance available. Then, I recognize that I have been always forced to gravitate toward the West/U.S.America in the post-second world war context. Suganuma (2012) asserts: "The West functions as a sort of mirror which reflects the realities of Japan's queer cultures" (p. 180). The post-second world war momentums of global capitalism gradually erased the localized nuances and practices of male–male homoerotism called *danseidōuseiai* (男性同性愛) [literally, male same-sex love]. The contemporary formations of Japanese male same-sex sexual cultures illustrate the discursive and material effects of Western/U.S.American gay imperialism—"the way certain normative gay identities are incorporated into the imperialist nation-state" (Chávez, 2013, p. 87). The Western/U.S.American gay identity and life-style function as *progressive* and *advanced* models for the on-going development and negotiation of Japanese male same-sex sexual cultures and identities (Suganuma, 2012). An on-going interplay of the push-and-pull between the homogenizing and heterogenizing discursive forces of power is at play. The localized new-half cultures and communities are being pushed to the margin in the historical continuum of globalization.

Accordingly, I suggest that what has been imported to [queer] Japan along with Western/U.S.American gay imperialism is the homoerotic performance of *Orientalism*. Said (1978) asserts that "the Orient was almost a European invention, and had been since antiquity a place of romance, exotic beings, haunting memories and landscapes, remarkable experiences" (p. 1). The Orient mirrors the essential separation of East from West as it homogenizes the multiplicity of Eastern cultures, people, and ideas. This historical and ideological invention of Asia coincides with the hierarchal productions of queer desire, intimacy, and relationally embedded in the materiality of Western/U.S.American gay imperialism. Cissexual Asian men are both problematically and collectively homogenized as feminine and submissive *Others* for the Western/U.S.American gaze (e.g., Eguchi, 2015; Han, 2015; Hoang, 2014; Lim, 2014). The eroticized scripts of Asian cissexual men are sexual bottoms desiring Western/White phalluses inside their Eastern/Asian anuses.

For example, I vividly remember when my friend and I had gone to Tokyo's international lesbian and gay movie festival in July 2000, ten months before I moved to the U.S. Most of the films shown at the event were Western productions. We selected a collection of short films to watch on that day. The British-produced film, *Yellow Fever*, was quite memorable. A Chinese man living in London, Monty, used to date only White men. However, he begins to shift his desire as he develops a relationship with a Chinese neighbor. From this storyline, what I have not yet forgotten is Monty's monologue. Monty says that Asian men over 30 years old are no longer attractive and desirable to any White men because Asians are supposed to be *bottom, young, feminine*, and *submissive*. Consequently, post-30-year-old Asian men must begin to seek out other Asian men because non-Asian men would not want to talk to them. I remember that I was becoming both angry and confused. At the same time, I learned that the

82 *S. Eguchi*

bodies, resembling mine, portrayed in the film, signify *second-class citizen* status in Western gay culture.

This rhetoric of debasement surrounding my body was a turning point for me to shift my attention from the local to the global and from the domestic to the international. As Stockton (2006) maintains, "debasement is a fully indispensible informant" (p. 8). Consequently, I have distanced myself from becoming and being an *onē* like Matsuko because I (un)consciously internalized that *onē* is a discursive phenomenon marking Japan's social point of view as "behind the West." In Tokyo's historically well-known red light district, *Shinjuku-Nichoume* (新宿二丁目), for example, there are a number of famous male-queer bars and clubs, such as *Dragon* and *Arty Farty*, specifically known as destinations for international residents and tourists. In these *special-taste* bars, Japanese male same-sex sexual subjects seek foreign/Western/U.S.American men in order to have access to the capital of Western/U.S.American gay culture. I argue that this relational landscape resembles what Han (2015) has observed in U.S.American gay bars and clubs: Asian/American men are waiting to be chosen instead of doing the choosing. Additionally, Western/U.S.American hit chart music is played in these Japanese queer spaces. Japanese songs are rarely played because they are not *sexy* and *cool* enough for these bars and clubs. Moreover, various Western/U.S.America-based gay designer fashion goods and magazines are available in *Shinjuku-Nichoume*'s retail stores. In these material effects of global capitalism, the West is the cultural background from which I construct my "ordinary" cissexual Japanese queer subjectivity. Consequently, I have been both *naturally* and *easily* shifted to perform the colonized script of the effeminized Asian cissexual male rather than accept the localized script of *okama* onto my body. Thus, foreign/Western/U.S.American male subjects can desire my cissexual body made in Japan.

I argue that this citationality is the paradoxical way in which Orientalism reproduces Occidentalism—the homoerotic and fetishized images of the West. The rhetoric surrounding the Orientalist power of foreign/Western/U.S.American gay masculinity signifies the *penetrating* domination of phalluses that require the subordination of non-Western anuses. Suganuma (2012) maintains that "the Japanese male-queer gender is situated as abject with respect to 'hegemonic masculinity'" (p. 163). Thus, I critique my voluntary participation in the Orientalist narrative of feminine Asian bottom. I have clearly internalized my Occidentalist fantasy about the penetrating power of foreign/Western/U.S.American phalluses to perform the transnational constructions of "gaysian [gay Asian] fabulosity" (Lim, 2014, xiii). In other words, I have been a Japanese queer subject who participates in, supports, and gets incentives from the power of Western/U.S.American gay imperialism. Accordingly, Japanese popular culture productions of *onē-kei* talents signify what I should not be and should not become. Therefore, I acknowledge and critique the paradox within which I make sense of my embodiment of Japanese male-queer femininity in the age of gay imperialism as I consume Matsuko's live show appearance in *Gojinimuchuu* (5時に夢中).

Closing remarks

I began this chapter by introducing the performative rhetoric of Matsuko as an *onē-kei* talent. More precisely, I have engaged in autoethnographic reflection on the Japanese mainstream media commodification of Matsuko as an *onē-kei* talent that ignores, blurs and/or erases the multiple, unstable, and fluid practices of Japanese male-queer femininity. The popularity of Matsuko as an *onē-kei* talent in Japanese media and popular culture today signifies the homogenized and essentialized framing of queer men as *okama*, who want to be like *women*. This line of misconception is strategically materialized for the heteropatriarchal needs of the culture industry. Simultaneously, this non-heteronoromative commercial and makertable label, *onē-kei*, allows us to identify with and critique undisrupted Japanese cultural and communicative processes and the practices of gender/sex and sexuality. The performative rhetoric of Matsuko, an *onē-kei* talent, points to the push-and-pull between the homogenizing and heterogenizing discursive forces of power that strategically re/secure the elitist, ethnocentric, and heteropatriarchal scripts of Japanese cultural tradition, authenticity, and identity as the center.

Still, I find that the hyper-visibility of Matsuko as an *onē-kei* talent is necessary to create a potential medium for social justice in Japan. The media appearances and performances of Matsuko temporarily diversify the homogenized ideas and/or social relations embedded in the material conditions of Japanese culture and communication. With this in mind, I assert that the performative rhetoric of Matsuko as an *onē-kei* talent serves as a politics of disruption in the historical continuum of Japanese elitist, ethnocentric heteropatriarchy. As Muñoz (2009) emphasizes: "Queerness is that thing that lets us feel that this world is not enough, that indeed something is missing" (p. 1). Thus, I end this chapter by celebrating Matsuko Deluxe, who paradoxically offers potential spaces of queerness to identify the holes in and failures of Japanese society and identity for a future "that is a spatial and temporal destination" (Muñoz, 2009, p. 185). I urge other theorists, scholars, and activists to join me in critiquing the personal/political as a critical/cultural method of remapping the world of queer worldlessness.

References

Alexander, B. K. (2012). *The performative sustainability of race: Reflections on Black culture and the politics of identity.* New York: Peter Lang.

Boylorn, R. M. (2008). As seen on TV: An autoethnographic reflection on race and reality television. *Critical Studies in Media Communication, 25*(4), 413–433.

Buckland, F. (2002). *Impossible dance: Club culture and queer world-making.* Middletown, CT: Wesleyan University Press.

Butler, J. (2006). *Gender trouble* (2nd ed.). New York: Routledge.

Calafell, B. M. (2012). Monstrous femininity: Constructions of women of color in the academy. *Journal of Communication Inquiry, 36*(2), 111–130.

Calafell, B. M., & Moreman, S. T. (2010). Iterative hesitancies and Latinidad: The reverberances of raciality. In T. K. Nakayama & R. T. Halualani (Eds.), *The handbook of critical intercultural communication* (pp. 400–416). Chichester, UK: Wiley-Blackwell.

84 S. Eguchi

Chávez, K. R. (2009). Embodied translation: Dominant discourse and communication with migrant bodies-as-text. *Howard Journal of Communications, 20*(1), 18–36.

Chávez, K. R. (2012). Doing intersectionality: Power, privilege, and identities in political activist communities. In N. Bardhan & M. P. Orbe (Eds.), *Identity research and communication: Intercultural reflections and future directions* (pp. 21–32). Lanham, MD: Lexington Books.

Chávez, K. R. (2013). Pushing boundaries: Queer intercultural communication. *Journal of International and Intercultural Communication, 6*(2), 83–95.

Darling-Wolf, F. (2004). SMAP, sex, and masculinity: Constructing the perfect female fantasy in Japanese Popular Music. *Popular Music and Society, 27*(3), 357–370.

Eguchi, S. (2015). Queer intercultural relationality: An autoethnography of Asian-Black (dis)connections in White gay America. *Journal of International and Intercultural Communication, 8*(1), 27–43.

Eguchi, S., Calafell, B. M., & Files-Thompson, N. (2014). Intersectionality and quare theory: Fantasizing African American men's same-sex relationships in *Noah's Arc: Jumping the Broom. Communication, Culture, & Critique, 7*(3), 371–389.

Eng, D. L. (2010). *The feeling of kinship: Queer liberalism and the racialization of intimacy.* Durham, NC: Duke University Press.

Gannon, M. J. (2001). *Understanding global cultures: Metaphorical journeys through 23 nations* (2nd ed.). Thousand Oaks, CA: Sage.

Han, C. W. (2015). *Geisha of a different kind: Race and sexuality in gaysian America.* New York: New York University Press.

Hoang, N. T. (2014). *A view from the bottom: Asian American masculinity and sexual representation.* Durham, NC: Duke University Press.

Holman Jones, S., & Adams, T. E. (2010). Autoethnography and queer theory: Making possibilities. In N. K. Denzin & M. D. Giardina (Eds.), *Qualitative inquiry and human rights* (pp. 136–157). Walnut Creek, CA: Left Coast Press.

Johnson, E. P. (2001). "Quare" studies or (almost) everything I know about queer studies I learned from my grandmother. *Text and Performance Quarterly, 21*(1), 1–25.

Johnson, J. R. (2013). Cisgender privilege: Intersectionality, and the criminalization of CeCe McDonald: Why intercultural communication needs transgender studies. *Journal of International and Intercultural Communication, 6*(2), 135–144.

Lee, W. (2003). Kuaering queer theory: My autocritography and a race-conscious womanist, transnational turn. In G. A. Yep, K. E. Lovaas & J. P. Elia (Eds.), *Queer theory and communication: From disciplining queers to queering the discipline(s)* (pp. 147–170). Binghamton, NY: Harrington Park Press.

Lim, E.-G. (2014). *Brown boys and rice queens: Spellbinding performances in the Asias.* New York: New York University Press.

Madison, D. S. (1993). "That was my occupation": Oral narrative, performance, and black feminist thought. *Text and Performance Quarterly, 13*(3), 213–232.

Maree, C. (2008). Grrrl-queens: One-kotoba and the negotiation of heterosexist gender language norms and lesbo(homo)phobic stereotypes in Japan. In F. Martin, P. A. Jackson, M. McLelland, & A. Yue (Eds.), *Asiapacific queer: Rethinking genders and sexualities* (pp. 67–84). Urbana and Chicago, IL: University of Illinois Press.

McCune Jr., J. Q. (2008). Out in the club: The down low, hip-hop, and the architexture of Black masculinity. *Text and Performance Quarterly, 28*(3), 298–314.

McLelland, M. J. (2000). *Male homosexuality in modern Japan: Cultural myths and social realities.* New York: Routledge.

Mitsuhashi, J. (2006). The transgender world in contemporary Japan: The male to female cross-dressers' community in Shinjuku. *Inter-Asia Cultural Studies, 7*(2), 202–227.

Moraga, C., & Anzaldúa, G. (Eds.). (1983). *This bridge called my back: Writing by radical women of color*. New York: Kitchen Table.

Moreman, S. T., & McIntosh, D. M. (2010). Brown scriptings and rescriptings: A critical performance ethnography of Latina drag queens. *Communication and Critical/Cultural Studies, 7*(2), 115–135.

Muñoz, J. E. (1999). *Disidentifications: Queers of color and the performance of politics*. Minneapolis, MN: University of Minnesota Press.

Muñoz, J. E. (2009). *Cruising utopia: The then and there of queer futurity*. New York: New York University Press.

Said, E. W. (1978). *Orientalism*. New York: Vintage Books.

Serano, J. (2007). *Whipping girl: A transsexual woman on sexism and the scapegoating of femininity*. Berkeley, CA: Seal Press.

Stockton, K. B. (2006). *Beautiful bottom, beautiful shame: Where "black" meet "queer."* Durham, NC: Duke University Press.

Suganuma, K. (2012). *Contact moments: The politics of intercultural desire in Japanese male-queer cultures*. Hong Kong: Hong Kong University Press.

Toyosaki, S. (2011). Critical complete-member ethnography: Theorizing dialectics of consensus and conflict in intercultural communication. *Journal of International and Intercultural Communication, 4*(1), 62–80.

Treat, J. W. (1996). *Great mirrors shattered: Homosexuality, orientalism, and Japan*. New York: Oxford University Press.

Yep, G. A. (2013). Queering/quaring/kauering/crippin'/transing "other bodies" in intercultural communication. *Journal of International and Intercultural Communication, 6*(2), 118–126.

5 Bleach in color

Unpacking gendered, queered, and raced performances in anime

Reslie Cortés

As a force of globalization, Japanese media has spread in popularity throughout much of Asia (Iwabuchi, 2002). When considering Japanese media influence in the U.S., I observed that anime has found an enormous fan base among adolescents and young adults. Its popularity began as early as the 1960s with the debut of *Astro Boy* or, as it was originally called, *Tetsuwan Atomu* (Gibson, 2012; Schodt, 2007). New technologies have introduced larger volumes and varieties of anime into the U.S., especially for those with access to the Internet or streaming access to speciality for-profit sites such as *Crunchyroll*. Mainstream sites such as Hulu and Netflix also offer hundreds of anime titles that are available for streaming (Chozick, 2011). Other fans turn to free streaming sites, e.g., *AnimeGet.com* and *Anime-Sub.com*, which offer subtitled versions of current titles and can meet fans' demand more quickly than English licensing companies. One reason many U.S. fans enjoy consuming anime is the introduction to and engagement with various cultural elements that are performed and represented, including Japanese language, food, and clothing, as well as other cultural artifacts (Fukunaga, 2006).

As a media text anime is embedded with artifacts, cultural performances and, therefore, discursive reproductions of Japanese cultural identities. There are clear possibilities for shaping anime consumers' perceptions of Japanese identity and culture. Despite the implications of anime as an intercultural media text, it has not been frequently examined in the field of intercultural communication. Thus, I am interested in identifying and critiquing the rhetorical implications for Japanese tradition, authenticity, and identity surrounding the textual materiality of anime as it is globally consumed. While Japanese national, cultural, and ethnic identity is (mistakenly) seen as singular and homogenous, I argue that transborder tensions of hybridity exist due to Japan's histories with the West and the rest of Asia. Due to the hybrid and global tensions within Japanese culture, anime often includes different races and ethnicities, thus potentially disrupting homogenizing discourses. Lu (2009) argues: "Many anime feature Caucasian-looking characters either from the West, or Orientals with Western names" (pp. 170–171). This ambiguous representation has been theorized as *mukokuseki* (無国籍, statelessness) (Fennell, Liberato, Hayden, & Fujino, 2012; Iwabuchi, 2001). Lu asserts that this is a deliberate choice on behalf of the creators in order to make anime more attractive in the global market. Thus, I maintain that a critical intercultural approach must consider the myraid ways in which national, cultural, and ethnic identities are constructed while attending to the identity relations represented within a context of globalism and capitalism.

More precisely, in this chapter I investigate textual representations of Japaneseness in the popular anime, *Bleach* (Abe, 2004). I cannot ignore my positionality as a non-Japanese, U.S. based anime *otaku* (nerd). Accounting for this, I should highlight the ways in which anime's cultural reproductions may be perceived by U.S. based otaku. In light of my positionality, I have chosen this series because of its consistent popularity both in the U.S. and in Japan. Although the series stopped airing in the U.S. in 2009 (2012 in Japan), it is still the third most watched anime series (Anime News Network). Additionally, the manga (comicbook) version of the series is still in production and, at the time of writing, its final chapter was due to be published in August 2016. A new live action movie is also set to release in 2018 (Alexander, 2016). This series is still relevant to anime fans in both Japan and the U.S., which makes it an important media text for the present analysis.

I was drawn to *Bleach* as it attributes a wide spectrum of gender performances and roles to both female and male characters. This series is part of the shounen genre of anime, frequently characterized by a male protagonist in an action/adventure plot. *Bleach* contradicts two important observed characteristics of anime, particularly the shounen genre. First, as Bresnahan, Inoue, and Kagawa (2006) suggest, shounen anime tend to have a disproportionately high number of male characters compared to other anime genres. However, this series has an almost equal number of female and male characters. Second, there is a perception that female characters in anime only perform very limited supporting roles (Lu, 2008). Considering that *Bleach* challenges these characteristics, I believe that it serves as an analytic artifact that can be examined for anime representations of emerging gender performances. In particular, I use representations of gender performance as a site of analysis to reveal the ways in which constructions of Japaneseness are articulated, defined, and imagined. In so doing, I aim to explore how *Bleach* can offer alternative possibilities and re-imaginings for Japanese authenticity and identity: to what extent, and for whom? While the series has a total 366 episodes, I focus my attention on the first *arc* of the series, which takes place in the first 80 episodes, as this is central to the development of the characters' intersectional identity performances.

Queer of color critique

In order to discover the performative constructions of sex, gender, and sexuality in anime, I ground my analysis in the genealogy of queer of color critique. Ferguson (2013) argues: "Queer of color critique approaches culture as a site that compels identifications with and antagonisms to the normative ideals promoted by the state and capital" (p. 121). This approach provides the tools to examine the ways in which sex, gender, and sexuality are constructed and performed

88   R. Cortés

within the discursive and material effects of the intersections of nationality, race, class, and ethnicity—within historical and ideological contexts. This lens combines queer theory, materialism, and women of color feminism to account for the fluidity of intersectional gender and sexual identity and the material realities of people of color. As I examine *Bleach*, I consider the conceptualizations of sex, gender, and sexuality set out below to better understand Japanese identity performance.

I emphasize that queer critique "calls expected values, beliefs, and relations into question" (Eguchi & Asante, 2016, p. 173), challenging static constructions of sexual and gender binaries. However, using queer critique alone fails to acknowledge the material realities of people of color and the role of intersectionality (see Alexander, 2004; Chávez, 2013; Eguchi, 2014; Eng, 2010; Ferguson, 2012; Johnson, 2005, 2013; Muñoz, 1999). As Johnson (2005) explains, "because much of queer theory critically interrogates notions of selfhood, agency and experience, it is often unable to accommodate the issues faced by gay and lesbians of color who come from 'raced' communities" (pp. 126–127). The material realities of queer of color are very different from those perpetuated by mainstream discourses dominated by White middle-class queer identity. Additionally, "queer critique favors universalizing views of sexuality over minoritizing ones" (Chávez, 2013); therefore, queer of color critique is necessary in order to examine diverse sexualities that fall outside mainstream (read: White, middle class, and frequently androcentric) identity constructions. This is especially important when considering U.S. perceptions of Japanese gender and identity performance in the media.

Queer of color theory uses historical materialism combined with intersectionality to contextualize the ways in which sexualities and gender performances of people of color are marginalized. Historical materialism allows scholars to critique capitalism and challenge the ways in which material realities are hegemonically and discursively shaped through White heteropatriarchy within historical and political contexts (Ferguson, 2013). It also challenges power relationships negotiated within the means of production. However, Marxist critique does not address the intersections of race, sex, gender, and ethnicity in the context of class (Muñoz, 1999). Queer of color critique brings in women of color feminism to consider the ways in which these identifications intersect. Hong (2006) draws our attention to the ways in which women of color feminism emphasizes the "intersecting and competing axes of identification and disidentification" (p. xxvi). Rather than considering each aspect of identity separately, women of color feminism complicates the ways in which each of these positions simultaneously work with or resist other positionalities. Together, three constructs complement each other—queerness, material realities within power relations, and intersectional identity construction and performance.

My utilization of queer of color theory benefits my examination of this intercultural text in two distinct but related ways. First, I use queer of color's combination of queer theory, historical materialism, and intersectionality in order to explore gender performance in the historical and social context of Japan. Second,

Bleach in color 89

I use queer of color theory in order to address my own positionality as a U.S. based scholar *otaku*. I give a short account of historical Japan–U.S. relations to address the second of these aims.

The history of Japan–U.S. relations includes a variety of classed, gendered, and sexed constructs that place Japanese/Asian bodies as inferior to and subordinated by White bodies (e.g., Eguchi, 2009; Eguchi & Starosta, 2012; Kang, 1993; Tajima, 1989; Toyosaki, 2011). For example, in a professional setting the *model minority* stereotype places Japanese/Asian Americans as superior to other racial minorities through their diligence and company loyalty. This also results in Japanese/Asians being perceived as hard working, smart, and nerdy but without the prestige or authority of White males (Eguchi & Starosta, 2012). However, these same qualities could be used to describe the performance of *salaryman* masculinity that reflects the hard working white-collar employee in Japan (Hidaka, 2010). Within a globalized context, these same characteristics are skewed and become power- and value-laden when Japanese men enter the predominantly White heteronormative masculine workplace (Eguchi & Starosta, 2012). In this context, the Japanese/Asian male is feminized through domestication (Nakayama, 2002).

Counter to the domestic, asexual, and submissive model minority stereotype attributed to Japanese men (Eguchi & Starosta, 2012), perceptions of Japanese/Asian women are sexualized and commodified for the White heteromasculine gaze (Washington, 2012). This includes the *Lotus Blossom* and *Dragon Lady* archetypes, which are both sexualized (and classed) in ways that may initially appear to differ although they equally uphold White heteropatriarchy. The Dragon Lady archetype characterizes a witty female with an unquenchable sexual appetite, but no need for emotional attachments (Kang, 1993). In contrast, the Lotus Blossom, also known as the *Geisha* when it refers to Japanese women, presents the loyal and loving submissive yet sexualized female stereotype (Tajima, 1989). These stereotypes have many implications for how Japanese identity is perceived in the U.S.

As a result of these stereotypes, U.S. based *otaku* have preconceptions of Japanese identity. However, when viewing anime they are also consuming competing identity constructions of Japanese embedded in the anime text. Japanese conceptualizations of national identity and authenticity inevitably become reproduced through Japanese media. This is where discourses of Japanese homogeneity are reproduced and subsequently consumed in Japan and abroad. Japanese identity and authenticity are critical to the formation of homogenous discourse in Japan and are inextricably linked to political and historical contexts (Kinefuchi, 2008, 2010). Just prior to World War II, Japan entered an isolationist phase that became foundational to ultra-nationalist discourse (Wahab, Anuar, & Farhani, 2012). These discourses cemented and solidified national sentiments of unity and, at the same time, reduced the visibility of racial and ethnic diversity in Japan. As a result, Japaneseness was defined through ethnicity, rooted in biological and cultural ancestry (Kinefuchi, 2008). This allowed Japan to maintain an *ethnically pure* workforce when the Japanese government limited immigrant

90   *R. Cortés*

workers to foreign nationals of Japanese descent. Therefore, the existence of other Asian identities, such as Korean and Chinese immigrants, indigenous Japanese, and other foreign nationals from the West, have been and continue to be discursively excluded from Japanese cultural belonging. This is potentially manifested through the lack of identity representation in media like anime. More contemporary conceptualizations of nationalism are described as a tension between modernization/Westernization and Japanese traditions of identity (Tanaka, 1993).

When I examine Japanese gender identity and performance, these material, historical, social, and global contexts must be taken into account. This makes queer of color critique imperative for this study. The framework also allows me to uncover the tensions between Japanese homogenizing and diversity discourses and establishes the ways in which identities do or do not conform with hegemonic expectations of Japanese authenticity and identity.

Some scholars have focused on the reproduction of gendered stereotypes and lack of representation of racial groups in anime (see Bresnahan et al., 2006; Choo, 2008; Fennell et al., 2012; Hiramoto, 2013; Lu 2008, 2009). Even a cursory glance at the list of characters in *Bleach*, however, shows racial and gender diversity. The pressing question is not whether the representations exist, but what ideologies these representations reproduce. With this in mind, I look at the identity performances of marginalized positionalities and alternative gender constructions in order to focus on the implications of representing difference.

Disidentifications and Japanese gender performance

In my examination of *Bleach*, disidentification becomes a primary strategy for characters to negotiate queer relational and gender identities in two distinct ways. First, the show demonstrates queer relational ambiguity as a way of challenging preconceptions about sexual and romantic relationships. Second, characters' gender performances counter assumptions regarding the gender binary.

Queer relational ambiguity

I argue that it is almost impossible to construct (queer) sexual identity without discussing relationality. In regard to *Bleach*, I specifically find that relationality is presented polemically. The three romantic/sexual relationships that are explicit are only referred to in the past tense. Additionally, they are all between men and women who are married. They also all end in tragedy, the wives dying in tragic scenarios. Of greater interest for the scope of this study is the other relational dynamic, which is romantic friendships that never develop into more explicit romantic or sexual relationships.

There are several characters who are expressive of affection and admiration for another character. These interests are shown both visually and through the plot. The visual aspect usually involves recurring scenes that show a character blushing while looking at the object of their affection. Certain plotlines may

Bleach in color 91

show acts of heroism and selflessness towards another character. The difficulty with examining these relational dynamics is that any sentiment is only implied. At no point in the series do any of the couples start dating or give themselves a more official status.

Perhaps the most obvious and hopeful romantic relationship is between Kurosaki Ichigo (黒崎 一護), the protagonist, and Inoue Orihime (井上 織姫). Not only are there several scenes that feature Orihime blushing at any kindness which Ichigo shows her, but one of the central plots in the series involves Ichigo going to great lengths to save her from the leader of the elite Hollow monsters. Another indication of the mutual feelings between this pair is how they talk to each other using the polite form of family name and Japanese honorifics. Some manifestations of affection are not as mutually evident. Abarai Renji (阿散井 恋次) frequently shows his fondness toward Kuchiki Rukia (朽木 ルキア) through a combination of protectiveness, loneliness in her absence, and staring in awe at a haloed or glittering Rukia. The irony of this visualization lies in the violent and sometimes abrasive way that Rukia interacts with most of her male peers. Rukia and Renji's exchanges favor intimate familiarity rather than the politeness demonstrated by Ichigo and Orihime. In both cases, there are romantic feelings that never escalate or are ever discussed explicitly between the characters. No confessions of love. No formal courtship of any kind.

The most richly described romantic (but not sexual) relationship in the series is between two female characters, Shihouin Yoruichi (四楓院 夜一) and Suì-Fēng (砕蜂). It is important to examine this duo for several reasons. The creators of the show dedicate a significant portion of multiple episodes detailing the history of their relationship. They are constructed as not ethnically Japanese. Suì-Fēng is a Chinese woman from a lower noble house in the spirit world—one of the few Chinese characters in the show. She belongs to the only lower noble house mentioned in the series, which is directly subjugated under the Shihouin clan. Contrary to stereotypes of Japanese authenticity, Yoruichi has a Japanese name but is a woman with dark caramel skin and golden brown eyes. That the producers spend more time solidifying this relational bond, showing scenes of physical (though not sexual) intimacy, challenges assumptions about normative romance. However, this singularity reflects real life global power dynamics between China and Japan by subjugating the only Chinese household in the series.

These three depictions show couples who do care for each other, but whose relationships are never specified as anything beyond friendship on a spectrum of gendered, sexed, and racialized identity constructions. The reluctance to label these relationships creates a site of disidentification through relational ambiguity. Muñoz (1999) characterizes disidentification as a cultural performance that creates new identity constructions within the tensions of assimilation of and opposition to hegemonic identity formations. In this case the tension lies between hegemonic and alternative modes of relational kinship. Furthermore, at no point do the characters seem uncomfortable or anxious about these seemingly vague relational dynamics. This offers the characters a kind of *queer futurity*

92   *R. Cortés*

where traditional labels of recognition and social acceptance are not the ultimate goal of their relational identity performances (Muñoz, 2009).

In the context of Japanese identity formation, these dynamics could be a reflection of contemporary relational trends in Japan. This is especially relevant as women in Japan are choosing to marry later in life, or not at all (Dales, 2014). While this has been an issue of national controversy, perhaps presenting this kind of queer futurity signals the bringing of single womanhood into Japanese identity and authentic citizenship. I suggest that U.S. viewers who only understand Japanese identity through popular media discourses could miss the salience of this.

Gender disidentifications

I argue that another form of disidentification that is significant in the series revolves around gender identity performances, rather than relationships. These disidentifications allow for reconstructions of identity performance that lean away from limiting stereotypes. By locating themselves within the dialectical tension of femininity and masculinity, minority subjects can navigate through their social realities in ways that escape the material violence inflicted on racialized, sexed, classed, and gendered bodies. As Muñoz explains,

> disidentification is meant to be descriptive of the survival strategies the minority subject practices in order to negotiate the phobic majoritarian public sphere that continuously elides or punishes the existence of subjects that do not conform to the phantasm of normative citizenship.
>
> (Muñoz, 1999, p. 4)

This can mean *passing* in ways that allow minority subjects to inhabit spaces they could not otherwise access. Several characters use this strategy to navigate their social worlds.

Kuchiki Byakuya (朽木 白哉) is a character who performs femininity and masculinity at the same time. He negotiates the heteromasculine performance expected of the noble family while, at times, simultaneously performing femininity. His stoic nature and fighting ability position him within masculinity. Belying this heteronormativity, his sword takes the form of pink cherry blossom petals, emblematic of its name, *senbonzakura* (千本桜), meaning 1,000 (long/pointy) cherry blossoms. Although beautiful, his skill with this weapon makes him a deadly force. The tension between masculine ability with the sword and feminine beauty constructs an opposition and an alternative way of performing both femininity and masculinity simultaneously. By using disidentification, the binary between femininity and masculinity is disrupted. This performance shows both genders being performed concurrently. Not only does this dialectic allow Byakuya to maintain his social status, but it also positions him as one of the strongest *taichou* (隊長, captain or commander) in Soul Society (an alternate dimension where the soul goes after death and where the death gods live).

Ayasegawa Yumichika (綾瀬川　弓親) is constructed within performances of disidentification that make some aspects of femininity more visible and other aspects less so. This is only possible in the series through the feminization of spiritual abilities (*kidou*, 鬼道, spirit way) versus physical abilities. The devaluing of *kidou* becomes a central crisis for Yumichika, an officer of the Gotei 13, the army of the spirit world. His primary concern in life is beauty. He is tall and slender with large expressive eyes and straight, short, black hair. His eyelashes and brows are adorned with colorful feathers. He strategically uses these visual feminine markers to make his feminized spiritual abilities less visible. This is important as his military division has a strong preference for physical rather than spiritual abilities. As a result, he has never revealed to his comrades the true nature of his ability, which allows him to absorb his opponent's energy. In one scene, Yumichika meets with his captain after an intense battle and proceeds to celebrate his victory by swaying his hips and spinning around on tiptoe while he hums in excitement. His posture accentuates the curve of his hips and bottom. His captain immediately orders him to stop his "disgusting" dancing before realizing he won the battle without a scratch and looks refreshed and dewy skinned. Once again, he redirects attention away from his feminized spiritual ability and toward his physical feminine performance by explaining he got dirty and had to go home to change his clothing. This performance reveals how disidentification can be used to avoid some of the material implications of performing minority identities.

These two characters, Yumichika and Byakuya, as well as a third who also follows similar disidentification, perform alternative gender construction. However, there are also racialized and classed discourses at play. Though most characters in the series have Japanese names, these men also share ethnically Japanese features such as black hair, dark eyes, and light skin. Conversely, other men of color are limited to masculine and hypermasculine identity performances. Sado Yasutora (茶渡 泰虎), Tousen Kaname (東仙 要), Yammy Llargo, and Abirama Redder are all men racialized as non-White and ethnically non-Japanese. Besides darker skin, they share similar performances of masculinity that manifest through stoicism or hot-headedness. This suggests that Japanese male characters are given a layer of complexity which is not offered to other men of color. It can be argued that this reflects the dialectical tension of Japanese identity, situated between Westernized and Japanese traditions (Tanaka, 1993), particularly when the ways in which U.S. media perpetuates similar racialized and sexed stereotypes is considered (Washington, 2012).

Monstrous femininity

Many more women than men in the series navigate the dialectical tensions of masculinity and femininity. Unlike the men in the series, these tensions are not reserved for non-Japanese women of color. I argue that non-Japanese women of color are more likely to be presented in this way; they use slightly different tactics to navigate their social spaces than the male characters, often in the form

94   *R. Cortés*

of *monstrous femininity*. This is an alternative gender performance to hegemonic femininity that "reflect[s] the anxieties of [our] time" and addresses the ways in which women of color are "animalized, exoticized, tokenized, and sexualized" (Calafell, 2012, p. 112). Calafell argues that monstrous femininity represents a breaking away from hegemonic White femininity through the use of monstrous, aggressive, and even angry gender performance. While disidentification can be used to reduce the recognition of specific identity positions, monstrous femininity is a performance that highlights racial otherness. Monstrous femininity is a performative strategy in its own right, but when juxtaposed with disidentification it subverts hegemony in similar ways.

In *Bleach*, Shihouin Yoruichi (四楓院 夜一) is initially presented as an old black (male) cat. The other characters (and the viewer) are led to believe she is male because her speaking voice is very deep in her cat form and her speaking style mimics that used by older Japanese males. However, these presumptions are dispelled when she transforms into a human, revealing that she is actually a dark-skinned woman. By constructing Yoruichi as transcending the division between animal and human, she breaks out of the confines of normative gender performance. Additionally, her status as a fugitive and outlaw constructs her animalistic body as a site of rebellion against the patriarchal order of the Gotei 13. Not only has she rejected the policies of the Gotei 13, but she is able to escape sexual objectification in her animal form. Her animal form is constructed and performs gender in ways that resist the sexualization of women of color. Instead, Yoruichi can be viewed as a complex character who is extremely smart, the fastest *hohou* (flash step) user in the *Bleach* universe, skilled in hand-to-hand combat and *kidou*, and a mentor to the main protagonist and his friends. If she did not perform femininity in this way it is possible that these complexities and roles would not be accessible to her.

Shiba Kukkaku (志波 空鶴) is another woman in Soul Society who strikes fear into the hearts of the other residents, but her performance is symbolic rather than literal. She rejects expectations of male deference and submissivity by taking the leadership role within her clan and displacing the men from positions of authority. The rumors surrounding Kukkaku construct her as vicious, feared by all, and lacking sound judgment. This is exemplified flawlessly through her occupation as a bomb-maker. Her explosive escapades have left their marks on her body, with one arm having been replaced with a prosthetic. Yet her love of ammunition is never curtailed by the risks or rumors, giving her a reputation for recklessness. Unlike Yoruichi, she matches the cultural imagery of Japanese ethnicity and authenticity. Kukkaku offers a different form of Japanese femininity that potentially frees her from expectations of submissivity and male deference, as well as from the hierarchy of the Gotei 13. However, her gender performance is both a blessing and a curse. Although she is able to be a leader for her clan she becomes an outcast within Soul Society. Still, she appears to be content living as a reject of the patriarchal society, once again giving rise to queer futurity. Her performance of monstrous femininity offers a sense of freedom from the desire for acceptance.

Some monstrous transformations come in very physical and material forms. One such example is the Tres Bestias (Spanish for "three beasts"), a trio of elite women in the Hollow army. When they enter their evolved state, they manifest animal affinities. The Tres Bestias's animal forms are a snake, a deer, and a lion. Compared to the rest of the elite Hollows, however, this trio has an additional unique skill they share. By ripping off their right arms, they are able to summon an enormous chimera that bears resemblance to each of them. The monster nearly annihilates the Gotei 13, an organization made up mostly of men, momentarily disrupting the patriarchal order. While summoning a monster that towers over skyscrapers is beastly in itself, the required penance for doing so makes this a grotesque act. By shedding normative performance of femininity and taking up monstrosity, they are able to overpower their opposition.

While most of the Japanese-looking female characters are shown to perform normative femininity, some of them take up monstrous femininity in order to break away from racialized expectations of gender performance. This provides an opportunity to dislodge notions of homogenous gender performance for those who are seen to be Japanese. At the same time, other characters of color are written in ways that bar them from hyperfeminine performance, pushing characters with darker skin to the more masculine end of the gender spectrum. Together these women and their bestial performances disrupt notions of femininity and patriarchal dominance, but continue to reproduce racialized gender stereotypes. These performances of femininity are frequently met with derision from the wider society in the series, so that the inclusion of these gender performances allows for the appearance of gender diversity while still maintaining the status quo (Ahmed, 2012; Eng, 2010; Ferguson, 2012). This closely mirrors the tension between homogeneity and diversity, between modernization/Westernization and Japanese authenticity.

Concluding remarks

At first glance it is easy to watch this series and see diversity as being present in race, gender identities, sex, sexuality, and ethnicity. However, I argue that discourses of power are still clearly reflected in these representations of difference. Japanese characters and characters that occupy upper social classes can more easily access a broad spectrum of gender and sex constructs. Other characters of color, on the other hand, are consistently presented in masculine or hypermasculine ways, so that while the *Bleach* universe centers on conflict between spiritual races it never comes to terms with the material realities of racial diversity in Japan.

By limiting non-Japanese characters of color within intersections of gender identity, I also found that the series engages the discourses of *Orientalism*. Said (1979) conceptualizes Orientalism as discourses that primitivize and romanta-cize Eastern culture and bodies in ways that justify colonization by the West under the premise of civilizing. This may seem counterintuitive considering that anime is produced in Japan; however these raced gender constructs reflect

96 R. Cortés

Japanese Westernized influence, domination, and desire (e.g., Darling-Wolf, 2004; Iwabuchi, 2002; Kinefuchi, 2008; Tanaka, 1993; Toyosaki, 2011). This ideology can be conceptualized as *self-Orientalism* as it is perpetuated through Japanese produced media (Feighery, 2012).

Informed by Eguchi, Calafell, and Files-Thompson (2014), I conclude that the representations of alternative gender constructions in media create *queer fantasy* when material realities and intersectionality are not carefully addressed. More specifically, *Bleach* offers us a variety of queer relational dynamics and gender performances that rarely result in negative material consequences. At the same time, the series fails to represent the intersections of Japanese diversity by erasing the material realities of marginalized others. Finally, I reiterate that what we consume is an illusory materiality of diversity that heightens the dialectical tensions between homogenous and diversity discourses for Japanese and U.S. consumption.

References

Abe, N. (Director). (2004) *Bleach* [Television Series]. Mitaka, Tokyo: Studio Pierrot.

Ahmed, S. (2012). *On being included: Racism and diversity in institutional life.* Durham, NC: Duke University Press.

Alexander, B. K. (2004). Bu(o)ying condoms: A prophylactic performance of sexuality (or performance as cultural prophylactic agency). *Cultural Studies ↔ Critical Methodologies 4*(4), 501–525.

Alexander, J. (2016, August 19). Live-action Bleach movie in development at Warner Bros. *Polygon.* Retrieved August 20, 2016, from www.polygon. com/2016/8/19/12555420/live-action-bleach-movie-in-development-at-warner-bros.

Anime News Network. (n.d.). *Bleach (TV).* Retrieved August 28, 2016, from www. animenewsnetwork.com/encyclopedia/anime.php?id=4240.

Bresnahan, M. J., Inoue, Y., & Kagawa, N. (2006). Players and whiners? Perceptions of sex stereotyping in anime in Japan and the US. *Asian Journal of Communication, 16*(2), 207–217.

Calafell, B. M. (2012). Monstrous femininity: Constructions of women of color in the academy. *Journal of Communication Inquiry, 36*(2), 111–130.

Chávez, K. R. (2013). Pushing boundaries: Queer intercultural communication. *Journal of International and Intercultural Communication, 6*(2), 83–95.

Choo, K. (2008). Girls return home: Portrayals of femininity in popular Japanese girls' manga and anime texts in the 1990s in *Hana yori Dango* and *Fruits Basket. Women: A Cultural Review, 19*(3), 275–296.

Chozick, A. (2011, October 29). Animation gives an edge to streaming services. *New York Times*, p. 1. Retrieved November 3, 2016, from www.nytimes.com/2011/10/29/ business/media/hulu-and-netflix-gain-an-advantage-with-anime.html.

Dales, L. (2014). Ohitorisama, singlehood and agency in Japan. *Asian Studies Review, 38*(2), 37–41.

Darling-Wolf, F. (2004). Sites of attractiveness: Japanese women and westernized representations of feminine beauty. *Critical Studies in Media Communication, 21*(4), 325–345. doi: 10.1080/0739318042000245354.

Eguchi, S. (2009). Negotiating hegemonic masculinity: The rhetorical strategy of "straight-acting" among gay men. *Journal of Intercultural Communication Research, 38*(3), 193–209.

Eguchi, S. (2011). Cross-National identity transformations: Becoming a gay "Asian-American" man. *Sexuality & Culture, 15*(1), 19–40.

Eguchi, S. (2013). Revisiting Asiacentricity: Toward thinking dialectically about Asian American identities and negotiation. *Howard Journal of Communications, 24*(1), 95–115.

Eguchi, S. (2014). Disidentifications from the West(ern): An autoethnography of becoming an Other. *Cultural Studies ↔ Critical Methodologies, 14*(4), 279–285. doi: 10.1177/1532708614527562

Eguchi, S., & Asante, G. (2016). Disidentifications revisited: Queer(y)ing intercultural communication theory. *Communication Theory 26*(2), 171–189.

Eguchi, S., & Starosta, W. (2012). Negotiating the model minority image: Performative aspects of college-educated Asian American professional men. *Qualitative Research Reports in Communication, 13*(1), 88–97.

Eguchi, S., Calafell, B. M., & Files-Thompson, N. (2014). Intersectionality and quare theory: Fantasizing African American same-sex relationships in *Noah's Arc: Jumping the Broom. Communication, Culture, & Critique, 7*(3), 371–389.

Eng, D. L. (2010). *The feeling of kinship: Queer liberalism and the racialization of intimacy.* Durham, NC: Duke Univerity Press.

Feighery, W. G. (2012). Tourism and self-Orientalism in Oman: A critical discourse analysis. *Critical Discourse Studies, 9*(3), 269–284.

Fennell, D., Liberato, A. S., Hayden, B., & Fujino, Y. (2012). Consuming anime. *Television New Media, 14*(5), 440–456.

Ferguson, R. A. (2012). *The reorder of things: The university and its pedagogies of minority difference.* Minneapolis, MN: University of Minnesota Press.

Ferguson, R. A. (2013). Introduction: Queer of color critique, historical materialism, and canonical sociology. In D. E. Hall & A. Jagose (Eds.), *The routledge queer studies reader* (pp. 119–133). New York: Routledge.

Fukunaga, N. (2006). "Those anime students": Foreign language literacy development through Japanese popular culture. *Journal of Adolescent & Adult Literacy, 50*(3), 206–222.

Gibson, A. (2012). Atomic pop! *Astro Boy*, the dialectic of enlightenment, and machine modes of being. *Cultural Critique, 80*, 183–204.

Hidaka, T. (2010). *Salaryman masculinity: The continuity of and change of hegemonic masculinity in Japan.* Boston, MA: Brill.

Hiramoto, M. (2013). Hey, you're a girl?: Gendered expressions in the popular anime *Cowboy Bebop. Multilingua: Journal of Cross-Cultural and Interlanguage Communication, 32*(1), 51–78.

Hong, G.K. (2006). *The ruptures of American capital: Women of color feminism and the culture of immigrant labor.* Minneapolis, MN: University of Minnesota Press.

Iwabuchi, K. (2001). Becoming "culturally proximate": The a/scent of Japanese idol dramas in Taiwan. In B. Moeran (Ed.), *Asian media productions* (pp. 54–74). Honolulu: Hawaii University Press.

Iwabuchi, K. (2002). *Recentering globalization: Popular culture and Japanese transnationalism.* Durham, NC: Duke University Press.

Johnson, E. P. (2005). "Quare" studies or (almost) everything I know about queer studies I learned from my grandmother. In E. P. Johnson (Ed.), *Black queer studies: A critical anthology* (pp. 124–157). Durham, NC: Duke University Press.

Johnson, J. R. (2013). Cisgender privilege, intersectionality, and the criminalization of CeCe McDonald: Why intercultural communication needs transgender studies. *Journal of International and Intercultural Communication, 6*(2), 135–144.

98 *R. Cortés*

Kang, L. H. (1993). The desiring of Asian female bodies: Interracial romance and the cinematic subjection. *Visual Anthropology Review, 9*(1), 5–21.

Kinefuchi, E. (2008). From authenticity to geographies: Unpacking Japaneseness in the construction of *Nikkeijin* identity. In L. A. Flores, B. J. Allen, & M. P. Orbe (Eds.), *Intercultural communication in a transnational world* (International and intercultural communication annual, vol. 31, pp. 91–119). Washington, DC: National Communication Association.

Kinefuchi, E. (2010). Finding home in migration: Montagnard refugees and post-migration identity. *Journal of International and Intercultural Communication, 3*(3), 228–248. doi: 10.1080/17513057.2010.487220.

Lu, A. S. (2008). The many faces of internationalization in Japanese anime. *Animation: An Interdisciplinary Journal, 3*(2), 169–187.

Lu, A. S. (2009). What race do they represent and does mine have anything to do with it? Perceived racial categories of anime characters. *Animation: An Interdisciplinary Journal, 4*(2), 169–190.

Muñoz, J. E. (1999). *Disidentifications: Queers of color and the performance of politics.* Minneapolis, MN: University of Minnesota Press.

Muñoz, J. E. (2009). *Cruising utopia: The then and there of queer futurity.* New York: New York University Press.

Nakayama, T. (2002). Framing Asian Americans. In C. Mann & M. Catz (Eds.), *Images of color: Images of crime* (pp. 92–99). Los Angeles, CA: Roxbury.

Said, E.W. (1979). *Orientalism.* New York: Vintage Books.

Schodt, F. L. (2007). *The Astro Boy essays.* Berkeley, CA: Stone Bridge Press.

Tajima, R. (1989). Lotus blossoms don't bleed. In A. W. California (Ed.), *Making waves: An anthology of writings by and about Asian American women* (pp. 308–318). Boston, MA: Beacon Press.

Tanaka, S. (1993). *Japan's Orient: Rendering pasts into history.* Berkeley, CA: University of California Press.

Toyosaki, S. (2011). Critical complete-member ethnography: Theorizing dialectics of consensus and conflict in intercultural communication. *Journal of International and Intercultural Communication, 4*(1), 62–80.

Wahab, J. A., Anuar, M. K., & Farhani. (2012). Global media product and construction of "Japanese identity": A case study of anime on Malaysian television. *Malaysian Journal of Communication, 28*(2), 1–19.

Washington, M. (2012). Interracial intimacy: Hegemonic construction of Asian American and Black relationships on TV medical dramas. *Howard Journal of Communications, 23*(3), 253–271.

Part III

Inclusiveness and Otherness

6 The discursive pushes and pulls of J-pop and K-pop in Taiwan

Cultural homogenization and identity co-optation

Hsun-Yu (Sharon) Chuang

"I gotta go! *Sailor Moon* will be on in 10 minutes and then *Doraemon* after that!" Getting ready to run, I stood up hastily and shouted at my playmate in her house. I was in elementary school, probably around ten years old (in the mid-1990s). Watching Japanese *anime* (cartoon, animation) on TV in the early evening hours on weekdays was a ritual for me and my sisters after school. We also borrowed and read Japanese *manga* (comic books), and used Japanese imported goods. Japanese media culture was omnipresent and part of my childhood. I did not question why because I was born into a "hybrid culture" of Japan and Taiwan (Huang, 2011).

As a country geographically close to and once a colony of Japan (between 1895–1945) (Huang, 2011), Taiwan has, both willingly and unwillingly, accepted Japanese popular culture ("J-pop" hereafter, cf. Japanese pop music genre) (Iwabuchi, 2001a). Through several outlets such as mass media, fashion, and the manufacturing industry, J-pop made its way into Taiwanese people's daily lives in the 1980s (Huang, 2011). However, approximately two decades or so ago (the late 1990s to 2000s), Korean popular culture ("K-pop" hereafter, cf. Korean pop music genre) emerged and began to have a comparable, if not greater, cultural impact in Taiwan (Huang, 2011). I was in high school when K-pop began to slowly take over the presence and prominence of J-pop, especially via popular TV dramas. Huang (2011) provides a clear historic trajectory of how J-pop and K-pop took roots in Taiwan, which will be discussed later. However, there has been little research examining the push-and-pull dynamics of these two pop cultures in Taiwan, their influences on Taiwanese identity construction, and the discourses Taiwanese employ to embrace and/or resist these cultural impacts.

In this research project, I focus on interpretive and critical interrogations of pop cultural impacts among Taiwanese participants. As a Taiwanese and J-pop and K-pop consumer myself, I also analyze my own lived experiences in order to investigate the discursive pushes and pulls of J-pop and K-pop in Taiwan. In keeping with the scope of this book, I foreground the analysis on how Japanese and Korean culture and people are homogenized in the eyes of Taiwanese, and on how Taiwanese national identities and self-perceptions are co-opted in such pop cultural consumptions. In essence, Taiwanese' discourses that discuss K-pop solidify the homogenization of Japan. In the following section, I review pertinent

102 H.-Y. Chuang

research to gain background knowledge regarding historical developments and
the flows of J-pop and K-pop in Asia, especially in Taiwan.

Historical development and intra-Asia flow of J-pop
and K-pop

Japanese (pop) culture, its development, and its dissemination in Asia
and Taiwan

Japanese culture, especially its (pop) cultural products, experienced several shifts
and reconstitutions before its omnipresence in Asia. According to Huang (2011),
Japan was the first non-Western country to recover from World War II and
experience fast economic growth and development. To accelerate the modernization process, the strategy which the Japanese government employed was
hybridism; that is, synthesizing Western cultures (specifically that of the U.S.)
with the distinctiveness of Japan-ness (Iwabuchi, 2001b). In the 1980s, the now-
famous Japanese *trendy dramas* (or so-called *idol dramas, "idol dorama"* in
Japanese) (Hu, 2005) started to capture the attention of increasing numbers of
working women and young females in Japan. These trendy dramas featured
tragic and romantic love stories as their central storylines, accompanied by
famous landmarks in Japan (e.g., Tokyo Tower) and affective music (Huang,
2011). *Tokyo Love Story* and *Long Vacation* were two of many well-received
Japanese dramas in Asia (Iwabuchi, 2001b). These trendy dramas later became
one of the main reasons for the increase in Japanese tourism business in East and
Southeast Asia in the 1990s. In addition to these well-known Japanese dramas
(J-dramas), the consumption of Japanese *manga* and *anime* among young adults
in Asian countries was as significant in propelling J-pop and its dissemination
(Eriko, 2012; Huang, 2011; Nakano, 2002).

Other reasons, such as cultural proximity, pirated video compact discs
(VCDs), and the audience's association between J-dramas and local reality,
played a pivotal role in the penetration of J-pop in Asia. "Cultural proximity"
(Straubhaar, 1991, p. 39) references how media consumers tend to choose TV
programs that closely match or resonate with their cultural, national, or regional
identities (see also Eriko, 2012; Hu, 2005). During the early- to mid-1990s, the
storming effects of J-dramas and Japanese cultural presence swept across East
and Southeast Asian countries (Iwabuchi, 2001b) such as China, Hong Kong
(Leung, 2002), Malaysia (Eriko, 2012), Singapore, South Korea, and Taiwan
(Hu, 2005; Huang, 2011). Beyond the factor of cultural proximity, young people
in Asia found pirated VCDs and online distribution to be ways of defying cable
TV channels (Hu, 2005; Iwabuchi, 2001a; Leung, 2002; Otmazgin, 2008).
Iwabuchi (2001a, 2001b) contends that Taiwanese audiences in particular consumed J-dramas because they made conscious choices to associate the central
themes in these dramas with their lifestyles and realities (for a view on this with
regard to Malaysians, see Eriko, 2012). Following the successful distribution of
J-dramas (legally or not), Japanese idols, pop songs, and other commodities (e.g.,

Japanese imported stationery, snacks and Hello Kitty—a famous J-pop icon, a cartoon cat designed by Yuko Yamaguchi) gained popularity outside Japan in the late 1990s. Taiwan was considered the biggest Asian market to which Japanese music was exported (Huang, 2011) and in which pirated J-dramas were distributed (Hu, 2005).

Through a combination of the aforementioned factors, a myriad of Japanese commodities and pop cultural products took root in Taiwanese people's lives. Almost anything Japanese, such as *anime*, clothing, cosmetics, food, goods, music, *manga*, memorabilia, and technological gadgets have been welcomed and embraced as ways for Taiwanese to connect with "Japanese styles." Many Taiwanese TV variety shows have even been modelled on Japanese TV programs (Iwabuchi, 2001a; Otmazgin, 2008). This vehement craze for Japan-ness is what Huang (2011) terms "Japan-mania" or what many Taiwanese call *"hari"* (哈日) [*ha*: craving and *ri*: Japan].

Taiwanese' admiration for J-pop and Japan-ness have promoted the tourist industry in relation to Japan. Many Taiwanese make countless pilgrimages to visit Japan's famous cities and towns to purchase "authentic" Japanese products, to embrace traditional Japanese lifestyles, and to enjoy the scenes that have been filmed in the J-dramas. According to the Tourism Bureau of Taiwan (2016a), the number of Taiwanese tourists visiting Japan grew from 498,565 in 1995 to 1,180,406 in 2005. The number has continued to grow in recent years, reaching the astonishing figure of 3,797,879 by 2015 (Tourism Bureau of Taiwan, 2016a). Needless to say, J-pop has penetrated the lives of many Taiwanese and continued to do so even after Japan-mania "cooled down" when the Korean wave competed with much success in the 2000s (Hu, 2005).

Concurring with the timeframe I have observed, Otmazgin (2014) describes the 1990s and early 2000s as "the heydays" of J-pop in Hong Kong (p. 323), before the Korean wave hit. Huang (2011) succinctly summarizes: "If Japan-mania signals Japan's return to Asia, the Korean wave elevates Korea's status in Asia" (p. 7).

Korean wave, its development, and its dissemination in Asia and Taiwan

South Korea's popular culture industry was considerably affected by the model of J-pop (Huang, 2011; Otmazgin, 2008; Shim, 2006). According to Yasuo Yamaguchi (cited in Katsumata, 2012, p. 139), "Japanese *anime* production houses began to outsource some of their works ... to companies in South Korea" in the 1970s until the wages there increased in the 1990s. Like Japan's move to modernization, Korea's efforts at reconstructing Korean-ness in the 1990s were hybridized to prevent national culture from dissolving in the flood of U.S. American products (Huang, 2011; Iwabuchi, 2010; Ryoo, 2009; Shim, 2006).

Imitating J-dramas (Huang, 2011; Iwabuchi, 2010; Otmazgin, 2008), the Korean TV industry created Korean dramas (K-dramas) and started disseminating them to other Asian countries, such as China and Taiwan, in the early 1990s.

104   *H.-Y. Chuang*

This move did not achieve much popularity in Taiwan at first (Huang, 2011). However, due to the rising costs of licensing J-dramas in the late 1990s (Shim, 2006), K-dramas eventually created an unstoppable wave in the 2000s, both domestically in South Korea and across East Asia. The popularity of K-dramas in Asia boosted South Korean's national economy, tourism, and its national identity and pride (Joo, 2011; Shim, 2006). Marketing strategies such as disseminating free K-dramas to multiple countries and selecting idols from K-dramas to represent Korean products and to visit different countries led Korean brands to be recognized across the world (Huang, 2011; Iwabuchi, 2010).

Because of the wide acceptance of K-drama in Asia, many Chinese (Hu, 2005; Leung, 2002), Japanese, Singaporean, Taiwanese (Hu, 2005), and Vietnamese have, since the late 1990s, willingly consumed K-pop and its derivative cultural products (Shim, 2006; Otmazgin, 2014). Just as J-dramas attracted innumerable Asian audiences, Ryoo (2009) considers cultural proximity to be the main force that accelerated K-pop's distribution, especially K-dramas. Many K-dramas featured tear-jerking storylines around family and friendship, highlighted the traditional Asian values of Confucianism (Ryoo, 2009), and focused on the theme of (tragic) romance—sometimes in an almost "too melodramatic" fashion (Leung, 2002, p. 74). *Autumn in My Heart*, *Winter Sonata*, and *Jewel in the Palace* were all mega-hit K-dramas in Asia.

The wide acceptance of Korean products and Korean-ness was dubbed the "Korean wave" or the so-called "Hallyu" or "Hanryu" in Korean and "Hanliu" (韓流) in Chinese (Hu, 2005; Huang, 2011; Shim, 2006). As Ryoo (2009) puts it, the Korean wave was an indication that Asian countries were starting to accept and consume cultural products in neighboring countries with similar cultural, historical, and economic backgrounds (see also Iwabuchi, 2010). The Korean wave washed over many Asian countries (Onishi, 2005), including Taiwan. K-pop products almost engulfed the major pop culture market once dominated by J-pop (see Ryoo, 2009). Huang (2011) further describes how K-pop influenced Taiwanese business and marketing strategies, one of which was that "Taiwanese businesses … mimic … Korean styles in marketing their own commodities, [and] promoting … plastic surgery to achieve a Korean look" (p. 8; see also Shim, 2006). To attest to the latter claim, I have indeed noticed large billboards with plastic surgery advertisements, printed with Korean pop stars' photos, hanging outside tall buildings and shrieking silently yet ostentatiously at passers-by in metropolitan areas of Taiwan.

Once K-dramas had successfully captured the attention of Taiwanese audiences (in the early 2000s), numerous (cultural) products representing Korea were promoted and the tourist industry also flourished. Products such as pop music, Samsung cell phones, cosmetics, fashion lines, Hyundai cars, and LG home appliances soon competed with Japanese products. In the early 1990s, Korean cosmetics were difficult to sell in Taiwan because "most Taiwanese people thought [the Korean] brand was inferior to Japanese products" (Chen, cited in Huang, 2011). Undeniably, the Korean wave brought changes. Several Korean cosmetics brands started to enter Taiwan's department stores in 2005 (Huang,

2011). Moreover, the number of Taiwanese tourists visiting South Korea increased from 108,831 in 2000 to 500,100 in 2015 (Tourism Bureau of Taiwan, 2016b). This represented an astonishing 500 percent increase over 15 years.

I conducted this research to study Taiwanese' experiences and consumptions of the two (pop) cultures and to further examine the discursive pushes and pulls of J-pop and K-pop in Taiwan. Next, I briefly describe the research design and procedures.

Research design and procedures

To investigate Taiwanese' experiences, I mainly followed the line of four research questions: (a) How and when did the transition to J-pop and K-pop take place?; (b) What cultural images do Taiwanese construct of J-Pop and K-Pop?; (c) How have Taiwanese people's self-perceptions been influenced by J-Pop and K-Pop?; and (d) How do Taiwanese construct their perceptions of their cultural others—Japanese and Koreans—through popular cultures?

To answer these guiding questions, I employed an online qualitative survey. The questionnaire was designed in a bilingual (Mandarin Chinese and English) format and made accessible to Taiwanese participants through "Google Docs." I included two main sections in the questionnaire: (a) participants' demographic information; and (b) a series of open-ended questions. The latter was further divided into two sub-sections to elicit participants' experiences with J-pop and K-pop, respectively. The online qualitative questionnaire allowed participants to provide answers freely and in their own time (Frey, Botan, & Kreps, 2000). It is also a useful measure for understanding participants' stated identities and interpretations of others' behaviors, in that such responses represent their private and subjective accounts (Burnett, 1991).

To help participants feel comfortable, I invited them to choose their preferred language (either Mandarin Chinese or English, or code-switch between the two) to describe their experiences and opinions. Some of the participants chose to respond in Mandarin Chinese; therefore, I translated their responses into English for the purpose of data presentation. All the responses remained anonymous and were recorded and stored in an online database.

In total, I received 29 survey submissions.[1] I read through the responses and identified persistent and recurring words, phrases, and concepts in order to recognize significant and shared experiences. Furthermore, I employed critical discourse analysis (Cameron, 2001) to delve into participants' responses in revealing underlying domination, power, prejudice, and (mis)representation in the pushes and pulls of J-pop and K-pop, which ultimately linked to the homogenization of Japan and Taiwanese' identity co-optation. In the following section, I discuss the findings.

106 H.-Y. Chuang

Findings and discussions

First encounters with J-pop and K-pop and transitions to pop cultural domination

I found that my study's participants had consumed, witnessed, and/or experienced the dissemination of and the transition of cultural domination from J-pop to K-pop in Taiwan. In line with J-pop's historical dissemination, all the participants described their first encounter with J-pop in Taiwan during the 1990s. They had all first consumed J-pop through the major avenues of TV programs, TV dramas, cartoons (*anime*), and comic books (*manga*). I was born in the early 1980s, and I also first encountered J-pop through watching *anime* and Japanese TV programs. One participant, Feng-Rui,[2] stated that his first contact with J-pop dated back to the time when he became a fan of Namie Amuro, a female Japanese pop singer, who made her first debut album in 1995. The youngest participant, Yo-Ting (born in 1993), jokingly wrote that he encountered J-pop when he was still "crawling on the floor" (my translation), which indicates that he was born into the era when J-pop had already arrived in Taiwan. As for K-pop, participants recollected that their first encounters with it were between 1998–2004, mostly via K-dramas. Their experiences largely match the timeframe when the Korean government invested heavily in K-dramas and other K-pop cultural products for intra-Asia exportation (Huang, 2011).

Examining participants' first encounters with J-pop and K-pop further, I observed that J-pop received a higher rate of consumption and through more avenues (including TV programs, TV dramas, *anime*, and *manga*) compared to those for K-pop (at a lower consumption rate and mainly through K-dramas). Based on this observation, J-pop was more conspicuously accepted and diffused locally when the two pop cultures first made their way to the neighboring land of Taiwan.

Although widely accepted and deeply penetrated in Taiwan for a decade or so, J-pop eventually had to make way for K-pop. Along with the participants, I had witnessed the temporal point of J-pop losing domination to K-pop during the late 1990s and early 2000s. It was when K-dramas on cable TV overtook the dominance of J-dramas. According to Shim (2006), it only cost a quarter of the price to license K-dramas compared to J-dramas. With such affordable prices, the exportation of K-dramas became an important force that propelled the distribution of K-pop. One participant, Ning-Wei, commented, "J-pop ... led how young people [thought] until K-pop came" while another, Chun-Sho, wrote: "I think Taiwanese people lost their interest in J-pop when K-dramas came to Taiwan" (my translations). Although the transition in pop cultural domination was apparent and observable to many Taiwanese, J-pop did not disappear completely. K-pop did, however, replace its cultural prominence and dominance in Taiwan. Despite the wax and wane of the domination of J-pop and K-pop, the (presumed) widespread cultural contact in Taiwanese people's lives became simulacra that lead to the homogenization of Japan and Korea.

Taiwan's homogenization of Japan and Korea

I further observed that part of the simulacra had already became rooted in the participants' construction of cultural Others (Japanese and Koreans). The cultural images of Japanese and Koreans were profoundly affected by the (mis)representations of their pop cultures. Many participants described J-pop and Japanese products as "cute," "delicate/detailed," "high-quality," "fashionable," and "creative/innovative." These images not only applied to J-pop cultural products, but also affected how Taiwanese construct images of Japanese people and culture. In essence, Japan is homogenized in the eyes of Taiwanese pop culture consumers, who rely mainly on the cultural images in J-pop and rarely question the limitations of this cultural information. One participant, Wei-Hao, suggested: "Because JP [Japanese] people potentially like [things portrayed in J-pop], J-pop grows in this way." He believed J-pop to be a faithful representation of Japanese people and culture.

Numerous pro-Japan discourses from participants' responses further point to how Taiwanese homogenize Japan and Japanese people. As one participant, Ya-Ting, opined: "[Japanese people] push their limits all the time," thus complimenting Japanese peoples' characteristic ability to persevere and endure at difficult times. Furthermore, I share the same cultural images with several other participants, who constructed Japanese people as "serious," "persistent," "diligent," "polite," and "organized." Another participant, Yi-Chun explained that she understood Japanese as people who placed a strong emphasis on self-discipline and personal reputation. Using a metaphor, she compared Japanese people to the cultural image of *samurai* (Japanese warriors), who would commit suicide to protect their pride if they were captured by enemies or defeated in battle. Again, the cultural reference of samurai was easily accessible from the TV programs and dramas that feature Japanese historical eras. Three participants, Yao-Hao, Ning-Wei, and Han-Ting, further avowed that they were willing to pay more to purchase Japanese products because "[Japanese] products have good qualities."

I found some opposition to the outpouring of pro-Japan comments. For instance, Yao-Hao remarked: "Males are awkward at expressing their emotions and affections" and "Japanese society privileges men over women a lot" (my translations). Another participant, Chia-Jun, wrote: "They [Japanese] seem to be quite introvert[ed] and repressive between their duty and desire." Ning-Wei also suggested: "Sometimes it [Japanese culture] goes too wild like some nasty eating competitions and some weird 'inventions'." Herein, the Taiwanese participants were further homogenizing Japanese gender roles, normalcy, and disposition based on what they had perceived in J-pop. These anti-Japan critiques may seem like the efforts of heterogeneity; I argue that they contribute to the construction of homogeneity, but in an unfavorable manner. The homogenization of Japan is reified because many Taiwanese construct the entire nation of Japan and its people based on limited pop cultural images, which leads to the elimination and disregard of possible cultural varieties, especially those under-represented in mainstream media.

108   *H.-Y. Chuang*

Unlike the abundant pro-Japan and negligible anti-Japan responses from participants, there was a mixture of pro- and anti-Korean comments. Pro-Korean responses included "fashionable, and good at marketing"; "more straight-forward [than Taiwanese]"; and "handsome men and beautiful women [as seen in K-dramas]" (my translations). However, along with these favorable images there were quite a few unfavorable and harsh ones. The most significant unfavorable images were related to Koreans as "copy-cat" and "cheaters"; both of these recurred in various participants' responses. Although unfavorable, one participant, Shu-Ting, justified her viewpoint by suggesting, "Korean pop culture ... is ... a 'copy-cat' which makes them able to improve their products." Many other participants simply viewed K-pop as inferior as they believed J-pop to be "the real originator and the innovator."

I concur with many scholars, such as Huang (2011), Iwabuchi (2010), and Otmazgin (2008), who have claimed that the Korean TV industry successfully and effectively copied J-drama when creating K-dramas. The issue here, however, is how Taiwanese consumers view this success. On the one hand, the widespread dissemination of K-dramas in Taiwan offered Taiwanese people glimpses of Korean culture and lifestyles and attracted Asian tourists who were intrigued by K-dramas and specifically wanted to take "television theme tours" (which visit the places where famous K-dramas were filmed) (Onishi, 2005). On the other hand, participants' pro- and anti-Korea comments proved yet another example of how Taiwanese people derived cultural images of Korea from what they absorbed from K-pop and K-dramas, which results in another cultural homogenization.

How Taiwanese people homogenize Japan and Korea is inseparable from their consumption of J-pop and K-pop. As Cavallaro (2001) reminds us, we are already (mis)represented by our cultures and cultural texts, which reduces and, sometimes, eliminates the possibility of diversity and individuality. Taiwanese participants formed both favorable and unfavorable images of their cultural Others (Japanese and Koreans) based on their consumption of pop cultural texts. As discussed, many Taiwanese perceive Japanese people and culture more favorably than Korean. I suspect that Taiwan's colonial relationship with Japan may play a crucial role here. Although there are bitter memories of the colonial past (as my grandparents, who experienced the Japanese colonization, would attest), the Japanese government undeniably contributed to major infrastructure and established social systems that helped to modernize Taiwan. I still remember how, when I was little, my grandparents would often point out to me the buildings, bridges, and schools the "Japanese built" because these constructions still stood strong after more than 60 years.

As once a Japanese colony, Taiwan has been influenced by Japanese culture for more than 100 years. Although there was a temporary ban on Japan's presence in Taiwan due to a breakdown in diplomatic relations in 1972, the ban was lifted in 1993 (Huang, 2011; Otmazgin, 2008). Connected to this, I find Eriko's contention regarding the effects of accumulation in pop culture particularly apt in explaining Taiwanese people's ready acceptance of Japanese culture. She claims:

Pushes and pulls of J-pop and K-pop in Taiwan 109

Accumulation is an important part of media consumption of Japanese popular culture.... [It] refers to both the physical practice of collecting popular cultural products and the cognitive process that occurs over the years as one engages in consumption.

(Eriko, 2012, p. 206)

Comparing to K-pop, the period of time and the extent to which J-pop and Japanese culture became rooted in Taiwanese people's lives were not only longer but deeper, which has facilitated the cognitive process of accumulation and acceptance.

Equally important to the effects of accumulation, I suggest that participants' anti-Korean responses stem from national economic conflict. The timeframe of Korea's ascent in Asia happened to correspond to an economic downturn in Taiwan. Cultural proximity may have attracted Taiwanese to consume K-pop (Straubhaar, 1991) and be reflexive of our own social lives (Iwabuchi, 2010); it also has generated national and cultural competition and rivalry between Taiwan and South Korea (discussed below). Essentially, the Taiwanese' homogenizations of Japan and Korea are due to limited access and exposure to Japanese and Korean culture, historical constraints, and capitalistic relationships. Finally, I look at the connection between homogenizations of Japan and Korea and the co-optation of Taiwanese' identity and self-perception.

Taiwanese' identity co-optation and self-perception

Many of the participants denied that the consumption of J-pop and K-pop influenced their Taiwanese identity. One of the participants, Lin-Chia, argued, "to enjoy the food or appreciate their culture does not affect how I identify myself as a Taiwanese because I was born and raised in Taiwan," while another, Yen-Yi, stated: "[Consuming J-pop] [d]id not affect my Taiwanese identity; but I like to wear, use, listen to, and watch anything Japanese." These participants' remarks support Huang's (2011) claim that "national cultures are not necessarily washed away by a powerful foreign culture" (p. 4). However, a further participant, Yo-Jun, responded: "How the Japanese manage their pop culture makes me wish Taiwanese become better and better." Yo-Jun's reflection is strongly in agreement with Otmazgin (2008); for many Taiwanese, "the Japanese popular culture industries were seen as an example and a model, and have influenced the development of the indigenous industries, providing formats for local productions" (p. 92).

Based on the reflections and the pro-Japan responses, I recognize the nuances that suggest co-optations of Taiwanese identity and self-perception. In the questionnaire, I asked participants to describe their reactions if others commented on them being "Japanese-like" (including mannerisms, fashion/style, lifestyle, etc.). The responses were overwhelmingly positive: "very happy," "taking it as a compliment," and (that meant they were) "fashionable," "polite," and "diligent." There were no negative reactions. Behind these affirmations lay adverse identity

110   H.-Y. Chuang

co-optation and self-depreciation. The high praises for being Japanese-like inherently co-opted Taiwanese identities as inferior, less modernized, not as fashionable, and/or not as diligent or polite as Japanese. Ultimately, the positive reactions to being considered Japanese-like are linked to the denigration of Taiwanese identity and self-perception.

In the questionnaire, I also asked how participants would react if they were commented on as being "Korean-like." Connected with their views of Korean culture and people, the reactions to being considered Korean-like included both favorable and unfavorable ones, with an inclination toward the unfavorable. There were neutral responses, such as "no comments" or "never been commented that way." There were a few relatively favorable responses, such as participants' associations with fun and politeness. Quite a few female participants replied that they would feel pleased because it meant they had dressed in a fashionable way, although several of them supplemented this with postscripts that they would feel happy *only if* they resembled Korean idols or those who had undergone plastic surgery. There were several others who articulated overtly unfavorable remarks, such as feeling "unhappy" or "angry," particularly if they were commented on as resembling Koreans in attitude, mannerisms, or before plastic surgery. The unfavorable reactions were mainly associated with their (doubtfully accurate) homogenized views of Koreans as "cheaters in sports," "copy-cats," and/or "fake."

Unlike Taiwanese' adverse identity co-optation in relation to Japanese, I recognize that the anti-Korean reactions boost Taiwanese' identity construction as "honest" and "original" (not "cheaters" or "fake"). I argue that anti-Korean comments about "cheating in sports games" are interrelated with Taiwanese people's nationalistic ideology and patriotism. Due to the geo-political cultural proximity between the three nations, Taiwanese sports teams, such as baseball and Taikwondo, often compete against Japanese and Korean teams. Before South Korea rose in the early 2000s, Taiwan did not seem to be bothered by the sports teams as much, nor was there obvious resistance to Korean culture. As the Korean wave gradually generated enough economic and cultural power to threaten Taiwan, I noticed more and more anti-Korea discourses whenever there were sports games between Taiwan and South Korea. At the same time, Taiwanese people have not expressed the same amount of anger or grief when defeated by Japan in sports, as if it was "normal" to be defeated.

Examining these discourses, I concur with Iwabuchi's (2010) contention that "...growing mediated interconnectedness under globalization has reactionarily evoked the sense of national pride and belonging" (p. 207). It is noteworthy that such national pride and belonging are hierarchical in Asia, which leads to rivalry. In a homogenized sense, Taiwanese people believe Japan to be a "better" country with everything "more advanced," whereas South Korea's position is considered to be somewhat similar to Taiwan's. The similarity and cultural proximity added fuels to cultural rivalry and resistance. Essentially, the rivalry between Taiwan and South Korea renders Japan the privileged nation on top of the pyramid. Iwabuchi (2010) explicitly states that, in terms of economic and cultural power,

Pushes and pulls of J-pop and K-pop in Taiwan 111

Japan seems to occupy the highest position in the hierarchy in Asia whereas the rest (of the Asian countries) are left to compete with each other. To many Taiwanese, Japan has long been conceived as the most modern and Westernized (like "the West" in Asia) (see Toyosaki, 2011). Neither Taiwan nor South Korea has reached the same level. To try to attain that level, Taiwanese rival and compete with Koreans without questioning or challenging the homogenized images we (Taiwanese) have constructed of Japanese people and culture.

Although cultural homogenization should be challenged and diversity should be promoted, for the rivalry to become established and enacted people need the homogenized image. The relationship of rivalry and competition (economically and athletically) between Taiwan and South Korea essentially helps to solidify the homogenized images and culturally supreme status of Japan. Just as non-white races rival each other to uphold whiteness in whiteness studies (Du Bois, 1920/2007), Japan's homogenization is socially constructed and supported by the conflict among non-Japan nations in Asia, such as Taiwan and South Korea. It is indicative how, even with pushes and pulls of J-pop and K-pop, many of Taiwanese accept and believe in the pop cultural images that constitute the homogenization of Japan and Korea. In a way, there needs to be cultural homogenization for identity co-optation to hold on to; otherwise, we are all discursively and fragmentationally the same.

Conclusion

In Taiwan, Japanese homogenization prevails favorably as the "standard/real/innovative/first" in relation to that of Korean ("the copy-cat/cheater"). I still hear how Taiwanese friends prefer purchasing Japanese products because they are cute, reliable, high quality, high-tech, and fashionable. Although less favorable to some Taiwanese, the arrival of K-pop during the last two decades has shattered the solid ground on which J-pop stood for so long. Korean products have undeniably taken up considerable space in Taiwan's foreign import market, once occupied by Japan and the U.S.

I have experienced the cultural domination of the transition from J-pop to K-pop in the early 2000s as well as the Taiwanese participants in this research, all adults in or around our thirties. We have consumed the two pop cultures through different channels, although some of us have been resistant toward K-pop. Heavily influenced by our pop culture consumption, Taiwanese people have largely homogenized Japanese and Korean people and cultures based on the cultural images represented in J-pop and K-pop. Such homogenizations, reversely, co-opt Taiwanese identities and self-perceptions. With only limited anti-Japan critiques, the sheer volume of pro-Japan admirations inherently denigrates Taiwanese identities the self-perceptions, whereas the anti-Korean discourses elevate Taiwanese identities.

Even though "Japan mania" calmed down after the Korean wave hit Taiwan, many Taiwanese still favor J-pop over K-pop while we compete with South Korea. From a critical intercultural communication perspective, the Taiwanese

112 H.-Y. Chuang

people have aided and upheld the homogenization and superiority of Japan. As a Taiwanese scholar, I cannot ignore the fact that the colonial past also influences how we idolize Japanese ideologies. The colonizer's (Japanese) power upon the once colonized (Taiwanese) is still indispensable in explaining pro-Japan discourses.

Taiwanese people have not pushed J-pop away, but the power of J-pop has certainly been diminished by the pull of K-pop in Taiwan. Although K-pop and Korean culture have experienced "pushes" (i.e., resistance) from many Taiwanese people, there are those who embrace them. We cannot underestimate Korea's potential, both regionally and internationally. We also must be cognizant of how pop cultures reflect only limited images of a nation, its culture, and its people.

Notes

1 Of the 29 participants, two were in their early twenties, five were in their late twenties, and 22 participants were in their thirties. This distribution means that the participants were either at a young age or were born at the time when J-pop made its way to Taiwan.
2 All participants' names in this chapter are pseudonyms.

References

Burnett, R. (1991). Accounts and narratives. In B. M. Montgomery & S. Duck (Eds.), *Studying interpersonal interaction* (pp. 121–140). New York: Guildford Press.
Cameron, D. (2001). *Working with spoken discourse.* London: Sage.
Cavallaro, D. (2001). *Critical and cultural theory.* London: Athlone Press.
Du Bois, W. E. B. (1920/2007). The souls of white folk. In W. E. B. Du Bois, *Darkwater: Voices from within the veil* (pp. 17–29). New York: Cosimo.
Eriko, Y. (2012). Accumulating Japanese popular culture: Media consumption experiences of Malaysian young adults. *Media Asia, 39*(4), 199–208.
Frey, L. R., Botan, C. H., & Kreps, G. L. (2000). *Investigating communication: An introduction to research methods* (2nd ed.). Needham Heights, MA: Allyn & Bacon.
Hu, K. (2005). The power of circulation: digital technologies and the online Chinese fans of Japanese TV drama. *Inter-Asia Cultural Studies, 6*(2), 171–186.
Huang, S. (2011). Nation-branding and transnational consumption: Japan-mania and the Korean wave in Taiwan. *Media, Culture & Society, 33*(1), 3–18. doi: 10.1177/0163443710379670
Iwabuchi, K. (2001a). Becoming "culturally proximate": The a/scent of Japanese idol dramas in Taiwan. In B. Moeran (Ed.), *Asian media productions* (pp. 54–74). Honolulu: University of Hawaii Press.
Iwabuchi, K. (2001b). Uses of Japanese popular culture: Trans/nationalism and postcolonial desire for "Asia." *Emergences, 11*(2), 199–222. doi: 10.1080/10457220120098955
Iwabuchi, K. (2002). "Soft" nationalism and narcissism: Japanese popular culture goes global. *Asian Studies Review, 26*(4), 447–469.
Iwabuchi, K. (2010). Globalization, East Asian media cultures and their publics. *Asian Journal of Communication, 20*(2), 197–212.
Joo, J. (2011). Transnationalization of Korean popular culture and the rise of "pop nationalism" in Korea. *Journal of Popular Culture, 44*(3), 489–504.

Pushes and pulls of J-pop and K-pop in Taiwan   113

Katsumata, H. (2012). Japanese popular culture in East Asia: A new insight into regional community building. *International Relations of the Asia-Pacific, 12*(1), 133–160.

Leung, L. Y. M. (2002). Romancing the everyday: Hong Kong women watching Japanese drama. *Japanese Studies, 22*(1), 65–75. doi:10.1080/103713902201436750

Nakano, Y. (2002). Who initiates a global flow? Japanese popular culture in Asia. *Visual Communication, 1*(2), 229–253.

Onishi, N. (2005, June 28). Roll over, Godzilla: Korea rules. *New York Times*. Retrieved from http://query.nytimes.com/gst/fullpage.html?res=9505E2D6143AF93BA15755C0 A9639C8B63.

Otmazgin, N. K. (2008). Contesting soft power: Japanese popular culture in East and Southeast Asia. *International Relations of the Asia-Pacific, 8*, 73–101.

Otmazgin, N. (2014). A regional gateway: Japanese popular culture in Hong Kong, 1990–2005. *Inter-Asia Cultural Studies, 15*(2), 323–335. doi: 10.1080/14649373.2014. 918700

Ryoo, W. (2009). Globalization, or the logic of cultural hybridization: The case of the Korean wave. *Asian Journal of Communication, 19*(2), 137–151.

Shim, D. (2006). Hybridity and the rise of Korean popular culture in Asia. *Media, Culture, & Society, 28*(1), 25–44. doi: 10.1177/0163443706059278

Straubhaar, J. D. (1991). Beyond media imperialism: Asymmetrical interdependence and cultural proximity. *Critical Studies in Mass Communication, 8*(1), 39–59. doi: 10.1093/ irap/lcm009

Tourism Bureau of Taiwan (2016a). *Outbound departures of nationals of the Republic of China by year* [to Japan]. Retrieved from http://recreation.tbroc.gov.tw/asp1/statistics/ year/INIT.ASP.

Tourism Bureau of Taiwan (2016b). *Outbound departures of nationals of the Republic of China by year* [to Korea]. Retrieved from http://recreation.tbroc.gov.tw/asp1/statistics/ year/INIT.ASP.

Toyosaki, S. (2011). Critical complete-member ethnography: Theorizing dialectics of consensus and conflict in intracultural communication. *Journal of International and Intercultural Communication, 4*(1), 62–80.

7 "Hating Korea" (*kenkan*) in postcolonial Japan

Andre Haag

Two of the first protestors out of the gate held up a large banner proclaiming: "Stop the Korean Wave! Drive Out the Korean Malcontents!" Thus commenced a demonstration, on February 9, 2013, that pledged to cleanse Japan of both the Korean pop culture boom (*Hallyu*) and the Korean subversives (*futei senjin*) allegedly lurking in Tokyo. The provocative march, held in the heart of Tokyo's Shin-Okubo ethnic Korean neighborhood, was organized by new Japanese nationalist groups that style themselves as "action conservatives," most prominent of which is the Citizens' Association against Privileges for Resident Foreigners (*Zainichi Tokken o Yurusanai Shimin no Kai*, abbreviated as Zaitokukai). As rows of police looked on, marchers paraded through the streets shouting offensive chants and brandishing placards with such provocations as "Death to the Descendants of Those Who Stole Japanese Land and Property," "Koreans, Hang Yourselves, Drink Poison, Jump Off a Building!" and, in English, "F**K KOREA." Perhaps the most shocking sign declared: "Good Koreans, Bad Koreans, Kill Them Both" (*Yoi Chōsenjin, warui Chōsenjin, dochira mo korose*). Such demonstrations have become increasingly commonplace in Japanese cities today, and this anti-Korean rally was neither the first nor the last of its type that year. The marchers appear at first glance to have no specific political goals other than voicing the protesters' resentment at the presence of non-Japanese people and non-Japanese culture in their midst. Their nation, as they see it, has been hijacked by anti-Japanese forces who distort history and undermine public safety (Sakurai, 2015).

A striking characteristic of xenophobic nationalism in contemporary Japan, clearly captured in the rhetoric of the February 2013 rally, is the primary target of hate: the new nationalism tends to be specifically anti-Korean rather than generally anti-foreign. This antipathy stands out given that not only is the Korean peninsula among Japan's closest neighbors geographically and culturally, but that relations with Korea and its people have constituted a key component of Japanese diversity, historically and in the present (Oguma, 2002). Reflecting the anti-foreign right's fixation on Korea is the circulation in Japanese of a term for "Hating Korea": *kenkan* (嫌韓). As an object of loathing under the expression *kenkan*, the entity "Korea" is nebulous and encompassing. Distinctions between North and South Korea, or the postcolonial *Zainichi* Korean

"Hating Korea" 115

minority community in Japan, are relatively unimportant to self-identified Korea haters; anything associated with the geographical, historical, and ethnic entity of Korea can inspire animosity. As Japanese ethnologist Ōtsuki Takahiro admitted: "Okay, let's just say it. We hate Koreans [*Chōsenjin*]. Not South Koreans, not North Koreans. It's 'Koreans.' There is no north or south. The two countries' behavior is quite similar, transcending differences in state or regime" (Yamano, 2005, p. 234).

An increasing number of studies across disciplines have tackled the problems of Japanese xenophobic nationalist movements and hate speech, with sustained focus on organizations such as the Zaitokukai (Morris-Suzuki, 2013; Higuchi, 2014; Yamaguchi, 2013; Itagaki, 2015; Shibuichi, 2015; Yasuda, 2015). Yet, the anti-Korean street demonstrations organized by a minority fringe of activist conservatives simply represent the most visible manifestations of a larger cultural phenomenon and discourse associated with *kenkan*: public opinion polls reflect a rising disdain and distrust of Japan's peninsular neighbors (Nogawa & Hayakawa, 2015). There has been a publishing boom in "*kenkanbon*," or Korea hating books (Ooizumi, Kajita, & Kato, 2015), led by Korea-bashing comics like the 2005 bestseller *Manga Kenkanryū*. Meanwhile, anti-Korean comments have long thrived on anonymous internet discussion boards dominated by Japan's "net rightists" (*netto uyo*) (Sakamoto, 2011).

Consequently, in this chapter I trace the origins and development of the discursive phenomenon of *kenkan* or Korea hating across a spectrum of cultural fronts during the last three decades. I will focus in particular on how the articulation of *kenkan* in the present has been mediated by narrations of the contested past between Japan and Korea. Korea was formally a part of the territory of the Empire of Japan for 35 years from 1910 to 1945, and understandings of this colonial past clearly shape mutual attitudes between both former imperial suzerain and former colonial subjects. Itagaki (2015) has argued that forms of anti-Korean cultural racism, which he dubs "Korea-phobia," can be traced back "at least to the first half of the twentieth century when Japan seized Korea as a colony" (p. 50). As evidence of continuity, he points to the Zaitokukai's revival of discriminatory terms from this past inscribed with hatred, suspicion and fear of Korean identities—namely the colonial policing sign *futei senjin* (不逞鮮人, Korean malcontents) and the early postwar epithet *sankokujin* (三国人, third country nationals).

While acknowledging the clear links to this history and terminology of colonial xenophobia, my analysis questions whether recent trends are simply the newest expression of old hatreds and fears, and seeks to draw attention to the ambivalent undercurrents beneath homogenizing and exclusionary discourses. This chapter's premise is that "*kenkan*," enunciated in this specific way, is a distinctly postcolonial, post-Cold War formation, though one that is explicitly (if selectively) in negotiation with mediated memories of the past. Focusing on three periods in the growth and transformation of this phenomenon, I examine how "*kenkan*" was from its inception symbiotically linked with the neonationalist historical revisionism that appeared in the 1990s in response to the

116   *A. Haag*

perceived imposition of foreign subjectivities and narratives deemed to be "anti-Japanese," i.e., "*hannichi*" (反日). As I will demonstrate, contemporary Korea hating discourses have been co-figured relationally and dialogically against this symbol of *hannichi*, in order to reject "deimperialization" (Chen, 2010) and nostalgically identify with Japan's colonial empire. *Kenkan*'s co-figuration thus negotiates with the push-and-pull dynamic between homogenizing and heterogenizing vectors by drawing from and identifying with the multiple past legacies (inclusive and exclusive, Korea-phobic and Korea-philic) bequeathed by the Japanese colonial empire.

The origins of *kenkan:* a brief history of hating Korea

Any attempt to trace a lineage of Japanese contempt, disdain, or fear vis-à-vis Korea and Korean people would quickly lead back to at least the beginnings of the modern Japanese state, and the perceptions of the peninsula as a source of instability and danger that surfaced in the 1873 "Chastise Korea Debates" (*Seikan-ron*) and developed into Meiji Japan's longstanding preoccupation with its "Korea Problem" (*Chōsen mondai*). In the decades prior to the 1910 colonization, the Korean nation was derided as backwards and barbaric by intellectuals influenced by Western Social Darwinism, perhaps most prominently by Fukuzawa Yukichi in "Datsu-A ron" (1885). Consequently, images associating Korea with "laziness, filth, and stagnation" circulated throughout the colonial era (Nakane, 2004, p. 25), underpinning a form of racism based on culture and "sensibility" rather than biology (Henry, 2013) which endured after decolonization into the postwar era (Itagaki, 2007, 2015). While contemporary anti-Korean sentiment has links with this legacy, the mode of articulating resentment for Korea as "*kenkan*" emerged as a distinct configuration that can be most effectively probed by clarifying when the Japanese term for this sentiment was first coined, disseminated and problematized. The use of "*kenkan*" to describe a new affective mode of responding to Korea was introduced into Japanese print in the early 1990s, at a time of flux in the immediate wake of the end of the Cold War. *Kenkan* was invoked in response to demands that Japanese people finally confront the legacy of the prewar Japanese empire, and internalize the pain and resentment it engendered among those nations that had been invaded and colonized.

The earliest notable invocation of the term *kenkan* was a 1992 published dialogue (*taidan*) between Tanaka Akira and Sato Katsumi that appeared in the monthly magazine *Bungei Shunjū* under the title "Japan–South Korea relations worsen the more we apologize." The immediate catalyst for the dialogue was Prime Minister Miyazawa Kiichi's January visit to South Korea, and the series of apologies Miyazawa had offered there for Japanese colonial rule, which included the then newly re-energized issue of Korean former comfort women. The victimization of Korean comfort women, used as sexual slaves by the Japanese military, had at that time recently become a flashpoint of the conflict between the two countries, as it came to "epitomize Japan's systemic exploitation of the Korean people during colonial rule" (Soh, 2004). Responding to the

"Hating Korea" 117

difficulties of historical reconciliation raised by Miyazawa's visit, which was greeted in Seoul by anti-Japanese protests that burned an effigy of the Japanese emperor, Tanaka opined that: "South Korea's repeated demands for apologies, and Japan's repeated apologies, have only intensified Japanese people's feeling of opposition to Korea [*hankan*] and hatred for Korea [*kenkan*]" (Tanaka & Sato, 1992, p. 134). Here Tanaka created, or at least popularized, the neologism *kenkan* to describe a new "national mood" of anti-Korean resentment in Japan, as South Korean newspaper reports quickly picked up on this new form of anti-Korean sentiment, translated into Korean as "*hyeomhan*" (Chŏngsindae munje, 1992). From this time, the word began to appear in both Japanese and Korean print media stories that voiced concern about the worsening of public sentiment between the two countries amid the seemingly endless cycle of (Korean) recriminations and (Japanese) apologies for the past.

At this early stage, *kenkan* sentiment is described not as a pre-existing or deeply-rooted Japanese loathing for Korea, but rather, in the words of Sato Katsumi, as "frustration" (Tanaka & Sato, 1992, p. 141) that only arises in reaction to Korean "anti-Japanese" (*hannichi*) narrations of the past. Rarely discussed in isolation, the notion of *kenkan* was, at this time, consistently framed as one half of a complex with Korean *hannichi* that placed the two in an acrimonious dialogue of co-figuration. Conservative magazine *SAPIO*, in analyzing the confrontation between Japanese Korea-hating (*kenkan*) and Korean animosity for Japan (*hannichi*) presented concise definitions of the two terms as follows: "*Hannichi* describes the mode of reception for Japanese culture in South Korea, and *kenkan* refers to Japanese people's irritation at *hannichi*" (Hannichi kenkan, 1992, p. 10). The two forces were not framed as perfectly equal or symmetrical halves (Nogawa & Hayakawa, 2015, p. 172), however, as *hannichi* was implied to be the more entrenched and problematic sentiment of the two. Japanese feelings of frustration and resentment, identified in terms of *kenkan*, were framed as the unfortunate but inevitable reaction to Korea's anti-Japanese attacks. Yet, crucially, at this point in the 1990s, intellectuals and journalists were simply describing and problematizing the dynamics by which a "national mood" of *kenkan* might arise, and they were unable to indicate any clear manifestations of Korea hating discourse or swings in public opinion toward Korea.

From the start, the imagined arena of confrontation between *kenkan* and *hannichi* was the colonial past. When tentatively coining the term *kenkan* in 1992, Tanaka Akira predicted that "completely unreasonable demands" from South Korea—for apologies and compensation—would provoke a response of "*haigaishugi*" (exclusionism, xenophobia) among Japanese people (Tanaka & Sato, 1992, p. 135). Korean demands for historical accounting are refigured in this discourse as anti-Japanese attacks that employ the past as a weapon. Among conservative intellectuals, these provocations spur, in turn, re-articulations of the past that reject the imposition of foreign narratives and privilege Japanese national subjectivities. *Kenkan* dovetails with the rise of contemporary neo-nationalist movements to "correct" narratives of Japan's modern history, which is usually dated to the mid-1990s formation of organizations led by the Japanese Society

118 *A. Haag*

for History Textbook Reform (*Atarashii Rekishi kyōkasho o tsukuru kai*). This movement called for the rejection of externally imposed, "masochistic" (*jigyaku*) views of the Japanese past and the restoration of a distinctly Japanese national history that could instill a sense of national pride and empathy (McCormack, 2000; Nathan, 2004). The close ties between anti-Korean movements and revisionism have been identified in previous studies (Yamaguchi, 2013; Higuchi, 2014; Itagaki, 2015; Shibuichi, 2015), but *kenkan* and historical revisionism were two sides of the same coin from a point in the early 1990s, before either trend developed into distinctive movements. The two were paired reactions to the same moment in which calls from former colonial subjects to face history collided with the challenge of negotiating a new postimperial national identity for Japan that could accommodate this past.

Revisionist narration of history was the form that early Korea hating took, and was formulated as the antidote to *hannichi*. *SAPIO*'s recurring series of special reports probing the issue of mutual hatred between Japan and Korea (framed as the *hannichi–kenkan mondai*), featured not only essays critiquing the anti-Japanese orientation of South Korean politics and society, but also revisionist challenges to the view that Japan's colonization of Korea was irredeemably oppressive and evil. Tinged by a frustrated imperial nostalgia, these re-tellings shifted attention away from the darker aspects of colonial rule—such as the comfort women—to identify with the prewar Japanese empire, the modernizing savior of a troubled Korean nation. Conservative intellectual Kase Hideaki's contribution to the November 1993 issue of *SAPIO*, for example, was titled "Were Korea's 36 years under the Japanese empire really all bad?" This reappraisal recalls how Korea was saved from the "utterly bankrupt" and tyrannical administration of the late Chosun dynasty by the Japanese empire, a force for progressive reform. "Japan brought about "modernization" in Korea," and many Koreans welcomed Japanese tutelage (Kase, 1993). This is a quite conventional revisionist narrative that idealizes the colonial era, and reproduces its official discourse. Yet, for justification, Kase draws explicitly from a text billed as "the first anti-Korean [*hankan*] book written by a Korean person," Pak T'ae-hyŏk's 1993 monograph *The Ugly Korean* (*Minikui Kankokujin*). The book's premise is that today's South Koreans are "ugly" (*minikui*) because they complain too much about the evils of past Japanese oppression, and refuse to accept their own flaws or responsibility. Pak argues in part that Korea benefitted from Japanese rule, and that South Koreans today must let go of their grudge against Japan. Published in Japanese, *The Ugly Korean* was for a time a bestseller in Japan, anticipating the success of *kenkanbon*, though doubts long lingered about whether it had really been written by a Korean journalist (under the pseudonym "Pak T'ae-hyŏk"), or a Japanese critic assuming a Korean persona (Lewis, 2002).

A closer look reveals that these revisionist narratives of the colonial past are not, however, premised on a wholesale rejection of Korea or Korean people. On the contrary, they come from an ambivalent space between a desire to re-assimilate the colonial Korea of the past into narratives of the Japanese nation, and the need to exclude critical Korean historical subjectivities. Overall, this

"*Hating Korea*" 119

form of early post-Cold War revisionism is more inward looking than overtly xenophobic. The aim is to rescue a positive sense of national identity from history, rather than to fan hatred of Korean people who, during the era in question, were Japanese subjects. Revisionist texts from this era such as *The History Not Taught in Textbooks* frequently highlighted instances of cross-ethnic cooperation and harmony with Korea as proof of how inclusive and tolerant the prewar Japanese empire was (Fujioka & Jiyūshugi shikan kenkyūkai, 1996, p. 108). Rather than rejecting Korea, they reject "*hannichi*." "*Hannichi*" historical subjectivities must be completely excluded because, as one revisionist put it, "underlying the anti-Japanese perception of history is the categorical negation of Japan" (Japanese Society for History Textbook Reform, 1998, p. 14).

Yet, crucially, the discourse of *kenkan* initiates a process of reconfiguring postcolonial Korean identity as essentially *hannichi*. To be Korean today has come to be equated with being opposed to Japan. The anti-Japanese nature of Korean identity was progressively emphasized in subsequent writings such as Kuroda Katsuhiro's 1995 book *South Korea's Anti-Japanese Syndrome* (*Kankoku hannichi shindoromu*), which pathologized contemporary Korean nationalism as rooted in hatred of Japan. Similar books critiquing Korean politics, society and culture in terms of *hannichi* appeared regularly in the next 20 years. Under the sign of *kenkan*, the object of resentment, hatred and ultimately fear is Korean *hannichi*, configured as a threatening form of anti-Japanese xenophobia. This logic makes it possible to disavow Japanese xenophobia, while projecting that xenophobia onto Koreans in a way that justifies moves to maintain the integrity of a purely Japanese historical narrative of the colonial past.

Kenkan goes pop: the rise of the anti-Korean wave

In the 2000s, the discourse and mood of hating Korea, first discussed a decade before using the term *kenkan*, finally surfaced in a concrete form. Nothing heralded this turn as much as the 2005 appearance of Yamano Sharin's controversial comic *Manga Kenkanryū* (literally the "Hating-Korea-Wave" or "Anti-Korean Wave"). *Manga Kenkanryū* depicts the story of one Japanese student's awakening to *kenkan*, as he discovers the truth about both a despicable neighboring country and the hidden past. The stir caused by *Manga Kenkanryū*, its arguments, and sales, brought national and international attention to Japan's Korea hating tendencies, interpreted as the sign of a new xenophobic nationalism among Japanese youth (Onishi, 2005). In light of the subsequent spread and intensification of *kenkan* discourse, the mid-2000s and the publication of *Kenkanryū* appear as epoch-making turning points for the breakthrough of *kenkan*.

An analysis of this period's popularization of *kenkan* and anti-Korean revisionism, through its urtext *Manga Kenkanryū*, must take into account the important role of new media platforms in articulating resentment, combined with the surge in mediated contact with Korean culture and viewpoints. As suggested above, in the early 1990s the framing of the term "*kenkan*" in print media

120 A. Haag

appeared to precede any overt manifestation of the phenomenon itself. The diffusion of internet comment boards in the late 1990s offered a key platform for voicing *kenkan* sentiment. By 2000, there was already a discernible trend toward anti-Korean discourse on sites such as 2-channel, heralded by the rise of "Korean hating trolls" (*kenkanchūbō* or *kenkanchū*) (Ōtsuki, 2005). Anonymous bulletin boards opened a space for critiques of Korea and alternate historical narratives of Japanese and Korean history that were treated as taboo in other media. As previous research explores, *Manga Kenkanryū* was born on the internet and maintained close ties to that medium (Sakamoto & Allen, 2007; Raddatz, 2013). The comic might be read as the print repository of a larger and more diffuse online discourse of anti-Korea attacks and revisionism that is otherwise difficult to apprehend.

Paradoxically, the Korea hating boom made visible by *Manga Kenkanryū* exploded precisely at a time when there seemed to be unprecedented prospects for friendly reconciliation between Japan and South Korea. Many consumers were embracing the Korean wave (*Hallyu*, Ja. *kanryū*) entertainment exports, such as *Winter Sonata* and other South Korean TV dramas that hit Japan in 2002—a phenomenon that the title *Manga Kenkanryū* gestures to. The intensification in mediated contact with Korean culture and viewpoints, however, did not uniformly foster positive feelings or construct healthier relations. On the contrary, some individuals who later joined anti-Korean movements pointed to the Japan–Korea breakthroughs of the early 2000s as their awakening to *kenkan*. Yet, any understanding of this as a backlash against multiculturalism is complicated by the same affective dynamics described above in the early 1990s whereby, for some, exposure to and knowledge of Korean viewpoints and narratives of the past meant encountering Korean "*hannichi*" nationalism and reacting with *kenkan* resentment. With respect to both, the *Hallyu* wave and the 2002 Japan–South Korea jointly sponsored World Cup generated *kenkan* resentment in some circles because of a sense that the Japanese public's unilateral moves toward rapprochement—i.e., consuming Korean culture or cheering for the South Korean soccer team—were not reciprocated by the other side. Instead, such overtures were found to be met with anti-Japanese hatred and a historical grudge, encountered under the banner of *hannichi*; indeed, some claimed to have loved South Korean language and culture until discovering on the internet how Korean people really felt about Japan. Similarly, Ogura (2016) found that online Japanese language versions of South Korean media outlets offered Japanese readers an opportunity to access Korean news coverage but this led to *kenkan* rather than deeper understanding. *Manga Kenkanryū* gave voice to the doubts and latent resentment that some harbored about the *hannichi* ideologies of Japan's closest neighbors.

Furthermore, in 2005, the year that *Kenkanryū* appeared, there were also major anti-Japanese protests across northeast Asia that erupted in response to both geopolitical tensions and the revisionist history textbook published by the Japanese Society for History Textbook Reform. Although most intense in China, protests in South Korea were also reported in exaggerated form in conservative media in Japan (Park, 2008, p. 196). *Manga Kenkanryū*, the urtext of hating Korea in the 2000s, is fundamentally a work of popular historical revisionism focused on the colonial legacies that divide Japan and Korea. In its approach to re-telling history, the graphic narrative presents ambivalently doubled visions of the Korean peninsula and its people. On the one hand, Korea, as part of the Japanese empire, is typically portrayed in the manner of imperial nostalgia, as a site of reform and harmony that united Japanese and Koreans. On the other hand, contemporary South Korean characters are visualized as angry, ugly and irrational thugs driven by *hannichi* and a warped sense of history (Itagaki, 2007; Sakamoto & Allen, 2007). In between is positioned the *Zainichi* Korean minority in Japan, a population that links these two characterizations through history and ideology.

Signaling the undertone of imperial nostalgia that colors the *Manga*'s approach to colonial Korea, history is first introduced to the text in the figure of protagonist Kaname's elderly grandfather who suddenly confides in his grandson, telling him that he had grown up in Korea when it was part of Japan. The smiling grandfather is shown looking over photos of his time in the colony as he reminisces, "Oh, those were the good old days" (*ano goro ga natsushii nō*) (Yamano, 2005, p. 25). Then a panel shows an image of grandpa as a youth standing next to a Korean young man with the caption: "I had a lot of great friends among the Korean students, and we vowed to each other that we'd devote our lives to modernizing Korea" (Yamano, 2005, p. 26). Ultimately, a drawing of bustling, modern Seoul (which appears repeatedly during the graphic narrative) is juxtaposed with close-ups of grandpa's increasingly sad face as he notes that although "we worked together to modernize Korea," people today refuse to acknowledge this legacy. The familiar historical argument that drives *Manga Kenkanryū* is that the Japanese empire accomplished modernizing reforms that brought material benefits to the Korean people. Furthermore, fragments like these drive home idealized images of cooperation between Japan and Korea that portray Koreans as diligent partners, not enemies. Calling into question the xenophobic nature of the narrative, characters also acknowledge the imperial Japanese ideologies of inclusiveness and the reality that the Japanese multiethnic, multicultural empire included ethnic Koreans and other non-Japanese, albeit in subordinate positions. For example, "Korea wasn't a colony, it was Japan! It is only natural that Koreans then had voting rights in Japan, given their position as Japanese nationals" (Yamano, 2005, p. 194). It should, of course, be noted that this legacy is strategically invoked by *Manga Kenkanryū* to counter critical accusations about the nature of Japanese rule; but there is also a sense of nostalgic longing to identify with the hybrid legacy of the empire.

Kenkanryū pursues a parallel line that re-figures contemporary Korean identity in terms of a threatening *hannichi* nationalism inimical to Japanese national and historical subjectivity. The divide between the good Korean subjects of the past and today's enemies is effected through the comic's narration of the severing of imperial ties in 1945. This moment is positioned within the history of the *Zainichi* ethnic Korean population. Relating the process by

122   *A. Haag*

which Koreans ceased to be Japanese after the fall of the empire, one of the comic's interlocutors states that: "After Japan's defeat, some Korean people claimed that they were a victorious nation, styled themselves the 'Korean Occupation Army,' and perpetrated savage acts of predation and violence all over Japan" (Yamano, 2005, p. 81). The accompanying illustration depicts a smiling Korean man cutting down a Japanese in a suit, black blood spraying from head and chest. A subsequent panel elaborates that "Korean people, who were Japanese nationals at that time, betrayed defeated Japan and ran amok, while misrepresenting themselves as a victorious power." This "betrayal" at a time of national vulnerability for Japan is located as the origin of a dangerous postcolonial Korean identity, and the beginnings of *hannichi*. Later in the chapter, the narrator observes that this memory of postwar Korean violence caused "a negative image [of resident Koreans] to become rooted. It's unfortunate, but there certainly was a tendency in Japan to think that 'Koreans are scary,' and try to avoid them" (Yamano, 2005, p. 91). Postwar discrimination, marginalization and ultimately *kenkan* are normalized as the unfortunate but inevitable results of resident Koreans' turning against Japan. In a later visual, the unreliability of ethnic Korean identity is cited as a reason to deny permanent Korean residents in Japan the right to vote in local elections—the prospect of which would ultimately galvanize a sense of crisis among anti-foreign groups such as the Zaitokukai (Higuchi, 2014).

Yamano's *Manga Kenkanryū* draws on re-articulated pasts to actively construct a crisis and a threat, progressively associating Korean identities with violence and *hannichi* thought that, with extrapolation, potentially pose an existential threat to the Japanese nation. At the same time, in *Manga Kenkanryū* the delineation of ethno-national boundaries between Japan and Korea is always fundamentally ambivalent due to the mediation of imperial nostalgia; thus the lines are perennially blurred. The comic's investment in an idealized vision of a Japanese empire that could include ethnic Korean subjects makes untenable any explicit rejection of Korean people across the board on immutable, racialized grounds. Rather, the basis for rejection is the form of Korean identity defined by an ideology of *hannichi*, which is by definition incompatible with a native sense of Japanese history and identity.

Xenophobic revisionism: "all of Korea's heroes are terrorists"

Since *Manga Kenkanryū*, the discourses associated with *kenkan* have become ever more toxic and unequivocal in their calls for the exclusion of Korean people, Korean culture and Korean viewpoints. This final section considers how the current incarnation of *kenkan*—the unalloyed form of Korea-phobia heralded by the Zaitokukai's hate speech demonstrations—might be understood in terms of paired shifts in nationalist historical revisionism that turn away from imperial nostalgia. That is, in contrast to the relatively inward-looking nationalist histories of the 1990s, new *kenkan* revisionism employs re-articulations of a different

"Hating Korea" 123

set of narratives and vocabularies from the past to reconstruct former colonial subjects as rebels and terrorists.

This shift is strikingly distilled in a single issue of the conservative magazine *Rekishitsū* (History Buff) from November 2012, just months before the surge in anti-Korean demonstrations by the Zaitokukai that brought increased attention to the issue of hate speech in Japan. The special focus in this issue was the "*Kenkan taifū*," or "Hating Korea Typhoon," a series of essays critical of Korea, past and present. The headline features of the issue included an article titled "All of South Korea's heroes are terrorists" (*Kankoku no eiyū wa terorisuto bakari*). Supporting this was a multi-page color photospread featuring "Profiles of malcontented Koreans." The prefatory remarks, "Have a look at this historical panorama that displays the ethnic character of a nation that worships terrorists as heroes," were followed by a line-up of Korean rebels, assassins, bomb-throwers and criminals, all of whom had sought to undermine Japan between 1909 and 2012 (Futei Chōsenjin retsuden, 2012, p. 9). The first was An Jung-geun, the famous patriot who fatally shot Japanese statesman Itō Hirobumi on the eve of the annexation of Korea in 1909. The final "Korean malcontent" profiled was Lee Myung-bak, then president of the Republic of Korea, who was presented as the ringleader behind the latest anti-Japanese campaign.

Such a line-up functioned to connect contemporary South Korean critics of Japan to a much longer timeline of violent outrages, and drive home that Korea is a perennial menace worthy of *kenkan* sentiment. Simultaneously, the historical figures profiled as terrorists were invoked in ways that explicitly underline the unbridgeable gap in national historical subjectivity between Japan and Korea. The captions repeatedly emphasize that anticolonial Korean assassins and activists executed by Japan for violent crimes or treason were posthumously awarded state honors by South Korea. Not content with the bromide that "one man's terrorist is another man's freedom fighter," this sort of writing gestures to the impossibility of historical reconciliation with "a country that worships criminals and terrorists." Watanabe's essay, "All of South Korea's heroes are terrorists," argued that Korea is a nation that can claim "no heroes other than terrorists" because it has always been a "vassal state" (*zokukoku*) of stronger powers (Watanabe, 2012, p. 36). All Koreans can boast, he continues, is a pent-up sense of "*han*" (恨), a grudge against Japan that is waiting to explode into violence. Watanabe concludes that Japanese people must abandon hope of historical reconciliation, because Korea is "without a doubt an enemy state" (p. 37).

This discourse signals the rediscovery by *kenkan* nationalists of the history of Korean anticolonial resistance to Japanese rule. Earlier revisionist histories generally avoided the topic of the Korean independence movement, because it did not square with the nostalgic vision of harmony and progress under the empire. The changing figuration of An Jung-geun, the embodiment of nationalist, anticolonial resistance in South Korea, is illustrative of the trend. For the first wave revisionist nationalists in the 1990s, An Jung-geun was a figure of ambivalence and potential reconciliation, not fear and loathing. A story about An in the 1996 revisionist publication *The History Not Taught in Textbooks*

124   *A. Haag*

relates how An Jung-geun's Japanese jailor, Chiba Tōshichi, was "able to build a close friendship with an assassin whom he should have despised," by recognizing that the Korean's act was driven by a love of a country not unlike his own (Fujioka & Jiyūshugi shikan kenkyūkai, 1996, p. 108). Under the banner of *kenkan*, however, An Jung-geun is labeled a "terrorist," and the stories and vocabularies deployed against the prewar Korean independence movement are actively drawn upon to sustain hatred and justify exclusion in the present. As Itagaki (2015) notes, one key term from the colonial lexicon of xenophobia which has been revived in Korea hating discourse is *"futei"*—meaning insubordinate, lawless, and malcontented—which was employed by imperial officials and journalists in the compound *"futei senjin"* (Korean malcontents) to label subversives associated with the independence or socialist movements. Brooks (1998) locates *"futei senjin"* at the center of a "discourse of the ruler's fear of the colonized," but points out that this discourse of bad Koreans was "implicitly opposed to one about the good, poor, primarily agricultural Koreans in the empire" (p. 30). In imperial Japan, narratives of Korean exclusion and Korean inclusion coexisted uneasily but symbiotically. Yet, as a discourse of "malcontents," they present contemporary Korean haters with a historical analogue to the label *hannichi*, and one that is intimately associated with crime, terrorism and fear.

Yet, how did that specific term *futei senjin* re-enter the lexicon of *kenkan* today, given that it was rarely used after Korea's liberation in 1945, and long lay dormant and half-forgotten during the postwar era? One vector of dissemination can be found in the new directions taken by popular revisionist historiography since the late 2000s. The appellation *futei senjin* is most closely associated in popular memory with the explosion of ethnic animus and panic against ethnic Koreans after the Great Kantō Earthquake (*Kantō Daishinsai*) of September 1, 1923. Post-disaster rumors and demagoguery about violence by *"futei senjin"* motivated the public to mobilize into vigilante squads to hunt down and kill *"futei senjin"* (Ryang, 2007). There has been a general consensus, reflected even in Japanese school textbooks, that thousands of ethnic Koreans were massacred as a result.

In the age of *kenkan*, however, the consensus narrative that there were tragic massacres in 1923 has been challenged by revisionist writers. In 2009, Kudō Miyoko, a supporter of the Japanese Society for History Textbook Reform, published *The Truth About the Great Kantō Earthquake 'Korean Massacres.'* The "truth" offered by Kudō is that the alleged massacre of Koreans is an anti-Japanese fabrication. Conversely, the book insists that there were actually acts of violence and terror plots carried out by *"futei senjin"* in the wake of the earthquake. Overturning the accepted understanding that groundless rumors spurred indefensible violence against the colonized, Kudō claims that

> terror and crimes were occurring right before people's eyes. The rumors spread because people feared [Korean terror and crimes]. And these were not simply rumors. There actually were incidents of arson, murder and rape

"Hating Korea" 125

immediately after the earthquake. It is necessary to recognize the legitimacy of self-defense.

(Kudō, 2009, p. 90)

According to this logic, any Korean people killed after the earthquake were "terrorists," and their killing was not a "massacre" but justifiable self-defense.

The motivation behind this revisionist reading is touched on in Kudō's original introduction. Drawing on the logic of neo-revisionism, the author regards the "massacres" as the "origin of masochism" (*jigyaku no genten*), which can never be defeated unless the truth is exposed (Kudō, 2009, p. 8). The massacres must be dismissed as a fabrication, because to acknowledge Korean victims would bring self-hatred and fuel *hannichi* narratives by the nation's enemies. The magnitude of this revisionist turn is suggested by how an incident from *The History Not Taught in Textbooks* (1996) approached the Kantō massacres (Fujioka & Jiyūshugi shikan kenkyūkai, 1996). The story "The police chief who protected Koreans after the Great Earthquake" implicitly accepts the established narrative that thousands of innocent Koreans were killed after the quake by panicked, hateful mobs. Rather than denying or attempting to justify that violence, however, this revisionist narrative finds national redemption for Japan in the example of Ōkawa Tsunekichi, a Yokohama police captain who risked his life to save the lives of hundreds of ethnic Koreans threatened by the mobs because, "[w]hether Japanese or Korean, human life is human life" (Fujioka & Jiyūshugi shikan kenkyūkai, 1996, pp. 126–128). Kudō's more recent denialism reflects the shift from a historical revisionism that eulogizes the inclusive spirit of the Japanese empire, to one focused on refiguring former colonial subjects as objects of fear and loathing.

The arguments developed by Kudō to deny the massacre of Koreans following the Kanto earthquake, though far-fetched and generally unpersuasive, have been embraced by Korea haters because they resonate with their fixation on anti-Japanese conspiracies. Kudō's work has been one vector re-introducing the topics of the Great Kantō Earthquake and *futei senjin* to a new generation of internet users and activists. Since 2009, anti-Korean net rightists have taken up Kudō's talking points in blogs and videos with titles such as "The truth about *futei senjin* rioting during the Kantō earthquake" and "Details about the Kantō earthquake slaughter of Japanese by *futei senjin* terrorists." Retold in this way, a colonial atrocity against past Korean subjects is justified as national self-defense, and provides more fuel to sustain hatred of Korean people in the present. What is troubling is that such popular historical revisionism has emerged in tandem with xenophobic political movements that organize marches where people openly call for Koreans to be killed, and sometimes even threaten another massacre (Yasuda, 2015, pp. 133–134). At the same time, *futei senjin*, a slur that motivated actual violence in the past, is now deployed by hate groups to refer to their "anti-Japanese" Korean opponents today.

Zaitokukai founder Sakurai Makoto writes vaguely of the threat of "*futei senjin*" in his long-running blog, while his 2015 book *The Great Hating Korea*

126   *A. Haag*

Age laments that many Japanese citizens have become the victims of "crimes by *futei zainichi*" Korean residents of Japan, who are never deported because of their deft manipulation of "fictional histories" (Sakurai, 2015, p. 119). Sakurai's movement has often labeled their anti-Korean rallies "Campaigns to expel *futei senjin*!" Used out of its historical, colonial context, the term, like the scope of Korea hating and the label *hannichi*, is expansive, potentially encompassing all those with ethnic Korean roots. As one leader of a xenophobic group shouted during a political campaign, "what's scary about *futei senjin* is that you can't identify them on sight" (Yasuda, 2015, p. 243), thus echoing the paranoid discourse of the Great Kantō Earthquake. Yet, unlike the imperative of colonial-era discourses to make room for the "good Korean," contemporary Korea haters have given up on reconciliation, and see no need for such a distinction. Thus, it is possible for xenophobes to now openly declare "Good Koreans, Bad Koreans, Kill Them Both."

Although the most extreme Korea hating activists now adopt positions and rhetoric that are unequivocally exclusionary vis-à-vis Korea, the course that *kenkan* has followed since it was first enunciated emphasizes that it is an ambivalent and dynamic phenomenon that arose dialogically through co-figuration with its other, *hannichi*. Korea hating emerges at the nexus of negotiation between heterogenizing and homogenizing vectors in contemporary Japan, and is mediated by the process of attempting to digest a fraught past that is intertwined with its closest neighbor. At the beginning of the twenty-first century, Morris-Suzuki (2002) observed "a profound, though often tacit, contest over the redrawing of the boundaries of national inclusion and exclusion" (p. 176) in Japan; while "cosmetic multiculturalism" can be embraced, "foreignness" deemed political threatening is unacceptable. The discourse of *kenkan* demonstrates that contests over diversity in Japan revolve not merely around the inclusion of foreign bodies and culture (food, television, pop music), but also around the challenge of accommodating conflicting historical subjectivities that do not easily fit into the narration of nation and empire.

References

Brooks, B. (1998). Peopling the Japanese empire: The Koreans in Manchuria and the rhetoric of inclusion. In S. Minichiello (Ed.), *Japan's competing modernities: Issues in culture and democracy, 1900–1930* (pp. 25–44). Honolulu: University of Hawaii Press.

Chen, K.-H. (2010). *Asia as method: Toward deimperialization*. Durham, NC: Duke University Press.

Chŏngsindae munje Il chisigindŭl toere han'guk pip'an (1992, February 11). *Dong-A Ilbo*, p. 2.

Fujioka, N., & Jiyūshugi shikan kenkyūkai (1996). *Kyōkasho ga oshienai rekishi [The History Not Taught in Textbooks]*. Tokyo: Sankei Shinbunsha.

Futei Chōsenjin retsuden. (2012). *Rekishitsū, 29*, 4–21.

Hannichi kenkan, Simultation report. (1992, November 12). *SAPIO*, 10.

Henry, T. A. (2013). Assimilation's racializing sensibilities: Colonized Koreans as yobos and the "yobo-ization" of expatriate Japanese. *Positions, 21*(1), 11–49.

"Hating Korea" 127

Higuchi, N. (2014). *Nihongata haigaishugi: Zaitokukai, gaikokujin sanseiken, Higashi Ajia chiseigaku*. Nagoya: Nagoya University Press.

Itagaki, R. (2007). Manga Kenkanryū to jinshushugi-kokuminshugi no kōzō. *Zen'ya, 1*(11), 20–34.

Itagaki, R. (2015). The anatomy of Korea-phobia in Japan. *Japanese Studies, 35*, 49–66.

Japanese Society for History Textbook Reform. (1998). *The restoration of a national history: Why was the Japanese society for history textbook reform established and what are its goals?* Tokyo: The Society.

Kase, H. (1993, May 27). Nittei 36 nen wa hontō ni "aku" dake dattanoka. *SAPIO*, 14–17.

Kudō, M. (2009). *Kantō daishinsai: Chōsenjin gyakusatsu no shinjitsu*. Tokyo: Sankei Shinbun.

Lewis, J. B. (2002). The Japan that does not exist and the ugly Korean: An essay on the history of Korean–Japanese relations and their contemporary images of each other. In A. Sesay & J. B. Lewis (Eds.), *Korea and globalization: Politics, economics and culture* (pp. 102–153). London: RoutledgeCurzon.

McCormack, G. (2000). The Japanese movement to "correct" history. In L. E. Hein & M. Selden (Eds.), *Censoring history: Citizenship and memory in Japan, Germany, and the United States* (pp. 53–73). Armonk, NY: M. E. Sharpe.

Morris-Suzuki, T. (2002). Immigration and citizenship in contemporary Japan. In S. J. Maswood, J. Graham, & H. Miyajima (Eds.), *Japan—Change and continuity* (pp. 163–178). New York: Routledge.

Morris-Suzuki, T. (2013). Freedom of hate speech: Abe Shinzo and Japan's public sphere. *The Asia-Pacific Journal, 11*(8). Retrieved November 9, 2016, from http://apjjf. org/2013/11/8/Tessa-Morris-Suzuki/3902/article.html.

Nakane, T. (2004). *"Chōsen" hyōshō no bunkashi: Kindai Nihon to tasha o meguru chi no shokuminchika*. Tokyo: Shin'yōsha.

Nathan, J. (2004). *Japan unbound: A volatile nation's quest for pride and purpose*. Boston, MA: Houghton Mifflin.

Nogawa, M., & Hayakawa, T. (2015). *Zōo no kokoku: Uhakei opinionshi aikoku kenchu kenkan no keifu*. Tokyo: Godoshuppan.

Oguma, E. (2002) *A genealogy of "Japanese" self-images*. Melbourne: Trans Pacific Press.

Ogura, K. (2016). *Kenkan mondai no tokikata sutereotaipu o haishite kankoku o kangaeru*. Tokyo: Asahi Shinbun Shuppan.

Onishi, N. (2005, November 19). Ugly images of Asian rivals become best sellers in Japan. *New York Times*, pp. A1–A6.

Ooizumi, M., Kajita, Y., & Kato, N. (2015). *Saraba heitobon: Kenkan hanchubon buumu no uragawa*. Tokyo: Korokara.

Ōtsuki, T. (2005). Netto yoron to "kenkan" no rekishi. In R. Ino (Ed.), *Manga Kenkanryū no shinjitsu!: Kankoku, hantō tabū chōnyūmon* (pp. 30–34). Tokyo: Takarajimasha.

Park, C. H. (2008). Historical memory and the resurgence of nationalism: A Korean perspective. In T. Hasegawa & K. Tōgo (Eds.), *East Asia's haunted present: Historical memories and the resurgence of nationalism* (pp. 190–203). Westport, CT: PSI reports.

Raddatz, R. (2013). Hating Korea, hating the media: *Manga Kenkanryu* and the graphical (mis-) representation of Japanese history in the Internet age. In R. Rosenbaum (Ed.), *Manga and the representation of Japanese history* (pp. 217–233). Abingdon, UK: Routledge.

Ryang, S. (2007). The tongue that divided life and death: The 1923 Tokyo earthquake

128   A. Haag

and the massacre of Koreans. *The Asia-Pacific Journal: Japan Focus, 5*(9). Retrieved November 9, 2016, from http://apjjf.org/-Sonia-Ryang/2513/article.pdf.

Sakamoto, R. (2011). "Koreans, go home!" Internet nationalism in contemporary Japan as a digitally mediated subculture. *The Asia-Pacific Journal: Japan Focus, 9*(10). Retrieved November 9, 2016, from http://apjjf.org/2011/9/10/Rumi-SAKAMOTO/3497/article.html.

Sakamoto, R., & Allen, M. (2007). Hating "The Korean Wave": Comic books: A sign of new nationalism in Japan? *The Asia-Pacific Journal: Japan Focus, 5*(10). Retrieved November 9, 2016, from http://ro.uow.edu.au/cgi/viewcontent.cgi?article=2441&context=lhapapers.

Sakurai, M. (2015). *Daikenkan jidai*. Tokyo: Seirindo Books.

Shibuichi, D. (2015). Zaitokukai and the problem with hate groups in Japan. *Asian Survey, 55*(4), 715–738.

Soh, C. S. (2004). Aspiring to craft modern gendered selves: "Comfort women" and Chŏngsindae in late colonial Korea. *Critical Asian Studies, 36*(2), 175–198.

Tanaka, A., & Satō K. (1992). Shazai sureba suru hodo waruku naru nikkan kankei. *Bungei Shunju, 70*(3), 134–143.

Watanabe, S. (2012). Kankoku no eiyū wa terorisuto bakari. *Rekishitsū, 29*, 31–37.

Yamaguchi, T. (2013). Xenophobia in action: Ultranationalism, hate speech, and the internet in Japan. *Radical History Review, 117*, 98–118.

Yamano, S. (2005). *Manga KenKanryū*. Tokyo: Shin'yūsha.

Yasuda, K. (2015). Heito supīchi: "Aikokusha"-tachi no zōo to bōryoku. Tokyo: Bungei Shunju.

8 Japan's internationalization

Dialectics of Orientalism and hybridism

Satoshi Toyosaki and Eric Forbush

ERIC: "Konnichiwa!" I shouted with enthusiasm as my Japanese teacher entered the class. "Ah, Ee, Oo, Eh, Oh," I sounded out the five vowels of the Japanese syllabary. This was the way. This was how I could get out of America, out of my stupid white suburb, my close-minded community. This was my path to dreamland—to a society where my uniqueness would be embraced—where I would truly feel at home.

SATOSHI: My US-American teacher corrected my "at." With my Japanese accent, I pronounced "at" "Ah-t." With his Boston accent, he corrected my "at." I practiced and practiced because I thought English was *kakkō-ii* (cool) (Seaton, 2001). Speaking like a native English speaker was such an "elite" thing to do (Toyosaki, 2007).

ERIC: "I am here," I said, as I stared up at the bright stars over Sapporo. "I am actually here." Nothing could explain the feeling of being in Japan that first night.

SATOSHI: I sat on the step outside of a dorm on a Midwestern US-American university campus. I made it to the United States, the Midwest, like I was told to. And I had jetlag, like I was told I would. I sat outside. The sun was rising, reflecting off the dew on the grass. The grass released a familiar scent—green tea. I smiled and thought, "I am here."

In our duoethnography, we—a Japanese person who left Japan for the United States and a US-American person who left the United States for Japan—weave our lived experiences and cultural observations in order to make sense of and critique Japan's internationalization. In particular, we focus on the minute ways in which the global force of Orientalism (Ma, 2000; Macfie, 2000; Said, 1978, 1994) and Japan's hybridism (Iwabuchi, 1998) function as everyday performative choices of our own "internationalization." Specifically, we theorize such performative internationalization as complex and nuanced dialectics of national identity performance betwixt global Orientalism (Said, 1978) and Japan's strategic hybridism (Iwabuchi, 1998).

In brief, Orientalism refers to a collection of historical discourses and representations of the Orient as the "Other" of the West (Said, 1978, 1994, 2000). Said (1994) contends that "the relationship between Occident and Orient is a

130   *S. Toyosaki and E. Forbush*

relationship of power" (p. 5). The Orient was created by the West and for the West. Japan's hybridism is characterized as a form of fluid essentialism (Iwabuchi, 1998). That is, Japan is like "a sponge that is constantly absorbing foreign cultures without changing its essence" (p. 73). Using the theoretical cross-fertilization of Orientalism and hybridism, we hope to nuance and make sense of Japan's contemporary internationalization—more specifically, Westernization and Whitenization—in this chapter.

Methodological approach

Theorizing monolithic Orientalism lacks substance. The scope of Orientalism— "a monolithic Orientalism" and "a hegemonic Occidentalism" (Ma, 2000, p. xii)—often falls short in theorizing the particularity of such concepts in human communicative acts and intercultural contexts. The Orient manifests itself in many different forms, not simply in representational texts—the main focus of research on Orientalism (Marcus, 2001). The various ways through which Orientalist misrepresentations are produced and co-opted into identity management and negotiations of the Orientalized are far more complex and nuanced in their workings than can be described by the dichotomous tension between monolithic Orientalism and hegemonic Occidentalism. Studying Orientalized Asian US-American identity, Ma (2000) explains: "Ethnicity in either flaunting or masquerading becomes a performative act" (p. xxii). Becoming Orientalist gazers and Orientalized is a relational performative accomplishment, or a relationally constructed identity, "instituted through a stylized repetition of acts" (Butler, 1990, p. 270). Japan's strategic hybridism (Iwabuchi, 1998) comes to be relationally performed, based upon the boundary setting between "Japanese purity" and "foreign impurity." Orientalism and hybridism are politically relational and both rely on "Othering."

To give context to the theoretical cross-fertilization between Orientalism and hybridism and their relational and performative nature, we employ duoethnography (Norris, Sawyer, & Lund, 2012). In brief, duoethnography is a relational epistemology that has evolved from and contributes to a number of ethnographic approaches, such as autoethnography (Ellis, 1999; Jones, Adams, & Ellis, 2013), community autoethnography (Toyosaki, Pensoneau-Conway, Wendt, & Weathers, 2009), and collaborative autoethnography (Chang, Ngunjiri, & Hernandez, 2012; Pensoneau-Conway, Bolen, Toyosaki, Rudick, & Bolen, 2014). It is a method through which two ethnographers self-reflexively (Davies, 1999), dialogically (Bakhtin, 1981), and intersubjectively (Schrag, 1986) engage in cultural analysis, collaborative sense-making, and a critique of their lived experiences. We offer each other and layer our lived experiences in theorizing Japan's internationalization in a complex and nuanced manner. Duoethnography as a relational and cultural labor "offers us a way to relationally (duo) understand our cultural (ethno) bodies, lives, and identities and to critically [write (graphy)] the implicated present" into our becoming (Hummel & Toyosaki, 2015, p. 43). As we embark on our duoethnography as a critical labor, we hope

Japan's internationalization 131

to contextualize and historicize Japan's contemporary internationalization—its dance with the West.

Kokusaika: Japan's dance with the West

Kokusaika (国際化) is a Japanese word for internationalization. Although Japan's internationalization has taken place in many political, social, historical, intellectual, and economic landscapes all over the world, we focus here solely on Japan's internationalization as it relates to the concepts and practices of the "West" (broadly defined) and Westernization. We use "dance" in the section title above as a metaphor for pointing to the back-and-forth or push-and-pull characteristics between Japan's homogenizing and internationalizing/Westernizing discourses. In the following, we begin with the Edo period (1603–1868).

In the Edo period, Japan issued a *sakoku* ("country in chains") policy and limited its international contact with foreign nations (Donahue, 1998). Through strategically exclusive international trade agreements, Donahue explains, Japan developed a unique method of foreign borrowing and absorbing foreign concepts into Japanese culture. According to McCormack (2001), during the eighteenth century *kokugaku* ("national study") scholarship was intended to develop "a pure … Japanese essence" (p. 1). Following Edo, Japan's Meiji period formalized the country's internationalization, understood and embodied as Westernization. *Meiji-ishin*—the Meiji Restoration (1868)—saw Japan modernized primarily by way of Westernization. Thus, Japan continued to experience a pull between Westernization and *kokugaku* scholarship. Yukichi Fukuzawa, the intellectual father of modern Japan, promoted "Datsu-A nyū-O" (Onishi, 2005), translated as "Leave Asia, Enter the West." Such Westernization movements were found in many aspects of Japan's modern political, intellectual, military, and industrial landscapes (see Graburn & Ertl, 2008). Like Edo's *kokugaku* scholarship, a homogenizing movement took place in opposition to Japan's Westernization—the "*kokutai*" (national polity) (McCormack, 2001, p. 1) ideology. Progressing into the Shōwa period, Japan continued to develop a homogenized nationalism against Asia and the powerful West all the while advancing with a Westernized military. Japan's military ventures left countless tragedies, both nationally and globally (see Okano & Tsuchiya, 1999), ultimately resulting in defeat and the end of World War II (WWII). In the pre-WWII period, Japan's national identity was socially and discursively constructed within the pushes and pulls between Westernization and construction of a homogenous Japanese essence (McCormack, 2001).

Japan's internationalization in the post-WWII era was more complex and nuanced because the global village became more connected with various technological and political developments. Japan's speedy recovery from defeat (Haglund, 1988) built on democracy for its political and ideological principles, and its industrial production (Graburn & Ertl, 2008) necessitated a more complex approach to internationalization. Expressions such as *kokusai kōryū* (international exchange) and *kokusai kyōryoku* (international cooperation) entered Japan's everyday lexicon. Japan's internationalization was discursively framed

132 S. Toyosaki and E. Forbush

with the notion and practice of information exchange and collaboration "with benefit." The country launched many initiatives for its *kokusaika* (international-ization), which Graburn and Ertl (2008) describe as Japan's "second great encounter with the Western world" (p. 6). During this time, Japan became increasingly internationalized/Westernized as many Westerners visited Japan and many Japanese learned more about the West through language and cultural education and foreign travel (Suganuma, 2012). People and information traveled more freely, including US-American media in the 1960s (Schilling, 1997). However, just as Japan pushed back against Westernization during the Edo and Meiji periods with *kokugaku* and *kokutai*, respectively, *nihonjinron* emerged as the new post-WWII nationalist scholarship. This emerging literature was trans-lated in various ways ranging from "theories of the Japanese" (Hambleton, 2011, p. 31) to "phallocentric obsession" (Macdonald & Maher, 1995, p. 5). In the homogenizing *nihonjinron* literature, the United States was strategically used synonymously with the West or Westernization as it was constructed as a coun-terpart of Japan (Graburn & Ertl, 2008).

Thus, Japan's national identity was imagined and constructed within the dis-cursive bipolarized pulls between an essentialized and original "Japanese char-acter" and post-WWII Westernization. Particularly through the Tokyo Olympics (1964) and Osaka Expo (1970), Japan was constructed as "a bridge between the East and the West" (Wilson, 2011, p. 169), which signified that Japan was neither the East nor the West and both the East and the West. Japan as a concept has been and, in some cases, still is, imagined to exist phenomenologically as "a representative of Asia or more broadly of the non-Western world" (Wilson, 2011, p. 169). Japan's internationalization was forged as a cultural struggle between intellectual, political, economic, and strategic Westernization and historical obsession with "racial/ethnic purity" (Iwabuchi, 1998, p. 72). However, this characteristic of Japan's internationalization shifted with its eco-nomic boom while residual effects continued to be evident.

In the 1980s, Japan's growing economy, known as "the Bubble," rendered a unique middle-class stratification. Japanese people's global mobility toward the West became prominent (Befu, 2006). The Japanese middle class, as a social product of Japan's WWII recovery and consequential economic boom, was char-acterized as a paradoxical phenomenon emerging out of *both* populist *and* elitist/ cosmopolitan views (Satsuka, 2009). In this way, the West or Westernization became accessible to and a mundane part of middle-class Japan. Westernized ideas, such as the "American Dream," permeated Japanese society and the Japanese developed transferential desire (Sakai, cited in Satsuka, 2009). In the embodiment of Japanese people's transferential desire, the West and, in par-ticular, the United States, were "constructed as a normative interlocutor in the Japanese imagination. The particularity of Japan [was] always thought out in ref-erence to the generality or universality of the West" (Satsuka, 2009, p. 71). Thus, the development of Japan's paradoxical middle class forged the push-and-pull of the country's homogenization and Westernization into Japanese people's everyday performance of their national identity.

Duoethnography

The transferential desire of the populist and cosmopolitan Japanese middle class is a globally structured phenomenon of "gaze"—an intricate dance of gazing and being gazed at and a power contestation of whose gaze is desired. The political and economic presence of the United States in Japan in the post-WWII period and during Japan's rapid economic growth induced Japan's "American fever," where "Amerika" was constructed as *"kakkō-ii"* (cool) (Toyosaki, 2011).

SATOSHI: I was not a Christian. Neither was I religious at all. But I rode a train to go to this Church. I went there because US-American White missionaries gave free English lessons. Each lesson was bookended by a little talk about the Bible in English.

ERIC: When I decided to move to Japan "permanently," I thought "finally, I will *live* in Japan instead of just visiting." I was fortunate enough to be picked up from the airport by a Japanese girl I met while studying abroad the previous summer. She helped me carry my bags and find the guesthouse I was staying at in Tokyo. I honestly would have been lost without her. I remember the first time we met, and she stared at me as though I was some unreal being … as though I had descended from a world unknown to her. It was then that I first realized the amazing power I possessed.

SATOSHI: Standing next to White people—missionaries or not—was a special event to me—an event that had not happened before in my life. Sitting next to them, I spoke in broken English. A rush of excitement, like the feeling of catching a fish on a rod, went through my body as I uttered random English words, hoping they would make sense. I was happy that they paid attention to my broken English and to me, one of a million Japanese. Other Japanese people saw me as an English-speaking Japanese person.

ERIC: I discovered my newfound power—my *gaijin* (foreigner) power.

SATOSHI: I started going to a private English conversation school. My family's low but middle class status barely afforded my tuition through my mother's additional workload (Toyosaki, 2007). I wanted to learn English to get attention from *gaijin*—from US-Americans, White people, and probably from other Japanese people, to show I was not a mere Japanese, but that I was a "special" Japanese.

ERIC: I began using my power in order to receive free meals, trips to various places, and make new friends. The ease at which I could obtain anything I wanted was ten times what I could normally do in the United States. And, it's all thanks to my parents for giving birth to me as a blonde haired, blue eyed Westerner.

Satoshi's fascination with White/US-American standard English and Eric's friend's fascination for Eric are cultural epitomes of the transferential desire.

134 *S. Toyosaki and E. Forbush*

Japan's internationalization is, indeed, Whitenization—"the process of identifying with white Westerners and privileging white bodies" (Fujimoto, 2001, p. 2). Fujimoto goes on to say that in Japan, White, US-American, Westerner, and *gaijin* (foreigners) are often understood as "synonymous" (p. 11). Eric's understanding of his *gaijin* power was certainly performed as "*gaijin*/Whiteness power". Satoshi's fascination with standard US-American/White/Christian/middle-class English rendered a receptive cultural mechanism of *gaijin* power, while Othering non-English speaking Japanese as not *kakkō-ii* enough for Japan's internationalization.

Thus, the Japanese embodiment of transferential desire, as a form of their internationalization, is a desire to use the Western/US-American gaze in evaluating and constructing their new Japanese identity.

> Most Westerners probably could outline what this image of Japan is: a homogenous society, where hierarchy and formality continue to be important. A country where men still are dominant and all work for large companies as modern "samurai" businessmen. Japanese women are held to be gentle, submissive and beautiful, and yet also appear in the foreign media as pushy mothers obsessed with their children's education. Japanese children, by extension, must be miserable automatons who do nothing but study all day and half the night.
>
> (Martinez, 1998, p. 2)

These types of image construction, especially of Japanese women, are ubiquitous in Western media representations where Japanese women become fetishized.

ERIC: A few days before classes started in Japan, I met another American student who had already studied there for a semester. We met at an *Izakaya* (traditional Japanese drinking establishment) where other international students were gathered for a "get-to-know-each-other" party. He sat there with his head hung low, tired, and drunk, and then he looked at me and said, "God damn it, I'm going to become a host!" He told me how during his first semester he lied to himself that he was there for so many other reasons, but in the end he had to admit that he was just there to meet Asian girls. "Well, that's stupid," I thought. I continued thinking to myself: "If you want to be productive and make something out of yourself, you have to set your goals higher than that. I mean, who the hell comes half way across the world just to pick up women?" I couldn't believe such a guy ... but I couldn't help but feel comforted by what he said.

Eric's vulnerable honesty and his friend's confession point to the ways in which Japanese women become sexualized and fetishized to the point where people travel to Japan "just to pick up women." The Western image construction of Japan and Japanese—or the Western gaze—is often meant to be innocent for some, yet damaging for others, because such a construction relies on and perpetuates the power structure of influence.

Japan's internationalization 135

ERIC: "Oh, no! It's happening!", I screamed. I placed my middle and index fingers on the corners of my young blue eyes and pulled the skin towards my temples. "I'm turning Chinese!" My older sister and her Chinese friend, both 7 or 8 years old at the time, stared in horror at a 5-year-old white boy pretending to be Chinese.

SATOSHI: I used to get slapped on the shoulders quite a bit. Someone I held close to me slapped my shoulder and said, "Wake up!" Then she started laughing. I did not understand the joke.

ERIC: I did not know what racism was at the time, but I thought for sure that what I was doing was funny.

SATOSHI: I did not know what Orientalism was at the time. Her body performed it, probably without her conscious engagement in Orientalist thought. For her, the joke was probably scripted and meant as a sign of her felt closeness to me—a friendly joke. Maybe it was a joke she saw on TV.

ERIC: A strict lecture from my grandmother—a close friend of the Chinese girl's mother—would ensure that I never forgot what racism was, and how it was extremely inappropriate for little White boys to pretend to be Chinese.

SATOSHI: I could not fathom how to make sense of my eyes, accused of sleeping, which had not happened before I came to the United States. I learned to feel ashamed of my Asian eyes. I closed my eyes in shame. And then, from the relational pressure, I started laughing with her.

This Western gaze bestowed upon Japan, or Japan as a representative of Asia (Wilson, 2011) or the Far East (Donahue, 1998), is referred to as Orientalism (Said, 1978, 1994, 2000) or the "Other" of the West—as the eyes of Satoshi and Eric's sister's friend were Otherized and used to render Western eyes. The mechanism of this Othering was bodily shame wrapped with a social practice of "joking." Said (1994) states: "The Orient is an idea that has a history and a tradition of thought, imagery, and vocabulary that have given it reality and presence in and for the West" (p. 5). While he does not simply consider the Orient as "just" an idea without any corresponding reality, Said contends that "the relationship between Occident and Orient is a relationship of power, of domination, [and] of varying degrees of a complex hegemony" (p. 5).

The various image constructions of the Orient—"Orientalist *mis*representations" (Ma, 2000, p. xiii)—reflect the history of the power dynamics and subjugate "Oriental" or "Eastern" subjects and subjecthoods to the history.

SATOSHI: "Do you know any martial arts?" my US-American friend asked. I had actually practiced Kendo since I was little. I replied with a question, "Do you know Kendo?" He answered, "No. But I know Karate."

ERIC: My older sister came back from her friend's birthday party at a local gymnasium. Apparently, they had all learned how to do "Karate" that day. My mom couldn't stop raving about how great the instructor was with the kids. "How about we sign up Eric for karate?" my mother suggested to my dad.

136   *S. Toyosaki and E. Forbush*

SATOSHI: I tried to sell the idea that Kendo was cooler than Karate. "Kendo is like a sword fight, like Japanese *samurai*." I tried to pronounce "*sám-rai*." Then, I used my right hand to demonstrate some sword movements and made my best vocal sound effect for my hand sword cutting through the air: "Shoo, shoo." After all of this, I only observed his awkward smile for my cultural performance.

ERIC: I made fart sounds, I fell on the floor, I ran around in circles, and I joked with the other kids. My *sensei* did nothing. He was not phased, even a bit, by my rambunctious behavior. Instead, he smiled at me, laughed, and said: "You're never going to get a bit of color on that belt." All I could think of was, "like hell, I won't."

SATOSHI: "Karate is cool, too," I said, as to respond to the awkwardness. Since I did not know Karate, I faked. "Hi-ya, Wha-tah." I might have sounded like Bruce Lee.

ERIC: Eight years after I was making fart jokes and bouncing off the wall, my *sensei* wrapped the heavy black belt around my waist and said: "Nobody can ever take this away from you."

SATOSHI: My friend smiled.

Satoshi autoreferentially subjugated his selfhood in order to fulfill the Orientalized expectation. In this moment of autoreferential subjugation, Satoshi validated his friend's awkward smile as a relational guide to "autocorrect" his cultural performance and to meet the expectation of his friend's Orientalist gaze. Karate had been constructed as culturally different and cool for many US-Americans as it was Orientalized and used to impress kids at a birthday.

Ultimately, Orientalism is not really about the Orient; it is about sustaining the West (Turner, 2000, p. 370) and its interest in upholding Occident–Orient power dynamics. Satoshi's friend's joke about his eyes was not really about Satoshi's Orientalized eyes; it was about her Western "aesthetically pleasing" eyes, predicated on the White body aesthetics that had been historically constructed and protected (Dyer, 1997). Satoshi's friend's fondness of Karate and Satoshi's fake show of being an expert practitioner were not really about Karate in its ontological and authentic sense. They were about the Western rendition/image/fascination with Karate. Eric's black belt may perhaps function as an Orientalized symbol, coded from the Western representational positionality. These incidents did not challenge, but ended up upholding, the Orientalizing discourses of Asian eyes and Karate.

This upholding, however, has consequences as "Orientalist *mis*representations conceivably become *self*-representations" (Ma, 2000) co-opted within, for example, Satoshi's Japanese identity constructed in the United States and Asian US-American identity constructions. The model minority image (Eguchi & Starosta, 2012) attributed to Asian US-Americans and their identity negotiation exemplify the ways through which gazers' misrepresentations become co-opted into the identity constructions of the gazed, potentially as a defense mechanism or survival skill. Understood on an international scale, this power relationship between the Occidental gazers and the Oriental gazed could explain the Japanese fascination with the West and the transferential desire (Sakai, cited in Satsuka, 2009) observed and embodied among the populist *and* cosmopolitan middle class during Japan's "bubble" economy—both of which have been celebrated as international symbols of Japan's recovery from defeat after WWII.

While Said's (1978) Orientalism is theoretically informative of Japan's contemporary internationalization/Westernization, we find revisions/critiques helpful in developing Orientalism further. In particular, we are drawn to the question of agency. Said (2000) himself writes: "The challenge to Orientalism ... was a challenge to the muteness imposed upon the Orient as object" (p. 349). Have Japanese people been subsumed, through their desire for the West (probably a cultural product of Orientalism), within the global and historical discourse of Orientalism? Are Japanese people the "silent Other" (Said, 2000, p. 349) of the Occidental speakers/gazers? How do we theorize agency of "Oriental/Orientalized" people?

Giving attention to the agency of the Orientalized and intentionally complicating Orientalism, we resort to an intercontextual theory of hybridity (Kraidy, 2002) and hybridism (Iwabuchi, 1998). Our theoretical move to hybridity and hybridism corresponds to the general observation about Japan during the post-Bubble period (1980s onward): Japan is characterized as metropolitanized and culturally hybridized (McCormack, 2001), rather than simply Westernized. However, we do not mean hybridity in the simple, idealistic, and unrealistic sense of cultural mixture or the "third space," produced through power-neutral means and contexts, of which both Iwabuchi (1998) and Kraidy (2002) are critical. Hybridity has been conceptualized as "a site of democratic struggle and resistance against empire" or critiqued as "a neocolonial discourse complicit with transnational capitalism" (Kraidy, 2002, p. 316).

Iwabuchi (1998) observes that the common application of hybridity fails to capture Japanese contemporary experience of its Westernization due to the general obsession with ethnic purity/homogeneity and because hybridity connotes impurity/heterogeneity.

SATOSHI: I was born and raised in Japan. I came to the United States early in my twenties. I have now lived in the United States longer than in Japan. This past summer, I had an opportunity to visit the Hiroshima Peace Memorial Park. As a Japanese person, I had been wanting to go there, learn the history in an embodied manner, and pay my respects to those who had passed away. Walking in the park by myself, I saw many elementary school students; some of them were wearing red hats and others were carrying school bags. I thought to myself: "I am here for the first time in my forties—What are they learning at such a young age?" This question was not meant to challenge their intelligence. I was simply curious about what they were learning from this experience. Some students were chasing dragonflies. As they passed by, they said "Hello" to me—a walking

138   *S. Toyosaki and E. Forbush*

body—in English. They obviously read my walking body's Westernized and hybridized impurity. At an early age, they had already learned to detect subtle cultural impurities that I, unconsciously, had picked up from living in the United States.

According to Iwabuchi (1998), Japan's Westernization is described, understood, and performed as "appropriation, domestication and indigenization of the West" (p. 72). Satoshi's friends and family often say, "Your body is Americanized (their perception)," pointing to his hairy and rather enlarged body. For them, Satoshi has lost the "essence" of a Japanese body: it is a body that has been Westernized, instead of a Japanese body that domesticates the West; for example, a stereotypical Japanese body—smooth and skinny—wearing US-American fashion. Iwabuchi calls the domestication of the West strategic hybridism: "Japanese hybridism aims to discursively construct an image of an organic cultural entity, 'Japan,' that absorbs foreign cultures without changing its national/cultural core" (Iwabuchi, 1998, p. 72).

ERIC: A friend once said to me, "I wasn't racist until I came to Japan." I laughed when he said this because I understood exactly what he meant. He was not relaying any serious feelings of hatred towards Japanese people, but rather conveying his (and my) struggle with being discriminated against as *gaijin* in Japan. As White, heterosexual, cisgender, educated, upper-middle class males, the term "discrimination" never really had a place in our lives (at least, not aimed in our direction). So you might imagine how strange it was for us to be told we weren't allowed somewhere because of our ethnic and national identities.

SATOSHI: I took a picture of a sign at a public bath at the hotel where I stayed in Japan. The hotel was relatively reasonable, and many "*gaijin*-looking" (to my sensibility) travelers used it while I was there. I sent the picture to my US-American friend, who had a tattoo. The sign said something like, "People with *irezumi* and tattoos are not allowed." Playfully, I sent a text: "You cannot get in here."

While people with tattoos are not equated to *gaijin* or Westerners, the image construction of the term "tattoo" in *katakana* signifies the foreign and the West (*katakana* is used to write words that are foreign to the language and/or that are foreign to Japanese people). Satoshi's playful text message certainly reminded his friend of his outsider—and forever outsider—status, which is similar to Eric's experience. While the hotel where Satoshi stayed had a cosmopolitan façade, the bath was reserved as a culturally sacred space to which bodies with "alterations" were not allowed.

The construction of *gaijin* as forever outsiders is a product of Japan's hybridism and its incapacity to transform its national and culture core in relation to shifting demographic and political landscapes. This is because Japan's hybridism is essentially about boundary making. On this point, Iwabuchi writes:

Japan's internationalization   139

Japan's *hybridism* is more intentional and strategic from the outset.... It attempts to suppress the ambivalence of the colonial encounter by relentlessly linking the issue of cultural contamination with an exclusivist national identity. It does not create a liminal space which blurs fixed and exclusive national/cultural boundaries. Rather, it reinforces the rigidity of these boundaries.

(Iwabuchi, 1998, p. 72)

In other words, Japan's hybridism, while having a façade of cultural assimilation or mixing, engages simultaneously in cultural Othering at the core. Iwabuchi (1998) understands it as a fluid essentialism.

ERIC: *Gaijin* cannot own property or rent an apartment in Japan without express written sponsorship from a guarantor. A *gaijin* is either a student learning Japanese, an English teacher, a model/actor, or the token non-Japanese employee of a Japanese company. I still remember when my favorite Japanese professor at a university in Tokyo told me something like the following: Japan has an annual immigrant population of zero because to immigrate, in his opinion, you must be able to attain citizenship at some point. If this is impossible, you have never truly immigrated, and will forever be "visiting." You could marry a Japanese person, have kids in Japan, work for a Japanese company, and live in Japan until the day you die, but you will always be visiting. You will always be a *gaijin*.

SATOSHI: The day will come: the day I need to choose either to become a US-American or stay Japanese. Japan seems to think that, if I choose to hold US-American citizenship, I am no longer Japanese in the purist sense. Will I become an impure Japanese?

ERIC: *Jus sanguinis*, a term that means your citizenship is determined by blood. If you have at least some Japanese blood inside you (i.e., one of your parents is Japanese) then you too can be Japanese (if you're born outside of Japan, you must decide by the age of eighteen if you want to be Japanese or not). I never bothered to do my own research on Japanese immigration law until now, but as it turns out, non-Japanese sanguineous *gaijin* can indeed become Japanese citizens through a very long and arduous naturalization process. The funny thing is, I never thought of questioning my professor because his reasoning resonated so strongly with my lived experience. I have yet to meet a *gaijin* who has become a Japanese citizen.

Japan's *Kokusaika*

Theoretical balancing of both Orientalism and strategic hybridism in our analysis—theoretical cross-fertilization—offers a more complex and nuanced picture of Japan's contemporary *Kokusaika* (Westernization in the case of this chapter) at the performative level. The theoretical cross-fertilization of Orientalism and strategic hybridism offers performative layers of various Otherings in

140   S. Toyosaki and E. Forbush

Japan's *Kokusaika* movement. Japan's *Kokusaika* is far more complex than Orientalism alone portrays—particularly around the theoretical axis of agency. Japan's strategic hybridism is instrumental in complicating Orientalism by theorizing Japan's agency in appropriating, domesticating, and indigenizing the West. However, we are cautious about theorizing Orientalism and hybridism as glocally oppositional discourses. While we may have fallen short in textualizing them in this chapter, we see them as relational and co-emerging constructs for understanding the performative dimension of Japan's *Kokusaika*. That is, Japan's hybridism simultaneously challenges Orientalism and re-Orientalize (Ma, 2000) by offering the site/essentialized cultural difference (such as a public bath) for Orientalist gaze and fetishizing. In return, such Orientalist gazing and curiosity sensitizes hybridism. Overall, we believe that the theoretical merger of Orientalism and hybridism offers intercultural communication scholars a more complex and nuanced picture of internationalization and details the hegemonic relationship between the Orient and the Occident.

References

Bakhtin, M. M. (1981). *The dialogic imagination* (M. Holquist, Ed., C. Emerson & M. Holquist, Trans.). Austin, TX: University of Texas Press.

Befu, H. (2006). Connditions of living together (*kyōsei*). In S. i. Lee, S. Murphy-Shigematsu, & H. Befu (Eds.), *Japan's diverse dilemmas: Ethnicity, citizenship, and education* (pp. 1–10). New York: iUniverse.

Butler, J. (1990). *Gender trouble: Feminism and the subversion of identity*. New York: Routledge.

Chang, H., Ngunjiri, F., & Hernandez, K.-A. C. (2012). *Collaborative autoethnography* (Vol. 8). Walnut Creek, CA: Left Coast Press.

Davies, C. A. (1999). *Reflexive ethnography: A guide to researching selves and others*. London: Routledge.

Donahue, R. T. (1998). *Japanese culture and communication: Critical cultural analysis*. Lanham, MD: University Press of America.

Dyer, R. (1997). *White*. London: Routledge.

Eguchi, S., & Starosta, W. (2012). Negotiating the model minority image: Performative aspects of college-educated Asian American professional men. *Qualitative Research Reports in Communication, 13*(1), 88–97. doi: 10.1080/17459435.2012.722166

Ellis, C. (1999). Heartful autoethnography. *Qualitative Health Research, 9*(5), 669–683.

Fujimoto, E. (2001). Japanese-ness, whiteness, and the "other" in Japan's internationalization. In M. J. Collier (Ed.), *Transforming communication about culture: Critical new directions* (pp. 1–24). Thousand Oaks, CA: Sage.

Graburn, N., & Ertl, J. (2008). Introduction: Internal boundaries and models of multiculturalism in contemporary Japan. In N. H. H. Graburn, J. Ertl, & R. K. Tierney (Eds.), *Multiculturalism in the new Japan: Crossing the boundaries within* (pp. 1–31). New York: Berghahn Books.

Haglund, E. (1988). Japan: Cultural considerations. In L. A. Samovar & R. E. Porter (Eds.), *Intercultural communication: A reader* (pp. 84–94). Belmont, CA: Wadsworth.

Hambleton, A. (2011). Reinforcing identities? Non-Japanese residents, television and cultural nationalism in Japan. *Contemporary Japan, 23*, 27–47. doi: 10.1515/cj/2011.003

Japan's internationalization 141

Hummel, G. S., & Toyosaki, S. (2015). Duoethnography as relational whiteness pedagogy: Human orientation toward critical cultural labor. *International Review of Qualitative Research, 8*(1), 27–48. doi: 10.1525/irqr.2015.8.1.27

Iwabuchi, K. (1998). Pure impurity: Japan's genius for hybridism. *Communal/Plural, 6*(1), 71–85. doi: 1320-7873/98/010071-15

Jones, S. H., Adams, T. E., & Ellis, C. (2013). Coming to know autoethnography as more than a method. In S. H. Jones, T. E. Adams, & C. Ellis (Eds.), *Handbook of autoethnography*, (pp. 17–48). Walnut Creek, CA: Left Coast Press.

Kraidy, M. M. (2002). Hybridity in cultural globalization. *Communication Theory, 12*(3), 316–339.

Ma, S-M. (2000). *The deathly embrace: Orientalism and Asian American identity.* Minneapolis, MN: University of Minnesota Press.

Macdonald, G., & Maher, J. C. (1995). Culture and diversity in Japan. In J. C. Maher & G. Macdonald (Eds.), *Diversity in Japanese culture and language* (pp. 3–23). London: Kegan Paul International.

Macfie, A. L. (Ed.). (2000). *Orientalism: A reader.* New York: New York University Press.

Marcus, J. (2001). Orientalism. In P. Atkinson, A. Coffey, S. Delamont, J. Lofland, & L. Lofland (Eds.), *Handbook of Ethnography* (pp. 109–117). London: Sage.

Martinez, D. P. (1998). Gender, shifting boundaries and global culture. In D. P. Martinez (Ed.), *The worlds of Japanese popular culture: Gender, shifting boundaries and global cultures* (pp. 1–18). Cambridge, UK: Cambridge University Press.

McCormack, G. (2001). Introduction. In D. Denoon, M. Hudson, G. McCormack, & T. Morris-Suzuki (Eds.), *Multicultural Japan: Palaeolithic to postmodern* (pp. 1–15). Cambridge, UK: Cambridge University Press.

Norris, J., Sawyer, R. D., & Lund, D. (Eds.). (2012). *Duoethnography: Dialogic methods for social, health, and educational research.* Walnut Creek, CA: Left Coast Press.

Okano, K., & Tsuchiya, M. (1999). *Education in contemporary Japan.* Cambridge, UK: Cambridge University Press.

Onishi, N. (2005, November 19). Ugly images of Asian rivals become best sellers in Japan. *New York Times*, pp. A1–A6.

Pensoneau-Conway, S. L., Bolen, D. M., Toyosaki, S., Rudick, C. K., & Bolen, E. K. (2014). Self, relationship, positionality, and politics: A community autoethnographic inquiry into collaborative writing. *Cultural Studies ↔ Critical Methodologies, 14*(4), 312–323.

Schrag, C. O. (1986). *Communicative praxis and the space of subjectivity.* Bloomington, IN: Indiana University Press.

Said, E. W. (1978). *Orientalism.* London: Routledge and Kegan Paul.

Said, E. W. (1994). *Orientalism* (25th anniversary ed.). New York: Vintage Books.

Said, E. (2000). Orientalism reconsidered. In A. K. Macfie (Ed.), *Orientalism: A reader* (pp. 345–361). New York: New York University Press.

Satsuka, S. (2009). Populist cosmopolitanism: The predicament of subjectivity and the Japanese fascination with overseas. *Inter-Asia Cultural Studies, 10*, 67–82. doi: 10.1080/14649370802605241

Schilling, M. (1997). *The encyclopedia of Japanese pop culture.* New York: Weatherhill.

Seaton, P. (2001). "Shampoo for extra damage": Making sense of Japanized English. *Japan Forum, 13*(2), 233–247. doi: 10.1080/09555800120081411

Suganuma, K. (2012). *Contact moments: The politics of intercultural desire in Japanese male-queer cultures.* Hong Kong: Hong Kong University Press.

Toyosaki, S. (2007). Communication *sensei*'s storytelling: Projecting identity into critical pedagogy. *Cultural Studies↔Critical Methodologies, 7*(1), 48–73. doi: 10.1177/1532708606288643

Toyosaki, S. (2011). Critical complete-member ethnography: Theorizing dialectics of consensus and conflict in intracultural communication. *Journal of International and Intercultural Communication, 4*(1), 62–80. doi: 10.1080/17513057.2010.533786

Toyosaki, S., Pensoneau-Conway, S. L., Wendt, N. A., & Weathers, K. (2009). Community autoethnography: Compiling the personal and resituating whiteness. *Cultural Studies↔Critical Methodologies, 9*(1), 56–83. doi: 10.1177/1532708608321498

Turner, B. S. (2000). From orientalism to global sociology. In A. K. Macfie (Ed.), *Orientalism: A reader* (pp. 369–374). New York: New York University Press.

Wilson, S. (2011). Exhibiting a new Japan: The Tokyo Olympics of 1964 and Expo '70 in Osaka. *Historical Research, 85*, 159–178. doi: 10.1111/j.1468-2281.2010.00568.x

Part IV
Media and framing

9 Ishihara Shintaro's manga moral panic

The homogenizing rhetoric of Japanese nationalism

Lucy J. Miller

On December 15, 2010, the Tokyo Assembly passed Bill 156 which gave the government the power to restrict the sale of manga, anime, and video games based on their perceived harmful effects on children. The passage of this bill was strongly supported by Then-Tokyo governor, Ishihara Shintaro. Ishihara was a successful novelist who served in the Japanese Diet for 25 years and as Tokyo governor from 1999–2012. Bill 156 revised the "Tokyo Metropolitan Ordinance Regarding the Healthy Development of Youths" to include representations of "sexual or pseudo sexual acts" (Kanemitsu, 2010d). The language of the bill framed the issue of the representation of sexual activity involving minors as common and easily accessible in purportedly mainstream content. The passage of Bill 156 responds not just to these internal concerns but also to the international perception of Japan as tolerant of child pornography and abuse of children. The U.S. State Department's (2015) "Country Reports on Human Rights Practices for 2015" says of Japan:

> No law addresses the unfettered availability of sexually explicit cartoons, comics, and video games, some of which depicted scenes of violent sexual abuse and the rape of children. Experts suggested a culture that appears to accept the depiction of child sexual abuse harmed children.

This American perception adds further context regarding why the issue was taken up by the Tokyo government; yet the dearth of actual content restricted after the bill was enforced in July 2011 suggests that the uproar that led to the passage of Bill 156 was a moral panic supported by Ishihara's nationalistic rhetoric.

In order to analyze Bill 156 and the statements related to it as a moral panic, I identify those members of the public and organizations constituted as "folk devils," who are at the center of the deviance the moral panic purportedly seeks to eliminate (Cohen, 2011, p. 2). Folk devils are "a category of people who, presumably, engage in evil practices and are blamed for menacing a society's culture, way of life, and central values" (Goode & Ben-Yehuda, 2009, p. 2). They are an important component of any moral panic by providing a focus for the outrage. The individuals and groups labeled "folk devils" are often excluded

146   *L. J. Miller*

from society and, in the case of Bill 156, Ishihara's labeling of certain groups as such connected the bill to the wider context of Ishihara's homogenizing nationalistic rhetoric on Japanese cultural and ethnic identity.

Horiuchi (2014) describes Ishihara as "perhaps the best known nationalist in Japan" (p. 36). His nationalistic stance has wide support from the Japanese people as a whole, as well as from hardline nationalists and conservatives, who consider him to be a "strong leader with [a] straightforward attitude and unwavering determination who is totally different from other politicians" (Horiuchi. 2014, p. 36). As with most nationalists, Ishihara defines true Japanese national identity through the exclusion of others. This is not limited to foreigners and immigrants but also to gays and lesbians, fans and creators of manga, anime, and video games, and the Japanese people as a whole when they fail to live up to his ideal for what it means to be Japanese. The purpose of this nationalistic rhetoric is to constitute a homogenous Japanese identity according to Ishihara's vision. Placing the moral panic over Bill 156 in the context of Ishihara's nationalistic rhetoric positions Ishihara as a moral entrepreneur, that is, an individual who has invested in creating societal rules that match his or her conception of what is best for society (Becker, 1963). The moral panic around Bill 156 fits with Ishihara's overall nationalistic project of constituting a homogenous Japanese national identity.

The intersections of moral panic and nationalism reveal the need for excluded others to be identified in order to maintain a homogenous national identity. Manufactured crises serve to make this exclusion appear warranted. In this chapter, I begin by analyzing Ishihara's nationalistic rhetoric, which seeks to constitute a homogenous Japanese cultural and ethnic identity. I then connect this homogenizing rhetoric to the statements made by Ishihara and others who have both supported and critiqued the proposal and passage of Bill 156, arguing that the uproar constitutes a moral panic. Finally, I review the moral panic over Bill 156 for what it reveals about modern anxieties over who constitutes a true member of a national community. National identity is partly constituted through the exclusion of others who are not included in the national community, and an analysis of Bill 156 as a moral panic demonstrates how the folk devils who are positioned as plaguing society serve as national Others who must be excluded.

Ishihara's homogenous national rhetoric

Nationalism is performative in the sense that "it creates something in the utterance, rather than describing something that is already there" (Hill, 2008, p. 4). It creates national identity by discursively determining who is included in that identity, not by just describing the objective reality of the nation. National identity is constituted through discourse by "demarcat[ing] those who belong and others who do not" (Marx, 2003, p. 6). Exclusion is as (if not more) important to determining national identity as inclusion. Critical intercultural communication scholars have broadened our understanding of identity construction (Darling-Wolf, 2004, 2005; Eguchi & Asante, 2016; Flores & Moon, 2002; Moon, 2016; Nakayama, 1994;

Ishihara Shintaro's manga moral panic 147

Sekimoto 2012, 2014). Carrillo Rowe (2008) reconceptualizes identity as *"differential belonging* – shifting the terms of interpellation from the individual subject to the spaces between them" (p. 28). Differential belonging allows for conceiving identity as the relationships between people from different groups rather than as an individualized possession. Nationalistic discourse "affirm[s] unique, collective identities by stressing that each national population differs from the people and cultures in all other nations" (Kramer, 2011, p. 11). The very aspects of national identity that inspire a close bond with fellow citizens can be used to exclude others (Cionea, 2007). Nationalism "is ultimately a double-edged sword, an efficient tool for promoting shared identity, perhaps, but one that may also encourage exclusion, intolerance, and even inhumanity" (Beasley, 2011, p. 5).

Queer theory extends our understanding of identity. Scholars have given particular attention to the ways in which queer people respond to exclusion (Bailey, 2014; Cohn, 1997; Namaste, 1994; Stone, 2013; Warner, 1993) and how queerness relates to nationalism (Berlant & Freeman, 1993; Chen, 2011; Mikdashi, 2013; Peterson, 2013; Puar, 2007). Members of marginalized groups often feel like "strangers" within the dominant culture (Ahmed, 2006, p. 141); Muñoz (1999) offers disidentification "as a response to state and global power apparatuses that employ systems of racial, sexual, and national subjugation" (p. 161). Queer theory adds depth to our understanding of the experience of exclusion for those left out of nationalist constructions of cultural and ethnic identity.

Once the status of the nation has begun to solidify, attention turns from external Others to the "otherness of the people-as-one" (Bhabha, 1990, p. 301). Having defined the nation as distinct from others, the performative project of nationalism turns to those who fail to embody the national ideal. The combination of defining the nation as distinct from other nations and excluding those within the nation who do not measure up to the national ideal are important features of Ishihara's nationalistic rhetoric.

One of the key goals of Japanese nationalism is to place a sense of Japaneseness at the forefront of citizens' minds, starting as early as childhood through revisions to school curricula and textbooks (Rose, 2006). Horiuchi (2014) contends: "Most nationalists simply want Japan to regain its national power and become a diplomatically and militarily influential state that can reject unfair foreign pressure, resolutely protect its own territory, and instill a strong sense of pride into its citizens" (p. 30). This sense of national pride found in Japaneseness, or what it means to be uniquely Japanese, can be understood through the concept of *Nihonjinron*, which Donahue (1998) defines as "a genre of thought in Japan that extols the uniqueness of the Japanese" (pp. 100–101). While the focus may be on Japanese uniqueness, this uniqueness is determined through comparison with other countries (Hambleton, 2011). Ishihara (1989) articulates the uniqueness of Japan in comparison to other countries when he addresses the issue of racial discrimination.

The American melting pot is a failed experiment. Racial discrimination may be a taboo topic there, but it is not for me. I said Japanese are probably

148   *L. J. Miller*

prejudiced, too. "Rather than make excuses, we should try to overcome these attitudes." And I told American[s] that Japan should be more responsive to the boat people and adopt a more flexible policy toward illegal unskilled Asian workers in the country.

(Ishihara, 1989, p. 144)

Ishihara acknowledges here that some discrimination targeted toward external Others like the Vietnamese and "illegal unskilled Asian workers" still needs to be addressed, though he qualifies this by stating that the Japanese are *probably* prejudiced while for Western nations, racial discrimination is "deeply entrenched in the Caucasian psyche" (Ishihara, 1989, p. 82). My purpose here is not to deny the ongoing realities of racial discrimination and oppression in the United States, but to better understand Ishihara's purpose in choosing racial discrimination as the comparison point with Western nations. Through his reference to the melting pot as a "failed experiment," Ishihara positions Japan's homogeneity as the reason the nation, as he perceives it, has been able to firmly address racial discrimination. Homogeneity is what makes Japan unique according to Ishihara's reasoning, and this homogeneity must be preserved by identifying Others to be excluded, whether they be external others or the folk devils of the manga moral panic.

Along with his attacks on manga, anime, and video game fans and creators as immoral, in constituting them as the folk devils for his manga moral panic Ishihara also identifies other elements within Japanese society that he views as threatening the nation's homogeneity, not just racially/ethnically but also ideologically. Ishihara strengthened his attacks on gays and lesbians as part of his manga moral panic when a reporter asked for clarification, saying: "I feel that [homosexuals] are missing something. Maybe it has something to do with their genes. I feel sorry for them as a minority" (cited in Watanabe, 2011). Ishihara frequently places gays and lesbians, along with other minorities, outside the range of behavior that he believes is proper and acceptable for a Japanese citizen; by locating their perceived failure in "their genes," he removes any possibility of gays and lesbians being incorporated into the Japanese body politic because what separates them from the Japanese people is inherent and natural. From Ishihara's viewpoint, their identities cannot be conceived of as part of the true Japanese cultural and ethnic identity; this attitude permits discrimination against gays, lesbians, and other minority groups to continue unabated.

As much as Ishihara seeks to exclude minority groups from inclusion in Japanese national identity, he directs his harshest criticism toward the Japanese people as a whole for not living up to his ideals. He attributes the workaholic behavior of many Japanese business people to "collective avarice to compensate for individual spiritual poverty" and goes on to say that

[a]s a people, Japanese have developed a very sophisticated spiritual culture – the tea ceremony, Noh, Zen, and the martial arts, to mention a few aspects. However, frustrated by the gulf between this metaphysical dimension and

Ishihara Shintaro's manga moral panic   149

their mundane, uninspired daily lives, Japanese pour their energy into accomplishing corporate directives.

(Ishihara, 1989, pp. 100–101)

Spiritual poverty implies a disconnect between the everyday, lived experiences of many Japanese citizens and a higher ideal of what it means to be truly Japanese. This notion of the Japanese people placing material concerns above an almost spiritual existence that should typify Japanese life can be seen in one of Ishihara's most notorious statements after a 9.0 magnitude earthquake and resulting tsunami devastated eastern Japan and led to the meltdown of the Fukushima Daiichi nuclear plant in 2011. He commented: "The identity of the Japanese people is selfishness. The Japanese people must take advantage of this tsunami as [a] means of washing away their selfish greed. I really do think this is divine punishment" (Ishihara, cited in Loo, 2011). Sounding like an American televangelist railing against gay people for causing a hurricane, Ishihara portrays an earthquake as punishment for the behavior of the Japanese people, not as a devastating natural disaster.

These appeals to a higher spiritual calling reveal the homogenous national identity Ishihara is seeking to create as one based not solely on identity politics but also on behavior, thus enabling him to invoke "divine punishment" whenever he witnesses behavior that he feels does not meet the ideals of Japanese identity. By defining his ideal in response to the external/internal Other and the behavior of the people, Ishihara is able to remain vague on how it is constituted; this allows him to employ this appeal whenever he chooses rather than being held to specific qualities or principles. Placed within the context of Ishihara's nationalistic rhetoric, the moral panic over Bill 156 serves as yet another example of how he seeks to chastise Japanese citizens for failing to live up to his ideal. Despite his claims of fighting to protect children, the manga moral panic served chiefly to reinforce Ishihara's view of a homogenous Japanese identity.

Bill 156 as a moral panic

Cohen describes a moral panic as a situation in which a

condition, episode, person or group of persons emerges to become defined as a threat to societal values and interests.... Sometimes the object of the panic is quite novel and at other times it is something which has been in existence long enough, but suddenly appears in the limelight.

(Cohen, 2011, p. 1)

Moral panic has been examined in a wide variety of contexts (see, for example, Springhall, 1998). The objects of the moral panic around Bill 156 (manga, anime, and video games) have long been a prominent feature of Japanese popular culture, particularly the cultural exports organized around the Cool Japan campaign which Iwabuchi (2015) criticizes for presenting a "one-way projection of appealing Japanese culture" (p. 425). That key cultural products used to promote Japan internationally, as well as their fans, could provoke a moral panic confirms that even established parts of society can become objects of concern when framed from a particular viewpoint. Ishihara paints the passage of the bill as intrinsic to Japanese national identity, saying that it was "natural" that the legislation had been passed. "It's the conscience of the Japanese," he said afterwards. "You cannot possibly show such things to your own children" (cited in Tokyo introduces manga restrictions, 2010). This manner of "moral indignation" serves to signify the object of the moral panic as both a threat to Ishihara's view of Japanese identity (the perverse content is leading people astray) while also confirming it (true Japanese people are not interested in such grotesquely sexual material) (Hier, 2011, p. 4).

Sensitization toward potential acts of deviance and delinquency is often part of the process of a moral panic. Cohen (2011) suggests the "phenomenon of sensitization … entails the reinterpretation of neutral or ambiguous stimuli as potentially or actually deviant" (p. 81). The passage of Bill 156 serves to sensitize the Japanese people toward the issue of sexual content in manga and other media; the content has been available for a long time, but it is only when there is debate over the bill that the people's attention is focused on the issue. They are sensitized as a result of a particular event or action but, for the agents of social control, their actions are not reactions in the moment to an act of deviance but serve as "an organized reaction in terms of institutional norms and procedures" (Cohen, 2011, p. 89).

Before the passage of Bill 156, the Tokyo government had already made laws restricting minors' access to pornographic and other potentially harmful content, such as depictions of suicide (Kanemitsu, 2010a). *The Wall Street Journal* found that:

> The Tokyo government monthly sends officials to bookstores to pick up 120–130 publications, 80% of which are comics that look pornographic but aren't labeled as such. The government then has a special committee discuss whether the publications should be labeled as unwholesome before the governor makes a final decision.
>
> (Sanchanta, 2010)

The purpose of Bill 156 was to expand the scope of content that is subject to review by the government. It is this widening scope that concerned critics of the bill, with opponents of an early version claiming that "restricting all fictional depictions that involve youth in sexual situations is far too broad, so more deliberations were necessary" (Kanemitsu, 2010e). Manga author Chiba Tetsuya framed his opposition to the bill around the issue of freedom of expression, saying, "I'm really concerned about the planned stricter law, as it would certainly discourage manga and anime creators to vividly express themselves—and it would sap them of life" (cited in Sanchanta, 2010).

Critics of the bill and the discourse surrounding it continue to offer the wide scope of content that falls under the bill's purview and the small amount of material restricted once the bill came into effect as evidence. In the first announced review of titles in May 2011, six titles were identified as being considered for restriction (1st Manga to be restricted by revised Tokyo law listed, 2011). None of the titles were formally restricted (No manga formally restricted by Tokyo's one-year-old youth ordinance amendment, 2012). The first title to be restricted was not until 2014 and Kadokawa, the publisher, voluntarily recalled it from stores (Kadokawa recalls manga that Tokyo designated as "unhealthy," 2014). Anime researcher Ruh (2010) questions whether Ishihara understood that even though the language of the bill was rather broad, the actual scope of content that would be restricted was limited.

> When questioned about the bill by the *Weekly Asahi*, Ishihara defended it by saying that works that depict 7 or 8 year olds being raped have no justification whatsoever. Okay, I'm with him there (although I would still defend any such artistic work on free speech grounds). But Ishihara seems to think that manga and anime are rife with such images, which I can plainly tell you is false. You might find such images in the hardest of hardcore pornographic manga and anime, but it is certainly far from commonplace. And even if you wanted to get rid of such products, Bill 156 would not do the trick.
>
> (Ruh, 2010)

To critics of the bill, it is self-evident that mainstream manga and other media are not rampant with hardcore sexual imagery, that media products that do contain this kind of material are already restricted and not impacted by the bill at all, and that the purpose of the bill must be to stir up anger and anxiety among the Japanese people. However, moral panic should be understood as a sub-set of social problems in which "claims can be analyzed as rhetoric, dissected to determine which arguments are used to make the claim convincing" (Best, 2011, pp. 44–45). Moral panic as rhetoric works as a process of resignification (Reed, 2015). In this process, isolated incidents or individuals stand in for an entire group of people (synecdoche) and those who identify the moral panic are able to construct the narrative of the events or actions (metanarrative). When resignifying events as a moral panic, more powerful groups and members of a society have more success in defining morality and proper behavior in a way that is consistent with their worldview (Goode & Ben-Yehuda, 2009). Ishihara, as the most powerful individual in the debate around the bill, shaped the narrative that the restricted content was rampant to fit his view of Japanese identity (synecdoche) and functioned as a moral entrepreneur (metanarrative).

Ishihara's role as a moral entrepreneur pressing for the passage of Bill 156 is demonstrated in a statement from December 3, 2010, in response to a request by Japanese Parent-Teacher Association (PTA) groups that he continue to push for the bill's passage. He declared: "Japan has become far too untamed. I'll go forward with [this bill] with a sense of mission in heart" (cited in Kanemitsu,

2010c). As discussed earlier, a moral entrepreneur seeks to create societal rules that match his or her worldview (Becker, 1963). Moral entrepreneurs "work to define a social problem and increase its public visibility" (Buckingham & Jensen, 2012, p. 424), thus "generat[ing] public attention to their crusades by making claims, a process by which rhetoric is carefully crafted so as to shape a particular image of a perceived threat to society" (Welch, 2000, p. 131). When Ishihara states that the passage of the bill reflects "the conscience of the Japanese," he is making a claim for a particular view on the bill itself and the behavior it is intended to regulate.

The bill had wide public support because of the work of moral entrepreneurs like Ishihara in framing the issue of sexual content in media as a pervasive social problem, even though research has shown that the harmful effects of such content on minors is frequently exaggerated (Levine, 2002). The ultimate goal of a moral entrepreneur is to create organizations or change the rules of an organization (Becker, 1963), as Ishihara was able to do for the Tokyo government agencies tasked with regulating content available to minors. The main concern with moral entrepreneurs framing issues according to their own worldview is that by doing so, "political elites participate in the social construction of reality by restricting the perspectives available for public understanding of an issue" (Bonn, 2010, p. 25). By creating a moral panic over sexual content in manga and other media, Ishihara exaggerated the prevalence of such content and enabled the Japanese people to feel secure in their morality by taking a stand against those perceived as peddling obscenity. By emphasizing the prevalence of sexually explicit content, Ishihara stacked the deck against his opponents. Opposing Bill 156 meant being seen as supporting (or even being involved in the creation of) almost pornographic imagery and its exposure to children, and with the weight of Ishihara's role as a moral entrepreneur the Japanese people had no reason to doubt his claims that such content was widespread in manga easily accessible to children. The folk devils of the moral panic over Bill 156 may have been vindicated by the dearth of manga actually restricted once the bill was enacted, but during the debate they endured harsh criticism from Ishihara who positioned them as Others outside the norms of Japanese society.

In an interview with TV Asahi, Ishihara argued that if the network aired equally graphic imagery the people would understand that "regulating something like this [is] only natural" (cited in Kanemitsu, 2010b). Ishihara goes on to say

> [I'm] not saying people can't draw this stuff. I only approved [this legislation] because it was about not exposing this stuff to children. It's clear there are perverts in this world. Sad people with warped DNA. If these kind[s] of people with these kinds of tastes, if they want to read and draw this kind of stuff and get excited over it, that's fine by me, really. Although, I don't [think] Western societies would tolerate such things very much. Japan has become too uninhibited. But you know, this stuff is abnormal, isn't it?
>
> (Cited in Kanemitsu, 2010b)

Ishihara Shintaro's manga moral panic 153

Ishihara frames his support for the bill solely around a concern for children, implying that his opponents do not share his concern by choosing to express themselves in a socially undesirable manner. He allows for private creation and enjoyment of such material in an attempt to curtail criticism that the bill represents a restriction of freedom of expression before challenging the Japanese people to emulate their Western peers who would not tolerate such behavior. Ishihara, as discussed earlier, frequently takes on the role of moral disciplinarian, chastising the Japanese people for failing to live up to his ideals. His final statement ("this stuff is abnormal, isn't it?") reiterates the constituting of those who create and read such material as outside the normal behavior for a Japanese citizen, while providing an opportunity for those sympathetic to his position to nod in agreement.

By framing the Japanese people as partially responsible by being "too uninhibited," Ishihara highlights an important aspect of the folk devil's role in a moral panic: essentially, that they are "cultural strangers" long before they become folk devils (deYoung, 2011, p. 120). There is a history of social shaming of fans of manga, anime, and video games in Japan (Kam, 2013). In the statement to the PTA mentioned earlier, Ishihara makes the social Othering of his opponents clear by identifying another marginalized group that motivates his actions: "This isn't just about the kids. Gays are appearing on television no problem" (cited in Ashcraft, 2010). Folk devils are important in a moral panic "because they are successful in achieving the goals of those who use them" (Patry, 2009, p. 139). By invoking the specter of gay people on television, Ishihara reveals the instrumental purpose of his moral panic: to further his vision of how the Japanese people should be constituted. The supposedly widespread appearance of sexually explicit material in manga accessible to children is nothing more than an excuse for Ishihara to advance his nationalistic goals. (As noted earlier, the first manga title to be restricted was not until 2014, three years after the bill was enforced, and in that case the publisher chose to voluntarily remove the title from bookshelves; thus even this was not a clear victory for Ishihara's position.) Failing to stay focused on protecting children from sexually explicit material makes it clear that this was never Ishihara's goal; it was merely another way to fuel the fears of the Japanese people.

The folk devils, for their part, did resist Ishihara's attacks. Fans took action to oppose the passage of the bill, such as distributing self-published manga (*doujinshi*) parodying the politicians who supported the bill (Leavitt & Horbinski, 2012). The greatest public response came when ten manga publishers announced that they would boycott the 2011 Tokyo International Anime Fair, an international showcase for Japan's anime and manga industries, in protest at the passage of Bill 156 (10 manga publishers to boycott Tokyo anime fair, 2010). This was a substantial move because of the international attention and financial boost that the event brought to Tokyo. Then-Prime Minister, Kan Naoto, responded, saying: "Upbringing of youth is an important matter. But at the same time, it's also important to present Japan's anime to the world" (cited in Sanchanta, 2010). The role of manga, anime, and video games as cultural ambassadors for Japan was

154   L. J. Miller

reaffirmed here, and while the event was eventually cancelled after the 2011 Great East Japan Earthquake (Tokyo international anime fair 2011 cancelled, 2011), Kan's statement demonstrates that not everyone in Japan supported Ishihara's position. Still, the successful passage of the bill in December 2010 makes it clear that Ishihara's moral panic was effective. However, as this analysis of the rhetoric of that moral panic reveals, that effectiveness was not the result of objective truth about sexually explicit content in manga, but due to the wider fears that Ishihara's moral panic fueled. These fears are reflective of the homogenous national identity that Ishihara envisions for Japan.

Conclusion

The December 2010 passage of Bill 156 by the Tokyo Assembly provides an example of a moral panic in which concern over the exposure of children to sexual content was used to enlist support for the bill, and in which manga, anime, and video game fans and creators were constituted as folk devils whose behavior represented a threat to the nation. Then-Tokyo governor Ishihara Shintaro served as a moral entrepreneur during the panic, pledging to fight for the passage of the bill and attacking those groups constituted as folk devils. This role of moral entrepreneur meshed with Ishihara's broader nationalistic goals; these were, primarily, to promote a homogenous Japanese identity by excluding Others and chastising the Japanese people for failing to live up to his higher, almost spiritual, ideals. Ishihara (1989) has little issue with the label "nationalism," which he defines as "a strong sense of roots and identity," arguing that without it, "there cannot be internationalism, only a shallow cosmopolitanism" (p. 76). Ishihara may believe that nationalism is nothing more than national pride and that such pride can lead nations to engage with the wider global community; however, the need to exclude Others, including the entire national citizenry if it fails to live up to his ideals, that is found in nationalistic rhetoric and moral panic, underlies all attempts at creating a homogenous national identity. Manufactured crises, liked the moral panic around Bill 156, do not merely represent an expression of concern for the people and pride in the nation but serve, instead, to make the exclusions inherent in nationalism appear warranted.

More attention needs to be given in future research to how moral panics align with broader political and societal projects. Moral panic is often analyzed as a singular event, in an attempt to understand how a particular group was demonized or an event exaggerated out of proportion. Analyzing moral panic in conjunction with other perspectives and ideologies connects the panic to wider purposes. The rhetorical analysis of moral panic should also be pursued more thoroughly as a method for understanding how specific elements of message construction and audience conception lend persuasive force to the appeals made and lead to certain groups being constituted as folk devils. The discourse of a moral panic does not focus only on the instrumental goal of addressing a social problem, but also seeks to achieve the constitutive goal of defining a particular group as the source of the problem. Rhetorical analysis can add further depth to our understanding of how these goals are simultaneously pursued. In the moral panic over Bill 156, Ishihara Shintaro and other proponents of the bill sought to exclude particular groups that did not fit with their homogenized vision of Japanese identity. Moral panic serves such nationalistic projects by fueling fear and anger against groups who have yet to be fully incorporated into the body politic. Vigilance against such exclusionary projects must continue for any society to fully embrace its heterogeneity.

References

10 manga publishers to boycott Tokyo anime fair (2010, December 10). *Anime News Network*. Retrieved from www.animenewsnetwork.com/news/2010-12-10/10-manga-publishers-to-boycott-tokyo-anime-fair.

Ahmed, S. (2006). *Queer phenomenology: Orientations, objects, others*. Durham, NC: Duke University Press.

Ashcraft, B. (2010, December 7). Is this the man to "clean up" manga and video games? *Kotaku*. Retrieved from http://kotaku.com/5707875/is-this-really-the-man-you-want-to-clean-up-manga-and-video-games.

Bailey, M. M. (2014). Engendering space: Ballroom culture and the spatial practice of possibility in Detroit. *Gender, Place and Culture, 21*(4), 489–507. doi: 10.1080/0966369X.2013.786688

Beasley, V. B. (2011). *You, the people: American national identity in presidential rhetoric* (Reprint ed.). College Station, TX: Texas A&M University Press. Retrieved from http://muse.jhu.edu.ezproxy.library.tamu.edu/book/135.

Becker, H. S. (1963). *Outsiders: Studies in the sociology of deviance*. New York: Free Press of Glencoe.

Berlant, L., & Freeman, E. (1993). Queer nationality. In M. Warner (Ed.), *Fear of a queer planet: Queer politics and social theory* (pp. 193–229). Minneapolis, MN: University of Minnesota Press.

Best, J. (2011). Locating moral panics within the sociology of social problems. In S. P. Hier (Ed.), *Moral panic and the politics of anxiety* (pp. 37–52). New York: Routledge.

Bhabha, H. K. (1990). DissemiNation: Time, narrative, and the margins of the modern nation. In H. K. Bhabha (Ed.), *Nation and narration* (pp. 291–322). New York: Routledge.

Bonn, S. A. (2010). *Mass deception: Moral panic and the U.S. war on Iraq*. New Brunswick, NJ: Rutgers University Press.

Buckingham, D., & Jensen, H. S. (2012). Beyond "media panics": Reconceptualising public debates about children and media. *Journal of Children and Media, 6*(4), 413–429. doi: 10.1080/17482798.2012.740415

Carrillo Rowe, A. (2008). *Power lines: On the subject of feminist alliances*. Durham, NC: Duke University Press.

Chen, L. (2011). Queering Taiwan: In search of nationalism's other. *Modern China, 37*(4), 384–421. doi: 10.1177/0097700411409328

Cionea, I. A. (2007). The banality of nationhood: Visual rhetoric and ethnic nationalism in post-communist Romania. *Controversia, 5*(2), 77–92. Retrieved from http://idebate.org/sites/live/files/Controversia_52-web.pdf.

Cohen, S. (2011). *Folk devils and moral panics: The creation of the mods and rockers* (3rd ed.). New York: Routledge.

156 *L. J. Miller*

Cohn, C. J. (1997). Punks, bulldaggers, and welfare queens: The radical potential of queer politics? *GLQ: A Journal of Lesbian and Gay Studies, 3*(4), 437–465. doi: http://dx.doi.org/10.1215/10642684-3-4-437

Darling-Wolf, F. (2004). On the possibility of communicating: Feminism and social position. *Journal of Communication Inquiry, 28*(1), 29–46. doi: 10.1177/0196859903258146

Darling-Wolf, F. (2005). Surviving soccer fever: 2002 World Cup coverage and the (re)definition of Japanese cultural identity. *Visual Communication Quarterly, 12*(3–4), 182–193. doi: 10.1080/15551393.2005.9687456

deYoung, M. (2011). Folk devils reconsidered. In S. P. Hier (Ed.), *Moral panic and the politics of anxiety* (pp. 118–133). New York: Routledge.

Donahue, R. T. (1998). *Japanese culture and communication: Critical cultural analysis.* Lanham, MD: University Press of America.

Eguchi, S., & Asante, G. (2016). Disidentifications revisited: Queer(y)ing intercultural communication theory. *Communication Theory, 26*(2), 171–189. doi: 10.1111/comt.12086

1st manga to be restricted by revised Tokyo law listed (2011, May 16). *Anime News Network*. Retrieved from www.animenewsnetwork.com/news/2011-05-16/1st-manga-to-be-restricted-by-revised-tokyo-law-listed.

Flores, L., & Moon, D. G. (2002). Rethinking race, revealing dilemmas: Imagining a new racial subject in race traitor. *Western Journal of Communication, 66*(2), 181–207. doi: 10.1080/10570310209374732

Goode, E., & Ben-Yehuda, N. (2009). *Moral panics: The social construction of deviance* (2nd ed.). Malden, MA: Wiley-Blackwell.

Hambleton, A. (2011). Reinforcing identities? Non-Japanese residents, television and cultural nationalism in Japan. *Contemporary Japan, 23*(1), 27–47. doi: 10.1515/cj.2011.003

Hier, S. P. (2011). Introduction: Bringing moral panic studies into focus. In S. P. Hier (Ed.), *Moral panic and the politics of anxiety* (pp. 1–16). New York: Routledge.

Hill, C. L. (2008). *National history and the world of nations: Capital, state, and the rhetoric of history in Japan, France, and the United States.* Durham, NC: Duke University Press.

Horiuchi, T. (2014). Public opinion in Japan and the nationalization of the Senkaku Islands. *East Asia, 31*(1), 23–47. doi: 10.1007/s12140-014-9202-6

Ishihara, S. (1989). *The Japan that can say no.* (F. Baldwin, Trans.). New York: Simon & Schuster.

Iwabuchi, K. (2015). Pop-culture diplomacy in Japan: Soft power, nation branding, and the question of "international cultural exchange." *International Journal of Cultural Policy, 21*(4), 419–432. doi: 10.1080/10286632.2015.1042469

Kadokawa recalls manga that Tokyo designated as "unhealthy" (2014, May 16). *Anime News Network*. Retrieved from www.animenewsnetwork.com/news/2014-05-16/kadokawa-recalls-manga-that-tokyo-designated-as-unhealthy.

Kam, T. H. (2013). The anxieties that make the "otaku": Capital and the common sense of consumption in contemporary Japan. *Japanese Studies, 33*(1), 39–61. doi: 10.1080/10371397.2013.768336

Kanemitsu, D. (2010a, November 20). Sneak attack of the nonexistent youth bill. *Dan Kanemitsu's Paper Trail*. Retrieved from https://dankanemitsu.wordpress.com/2010/11/20/sneak-attack-of-the-nonexistent-youth-bill/.

Kanemitsu, D. (2010b, November 24). Governor Ishihara's alternative universe. *Dan*

Ishihara Shintaro's manga moral panic 157

Kanemitsu's Paper Trail. Retrieved from https://dankanemitsu.wordpress.com/2010/12/17/governor-ishiharas-alternate-universe/.

Kanemitsu, D. (2010c, December 4). The outspoken governor. *Dan Kanemitsu's Paper Trail.* Retrieved from https://dankanemitsu.wordpress.com/2010/12/04/the-outspoken-governor/.

Kanemitsu, D. (2010d, December 17). Bill 156's total scope. *Dan Kanemitsu's Paper Trail.* Retrieved from https://dankanemitsu.wordpress.com/2010/11/24/bill-156s-total-scope/.

Kanemitsu, D. (2010e, December 28). How Bill 156 Got Passed. *Anime News Network.* Retrieved from www.animenewsnetwork.com/editorial/2010-12-28.

Kramer, L. (2011). *Nationalism in Europe and America: Politics, cultures, and identities since 1775.* Chapel Hill, NC: University of North Carolina Press.

Leavitt, A., & Horbinski, A. (2012). Even a monkey can understand fan activism: Political speech, artistic expression, and a public for the Japanese dôjin community. *Transformative Works and Cultures, 10.* Retrieved from http://journal.transformativeworks.org/index.php/twc/article/view/321.

Levine, J. (2002). *Harmful to minors: The perils of protecting children from sex.* Minneapolis, MN: University of Minnesota Press.

Loo, E. (2011, March 14). Tokyo head: Tsunami is "divine punishment"—Haruhi Yamakan responds. *Anime News Network.* Retrieved from www.animenewsnetwork.com/interest/2011-03-14/tokyo-head/tsunami-is-divine-punishment-haruhi-yamakan-responds.

Marx, A. W. (2003). *Faith in nation: Exclusionary origins of nationalism.* New York: Oxford University Press.

Mikdashi, M. (2013). Queering citizenship, queering Middle East studies. *International Journal of Middle East Studies, 45*(2), 350–352. doi: 10.1017/S0020743813000111

Moon, D. G. (2016). "Be/coming" white and the myth of white ignorance: Identity projects in white communities. *Western Journal of Communication, 80*(3), 282–303. doi: 10.1080/10570314.2016.1143562

Muñoz, J. E. (1999). *Disidentifications: Queers of color and the performance of politics.* Minneapolis, MN: University of Minnesota Press.

Nakayama, T. K. (1994). Show/down time: "Race," gender, sexuality, and popular culture. *Critical Studies in Mass Communication, 11*(2), 162–179. doi: 10.1080/15295039409366893

Namaste, K. (1994). The politics of inside/out: Queer theory, poststructuralism, and a sociological approach to sexuality. *Sociological Theory, 12*(2), 220–231. doi: http://dx.doi.org/10.2307/201866

No manga formally restricted by Tokyo's 1-year-old youth ordinance amendment (2012, July 2). *Anime News Network.* Retrieved from www.animenewsnetwork.com/news/2012-07-02/no-manga-formally-restricted-by-tokyo-1-year-old-youth-ordinance-amendment.

Patry, W. (2009). *Moral panics and the copyright wars.* New York: Oxford University Press.

Peterson, V. S. (2013). The intended and unintended queering of states/nations. *Studies in Ethnicity and Nationalism, 13*(1), 57–68. doi: 10.1111/sena.12021

Puar, J. K. (2007). *Terrorist assemblages: Homonationalism in queer times.* Durham, NC: Duke University Press.

Reed, I. A. (2015). Deep culture in action: Resignification, synecdoche, and metanarrative in the moral panic of the Salem witch trials. *Theory and Society, 44*(1), 65–94. doi: 10.1007/s11186-014-9241-4

158 *L. J. Miller*

Rose, C. (2006). The battle for hearts and minds: Patriotic education in Japan in the 1990s and beyond. In N. Shimazu (Ed.), *Nationalism in Japan* (pp. 131–154). New York: Routledge.

Ruh, B. (2010, December 21). Youth brigade: Clearing up the Tokyo youth ordinance bill. *Anime News Network*. Retrieved from www.animenewsnetwork.com/braindiving/2010-12-21.

Sanchanta, M. (2010, December 16). Sparks fly as Tokyo fights racy manga. *The Wall Street Journal*. Retrieved from www.wsj.com/articles/SB1000142405274870409830457602109249941072 6.

Sekimoto, S. (2012). A multimodal approach to identity: Theorizing the self through embodiment, spatiality, and temporality. *Journal of International and Intercultural Communication, 5*(3), 226–243. doi: 10.1080/17513057.2012.689314

Sekimoto, S. (2014). Transnational Asia: Dis/orienting identity in the globalized world. *Communication Quarterly, 62*(4), 381–398. doi: 10.1080/01463373.2014.922485

Springhall, J. (1998). *Youth, popular culture and moral panics: Penny gaffs to gangsta-rap, 1830–1996.* New York: St. Martin's Press.

Stone, A. L. (2013). Flexible queers, serious bodies: Transgender inclusion in queer spaces. *Journal of Homosexuality, 60*(12), 1647–1665. doi: 10.1080/00918369. 2013.834209

Tokyo international anime fair 2011 cancelled (2011, March 16). *Anime News Network*. Retrieved from www.animenewsnetwork.com/news/2011-03-16/tokyo-international-anime-fair-2011-cancelled.

Tokyo introduces manga restrictions (2010, December 15). *BBC News*. Retrieved from www.bbc.com/news/magazine-11998385.

United States Department of State, Bureau of Democracy, Human Rights and Labor. (2015). *Country reports on human rights practices for 2015: Japan.* Retrieved from www.state.gov/j/drl/rls/hrrpt/humanrightsreport/index.htm?year=2015&dlid=252767.

Warner, M. (1993). Introduction. In M. Warner (Ed.), *Fear of a queer planet: Queer politics and social theory* (pp. vii–xxxi). Minneapolis, MN: University of Minnesota Press.

Watanabe, M. (2011, January 17). Tokyo LGBT community and supporters protest Ishihara's homophobic comments. *Japan Subculture Research Center*. Retrieved from www.japansubculture.com/tokyo-lgbt-community-and-supporters-protest-ishiharas-homophobic-comments/.

Welch, M. (2000). *Flag burning: Moral panic and the criminalization of protest.* New York: Aldine de Gruyter.

10 mixi and an imagined boundary of Japan

Ryuta Komaki

mixi[1] is a Japanese social network site (SNS[2]) similar to U.S.American-based Facebook. It has been commercially developed and is operated by mixi, Inc. as their flagship product. In this chapter, I present a detailed analysis of the SNS's user-facing interface, with a particular focus on its rendition from 2008, when it reigned as Japan's most used SNS. Launched in February 2004 as the first of its kind in Japan, mixi quickly rose to the position of the largest SNS in the Japanese market, gaining more than 13 million registered users by January 2008.[3] (GREE, its primary domestic competitor at the time, lagged far behind with four million users in February of the same year.[4]) With the addition of mobile- and smartphone-oriented services such as "mixi Check-in," the service retained this market position until around 2014, by which time it had started to lose users to its global competitors Facebook and Twitter—and later to more smartphone-specific services such as Line.[5]

Looking at this Japanese SNS with a specific focus on its web interface, I argue that mixi's interface imagines the boundary of the social network of an "average Japanese person"—who can be comfortably included and who is to be excluded—in effect setting criteria for what types of people can "fit in" in "Japanese society," or who can be "properly Japanese." A look back to 2008 is important. As an object on the Internet, mixi's web presence is both persistent and transient. A reconstruction of a historical snapshot is only possible through archiving and careful note taking. For my analysis in this chapter, I am returning to the screenshots and "fieldnotes" I took in August 2008. I have documented my experience as a registering and registered user, taking screen captures and notes as I navigated through the sign-up process, the home screen, and other sections of the SNS. In retrospect, the elements of mixi I collected were similar to what Papacharissi (2009) calls "social networking site architecture," which she defines as a "composite result of structure, design and organization" that is "all specified by programming code" (p. 205). I have also visited the "about" page of the service and the corporate website of mixi, Inc., and collected email communications to document how the company marketed the SNS.

The 2008 web interface of mixi reconstructed from my research archive and "fieldnotes" presents not only a throwback to when the SNS was at its

160   *R. Komaki*

peak, but also a unique moment in mixi's history. At this time, while keeping its original invitation system—which required any new users to receive an invitation from a "friend" who was an existing user—mixi retained a certain degree of global reach. Later, as the invite system was discontinued, mixi implemented a series of system and policy updates that lead to stricter enforcement of the requirement for users to link their mobile phone messaging address or device identification information with their usernames.[6] As mixi's system only accepts mobile phone credentials from domestic Japanese operators, the SNS has lost its reach to the global market and a global audience. In 2008, mixi was thus still navigating between the openness of "the Net" and pressure to homogenize the presentation of Japanese society. I intend to capture some of that dynamic.

The chapter is divided into two sections. In the first section, I reconstruct the process an individual user went through in 2008 when signing up with and logging on to mixi, and discuss how its web interface affects the actions and experiences of users, particularly members of various minority groups. In the second section, I explore the complex neighborhood of relations (Mackenzie, 2006) within and around mixi's interface.

Welcome to mixi

Signing up

mixi was a "closed" SNS when I gathered the snapshot of the service and the website. That is, an invitation from an existing user was required to sign up as a member. The SNS justified this by stating that: "at mixi, we think developing a healthy, safe and comfortable community is important. To attain this goal, the system does not allow new registrations without an invitation [from an existing user]."[7] To receive an invitation, one had to have a personal computer (PC) email address, or an email address tied to a mobile phone service in Japan. (By mid-2008, mixi's system and policy was updated to also require a signing-up user to have an internet-enabled mobile phone sold in the Japanese market to complete the process; individuals not living in Japan were thus practically barred from getting an account.)

An invitation email starts with: "Hello, this is the mixi management team. [A name of a user] is inviting you to a social networking service (SNS) 'mixi.' Below is a message for you. Check it out, and start using mixi" (my translation). It also includes brief introductions (and a sales pitch) to the service, such as the following (my translation):

> With mixi, you can activate relationships with people around you, and with your existing friends: catch up with your high school friends in communities, write your diary and tell your old friends living away from you what you are doing, and check out profiles of your co-workers and find out what they are interested in.

mixi and an imagined boundary of Japan 161

A click on a link in the invitation email directs you to a registration page. Registration is free; however, you are also given an option to purchase a premium membership for 315 Japanese yen (about US$3) per month. Premium membership gives you larger disk space for uploading photos, videos and diaries, enhanced search and diary writing functions, and unlimited message storing. For an initial setup, mixi asks a set of questions, which boyd and Ellison have also found in many of the SNSs they have studied:

> After joining an SNS, an individual is asked to fill out forms containing a series of questions. The profile is generated using the answers to these questions, which typically include descriptors such as age, location, interests, and an "about me" section. Most sites also encourage users to upload a profile photo.
>
> (boyd & Ellison, 2007, p. 213)

Though mundane, this is also where the interface starts to facilitate representation and expression of the racial/ethnic identities of users. On the new user registration screen, I am asked to fill out my real name, pick a screen name, enter where I live, identify my gender/biological sex (*seibetsu*), and type in some "self-introduction" (all the above are required fields in order to sign up), along with dealing with administrative issues (such as providing my active email addresses and choosing a password).

A noteworthy feature of the screen is the way it asks a registering user to enter her/his location of current residence. Instead of allowing free text entries, it has two drop-down lists from which a user must choose a geographical location. The first drop-down menu lists 47 prefectures in Japan. Once the user has selected a prefecture, the second drop-down menu interactively generates a list of cities, townships, and villages within that prefecture (the city, township, village level is optional). This appears to be a secure and foolproof method of collecting information about the user's current place of residence, without the user accidentally revealing too much (street address, etc.). It is also a useful way of seducing users to provide valuable marketing information, so that businesses can target a user with location-specific advertising (see below for further discussion on mixi's business model).

One of mixi's much publicized features, its ability to foster location-based social networking and community development, supports (or covers up, if you will) this data collection. The "Welcome to mixi" page[8] rather eloquently advertises this feature: "'The bakery shop near the train station just opened today!' A lively conversation with someone living in your neighborhood, someone you have never met before, may spring up from a one-sentence entry in your diary like this" (my translation). There is, however, a glitch. The method by which this interface gathers location information does not allow one particular set of users (however non-typical) to connect to location-specific social networks or communities in a meaningful way (or, in the advertised way): users not living in Japan. It is not that these users cannot enter their location information. The

162   *R. Komaki*

"prefecture" drop-down list has a 48th option at the bottom: "overseas." The place of residence, however, gets sorted into extremely broad categories. When you pick "overseas" as your "prefecture" the second "Cities, townships, villages" drop-down menu produces a list of countries. Since the screen has only two drop-down tiers, this is as specific as you can go with your location. An individual's attribute, here, is "menu-driven" (Nakamura, 2002). Nakamura discusses how expressions and representations of racial/ethnic identity become "menu-driven" on many "portal" sites on the Internet (such as Excite and Yahoo!, which were popular at the time she was writing). As she notes:

> It [the list] forces the user to choose "what" they are, and allows only one choice at a time. This interface feature enforces a menu-driven sense of personal identity that works by progressively narrowing the choices of subject positions available to the user.
>
> (Nakamura, 2002, p. 104)

In a similar manner, the mixi's interface narrows down the ways in which a person identifies and associates with a place, and limits non-typical users' ability to form networks that are meaningful in their own terms. In this instance, the interface feature affects all users living outside Japan, setting a "national" boundary. And, as I mentioned above, the current registration system excludes individuals who live outside Japan on a permanent or semi-permanent basis, who do not have access to internet-enabled mobile phones sold by Japanese carriers. mixi does not elaborate on why this has to be the case, but it is most likely partly for technological reasons and partly a marketing decision (see discussion below on mixi's marketing model). As the widely recognized boundary of the "Japanese market" overlaps with the regulatory boundary of "Japan" as defined by the Japanese nation-state, this also reinforces the territorial boundary of the Japanese nation.

After completing the process of user registration, you are asked more questions to populate your profile page. This includes date of birth (required), year of birth (required), blood type (optional), place of origin (optional), hobbies/interests (required—a choice is offered from a provided list and multiple choice is possible), work and institutional affiliations (optional), and up to three "My favorite [something]" (optional—the "[something]" is chosen from a drop-down list and the actual content is free text entry). Except for the screen name, blood type (an important conversation starter in Japan), hobbies/interests, self-introduction and "My favorites," which are automatically made available to all users of mixi, you can designate for each whether information is to be shared with all members, only with your mixi friends, or with friends and friends' friends.

Here again, the location of your birth has to be entered through a set of drop-down menus, which only allows you to specify a country as your "place of origin" if you are from "overseas." The interface acknowledges that regional differences mediate your experience of growing up in Japan. Nevertheless, it

mixi and an imagined boundary of Japan 163

neglects the fact that experiences of growing up in overseas locations also vary regionally and thus cannot simply be sorted into "countries." Furthermore, the interface assumes that individuals from a specific region in Japan share common experiences and memories; hence they can connect or reconnect using this information. What it leaves out is that race and/or ethnicity, as well as social class, also mediate memories and experiences. Ideas and ideologies, such as traditional discourses and the politics of inclusion and exclusion, corporate interests and the concept of the "Japanese market," designers' intentions, software prototypes, and users' actions and reactions are intertwined within and around mixi's interface design. I call this entwining the "neighborhood of relations," borrowing from Mackenzie (2006) (this is discussed further in the below). This mix of ideas and ideologies allows mixi's interface not only to reiterate the geographical boundary of "Japan," but also to draw a racial/ethnic boundary for "Japanese society." This interface feature affects various groups of minority users in different ways. The following narrates some of the possible scenarios.[9]

Immigrant workers

Although the Japanese government has not officially accepted the entry of non-skilled immigrant laborers, people fitting this category have existed in Japan in substantive numbers for many decades (Komai, 1999/2001). With the loosening of the restriction on the "return-migration" of foreign nationals of Japanese ancestry in the 1990s, the number of workers migrating from Central and South American countries (such as Peru and Brazil, which received many Japanese settlers in the late nineteenth to early twentieth centuries) rapidly increased.

The interface of mixi, with its "menu-driven" orientation, fails to recognize either the importance and nuances of these workers' location-specific experiences and memories, or their existing location-specific social networks, which they may have had in their home countries and may want to stay in touch with after their moving to Japan. Rather, their identities, experiences and memories become sorted into and fixed to a country. In addition, as their first languages are less likely to be Japanese, the Japanese-language-only nature of mixi's interface may hinder their ability to fully utilize the service. Users in this category may be able to locate other users in similar circumstances based on the place of origin data and share their experiences and reflections. It may also be possible for them to create "communities" centered on their national or regional origins. Such communities would, however, receive less publicity than other, more "general interest" communities, because of the way mixi categorizes communities (see below).

Zainichi *Koreans and other Japanese-born foreign nationals*

For historical reasons, *Zainichi* Koreans make up the largest ethnic minority group in Japan. The majority of this population is Japanese-born. There is also a substantive population of other Japanese-born foreign nationals (including the

164   *R. Komaki*

children of the immigrant workers mentioned above). On the one hand, because they were born and raised, and many remain, in Japan, this group of users may be able to connect to or reconnect with location-based social networks and communities using their place of origin or current location of residence as their "identity" (so long as their "interests" stay in a similar realm to that of other normative users' "interests"—that is, not mediated by race, ethnicity, nationality, class, or sexuality). On the other hand, since the interface does not allow other ways to express one's identity (except in the free-entry "self-introduction" section), it may be difficult for these foreign nationals to connect to or reconnect with social networks or communities based on shared racial, ethnic or national identities. Members of racial/ethnic minorities within a particular country have translocal networks, both in the form of traditional media (Lee & Wong, 2003) and computer-mediated forms (see, for example, Parker & Song, 2006), for sharing experiences, memories, and reflections specific to the population. mixi's interface does not recognize these forms of networking as a meaningful part of an individual's social network.

Okinawans and people of Okinawan descent

Okinawa is an official (and fully incorporated) territory of Japan, and Okinawans are Japanese nationals. This, however, is only an official designation. As Nakasone states:

> For many years Okinawa was part of an extensive international commercial, political, social, and religious network, and the Okinawan cultural fabric is therefore richly woven with North, East, and Southeast Asian motifs. And the American military presence brings another culture into the mix.
>
> (Nakasone, 2002, p. 23)

In addition to culture, the history of U.S. occupation and the continuing presence of U.S.American armed forces bring a different political agenda to the island and to people with ancestral ties to the island. As Okinawa is an official territory of Japan (it is one of the 47 prefectures), individuals of Okinawan origin can indicate this on mixi through the place of origin information, and may be able to create or join social networks or communities meaningful in their terms. There may, however, be additional obstacles for people of Okinawan descent (i.e., those born and/or raised outside Okinawa), because mixi's interface does not allow them to express their Okinawan heritage through the place of origin entry. In addition, even if they do manage to do this, their efforts to develop communities for sharing specific Okinawan experiences and memories may not gain sufficient publicity. As I discuss below, the "community" feature of mixi categorizes communities in a way that does not appreciate the meaningfulness of such conversations.

In sum, the interface of mixi imagines a typical user of the site to be an individual who grew up in Japan, currently lives in Japan, and has experiences and

mixi and an imagined boundary of Japan 165

memories mediated by regional differences (within Japan), and possibly by gender, but unmediated by race, ethnicity, or class (or sexuality). If a user fits this normative model, she/he can express her/his attributes and affiliations in a meaningful way, and can use this to develop social networks and communities; even if an individual is a member of a racial, ethnic or cultural minority, she/he can "fit in" with other typical users' social networks and be a part of the social network of an "average Japanese person." If an individual deviates from that model, however, her/his ability to do so becomes severely limited. Only those who can "successfully assimilate" can be "fitting members of Japanese society," in mixi's imagination.

Logging in

Once your user account has been fully set up and your profile fully populated, you can peruse all of mixi's features. In 2008, the full range of services offered through the SNS included a diary (a blog-like status update), communities (discussion forums), photo and video sharing, music playlist sharing, product review sharing, and news. When you log in, you are directed to your "home" page. At the top of the home page are navigation bars that include a link for each feature (as well as links to the help page, "Change my settings," and a page to check who has viewed your profile, diaries, videos and photos). Below that are a search field that performs a search within mixi and announcements from the management team. Your profile photo and the list of your mixi friends (called "My mixi") appear on the left-hand side. Latest diaries, messages and postings by or from your "My mixies" and members of the "communities" you subscribe to are in the middle of the page. The right-hand side displays several visual and text advertisements, latest news, top five keywords (the top five most mentioned words in members' diaries), and some help-related items.

One interface feature worthy of further attention is the "community" page. Here, communities are listed by categories, as designated by the community's owner(s). The categories are as follows (translations of category titles are mine):

For Fun: Music, Movies, Sports, Gaming, Books and Manga, Travel, Cars and Motorcycles, Fortune-Telling, Hobbies, Pets and Animals
Knowledge: PC and the Internet, Scholarship and Research, Business and Economy, Art
Living: Regional, Food and Drink, Fashion
Groups: Schools and Colleges, Companies and Associations, College Student Organizations, Age-Group
Entertainment: Stars and Celebrities, TV Programs, Comedy
Other: Other, Events.

As Silver (2000) notes, "communities—geographic and online—are defined not only by who and what are included but also by who and what are excluded" (p. 143). Importantly, there are no categories under which conversations on

166 R. Komaki

experiences and memories mediated by race, ethnicity or nationality, of being an immigrant worker in Japan, being a *zainichi* Korean, or having an Okinawan heritage, can apparently fit. (And, interestingly, there is no "Politics" category, under which some of the Okinawa-related topics could belong.) If you can express your identity through a proxy that matches one of the provided categories, a community that pertains to expression and representation of your identity may get sufficient and desired publicity. For instance, *zainichi* Koreans' social networks can be delegated to Korean-language schools, which properly fit into the community "Schools and Colleges." Considering the prevalence of hate speeches against Koreans and people of Korean descent on the Japanese Internet—as well as offline—creating and associating oneself to such a community may attract more undesirable audiences (i.e., hate speakers) than those who hope to connect and reconnect with their schoolmates. Nonetheless, if it cannot be expressed through such proxies, your community can only get an obscure placement under the heading "Other."

Here again, the normative bias of mixi's interface is apparent. The "Welcome to mixi" page[10] advertises: "mixi is very good at finding people with whom you have things in common. Take a peek at a community you find interesting. It is full of 'Yes! I feel the same way too'" (my translation). However, the interface only allows typical users to fully take advantage of this marketed benefit. If you have experiences, memories, interests and reflections mediated by race, ethnicity, or nationality, for instance, your chance of saying "Yes! I feel the same way too" diminishes significantly.

The neighborhood of relations

The section above showed that mixi's web interface has its own imagination about inclusion and exclusion and the ability to order users' actions and experiences based on that imagination. Rather than passively embodying the politics of its designers or reflecting inequalities in the wider society, this imagined boundary emerges because the interface stores a complex "neighborhood of relations" (Mackenzie, 2006).

In *Cutting Code* (2006), Mackenzie argues that software is "a densely populated neighborhood of relations" (p. 18). Influenced by authors such as Callon (1987) and Latour (1993/1996), and by the anthropological theory of art of Gell (1998), he writes:

> Software is a neighborhood of relations whose contours trace contemporary production, communication and consumption. Code is a multivalent index of the relations running among different classes of entity: originators, prototypes and recipients. These classes might include people, situations, organizations, places, devices, habits and practices. In code and coding, relations are assembled, dismantled, bundled and dispersed within and across contexts.
>
> (Mackenzie, 2006, p. 169)

mixi and an imagined boundary of Japan 167

One implication of this is that what is stored in software is far more complex and complicated than conventionally thought: software is not a mere representation of the intentions of designers, nor does it simply embody an abstract social force. As Mackenzie (2006) says, his analysis "complicate[s] any simple attribution or withdrawal of agency to programmers or recipients ('users') of software" (p. 178). Moreover, "viewed as an ensemble of relations, software is particularly susceptible to the incorporation of heterogeneous places.... No particular symbolism, socioeconomic order, territorial unity or politics absolutely dominates in software" (Mackenzie, 2006, p. 181). In short, Mackenzie invites us to take software seriously and, in doing so, not to reduce it to a symbol, to a mere reflection of human thought.

Traditional politics and discourses of inclusion and exclusion

Not unlike any other society, Japanese society has politics and discourses of inclusion and exclusion. One—and perhaps the most prevalent—of which is the myth of a homogenous and monoethnic population (Burgess, 2007). It is a myth because it is not an accurate description of the population that occupies the archipelago; nonetheless, the discourse is widely accepted. Not only does this conceal the existence of racial/ethnic minorities in Japan, but it also marginalizes their experiences, memories and interests (Lie, 2001). Additionally, as Yoshino (1992) points out, the ways in which Japanese identity is defined and discussed in Japan often emphasize a disconnection between the "Japanese people" and "others." As he notes:

> Mere emphasis of the Japanese difference from, and neglect of similarity with, other peoples as a way of defining Japanese identity promotes a strong and problematic feeling of "unique us." The assumption that uniquely Japanese modes of thinking and behaving are incomprehensible for non-Japanese tends to hinder social communication between Japanese and foreign residents and the latter's integration into social life in Japan.
>
> (Yoshino, 1992, p. 37)

Although mixi's interface may not explicitly embody these discourses, they are among the factors that assert an influence in this "neighborhood of relations." After all, many Japanese people, perhaps including designers and users of mixi, internalize the myth of a homogenous population and the type of cultural nationalism discussed above (see Yoshino, 1992; Lie, 2001). As such, these politics and discourses are strongly intertwined with influences that designers and users assert in this "neighborhood of relations."

Corporate interests and theories of the Japanese market

Nakamura (2002) observes that behind online collection of "menu-driven" demographic information are corporate interests: data thus gathered helps

168 *R. Komaki*

marketing companies to target niche markets with specific advertising. To be usable in this way, the data must be as "clickable" as possible. She writes:

> It appears that it's not only older taxonomies of racial identity that inform menu-driven racial identities: the need for precisely targeted demographic data, strategic advertising campaigns, and "tribal marketing" (a disturbingly colonial locution for describing the best way to sell beads to the natives) also drive the selections available in the "ethnicity" interface. The best way to sell is to know who your client is in the most empirical and quantifiable (or clickable) way possible.
>
> (Nakamura, 2002, p. 122)

SNSs are another smart way to carry out such data collection, as well as to deliver targeted advertisements. mixi follows this business model, and indeed is successful at generating profit from this practice. ITmedia (2007), quoting Kasahara Kenji, then CEO of mixi, Inc, reports (my translation):

> "Our projected sales for this term are 9.7 billion Japanese yen [approximately US$97 million]. I read somewhere that Facebook makes about US$150 million. In terms of profitability, we are not that far behind." Kasahara went on to say that most profit comes from advertising and that targeted advertisements based on user attributes, "community" based advertisements, and video advertisements are the most successful.

Theories of the Japanese market are also entwined with the politics and discourses of inclusion and exclusion. Gender, sexuality, locations and interests become the most important user attributes in a market rendered as "racially and ethnically homogenous." Racial and ethnic minorities and people living outside Japan are neglected partly because existing theories of the Japanese market do not currently recognize them as potential "niche markets." As mixi, Inc. began losing users and thus revenue from the SNS, it started to focus more on transitioning the platform to deliver social games, and later developing games of its own, rather than trying to expand its social network service to include a wider audience.[11] As Monster Strike, a mobile game mixi developed in-house, is experiencing much global success, it is unlikely that mixi will change course with its SNS in the near future.

Prototypes

Mackenzie (2006) notes that "software sometimes resembles or represents something else, a prototype" (p. 16). He also argues:

> [I]n the shifting permutations of agency associated with code, the originator [(designer)] can just as well be subject to the action of the prototype.... The Linux kernel in its very name combines originators: a programmer (Linus

mixi and an imagined boundary of Japan 169

Torvalds) and a prototype (Unix). The ongoing production of Linux relies on coupling prototype and originators.

(Mackenzie, 2006, p. 180)

Although mixi was the first Japan-based SNS, its interface did not emerge from nowhere. Models of social network services had existed before mixi, and it is based on these. As ITmedia (2007) notes, "[mixi was] built based on SNSs gaining popularity in the U.S. at that time [(around 2004)]" (my translation). mixi thus has features commonly found on U.S. based SNSs: each user has her/his/own "profile" page, and it displays the user's network of friends ("My mixies"). It is likely that original designers' ideas and ideals about social networks and social networking were incorporated into these models. The roles and influence of prototypes are, thus, also entwined in a complex manner with the roles of designers and the influences of theories of social networks and social networking (see below on the roles and influences of the designers of mixi).

Designers

While designers may not be God as Kolko (2000) makes them out to be under the "neighborhood of relationship" approach, their role and influence does become manifest through web interfaces. Kasahara, then mixi CEO, was quoted in ITmedia (2007) as saying (my translation):

Many SNSs in the U.S. and SNSs offered by other domestic companies were "static," only connecting people with people, but we thought we would not be able to sustain our service like that.... We aimed to build an SNS on which people could communicate, on top of being connected.

Such intentions of designers are clearly visible on the interface of mixi. As I documented above, in addition to the features that help users build and visualize their connections (the function to display one's "My mixi," for instance), mixi has mini-blogging ("diary") and discussion forum ("communities") features which, the designers of the service envision, make it possible for users to "communicate," make their interactions on mixi more "dynamic."

Users

Like designers, users may not be *the* agents of social and technological change as some technology studies literature suggests (e.g., Pinch & Bijker, 1987; Oudshoorn & Pinch, 2003), especially when we look at the complex and intertwined "neighborhood of relations." Nevertheless, the role of the users should not be ignored. mixi has a functionality through which users can request changes and additions. They are thus able to influence the way in which its interface is designed. Furthermore, users are not passive recipients of technologies. For instance, although in its 2008 rendition the SNS's interface had a particular

170 R. Komaki

imagination regarding inclusion and exclusion, minority users (at least some of them) seemed to appropriate mixi and attempt to build communities meaningful to them within it.

In short, the source of the imagination that the interface of mixi has regarding the boundary of Japanese society cannot be reduced to just one. It has the imagination because of the dynamic push and pull among the heterogeneous "neighborhood of relations" formed in and around it. Traditional politics and discourses of inclusion and exclusion, corporate interests, prototypes, designers and users all actively assert their influences through the interface in a complex and intertwined manner. As such, mixi's imagination is not a complete mirror image of politics that is embedded in more traditional modes of boundary drawing. From mixi's perspective, those who can, for instance, "assimilate" to the model of the "normal" user (born in Japan, living in Japan, having experiences, memories and interests unmediated by race, ethnicity, class or sexuality) can be "fitting members of Japanese society." While this is very problematic (as it forces assimilation), it slightly departs from the traditional, cultural nationalist mode of boundary making, which deems it impossible for "foreigners" to assimilate at all—see the quote above from Yoshino, (1992) (page 167). mixi's imagination also differs from official Japanese citizenship law. While the law recognizes Japanese nationals living abroad and children born outside of Japan to Japanese parents as fully Japanese, mixi refuses to acknowledge the experiences, memories, interests, and social networks of this group of people as also a meaningful part of other, more typical users. The latter are those who live within the overlapping territorial, regulatory, and marketing boundaries of Japan, who can be ascribed "clickable" identities and sorted into "niche" markets so that targeted advertising can be delivered.

Conclusion

As I have shown, although mixi's publicity states that it offers everyone "healthy, secure, and comfortable"[12] ways to develop online social networks and communities, as well as opportunities to build meaningful location- and interest-based associations, it only delivers this promise to a limited set of users. mixi's interface, in its 2008 rendition, does enable a typical user—an individual who was born and raised in Japan, who currently lives in Japan, and has experiences, memories and interests flavored by regional differences and gender, but *not* by her/his race, ethnicity or nationality (or class or sexuality for that matter)—to connect to or reconnect with social networks and communities as advertised. At the same time, however, mixi's interface renders those who deviate from this model as "non-fitting" parts of typical users', or "average Japanese people's," meaningful association. Prioritizing collection of the marketable, "clickable" identities of typical users, it ascribes much less importance to the ways in which non-typical users—those of non-Japanese origin, with non-Japanese genealogical ties, and/or whose current home is not in Japan—associate themselves with a place (or places). It does not give meaningful and visible category labels to

mixi and an imagined boundary of Japan 171

communities formed around experiences, memories and interests mediated by race, ethnicity and/or national origin. In other words, mixi's web interface renders them "non-proper members" of "Japanese society."

This is not simply because mixi's interface *embodies* pre-existing notions about Japaneseness and the politics of inclusion and exclusion that are prevalent in Japanese society. Rather, as I demonstrated above, it is because of a complex "neighborhood of relations" (Mackenzie, 2006), an intertwining of traditional discourses and politics, corporate interests and the concept of the "Japanese market," prototypes, and the intentions and actions of designers and users, residing in and around the interface. As such, the way mixi's interface draws a boundary around "Japan" differs from the ways in which other, offline modes of boundary making do so—although those offline (and more traditional) ways do assert their influences through the interface. mixi's web interface, thus, *has its own imagination* regarding the form and content of the online community (and in effect those of the Japanese society of which it is a part). Still, as in the case of "non-typical" users of mixi, there are those who have to confront this "imagination" that becomes ingrained in the online space in order to be there in the first place. They then face a struggle to form meaningful associations and organize for a cause in the space, amid offline discourses that tend to pull towards the myth of homogenous Japan, and even against (or because of?) the backdrop of the supposed "openness" of the Net.

Critical intercultural communication scholars have argued that "inter-"cultural communication does not take place in a vacuum (Rowe, 2010; Sorrells, 2010). Every intercultural encounter in the globalized world is "situated in particular historical, social, economic, and political contexts" (Sorrells, 2010, p. 192). Moreover, as Rowe (2010) argues: "Because the inter [of intercultural communication] marks the process of exchange in which differently located subjects encounter an/other, it is also a site enmeshed in power relations" (p. 236). In the neighborhood of relations "no particular symbolism, socioeconomic order, territorial unity or politics absolutely dominates" (Mackenzie, 2006, p. 181). However, it is no coincidence that the "non-typical users" mixi's interface tends to displace, those mentioned in this chapter, are those who have been brought into this "intercultural" communication setting through Japan's past legacy of colonial expansion (Okinawans and *zainichi* Koreans), and through differential access to the global labor market (immigrant workers in Japan and Japanese nationals outside Japan).

The study presented in this chapter suggests that an SNS and the design of its web interface not only present an uneven setting for "inter-"cultural communication, but also play significant roles in the dynamic push and pull between homogenizing and heterogenizing discursive forces themselves. Like any other intercultural encounter, interactions, alliance forming and expressions of identity in online settings do not happen in a space devoid of historical, social, economic, and political contexts. How the space is constituted with codes and coding differentially affects different groups of users. It is thus important to unpack the neighborhood of relations that goes into making up the space, although we as

172   *R. Komaki*

researchers should not "remove ourselves from the convergence of conditions and forces that constitute our lives and intercultural relations" (Sorrells, 2010, p. 192).

Notes

1 www.mixi.jp.
2 Following boyd and Ellison (2007), this chapter uses "social network sites" as the umbrella term for this type of service, rather than "social networking sites" or "social networking services" (mixi, Inc. uses the latter to describe its own service). boyd and Ellison (2007, p. 211) note:

> We chose not to employ the term "networking" for two reasons: emphasis and scope. "Networking" emphasizes relationship initiation, often between strangers. While networking is possible on these sites, it is not the primary practice on many of them, nor is it what differentiates them from other forms of computer-mediated communication.

While this characterization may not be completely applicable to mixi, I employ the term for the sake of consistency.
3 www.mixi.co.jp.
4 http://gree.jp/?mode=static&act=page&page=ext_history.
5 According to a report by Japan's Ministry of Internal Affairs and Communications (2014), the adoption rate of mixi and Facebook among 1,500 participants in a study was similar at around 17 percent (in 2012); however, Facebook (26.1 percent) surpassed mixi (12.3 percent) in the following year and the gap had widened to 28.1 percent (Facebook) and 8.1 percent (mixi) by 2014.
6 http://mixi.co.jp/press/2010/0301/15602/.
7 From an archived snapshot of http://mixi.jp/regist.pl. (my translation).
8 From an archived snapshot of http://mixi.jp/about.pl.
9 The author is aware of the existence of socially/culturally marginalized groups in Japan other than those mentioned here—such as Ainu, burakumin, the lesbian, gay, bisexual, trans and queer (LGBTQ) population, and the physically and mentally challenged—and that the "menu-driven" means of identity expression and representation on mixi also seriously affects these people. The omission here is simply due to the limited scope of the chapter and limitations on space and not because I attribute less importance to their experiences.
10 From an archived snapshot of http://mixi.jp/about.pl.
11 See, for example, http://mixi.co.jp/press/2014/0213/15389/.
12 From an archived snapshot of http://mixi.jp/regist.pl. (my translation).

References

boyd, D. M., & Ellison, N. B. (2007). Social network sites: Definition, history, and scholarship. *Journal of Computer-Mediated Communication, 13*(1), 210–230.

Burgess, C. (2007). Multicultural Japan? Discourse and the "myth" of homogeneity. *The Asia-Pacific Journal: Japan Focus, 5*(3). Retrieved from http://apjjf.org/-Chris-Burgess/2389/article.html.

Callon, M. (1987). Society in the making: The study of technology as a tool for sociological analysis. In T. E. Bijker, T. P. Hughes, & T. J. Pinch (Eds.), *The social construction of technological systems: New directions in the sociology and history of technology* (pp. 83–103). Cambridge, MA: MIT Press.

mixi and an imagined boundary of Japan 173

Gell, A. (1998). *Art and agency: An anthropological theory.* Oxford: Clarendon Press.

ITmedia (2007, November 15) *mixi wa naze hitori-gachi dekitano ka—Kasahara shacho ga kataru.* Retrieved from www.itmedia.co.jp/news/articles/0711/15/news115.html.

Kolko, B. E. (2000). Erasing @race: Going white in the (inter)face. In B. E. Kolko, L. Nakamura, & G. B. Rodman (Eds.), *Race in cyberspace* (pp. 213–232). New York: Routledge.

Komai, H. (2001). *Foreign migrants in contemporary Japan.* (J. Wilkinson, Trans.). Melbourne: Trans Pacific Press. (Original work published 1999).

Latour, B. (1996). *Aramis, or the love of technology.* (C. Porter, Trans.). Cambridge, MA: Harvard University Press. (Original work published 1993).

Lee, R. C., & Wong, S. C. (2003). Introduction. In R. C. Lee & S. C. Wong (Eds.), *Asian America.net: Ethnicity, nationalism, and cyberspace* (pp. xi–xxxv). New York: Routledge.

Lie, J. (2001). *Multiethnic Japan.* Cambridge, MA: Harvard University Press.

Mackenzie, A. (2006). *Cutting code: Software and sociality.* New York: Peter Lang.

Ministry of Internal Affairs and Communications (2014). *Heisei 26-nen joho tsushin media no riyo jikan to joho kodo ni kansuru chosa hokokusho.* Retrieved from www. soumu.go.jp/main_content/000357570.pdf.

Nakamura, L. (2002). *Cybertypes: Race, ethnicity, and identity on the Internet.* New York: Routledge.

Nakasone, R. Y. (2002). An impossible possibility. In R. Y. Nakasone (Ed.), *Okinawan diaspora* (pp. 3–25). Honolulu: University of Hawaii Press.

Oudshoorn, N., & Pinch, T. (2003). Introduction: How users and non-users matter. In N. Oudshoorn & T. Pinch (Eds.), *How users matter: The co-construction of users and technology* (pp. 1–25). Cambridge, MA: MIT Press.

Papacharissi, Z. (2009). The virtual geographies of social networks: A comparative analysis of Facebook, LinkedIn and ASmallWorld. *New Media and Society, 11*(1–2), 199–220.

Parker, D., & Song, M. (2006). New ethnicities online: Reflexive racialisation and the Internet. *Sociological Review, 54*(3), 575–594.

Pinch, T. J., & Bijker, W. E. (1987). The social construction of facts and artifacts: Or how the sociology of science and the sociology of technology might benefit each other. In T. E. Bijker, T. P. Hughes, & T. J. Pinch (Eds.), *The social construction of technological systems: New directions in the sociology and history of technology* (pp. 17–50). Cambridge, MA: MIT Press.

Rowe, A. C. (2010). Entering the inter: Power lines in intercultural communication. In T. K. Nakayama & T. T. Halualani (Eds.), *The handbook of critical intercultural communication* (pp. 236–246). Malden, MA: Wiley-Blackwell.

Silver, D. (2000). Margins in the wires: Looking for race, gender, and sexuality in the Blacksburg Electronic Village. In B. E. Kolko, L. Nakamura, & G. B. Rodman (Eds.), *Race in cyberspace* (pp. 133–150). New York: Routledge.

Sorrells, K. (2010). Re-imagining intercultural communication in the context of globalization. In T. K. Nakayama & T. T. Halualani (Eds.), *The handbook of critical intercultural communication* (pp. 191–209). Malden, MA: Wiley-Blackwell.

Yoshino, K. (1992). *Cultural nationalism in contemporary Japan: A sociological enquiry.* New York: Routledge.

Part V

Environment and movement

11 Historicization of cherry blossoms

A study of Japan's homogenizing discourses

Takuya Sakurai

Among the various discourses portraying Japan as a unique and homogenous country, one especially worthy of consideration is that Japan is "the land of the cherry blossom." Along with a large number of cherries growing in the wild, the Japanese have, from ancient times, made efforts to cultivate their favorite cherries, producing and multiplying garden varieties. Already in the Heian period (794–1185), when some classic anthologies of poetry were compiled after the establishment of the Imperial Palace in Kyoto, the imperial houses of many distinguished aristocrats decorated their gardens with choice specimens of cherry tree. The cherry flower has been one of the foremost objects of the nation's admiration ever since then. In early springtime, after the dark and dreary winter months, cherry blossoms burst open almost at once to full bloom with vivid white flowers, thus symbolizing the nation's vitality as well as the purity of life. The way in which the petals of cherry trees leave their calyx when still fresh and at the height of their vigor and beauty as if not afraid to die, unlike all other flowers whose petals cling to their calyx until they wither and rot, is also believed to represent the samurai spirit.

While cherry trees are not only found in Japan, no other country has exploited them as symbolically and ideologically. From ancient times until the present, many studies have sought to find a coherent Japanese culture in cherry blossoms (e.g., Arioka, 2007; Hayashi & Kuroda, 1997; Ohnuki-Tierney, 2002; Orikuchi, 1975; Sato, 2005; Yamada, 1942/1990). The relationship between cherry blossoms and Japanese culture has been discussed since the *Someiyoshino*, a cultivated variety of cherry tree, emerged in the market in the late Edo period (1603–1868) and was widely disseminated in the Meiji period (1868–1912). Once the *Someiyoshino* was accepted by the Japanese, various kinds of cherry varieties were replaced by this single variety. Today more than 80 percent of all cherry trees in Japan are *Someiyoshino* (Hiratsuka, 2005).

The *Someiyoshino* is particularly important to a historical understanding of the relationship between Japanese culture and cherry blossoms, for two reasons. First, *Someiyoshino* trees began to be widely disseminated around the 1880s, when Japan established its law and education system to become a modern nation state; they were symbolized as "an efflorescence flower of new era." Second, as every single *Someiyoshino* tree is identical (because they are

178   *T. Sakurai*

produced only by cultivation techniques such as grafting), this has changed the whole cherry landscape across the nation. Sato (2005) points out that the *Someiyoshino* has been favorably accepted by the Japanese because the way the tree blossoms and the flowers fall meets with what they associate with cherry trees. They bloom before the leaves come out with medium-sized, modest, pale pink single flowers, which makes the whole tree look pink. The flowers begin to fall all together right after blooming, like a shower of petals (*hanafubuki*). These characteristics of the *Someiyoshino* have complemented symbolized images and meanings utilized in art, literature, theater, and so forth (Arioka, 2007; Hayashi & Kuroda, 1997; Ohnuki-Tierney, 1998, 2002; Ogawa, 1988; Yamada, 1942/1990).

It is easy, then, to imagine that cherry blossoms in general and the *Someiyoshino* in particular affect Japan's homogenous national identity and construct its historically coherent story: "Japan is the land of cherry blossoms." In this chapter I add an insight into the nature of homogenizing discourse in the historical context of Japanese culture and cherry blossoms. The purpose of this chapter is twofold: (1) to demonstrate that the historical evolutional process in which the multilayered meanings of cherry blossoms are reduced to a singular homogenizing discourse; and (2) to show how cherry blossoms have successfully helped the Japanese construct their homogeneous identify. In this way, the present chapter attempts to portray the taken-for-granted assumption of Japan's homogeneity as a spur to further inquiry.

Historicization and critical intercultural communication

Nihonjinron, a set of discussions in pursuit of Japanese cultural uniqueness and homogeneity, has long portrayed Japan through various descriptions such as a "topsy-turvy land of opposites," "feudal yet postmodern," "peaceful yet violent," "diligent yet frivolous" (Hudson, 1999, p. 234), the "Outnation," and a "smallislandnation" (Rauch, 1992, p.86). At the same time, these attempts have often been questioned and criticized as they tend to serve as nationalistic and ideological "myths" or "discourses" for disseminating the "uniqueness" of "Japanese" culture (e.g., Befu, 2000; Burgess, 2007; Dale, 1986; Hudson, 1999, p. 234; Kramer & Ikeda, 1997; Moeran, 1990; Mouer & Sugimoto, 1986). Moeran (1990) even calls them "Japanism," borrowing Said's "Orientalism," and criticizes them as "a genre of quasi-academic literature." Recognizing nations as "imagined communities," Anderson (1983) emphasizes the discursive nature of nationalism and the powerful role of printed literature and its dissemination. In imagined nations, people rely on symbolic language (myths, symbols, the geometry of maps, etc.) rather than actual personal contact between them, and identify themselves as members of a nation that shares a homogenous collective history.

Critical intercultural communication approaches provide us with a view of the ways in which the structures and contexts of such discourses impact our historical identities (Halualani & Nakayama, 2010). Contrary to historicism, which

Historicization of cherry blossoms 179

assumes that the past determines us with its accumulated linguistic depth, the critical approach recognizes history as a crucial force shaping intercultural encounters (Halualani & Nakayama, 2010) and constructing cultural identity (Kinefuchi, 2010). To understand history as such requires us to historicize culture, that is, "to carefully analyze the processes and mechanisms of how certain social conditions and realities have come to be what they are" (Sorrells & Sekimoto, 2016, p. xviii). Culture is not "ahistorical," but "a product of a series and continuous interpenetration between the external/global and the local" (Ohnuki-Tierney, 2001, p. 238). To historicize culture allows us to see how culture is created, sustained, and reconstructed through interactions with cultural others. Ohnuki-Tierney (2001), furthermore, criticizes the notion and the term "hybridity" of culture because it presumes the existence of "pure culture." She claims: "From the beginning, culture is a process of interaction between the local and the external" (Ohnuki-Tierney, 2001, p. 238). Culture is "a site of struggle" where the local meets the global and the external, and it is a crucial locus where history is constructed.

Historicization is often facilitated through naturalization processes that present historical discontinuities as continuities. The term "naturalization" refers to a process whereby "cultural arbitrariness" becomes "natural" (Bourdieu, 1977), and the idea allows us to understand historical time as "discontinuous" (Mumford, 1934), "mutational" (Gebser, 1949/1985), and "fusional" (Kramer, 2000) in nature, as the linearity and universality of time are merely cultural constructs. Ohnuki-Tierney (2001) also points out: "A corollary to the mutually constituent nature of the global and the local in culture is that neither temporal nor ontological priority should be given to one of these false dyads, the 'global/local' and 'structure/event' " (p. 238).

These dichotomized views presuppose an initial understanding of culture and its various domains. Mickunas (2007) points to two types of projection of time in the presupposition "memory" and "projection of temporal possibilities," because they are the catalyst for modern historical consciousness. He explains:

> All events, depicted mechanically, follow a causal sequence. What is given now can be explained by previous causes. Yet at present the previous causes are no longer available; they require an introduction of awareness of the past called memory. The future not being at present also requires an awareness that is called projection of temporal possibilities.
>
> (Mickunas, 2007, p. 4)

Gebser (1949/1985) points out that what we now call "memory" comes from the rational structure of consciousness that is manifested in a presumed continuous historical time, and that it assumes there is a transcended historical aim above and beyond history. According to Mickunas (2007), "future final purpose is posited as a condition for the invention of necessary rules of historical development" and "one historical event cannot be the aim of the whole" (p. 5). The historical discursive tradition comprises "horizons" into which our own limited

180   *T. Sakurai*

horizons constantly merge, "horizons that are more extensive than our individual horizons, and at the same time ... show how they are related and converge" (Mickunas, 2007, p. 11).

In sum, in the realm of critical intercultural communication, I draw on the idea "horizon" to explore how the dominant cherry-blossom discourses are historically formulated into a singular coherent history and to explain why the homogenous discourse that Japan is "the land of the cherry blossom" has been largely accepted. Horizon refers to a discursive process, which Gadamer (1975/2004) calls a "fusional process." Mickunas (2007) explains: "We are always immersed in a horizon of past and future without sharp boundaries between them, and our theories of knowledge and reality merge into these horizons" (p. 8). To explore cherry blossoms as a horizon, I utilize critical intercultural communication as a methodological approach. The approach allows us to recognize history as a shaper of cultural construction and intercultural encounter and to clarify the mechanism at play in historicization as a series of intercultural encounters and "a process not of correspondence but of articulation" (Halualani & Nakayama, 2010, p. 7).

Cherry blossoms and the *Someiyoshino*

Cherry trees found in Japan, the so-called "Japanese flowering cherry," are botanically categorized into *Cerasus*. This consists of approximately ten wild and 20 naturally cultivated varieties and, stemmed from these cherries, more than 300 cultivated varieties have been recognized. The latter can be differentiated from agricultural plants in that they are raised for ornamental and practical use, excluding edible purposes. In the late Edo period, new varieties of plants such as azalea, primrose, morning glory, and camellia were widely cultivated and produced. Specific techniques such as layering, cutting, grafting, and suckering as well as seed selecting and selective breeding were also developed and had a great influence on the popularity of gardening.

Somei (now Komagome, Tokyo), a village of gardeners who gathered and developed knowledge and skills of selective breeding and landscape designs, emerged around the late Edo period and became a major production site for cultivated cherry trees. The emergence of cherry horticulture also capitalized on the market value of cherry blossoms. As seen in the name, Somei is also known as the birthplace of the *Someiyoshino* (*Prunus yedoensis*), a hybrid between the *Edohigan* (*Prunun pendula*) and the *Oshimazakura* (*Prunus speciosa*). *Someiyoshino* trees were first sold simply as "Yoshino" because Mt. Yoshino has been the most famous cherry-blossom place and a synonym for beautiful cherries since ancient times. The village name was added soon after a large volume of the cherry trees became available on the market. Since *Someiyoshino* trees are relatively easy to grow and can adapt to most environments, they were mass produced to meet a huge demand and planted in parks, on river banks, in monumental places, and in schools all over Japan (Arioka, 2007; Sato, 2005). Today, more than 80 percent of all cherry trees are said to have been replaced by the hybrid

Historicization of cherry blossoms 181

variety, even though there are more than 300 varieties of cherry in Japan, during the past 200 years (Arioka, 2007; Hiratsuka, 2005; Sato, 2005).

Since the *Someiyoshino* is the name of a particular cherry tree, if a cherry tree grows from the *Someiyoshino* seed it is not recognized as a *Someiyoshino* tree. The cherry tree is not a self-fertilizing plant, which means that it cannot be pollinated from the same tree. All seeds have to be mixed with genes from another tree. Therefore, a cherry tree cannot be identical when it grows from seed. *Someiyoshino* trees are produced only through selective breeding techniques such as grafting. That is, all *Someiyoshino* trees, not only across Japan but also all over the world (such as those in Washington, D.C.), are from the same tree (i.e., have the same DNA). This is why *Someiyoshino* trees are considered to be "reproduced," which Sato (2005) and Arioka (2007) call "clone propagation." As all *Someiyoshino* trees come from the same tree the flowers, under the same conditions, come out simultaneously every year. According to Shirahata (2000), today's flower viewing (*hanami*) customs emerged when hundreds of cherry trees (the *Someiyoshino*) were planted in Ueno Park in Tokyo. People can now estimate the best days to watch cherry blossoming throughout Japan. The phrase "Cherry Blossom Front," borrowed from weather terminology, is an idea that emerged in the 1950s to report the daily progression of cherry blooming northward over the island in early spring. This implies that *Someiyoshino* trees have been disseminated all over Japan and have changed the national landscape. As every single *Someiyoshino* is identical, the landscapes are homogenous in nature. As a national icon or symbol of national identity, the cherry blossom is thus more or less reconstructed with the *Someiyoshino*; I call the impacts the *Someiyoshino* has on the discourses "the *Someiyoshino* lens."

A brief historical view of the dominant cherry-blossom discourse

The *Someiyoshino* is an influential cherry tree that reconstructs a history of how the Japanese lived with cherry blossoms before it existed. For example, we tend to believe that *Yamazakura* (mountain cherries) were the dominant cherry trees before *Someiyoshino* trees were disseminated across the nation. But, as Sato (2005) points out, this kind of historical speculation can be made only through the *Someiyoshino* lens. It involves projecting the past and presuming that one previous event has caused the present. In order to discuss the "projecting" impacts of the *Someiyoshino*, this section reviews the dominant historical discourses of cherry blossoms.

In ancient Japan, the cherry blossom was the most important part of the farming calendar; Ohnuki-Tierney (2002) calls it "agrarian productive energy" (p. 27). To the ancient Japanese, the cherry blooming was a sign that the mountain deities had come down to the rice paddies (which also indicated the rice-planting time). Shirahata (2000) provides some etymological analyses of the cherry blossom. The most widely accepted of these today is the division of cherry blossom (*sakura*) into *sa* and *kura*. In ancient Japan *sa* meant rice

182   *T. Sakurai*

paddies, while *kura* refers to a place for the deities. In folklore, *sa* in *satsuki* (May), *sanae* (rice sprouts), and *saotome* (rice-planting girl) all refer to the deities of rice paddies and are closely related to Shinto rituals (Wakamori, 1975). Ohnuki-Tierney (2002) claims that "a foreign element, rice, was turned into *the* maker of Japanese identity" (p. 28), gaining a connection with cherry blossoms which were not only Japanese indigenous plants, but also the mountain deities, the most sacred deities in Shinto.

Many studies have surveyed classical poetry in order to try to find the Japanese spirit in cherry blossoms (e.g., Arioka, 2007; Ogawa, 1988; Yamada, 1942/1990). The *Manyoshu*, the earliest collection of poetry complied in the eighth century, contains some 4,500 poems, 1,500 of which are about plants, while 118 poems are about plum blossoms, some 40 of them cherry blossoms. At that time, aristocrats preferred to compose poems about plum blossoms because they were imported from China, whose civilization was believed to be the most sophisticated (Yamada, 1942/1990). In the *Kokinwakashu*, a collection of poetry compiled in the early tenth century, cherry blossoms became a more popular motif than plum blossoms (60 cherry blossom poems, 28 plum blossoms poems). This transition was due to the abolition, in 894, of Japan's official delegations to China (*kentoshi*). The abolition officially minimized Chinese influence and provided the aristocrats with an opportunity to compose poems based on their own experience of nature and the climate (Arioka, 2007; Ogawa, 1988). By the time *Kokinwakashu* was compiled, the words "flower" and "this flower" in poetry began to refer explicitly to cherry blossoms. One of the most dominant characterizations of cherry blossom appeared in the collection: *mono no aware* (the fragility of life). For example, Ono no Komachi, a female poet, expressed her grief, comparing it to the falling petals of cherry blossom (*Traditional Japanese poetry: An anthology*, 1991, p. 208):

> Behold my flower: its beauty wasted away on idle concerns that have kept me gazing out as time coursed by with the trains.[1]

Folk cultures such as nō and kabuki during the Muromachi period (1336–1573) and the Edo period also played an important role in culturally and symbolically reconstructing Japanese images of "the land of cherry blossoms." Zeami (1363–1443) reconstructed the beauty of cherry blossoms in the theater arts and presented a new cosmology of cherry blossoms in the Muromachi period (Ogawa, 1988). The samurai loyalty to the lords was emotively illustrated with cherry blossoms in the kabuki theater. *Sakurafubuki* or falling petals of cherry blossom, like snow, became a theatrical device to stir an audience's emotions and shaped Japanese views of the cherry blossom as a dramatic symbol of death (Ogawa, 1988). The line "As among flowers the cherry is queen, so among men the samurai is lord"[2] was repeated in scenes of ritual suicide performed by samurai, or *seppuku*, in dramas. The scenes were adorned with many falling cherry blossom petals, like snowflakes on the stage. Portraying death with falling cherry blossom petals spread the idea of "dying beautifully." The woodblock

Historicization of cherry blossoms 183

prints of the late Edo period employed cherry blossoms as a major motif and enjoyed vast popularity (Arioka, 2007).

By the time of the Meiji Restoration, cherry blossoms were symbolically used to idealize the way the Japanese should live and behave. In the beginning of *Bushido* (1899/1905), Nitobe (1862–1933) finds the essence of bushido in cherry blossoms (p. 1):

> Chivalry [bushido] is a flower no less indigenous to the soil of Japan than its emblem, the cherry blossom.

Motoori Norinaga (1730–1801) connected cherry blossoms more explicitly, or more ideologically, with the Japanese spirit or *yamatodamashii*. He is probably cited more often than any other scholar in Japanese studies and was the first to attempt to unveil the core of Japanese culture rooted deep in Japanese history and to define the meaning of being Japanese. One of the Japanese core cultures he pointed to is *mono no aware*, derived from the poems about cherry-blossom: the temporal nature of life. Although Ogawa (1988) contends that Motoori did not see the cherry blossom itself, but the idealism in cherry blossoms, Motoori found the core of Japanese culture in ever-changing nature and composed the following poem (Matsumoto, 1970, p. 169):

> Should anyone ask me about the Japanese spirit, it is the wild cherry blossoms blooming in the morning sun.[3]

Some scholars claim that Motoori changed the value of cherry blossom from aesthetics to political ideology. However, Ogawa (1988) and Hayashi and Kuroda (1997) point out that Motoori tried to capture the core of Japanese culture in everyday life and simply thought that one of the most important Japanese cultural characteristics could be found in cherry blossoms, especially the *Yamazakura*.

Cherry-blossom discourses, such as the two mentioned above, were used intentionally by the government to promote Japanese militarism. After political and intellectual leaders had refashioned the warrior's way (*bushido*) and assigned cherry blossoms qua the Japanese soul as an exclusive possession of soldiers, the symbolic meanings of cherry blossom were subsequently changed (Ohnuki-Tierney, 2002). Until World War II, the Japanese government symbolized its military as cherry blossoms. Most of the military songs that were sung during wartime contained cherry blossoms in their lyrics and equated death with the beauty of the cherry blossom as its flowers fall down (Arioka, 2007; Ohnuki-Tierney, 2002). These military songs were sung throughout Japan, and the cherry blossom became a metaphysical flower symbolizing tragic death. Specially organized military teams were named *sakura-tai* or the "teams of cherry blossoms." The *tokkotai* pilots, or *kamikaze*, were taught that "you shall die like beautiful falling cherry petals for the emperor" and flew to their deaths with blooming cherry branches adorning their uniforms (Ohnuki-Tierney, 2002, p. 3).

184 *T. Sakurai*

Ogawa (1988) and Ohnuki-Tierney (2002) trace the way in which cherry blossoms have been used to evoke ideological nationalism and militarism.

Historicization of cherry blossoms

As Ohnuki-Tierney (1998, 2002) repeatedly argues, cherry blossoms were used to establish a Japanese identity distinct from the Chinese in ancient times and from West after the Meiji period. Conversely, intercultural encounters such as with Chinese and Western cultures have helped the Japanese to construct distinctive identities with cherry blossoms. Pure indigenous cultures are merely metaphysical phenomena because they are identifiable only when they become absolute, universal entities (Dale, 1986; Lebra, 1976; Ohnuki-Tierney, 2001; Wierzbicka, 1997); as Ohnuki-Tierney (2001) points out, the indigenous cultures are rather identified and constructed through reinterpreting them with cultural others. As seen above, cherry blossoms were a counterpart to Chinese plum blossoms in ancient times. Faced with Western culture, they represented a distinctly Japanese culture in the context of the indigenous religion, Shinto, and traditional poetic customs.

However, Shinto itself did not have a distinctive form or name before Buddhism and its corresponding Buddhist scriptures or sutras were officially imported from the Korean Peninsula (Aoki, 1976). The term *Shinto* (the way of *kami*) in ancient and medieval Japan did not, indeed, stand for an independent religion with explicit doctrines, but simply referred to those matters that concerned *kami*, who were reinterpreted to be avatars of Buddha for most of Japanese history. The Japanese have attempted to combine this belief with native or pre-existing cults that are lumped together under the term "Shinto." Buddhist clerics attempted to perpetuate their beliefs and practices, while Shinto competitors tried to popularize "pure" and "native" forms of worship and fought bitterly over ritual turf (Bernstein, 2006). Bernstein (2006) also points out that we cannot isolate Japan from foreign influences at any given time after Buddhist beliefs and practices came to the Japanese islands because Buddhist practices were integrated into the court's ceremonial complex over the next several centuries. At the center of this complex was the Yamato clan, an imperial lineage that traced its origins to the sun deity, *Amaterasu*. Piggot (1997) explains the long and complex history of this process. The Yamato clan dominated Japan, not only by exerting military force, but also by manipulating the native *kami* worship and by adapting institutions, technologies, and belief systems based on Buddhism from the Asian continent.

The Shinto tradition also plays an important role in portraying the Japanese unique understanding of Western technology and science. The Japanese attempted to adapt an alien science and technology while preserving the indigenous tradition under the saying "Japanese spirits, European science" or *wakonyosai*. Before encountering the West, the Japanese had knowledge of nature or *shizen*, which encompassed descriptive and explanatory elements as cosmological characteristics (Watanabe, 1976/1990). Ogawa explains:

Everything surrounding human life (for example, mountains, rivers, plants, trees, insects, fish, or animals) has its own spirit, which can communicate with each other as well as with the people living there. Thus, the special feelings summarized by the "one-bodiness," which means that human beings and every natural thing are one body in total, are felt by the Japanese.

(Ogawa, 1997, p. 176)

Watanabe (1976/1990) claims that nature is viewed through the eyes of traditional poetry, whose aim is to become one with nature. Japanese ancestors composed poems about the beauty of nature that they were never tired of looking at, while the West attempted to understand nature through paying attention, observing, and evaluating it in terms of its utility. Although the English word *observe* is translated into the Japanese word *kansatsu*, the latter implies a close spiritual kind of relationship (Aikenhead, 2001). It is very different from the objective relationship presupposed by Cartesian dualism (a mind/thing dichotomy) that forms the cornerstone of the Western scientific worldview. Therefore, fortified by a feeling of animism, the Japanese cannot regard natural things as mere objects of value-free inquiry.

The *Someiyoshino*, disseminated as a flower of Japan's Westernization movement during the Meiji era, was particularly effective when confronting the West, not only because the flowers were vivid and showy and indicated the coming new era of Western science and technology, but also because they were always part of the Shinto tradition, the unique Japanese way of understanding nature. The *Someiyoshino* has constructed a historical horizon that connects the past to the future image of Japan through science and technology. It clarified and purified this identity into a distinct form that is well supported by Shinto tradition. Across the nation, the *Someiyoshino* also provided a homogenous image of Japan as a united nation not only because of its identical appearances, but also through its symbolic capacity that reconstructed the various meanings of cherry blossom into a singular horizon that can be traced back to the origins of Japanese cultural traditions.

As seen above, the Japanese cherry-blossom culture was born and developed as a distinctive culture through its encounter with Chinese culture and recontextualized as an indigenous culture when it encountered Western culture. When different cultures meet, cultural horizons are fused and reconstructed, purifying the indigenous culture. Constructing the linear, continuous history of cherry blossoms is an extremely one-sided, perspectival, and materialistic endeavour. As Gebser (1949/1985) explains: "The word *history*, which is derived from the Greek *historia*, is based on the Greek verb *historeo*, meaning 'to inquire after something' and thus conveys a clear expression of being directed" (p. 192). Once we assume the origins of Japanese culture to be at a certain historical point, a historical discourse is reconstructed but only in an abstract form. Mickunas (2007) claims that all discourses must "justify themselves within the standards and rules established by a subject reflecting itself" (p. 12). Placing the

186   *T. Sakurai*

Someiyoshino on a boundary between the modern and the traditional and projecting the historically transcendent aim of seeking Japanese identities, the cherry blossom gains its spectacular temporal flow from the past to the present. Seeing cherry blossoms as a horizon, however, demonstrates that culture is not static and lineally continuous; rather, as Ohnuki-Tierney (2001) and Halualani and Nakayama (2010) point out, it is always in a process where the local meets the external and "a site of contestation where meanings are constantly negotiated" (Sorrells, 2010, p. 178). While different horizons are struggling for discursive truth, the cherry blossom is always being redefined. Recapturing such a process of constructing a history as a "horizon" allows us to see how one event discloses other events and itself, supervenes upon other events, subtends them, or how various events intertwine.

Concluding remarks

In this chapter I reviewed how cherry-blossom discourses have been constructed, maintained, and shared with a focus on the *Someiyoshino*. I also discussed how the history of cherry blossom is reconstructed when encountering cultural others. To this end, I examined the historical horizon of cherry blossoms that has been shared by the Japanese, placing a particular focus on the transformation that occurs when encountering cultural others. What is revealed through the horizon is not a simple chronological description, but a certain coherent logic that is often considered to be a "tradition." Husserl (1954/1970) calls this the "we-horizon," where "the whole cultural world, in all its forms, exists" (p. 354). Mickunas (2006) claims that each culture has its own ways of experiencing and articulating universality under its own logic, within which individuals tend to interpret and locate other cultures. This logic is articulated as a homogenizing discourse that "provides an interpretation of events that allows human reality to have sense, value, ethics, and purpose—indeed a final and ultimate purpose" (Mickunas, 2006, p. 21). Homogenizing discourse is one of the major methods of the ethnic cultural revival, as it is related to the culture's naïve picture of the world; it is necessary for living and socializing in a cultural group, but it is always manifested when encountering cultural others.

Notes

1 The original Japanese version is: *hana no iro wa/utsurinikeri na itadurani/wagami yonifuru/nagame seshimani*. I cite the English translation in *Traditional Japanese poetry: An anthology* (1991).
2 The original Japanese version is: *hana ha sakuragi/hito ha bushi*. I cite the English translation in Nitobe (1889/1995, p. 62).
3 The original Japanese version is: *shikishima no/yamatogokoro wo/hitotohaba/asahini nihofu/yamazakurabana*.

References

Aikenhead, G. S. (2001). Science communication with the public: A cross-cultural event. In S. M. Stocklmayer, M. M. Gore, & C. Bryant (Eds.), *Science communication in theory and practice* (pp. 23–45). Boston, MA: Kluwer.

Anderson, B. (1983). *Imagined communities: Reflections on the origin and spread of nationalism.* London: Verso.

Aoki, K. (1976). Zui tou bunka to nihon [The Zui and Tong cultures and Japan]. In M. Inoue, T. Haga, & T. Hayashiya (Eds.), *Nihon rettou no bunkashi* [Cultural history of the Japanese archipelago] (pp. 33–59). Tokyo: Kenkyusha.

Arioka, T. (2007). *Sakura* [Cherry blossoms]. Tokyo: Hosei University Press.

Befu, H. (2000). Globalization as human dispersal: From the perspective of Japan. In J. S. Eades, T. Gill, & H. Befu (Eds.), *Globalization and social change in contemporary Japan* (pp. 17–40). Melbourne: Trans Pacific Press.

Bernstein, A. (2006). *Modern passings: Death rites, politics, and social change in imperial Japan.* Honolulu: University of Hawaii Press.

Bourdieu, P. (1977). *Outline of a theory of practice.* Cambridge: Cambridge University Press.

Burgess, C. (2007). Multicultural Japan? Discourse and the "myth" of homogeneity. *The Asia-Pacific Journal, 5*(3), 1–25.

Dale, P. N. (1986). *The myth of Japanese uniqueness.* London: Routledge.

Gadamer, H-G. (2004). *Truth and method* (2nd ed. revised). (J. Weinsheimer & D. G. Marshall, Trans.). New York: Continuum. (Original work published 1975).

Gebser, J. (1985). *The ever-present origin* (N. Barstad & A. Mickunas, Trans.). Athens, OH: Ohio University. (Original work published 1949).

Halualani, R. T., & Nakayama, T. K. (2010). Critical intercultural communication studies: At a crossroads. In T. K. Nakayama & R. T. Halualani (Eds.), *The handbook of critical intercultural communication* (pp. 1–16). Malden, MA: Wiley-Blackwell.

Hayashi, C., & Kuroda, Y. (1997). *Japanese culture in comparative perspective.* Westport, CT: Praeger.

Heine, S., & Fu, C. W. (1995). From the beautiful to the dubious: Japanese traditionalism, modernism, postmodernism. In C. W. Fu & S. Heine (Eds.), *Japan: In traditional and postmodern perspectives* (pp. vii–xxi). New York: State University of New York Press.

Hiratsuka, A. (2005). *Nihon no sakura ga shindeyuku* [Japanese cherries are going to die]. Tokyo: Shinpusha.

Hudson, M. J. (1999). *Ruins of identity: Ethnogenesis in the Japanese islands.* Honolulu: University of Hawaii Press.

Husserl, E. (1970). *The crisis of European science and transcendental phenomenology: An introduction to phenomenological philosophy* (D. Carr, Trans.). Evanston, IL: Northwestern University Press. (Original work published 1954).

Kinefuchi, E. (2010). Layers of Nikkei: Japanese diaspora and World War II. In T. K. Nakayama & R. T. Halualani (Eds.), *The handbook of critical intercultural communication* (pp. 495–516). Malden, MA: Wiley-Blackwell.

Kramer, E. M. (2000). Cultural fusion and the defense of difference. In M. K. Asante & E. Min (Eds.), *Socio-cultural conflict between African American and Korean American* (pp. 182–223). New York: University Press of America.

Kramer, E. M., & Ikeda, R. (1997). What is a "Japanese"?: Culture, diversity, and social harmony in Japan. In E. M. Kramer (Ed.), *Postmodernism and race* (pp. 79–102). Westport, CT: Praeger.

188 *T. Sakurai*

Lebra, T. S. (1976). *Japanese patterns of behavior*. Honolulu: University of Hawaii Press.

Manyoushu [The ten thousand leaves]. (1981). (I. H. Levy, Trans.). Princeton, NJ: Princeton University Press.

Matsumoto, S. (1970). *Motoori Norinaga*. Cambridge, MA: Harvard University Press.

Mickunas, A. (2006). Hermeneutics of the other: The limits of modern Western education. In R. Elveton (Ed.), *Educating for participatory democracy: Paradoxes in globalizing logics* (pp. 1–25). Cresskill, NJ: Hampton.

Mickunas, A. (2007). Historical consciousness. In P. Dalton (Ed.), *Communication, comparative cultures, and civilizations* (pp. 1–18). Cresskill, NJ: Hampton Press.

Moeran, B. (1990). Rapt discourses: Anthropology, Japanism and Japan. In E. Ben-Ari, B. Moeran, & J. Valentine (Eds.), *Unwrapping Japan: Society and culture in anthropological perspective* (pp. 1–17). Manchester, UK: Manchester University Press.

Mouer, R., & Sugimoto, Y. (1986). *Images of Japanese society*. London: Kegan Paul International.

Mumford, L. (1934). *Technics and civilization*. Orlando, FL: Harcourt, Brace & World.

Nitobe, I. (1905). *Bushido: The soul of Japan* (10th ed.). New York: The Knickerbocker Press. (Original work published 1899).

Ogawa, K. (1988). *Sakura shi* [A journal of cherry blossoms]. Tokyo: Hara Publishing.

Ogawa, M. (1997). The Japanese view of science in their elementary science education program. In K. Calhoun, R. Panwar, & S. Shrum (Eds.), *International organization for science and technology education, 8th symposium proceedings, Vol. 2: Policy* (pp. 175–179). Edmonton, Canada: University of Alberta.

Ohnuki-Tierney, E. (1998). Cherry blossoms and their viewing: A window onto Japanese culture. In S. Linhart & S. Fruhstuck (Eds.), *The culture of Japan as seen through leisure* (pp. 213–236). New York: State University of New York Press.

Ohnuki-Tierney, E. (2001). Historicization of the culture concept. *History and Anthropology, 12*(3), 213–254.

Ohnuki-Tierney, E. (2002). *Kamikaze, cherry blossoms, and nationalisms: The militarization of aesthetics in Japanese history*. Chicago, IL: University of Chicago Press.

Orikuchi, S. (1975). *Orikuchi Shinobu zenshu* [Anthology of Orikuchi Shinobu] (Vol. 7). Tokyo: Chuokoronsha.

Piggot, J. R. (1997). *The emergence of Japanese kingship*. Stanford, CA: Stanford University Press.

Rauch, J. (1992). *The outnation: A search for the soul of Japan*. Brighton, MA: Harvard Business School Press.

Sato, T. (2005). *Sakura ga tsukutta nihon* [Japan, created by cherry blossoms]. Tokyo: Iwanami.

Shirahata, Y. (2000). *Hanami to sakura* [Flower viewing and cherry blossoms]. Tokyo: PHP.

Sorrells, K. (2010). Re-imagining intercultural communication in the context of globalization. In T. K. Nakayama & R. T. Halualani (Eds.), *The handbook of critical intercultural communication* (pp. 171–189). Malden, MA: Wiley-Blackwell.

Sorrells, K., & Sekimoto, S. (Eds). (2016). *Globalizing intercultural communication: A reader*. Thousand Oaks, CA: Sage.

Traditional Japanese poetry: An anthology. (1991). (S. D. Carter, Trans.). Stanford, CA: Stanford University Press.

Wakamori, T. (1975). *Hana to nihonjin* [Flowers and the Japanese]. Tokyo: Sogetsu Shuppan.

Watanabe, M. (1990). *The Japanese and Western science* (O. T. Benfey, Trans.). Philadelphia, PA: University of Pennsylvania Press. (Original work published 1976).

Wierzbicka, A. (1997). *Understanding cultures through their key words*. New York: Oxford University Press.

Yamada, Y. (1990). *Oushi* [History of cherry blossoms]. Tokyo: Koudansha. (Original work published 1942).

12 Alternative vs. conventional
Dialectic relations of the organic agriculture discourse

Saki Ichihara Fomsgaard

Agriculture is a contentious subject today. In addition to its indisputable significance for human survival, diverse interests—among others, environmental protection, safety, rural development, animal welfare, globalization, trade liberalization, and national identity—are intersecting, amalgamating, and competing within the social imagination of agriculture. In this study, I focus on the discourse of "organics" (*yūki*), i.e., the term depicting organic agriculture, food, and goods in general, and the organic agriculture movement[1] (*yūkinōgyōundō*) in Japan, which well demonstrate this increasing contention in agriculture. I intend to reveal the changes—homogenization and heterogenization processes—that are evolving along with the development of this discourse from a movement discourse toward a public discourse. Then, I aim to uncover the struggles, limits, and potential of the organic movement discourse that are emerging in the course of its development, by applying the dialectic-relational perspective of alternative vs. conventional.

In the following chapter, I first explain the theoretical and methodological framework of this study. This is followed by sections that look at the interplay between the organic discourse and the surrounding movement as well as the political and social contexts. Finally, I suggest some implications of this development.

Approach of this study

This study's approach to the organics discourse was particularly inspired by critical discourse analysis (CDA), which is based on the critical realist's transdisciplinary, dialectical, and relational envisagement (van Dijk, 1993; Fairclough, 2003; Wodak & Meyer, 2009). CDA treats discourse as a specific semiotic category that, by being enacted, inculcated, or materialized, designates the specific manner of representing a particular part of society. Here, discourse is firmly viewed as in a dialectic relationship with such cognitive and material elements as "activities, subjects and their social relations, instruments, objects, time and place, forms of consciousness, and values" (Fairclough, 2001, p. 1). Discourse and these other elements mutually appropriate—internalize and are internalized—through interaction, though they are not reducible to each other; in other

Organic agriculture discourse 191

words, they are "different but not discrete" (ibid., p. 3). This conception of dialectic relationship enables us to inquire into the particular modes of interplay between discourse and its surrounding material and discursive contexts without conflating them. Furthermore, CDA construes discourses to be "inherently positioned" by "differently positioned actors" in the social practice, so that they create a specific order of discourse—"a particular social ordering of relationships amongst different ways of making meaning" (ibid., p. 2). In this way, CDA envisages understanding and exposing co-relations in the change of semiotic processes and social, cultural, and political contexts; namely, how and to what extent such correlations take place, gain dominance, constitute, and shape social realities such as ideology, power, dominance (including social inequality among other outcomes), and representation.[2] Inspired by this conceptualization, I intend to approach the discourse of organics as in a dialectical relation with the changing contexts that were found to be relevant, i.e., the organic agriculture movement and the social and political/policy environments.

To pursue such relations effectively, I particularly focus on a *dialectic of alternative/conventional*. This is inspired by the dialectic-relational approach of Martin and Nakayama (1999, 2013), which suggests "holding two contradictory ideas simultaneously" (Martin & Nakayama, 1999, p. 14) in order to understand changing dialectical relations. This particular dialectic of alternative/conventional reflects current discussions in academia and in the organic movement community on the "conventionalization" of organics. That is, an argument supporting the tendency of organics to follow the productivist pathway of conventional agriculture (Buck, Getz, & Guthman, 1997; Tovey, 1997; DeLind, 2000; Guthman, 2004). This conventionalization argument claims that the world-wide homogenization process of economic globalization propels the penetrating capitalist logic and commodity relations into the organic agriculture community. This process is understood to activate the mechanisms that the movement once explicitly opposed—e.g., mechanization, specialization, standardization, large-scale farming, and the domination of agribusiness—and ultimately transform organics into a mere niche commodity with fancy labels.

Conventionalization can also penetrate the movement. As its problematique becomes more integrated in the conventional socio-political framework, the movement typically faces the classic dilemma between "ethics based on conviction" (i.e., sustaining the initial movement ideologies) and a "logic of efficacy" (i.e., adoption of the conventional norms and practices to attain greater influence) (Touraine cited in Campbell, 2001, p. 353). In contrast, critics of this argument question the universality of homogenization, suggesting a more contextual and nuanced approach is required (Campbell & Liepins, 2001; Hall & Mogyorody, 2001; Kjeldsen & Ingemann, 2009). Although they are aware of the increasing dominance of economic globalization, they focus their attention on the ongoing persistence and/or rejuvenation of aspiration for being "alternative" to the conventional modes of food production, distribution, and consumption. This is represented by such practices as community supported agriculture (CSA),

192   S. I. Fomsgaard

farmers' markets, box and delivery schemes, small-farmers' collective organic certification programs, and consumer-owned farms.

Both conventional and critical perspectives have provided important insights: the former awakened awareness of the growing mismatch between the envisaged ideology and the practice of organics, while the latter properly portrays the complexity, context-dependency, and, indeed, co-existence of conventionalizing and alternativizing processes. Yet, having spent much energy on the ontological propriety of conventionalization, the discussion has often missed the opportunity to scrutinize the concomitant and mutual development between the move towards the conventional path and the aspiration for alternativeness. Considering this background, I find the dialectic of alternative/conservative a useful tool to capture the changing construction of organics as open-ended push and pull among competing social elements—both discursive and non-discursive—rather than a zero-sum game.

This study is based on interviews with 13 core members of the leading organic agriculture organization, the Japan Organic Agriculture Association (*nihonyūkinōgyōkenkyūkai*) (JOAA), as well as observations of many meetings and activities of this organization and other local organizations/groups. Information was also gathered from JOAA's publications—among others, editions of its monthly magazine, *Soil and Health* (*tsuchitokenkō*), since the organization's establishment in 1971—leading members/member organizations, and official policy documents.[3]

Evolution of organic agriculture discourse

Constructing the movement discourse: homogenization by the movement

The organic agriculture movement in Japan began with the creation of the JOAA in 1971 (Tabeta & Masugata, 1981; Suzuki, 1995). Some attempts at non-chemical farming had already existed before that—most prominently, nature farming promoted by the Shinto sect *sekaikyūseikyō* since around the end of World War II. Yet, JOAA articulated its own movement with a new term, *yūki* (the Japanese equivalent to organic), thus distinguishing itself from existing religion-based alternative farming. *Yūki* was not in common parlance for a while, but it soon came to represent the general attempt at alternative agriculture.

The founding phase of JOAA was clearly elite driven, often described as a "salon for academics" (Tabeta & Masugata, 1981, p. 26). This owed much to the leader, Teruo Ichiraku, who had an eminent career profile as the top executive at the agricultural cooperative bank. Soon, the organization experienced rapid growth, and consumers and farmers began to outnumber the elites. Consumers' participation in the organic agriculture movement boomed around the mid-1970s, when Japan faced serious incidents such as large-scale industrial pollution (*kōgai*), two oil shocks, and a series of food scandals (represented by the lawsuit regarding arsenic contamination of powdered milk). Another event that

Organic agriculture discourse 193

triggered the boom was the 1974 novel (that first appeared in a major daily newspaper in serialized form), *Multiple Pollution (fukugōosen)*, by Sawako Ariyoshi, which revealed the consequences of pesticides—among others, the deteriorating health of farmers.

Constructions of organic agriculture at JOAA have been widely recognized as the common ground for the movement. These were, first of all, characterized by the explicit criticism of "modernized" agriculture. This criticism was based on a clear picture of modern society as divided between industry and agriculture as well as between urban and rural, wherein the former dominates the latter. Based on this view, JOAA underlined that agriculture is qualitatively different from industry; i.e., agriculture essentially works with the natural environment and *creates life*, while industry is inorganic, abiotic and lifeless. This point was illustrated in the following words by Ichiraku.

> I have just told you "to nurture *(sodateru)* crops." This is generally equivalent to "produce agricultural produce." But we don't say "to produce a child (as we do for industrial products)," right? Children must be nurtured. It is same for food, since it is the source of life and it is made by nurturing lives. It is fundamentally different from industrial products.
>
> (Ichiraku in JOAA, 1989, p. 66, my translation)

JOAA has been persistent with the focus on life, and this has constituted the common formulation of organic agriculture as a movement for *"retrieving the authentic agriculture."* Conventional agriculture, which "industrializes" agriculture in the name of "modernization," was depicted as a diversion from its innate disposition. Based on this problematique, the organization asserted that "retrieval of agriculture's autonomy from industry" was essential.

For JOAA, however, this deviation was more firmly rooted in the dominant policy paradigm of "economic rationalism," which reduced people to "homo economicus" who ignore the non-economic value of agriculture, most importantly, its contribution to life and health. From this viewpoint, it is prevailing norms and practices that systematically hinder agriculture from pursuing sustenance and the enhancement of life. For this reason, JOAA demanded a radical transformation of the *whole* system, which encompasses farming methods, economic practices, paradigms, values and lifestyle (Yasuda, 1986; Minamida, 1995). Such a transformation would envisage a food system that prioritizes "human health and survival of a nation" over "the economic values and considerations." Based on this vision, JOAA primarily called for a "cognitive revolution" that would liberate agriculture from materialism–orthodox economics, market competition, and commodification.

JOAA originally envisaged a farmer-led movement. As stated in the "Prospectus of the Organization," farmers were, in its founding phase, drawn to the organization as the lead actors in implementing "authentic agriculture." Later, with the rise of housewives' activism in big cities around building co-partnerships with farmers for the availability of non-chemical produce, JOAA

194 *S. I. Fomsgaard*

started to put more emphasis on the reciprocal relationship between farmers and consumers as the core component of the movement. This relationship was termed *teikei* (meaning cooperation in Japanese) and the ideal was defined in the "Ten Principles of Teikei" in 1978. Since then *teikei* has constituted the fundamental basis of the organic movement's ideology and practice.

The central elements of *teikei* are, first, the establishment of friendly and even family-like relationships between farmers and consumers by departing from the usual trade relationship. Instead of "purchasing," consumers should consider that they are "given" food by farmers. Exchanging money in this respect is a "reward" for receiving food. Second, JOAA envisaged this relationship to be based on mutual commitment. This led to the norm of "eating the whole farm," i.e., forming a co-partnership where consumers and farmers together make a plan for planting and consumers accept all the produce, regardless of the yield. In this way, farmers are secured the agreed payment. Here, consumers are expected to adjust their diet to the yields of the farm, and help with farm work as much as possible. Furthermore, distribution of farm produce is to be organized mutually by both sides. Through such direct commitment to farmers' daily work, close and friendly relationships would be established. This obviously called for a much deeper engagement, especially for consumers, than existing direct sales (*sanchoku*).

Teikei had long been the only defined principle of the organic movement. This seems to owe much to its highly abstract conceptualization of "authentic agriculture" without defining what this is. Due to the absence of established techniques and know-how, the movement has tended to concentrate on changes in people's mentality and lifestyle rather than on quantitative growth of organic agriculture and the development of this farming method. As a pioneer member of JOAA claimed:

> The organic movement is not a movement which aims merely for technical objectives under the slogan of non-pesticide agriculture, but a kind of civic movement based on the acute need of the well-being of farmers and consumers. Furthermore, I think it is indeed the movement for innovating everyday life, wherein the people across different positions unite for that.
>
> (Yasuda in JOAA, 1975, p. 28, my translation)

With this ideological foundation, the organic movement in Japan exhibited the characteristics of Japanese civil society organizations—small, locally-based, and run by the voluntary commitment of members (Hasegawa, 2014). It clearly displayed the typical orientation of Japanese civil society toward individual effort rather than policy advocacy (Pekkanen, 2006). Notably, due to its general focus on highly idealized voluntary practices between local consumers and farmers, its interaction with other movements, such as the wider consumer movement and the farmers' movement, was very limited.

Emergence of heterogenization

Since the mid-1980s, alternative agriculture has gradually been institutionalized in policy and the conventional market. One of the major reasons for this development was a drastic increase in self-declared organic and other added-value produce in the market, due to rising consumer demand for safe food, especially after the Chernobyl incident in 1986. By the late 1980s, between 20 percent and 40 percent of agricultural produce was estimated to be sold as organic at the Tokyo Central Wholesale Market, though most often without any credibility to this claim (Taniguchi, 1988).

The policy response to organic agriculture was, however, lukewarm throughout the 1990s. Some initiatives on organic agriculture were taken by the Ministry of Agriculture, Forestry and Fisheries (MAFF), politicians, agricultural cooperatives, and so forth, in the late 1980s. However, the new policy framework for "sustainable agriculture" (*kankyōhozengata nōgyō*) established in 1991 articulated a trajectory that treats organic agriculture along the same lines as other environmentally-friendly forms of agriculture, in which the use of chemicals and/or synthetic fertilizers was allowed though to a lesser degree than in conventional farming. This was contrary to the policy directions of European and North American counterparts, which chose to prioritize organic agriculture around the same time.

This overall policy direction represents a world-wide mainstreaming of sustainability discourse that competes with activists' ecology discourse (Eder, 1996). In the sustainability discourse, environmental protection and economic growth are articulated not as mutually exclusive but, on the contrary, as creating positive synergy effects. This new coupling, or "discourse coalition" (Hajer 1995), between ecology and economy, is most attractive for the policy community and for businesses, as it allows for environmental solutions without compromising the basic functions of conventional state and market systems.

The new policy initiative on sustainable agriculture exemplified the linking of economy, environment, and food safety. Under this union, the standardization of organic agriculture was set in motion. Soon after a legally non-binding guideline for labelling was introduced in 1992, a discussion on creating national organic standards began with the prospect of an international regulatory framework being introduced in the near future. Indeed, the growth in organic sales in Japan was among the fastest in the world, making it a key export target for foreign businesses. The international community heavily criticized the absence of internationally observed standards in Japan as evidence of protectionism. The intensifying of international negotiations for free trade, as represented by the process toward the General Agreement on Tariffs and Trade (GATT) Uruguay Round in 1994, added to this foreign pressure (*gaiatsu*).

The organic movement was clearly critical of this development. It is worth noting that the basic standpoint of the movement did not necessarily conflict with the policy's loose conception of "sustainable agriculture," as within the abstract formulation of "retrieving authentic agriculture" it did not consider the

196 S. I. Fomsgaard

elimination of chemicals as the first priority. However, it nonetheless found the new policy initiative fundamentally conflicted with the movement, primarily because it felt the major target of the policy-makers was profit making (JOAA, 1989). In the movement discourse, agriculture should be intrinsically location-dependent, and this connection is especially strong in Japan because of its rich geo-climate diversity. Farms in southern areas naturally tend to get more vermin and need more weeding than the cooler areas in the north; while the former can produce different produce all year around, the latter often cannot. Furthermore, farming in mountainous areas, which covers 70 percent of the land, is techni-cally challenging and less competitive. In addition, it is often not easy for farmers to change their planting routines, for technical as well as social reasons, as often the whole village is collectively specialized in particular produce which means efficiency and added value. In consequence, conversion to organic methods can impinge on the norms of local farming communities. Taking this into consideration, the movement presumed the implementation of unified national standards to be not only unrealistic but that it would also merely burden farmers. Furthermore, activists were suspicious about the commitment of established actors (notably, government, MAFF and agricultural coopera-tives) to a fair and reliable regulatory system. For them, the *teikei* system built upon mutual trust was sufficient for excluding "fake" produce. They thus believed the on-going development of *teikei* should be supported and not be disrupted by standards and fixed definitions which did not (and could not) comply with the movement's aspiration toward organic agriculture (JOAA, 2000).

However, while the leaders of the organic movement tried to hold on to their movement trajectory, the movement's growth turned into a steady decline after it hit a peak in the early 1980s. JOAA, which had 5,673 members in 1983, had reduced to under 3,000 by the late 1990s. This tendency was shared by many of its member organizations and local *teikei* groups. The movement's stagnation largely resulted from, on the one hand, the split and dissolution of *teikei* groups caused by the increased availability of organic or non-chemical produce in the conventional market, and, on the other hand, the general decrease in full-time housewives as women's participation in the labor market increased (Hatano, 1998). In many ways, *Teikei* exhausted the members with practical work and was too slow in adapting to these changes. Furthermore, as long as *teikei* was considered a locally based practice, establishing a prospect for the nationwide diffusion of organic agriculture was difficult. The movement failed to provide convincing solutions to actual problems—for instance, how farmers in remote areas could find consumers, and how small, local organic initiatives could solve Japan's wider agricultural problems, including the acute decline in the farming population and national food self-sufficiency. Consequently, the movement's principle of relying heavily on *teikei* increasingly brought frustration in the community.

Such decline and stagnation prompted emerging diversity in the movement. One of the prominent actors in this regard was the so-called "organic entrepreneur" (Masugata & Kubota, 1989) who, unlike the first generation, did not totally reject the conventional trade and business system. Albeit they are basically business actors who trade organic goods as commodities, they have actively participated in organic movement activities, including JOAA. In particular, *Daichi*, which currently runs a box scheme (home delivery) of organic produce as its main business, set as its main objective from the start "to purge pollution by agricultural chemicals." Part of its profit has until today been used for this aim, as well as for other civic movements, such as the anti-nuclear movement and the sustainable energy movement. These organic entrepreneurs do not adhere to the rigid interpretation of, for example, the principles of *teikei* and non-materialistic values. The director of *Daichi*, Kazuyoshi Fujita, formerly a left-wing activist, has claimed, for instance, that a corporation is not necessarily a capitalist profit-making machine but "can be used for protecting the national agriculture by having conscious consumers and producers as shareholders" (Fujita, 2005, p. 111). The emergence of these new actors was not welcomed by the leaders of JOAA. Yet they did, and still do, constitute the fastest growing constituency of the organic movement community.

Split and diversification: re-construction of organic discourse

Despite protests, the national organic standards came into force in 2000. Around this time, standardization and commodification of organic agriculture was already widely recognized as an unavoidable reality by the movement community. Furthermore, the death of de facto leader Ichiraku in 1995, who was strongly opposed to this direction, also accelerated this recognition. Consequently, JOAA, along with many other organic organizations, reversed its total rejection of the national standards and organic trade in the conventional market, while shifting its focus to creating as much autonomy as possible within this environment. Such attempts included, for instance, the establishment of the organizations' own organic standards, which complied with the national standards, and the creation of non-profit organic certification agencies to provide a fair service for organic farmers who now had to pay for official certification to sell their produce as organic. The establishment of non-profit agencies was also a result of the Law to Promote Specified Nonprofit Activities (the so-called NPO Law) which came into force in 1998. With this new, but notoriously delayed law, civil society actors were able to obtain official corporate status. This stimulated the professionalization of civil society organizations wherein, unlike the traditional pro bono-based commitment, activism can constitute one's profession.

Yet, when discussion on the Organic Law to support organic agriculture started in the mid-2000s, internal splits within the movement became evident. Acknowledging the increase in political opportunities, activists who were critical of the movement's traditional orientation began to establish new organizations and alliance networks outside JOAA. Rei Ozaki, who led one of these initiatives, *Zenyūkyō*, asserted:

198 *S. I. Fomsgaard*

> We cannot step forward to the next stage without reconstruction of ... organic agriculture and the movement by verifying all its ideas, objectives, techniques, distribution, food, *teikei*, etc. Thirty years have passed since the movement started, and now we are in the time of generation change. We cannot avoid this process.
>
> (Ozaki in JOAA, 2005, p. 27, my translation)

Such reconstruction aspired to revise the ongoing apolitical, reactive, and narrow-focused orientation of the movement, which still continued to promote *teikei*. As such, the movement finally prioritized policy advocacy. Such new initiatives included actors that the organic community had traditionally excluded; namely, conventional farmers practicing reduced-chemical farming (i.e., so-called "eco-farmers" in MAFF's scheme), non-*teikei* consumer movements and organic food businesses. In these initiatives, *teikei* was not rejected, but it was expressed as just one possible path for the movement. Corresponding to this split, the number of JOAA's members with voting rights radically decreased to barely 300.

Implications

Such division in the organic movement can be seen as a new phase of homogenization and heterogenization for the construction of organics. Organic discourse, which was once shared only within the activist community, has now tuned into a public discourse. That is, this discourse is currently evolving in the open organic discourse market, wherein constant contestations around defining organics are taking place among diverse actors from both inside and outside the organic movement community (Eder 1996). We can detect evidence of a strong thrust toward conventionalization in this new construction: as organics become more standardized, a growing part of organic communication is preoccupied with expert technicalities (e.g., what substances it is permissible to apply and how much). Organics is frequently discussed within sustainability narratives that express the "multifunctionality" of agriculture, which discursively reconciles varied interests, such as growth, environmental protection, safety, security, and rural development. The growing dominance of standardization and the incorporation of growth as positive and benign is obviously suppressing the movement's formulation of organics as multi-directional; open-ended attempts at ideal agriculture ("authentic agriculture") are fundamentally different from conventional approaches. However, following recent developments, particularly since the late 1990s, some crucial processes which are pulling the conventionalizing force can be observed. I argue these processes signify evolving construction—heterogenization—of the organic discourse, wherein a mutual shaping of the conventional and the alternative is taking place. I further argue that this discursive construction is opening up new opportunities for the movement.

In this regard, we can, first, focus on the nation-wide diffusion of the conception of *physical proximity*, as represented by "produce locally, eat locally" *(chisan chisyō)*, "face-to-face relationship" (*kao no mieru kankei*), and "indivisibility of soil and health" (*shindofuji*). Indeed, these exact terminologies have long been nourished by the organic movement in its advocacy of establishing a local-specific food system based on a close consumer–farmer relationship. As such, the rising popularity of this conception represents the persistence of alternative envisagement. Compared with physical proximity as the desirable direction of food and agriculture policy, the prevailing standardization, which makes food faceless and disconnected, is questioned and devalued as erroneous. Thus, the organic movement can enhance the thrust of alternativeness by strengthening this conception of physical proximity in the evolving construction of the organic discourse.

Interlinked with physical proximity, we can, second, pay attention to the recent intersection of organic discourse with the emerging *"nationalist" food discourse* in the policy sphere (Tanaka, 2008; Kimura, 2011), which is manifested in policy frames such as "learning through eating" (*shokuiku*) and "the Japanese-style dietary life" (*nihongatashokuseikatsu*). This nationalist food discourse claims this policy direction as a "national movement" (Cabinet Office, 2015), and clearly idealizes the traditional dietary pattern—i.e., according to MAFF, the typical diet of the 1950s, which is based on rice as the staple food and a variation of fish-and-vegetable-based dishes cooked with less oil. Here, the Japanese "traditional" diet is nuanced as superior to the Westernized diet. The former is healthier, contains balanced nutrients, is low fat, and has many positive effects such as the prevention of lifestyle-related diseases, cancer, and cardiac disease; by contrast, the latter is unhealthy as it contains excessive (animal) fat and protein. Overall, the nationalist food discourse claims it is the moral obligation of the people to embrace their national culinary tradition, as it brings "positive social effects." That is, the more Japanese people appreciate and eat local region-specific food, the higher the social status of farmers; national food self-sufficiency as well as healthier lives can also be achieved.

This food nationalism suggests that the traditional food culture and Japan's natural environment are integrated as one: a nutritious and healthy food culture stems from the "Japan's rich diversity in nature" as well as a tradition that "respects nature." Traditional food, above all rice, is hereby promoted, since it not only best suits the local climate but also contributes to the protection of nature. Since the establishment of the Basic Law for Shokuiku in 2005, this connection of food, education, national culture, and nature has rapidly been integrated into the activities of school and regional authorities (Tanaka, 2008). Such emerging food nationalism is quite congruent with the organic movement discourse, which has advocated a "cognitive revolution" that leads to lifestyle change. In this advocacy, the linkage between region-specific ways of producing and eating, nature, and education has for a long time constituted the movement's core and manifested itself in *teikei*. Further concrete examples in this regard are pioneer organic consumer actions for reforming school meals on the basis of locally produced food and cooking meetings where people teach each other how to use the seasonal farm produce obtained from their *teikei* farmers (Ohe, 2006).

200 *S. I. Fomsgaard*

Crucially, this tendency towards physical proximity and food nationalism further intersects with the discourses of other critical movements that problematize issues such as trade liberalization (at the time of writing, the Trans-Pacific Partnership), U.S. dominance in Japanese institutional politics (e.g., the military base in Okinawa), and, more recently, nuclear energy (Hasegawa, 2014).[4] Notwithstanding the diversity on core issues, these movements share in common explicit criticism of economic globalization and the policies of the dominant Liberal Democratic Party (LDP). Such criticism resonates well with the organic movement, which finds the root cause of modern agricultural problems in capitalist economics and ideology as well as the policy community driven by them.

Yet, as the movement has long been homogenized as a cultural movement for cognitive change, it has traditionally isolated itself from the political scenes of institutional politics and civil society. In the case of the anti-nuclear issue, for instance, JOAA formerly could not reach consensus on collective action, as a considerable part of the organization preferred to separate themselves from the anti-nuclear movement (JOAA, 1988). However, having experienced stagnation, the death of its leader, an internal split, the growing penetration of norms and practices of conventional agriculture, and Fukushima in 2011, a significant part of the organic movement's orientation has shifted toward a more inclusive, cooperative, and, indeed, political direction. Such change can orient the discursive consolidation of the organic movement with other critical movements that politicize organics, and strengthen the pulling process of alternativeness, while the organic movement conducts critical reflection on its struggles, limits and stagnancy. The following words expressed collectively at the national assembly for organic groups and organizations in March 2006, titled "Change Agriculture!" (*Nō wo kaetai!*),[5] indicates this direction:

We envisage creating local visions and exchanging them for bringing solidarity between local communities. By appreciating difference in opinions as a sign of the movement's breadth, we envisage creating rich human relationship, which can oppose to globalization enforcing centralization of values. Let's exchange our ideas for the new generation's agriculture and gather inspirational experiences. Let's create the prospect for the nation-wide movement from there.

(Change Agriculture!, 2006)

Conclusion

Organic agriculture is still a minor part of national agriculture, estimated to be merely 0.4 percent of total agricultural land in Japan. Despite this limited achievement in practice, this study aimed to highlight the struggles, changes, and potential in the discursive construction of organics that emerges in the course of a social imagination of ideal agriculture. While I utiliize the rising potential of the movement's discourse, it is still unclear whether such discursive potential can be effectively enacted by the movement so that it can go beyond the

Organic agriculture discourse 201

traditional inward looking and apolitical trajectory. Indeed, as Kimura points out, the government's promotion of local-national food, for instance, could merely result in transferring responsibility to individuals, preaching to them to take care of their own health and well-being (Kimura, 2011). The organic movement could easily be absorbed into this reductionism, contributing only to the symbolic development of alternative conceptions. Furthermore, it is not clear whether the heterogenization of the movement—through the weakening of its long-term core, as represented by *teikei*—can lead to an empowerment of the organic movement. The potential is there, and the struggle for being alternative continues.

Notes

1 This study's understanding of "social movement" is based on Alberto Melucci's conception. He argues that social movement is an analytical category of collective actions, which is characterized by its orientation toward: (1) solidarity; (2) conflict with the system targeted; and (3) breaching the system's limits (Melucci, 1996).
2 More concretely, Fairclough proposes a three-dimensional model for studying discourse, which I utilize: (1) studying of the text (either written or spoken); (2) discourse practice-production, distribution, and consumption of the text; and (3) social practice—a relatively stable form of social activity (Fairclough, 2003).
3 This study is based on my Ph.D. dissertation, approved by the Doctorate Programme in Culture and Global Studies, Aalborg University, September 2014.
4 It worth noting that this critical increase is of interest to the opposition parties, as it clearly suggests voters' dissatisfaction with the government led by the Liberal Democratic Party (LDP). As such, the leading opposition party, the Democratic Party of Japan (DPJ), has been a leading supporter of organic agriculture.
5 This assembly was the preparatory step for establishing the new association for organic agriculture actors, *Zenyūkyō*, in December 2006.

References

Brand, K.-W. (1999). Dialectics of institutionalisation: The transformation of the environmental movement in Germany. *Environmental Politics, 8*(1), 59–80.
Buck, D., Getz, C., & Guthman, J. (1997). From farm to table: The organic vegetable commodity chain of Northern California. *Sociologia Ruralis, 31*(2), 3–20.
Cabinet Office, Government of Japan (2015). *The 3rd basic program for Shokuiku promotion*. Retrieved from www8.cao.go.jp/syokuiku/about/plan/pdf/3kihonkeikaku.pdf.
Campbell, D. (2001). Conviction seeking efficacy: Sustainable agriculture and politics of co-optation. *Agriculture and Human Values, 18*, 353–363.
Campbell, H., & Liepins, R. (2001). Naming organics: Understanding organic standards in New Zealand as a discursive field. *Soiologia Ruralis, 41*(1), 21–39.
Change Agriculture! [Nōwo kaetai!]. (2006). Declaration for Change Agriculture! *Change Agriculture! National Assembly in March*. Tokyo: Committee for Change Agriculture!
Coombes, B., & Campbell, H. (1998). Dependent reproduction of alternative modes of agriculture: Organic farming in New Zealand. *Soiologia Ruralis, 38*, 127–145.
DeLind, L. (2000). Transforming organic agriculture into industrial organic products: Reconsidering national organic standards. *Human Organization, 59*(2), 198–208.

202　*S. I. Fomsgaard*

Doherty, B. (1992). The Fundi-Realo controversy: An analysis of four European green parties. *Environmental Politics, 1*(1), 95–120.

Eder, K. (1996). *The Social construction of nature: A sociology of ecological Enlightenment*. London: Sage.

Fairclough, N. (2001). The dialectics of discourse. *Textus, XIV*(2), 231–242.

Fairclough, N. (2003). *Analysing discourse: Textual analysis for social research*. London: Routledge.

Fujita, K. (2005). *Revolution started with a stick of radish: 30 years of an environmental NGO*. Tokyo: Kōsakusha.

Guthman, J. (2004). The trouble with "organic lite" in California: A rejoinder to the "conventionalisation" debate. *Sociologia Ruralis, 44*(3), 301–316.

Hajer, M. A. (1995). *The politics of environmental discourse: Ecological modernization and the policy process*. New York: Oxford University Press.

Hall, A., & Mogyorody, V. (2001). Organic farmers in Ontario: An explanation of the conventionalization argument. *Sociologia Ruralis, 41*(4), 399–422.

Hasegawa, K. (2014). The Fukushima nuclear accident and Japan's civil society: Context, reactions and policy impacts. *International Sociology, 29*(4), 283–301.

Hatano, T. (1998). *Economics of the organic agriculture*. Tokyo: Nihon Keizai Hyōronsha.

Japan Association for Consumers. (2005). *Food Sovereignty*. Tokyo: Ryokufushuppan.

JOAA (1988). Minutes of the 16th general assembly of JOAA. *Soil and Health, 187*.

JOAA (1989). *Proposals for organic agriculture*. Tokyo: JOAA.

JOAA (1975). *Soil and Health, 32*, 31–32.

JOAA (2000). *"Basic organic standards 2000" and the development of the JAS certification system*. Tokyo: JOAA.

JOAA (2005). *Soil and Health, 373*.

Kimura, A. H. (2011). Nationalism, patriarchy, and moralism: The government-led food reform in contemporary Japan. *Food and Foodways, 19*, 201–227.

Kjeldsen, C., & Ingemann, J. H. (2009). From the social to the economical and beyond? A relational approach to the historical development of Danish organic food networks. *Sociologia Ruralis, 49*(2), 151–171.

Kondoh, K. (2015). The alternative food movement in Japan: Challenges, limits and resilience of the teikei system. *Agriculture and Human Values, 32*, 143–153.

Martin, J. N., & Nakayama, T. K. (1999). Thinking dialectically about culture and communication. *Communication Theory, 9*(1), 1–25.

Martin, J. N., & Nakayama, T. K. (2013). Intercultural communication and dialectics revised. In T. K. Nakayama & R. T. Halualani (Eds.), *The handbook of critical intercultural communication* (pp. 59–83). Malden, MA: Wiley-Blackwell.

Masugata, T. (2011). Development of "produce locally, eat locally" and organic agriculture in Imabari city: Creation of environmental ethics in local governance. *Bulletin of Shukutoku University, 45*, 177–203.

Masugata, T., & Kubota, H. (1989). *Study of diversified distribution channels of organic agricultural products*. Tokyo: Consumers' Union of Japan.

Melucci, A. (1996). *Challenging codes*. Cambridge: Cambridge University Press.

Minamida, S. (1995). Teikei or copartnership: A characteristic type of the producer–consumer relationship in the organic agriculture movement in Japan – Part one. *Journal of Chiba University, 49*, 189–199.

Ohe, M. (2006). School meals based on "produce locally, eat locally" and food and agriculture education. *Sekai, 9*, 302–311.

Organic agriculture discourse 203

Pekkanen, R. J. (2006). *Japan's dual civil society: Members without advocates.* Stanford, CA: Stanford University Press.

Suzuki, H. (1995). Locus of development and changes in Japanese organic agriculture. *Research and Inquiry (Chōsa-to-Kenkyū), 26*(1), 75–84.

Tabeta, M., & Masugata, T. (1981). *The organic agriculture movement in Japan.* Tokyo: Nihon Keizai Hyōronsha.

Tanaka. H. (2008). Delicious food in a beautiful country: Nationhood and nationalism in discourses on food in contemporary Japan. *Studies in Ethnicity and Nationalism, 8*(1), 5–30.

Taniguchi, Y. (1988). Can organic agriculture survive? *Soil and Health, 188*, 16–22.

Tovey, H. (1997). Food, environmentalism, and rural sociology: On the organic farming movement in Ireland. *Sociologia Ruralis, 37*(1), 21–37.

Une, Y. (2006). Enbrace non-materialistic values. In K. Nakajima (Ed.), *Logic of life and agriculture: Local development of organic agriculture* (pp. 33–57). Tokyo: Commons.

van Dijk, T. A. (1993). Principles of critical discourse analysis. *Discourse and Society, 4*(2), 249–283.

Wodak, R., & Meyer, M. (2009). Critical discourse analysis: History, agenda, theory and methodology. *Methods of Critical Discourse Analysis, 2*, 1–33.

Yasuda, S. (1986). *Japanese organic agriculture: Development of the movement and economic analysis.* Tokyo: Daiamondosha.

Part VI
Education and internationalization

13 A dialectic between nationalism and multiculturalism

An analysis of the internationalization discourse in Japan[1]

Ako Inuzuka

Since the mid-nineteenth century, internationalization has been an important national policy in Japan (e.g., the *"Datsu-A Nyu-O"* or "Leave Asia, Enter Europe" policy during the Meiji era, 1868–1912). A more recent example that shows how far reaching these efforts have been is the proposal, in 2000, by former Prime Minister Keizo Obuchi's advisory commission, to adopt English as an official language. In a political climate supportive of internationalization, Japanese universities emphasize "internationalization" and "globalization," employing the terms as key public relations slogans to attract potential students. However, despite a strong emphasis on these concepts both in government and in education, incidents indicating a lack of social tolerance are on the rise in Japan today (e.g., hate speeches against Koreans, a "Japanese Only" banner hung at a professional soccer stadium).[2]

In this chapter, I examine Japanese universities' and government's efforts to internationalize higher education—the planning and implementation of "super global universities" in Japan. In particular, I analyze 24 proposals submitted to, and later awarded grants by, the Japanese Ministry of Education, Culture, Sports, Science, and Technology (MEXT) in September 2014.

In April 2014, the Japanese government launched the Super Global Universities Creation Assistance Project, calling for submissions to be selected as "Top Universities" (universities that aim to be among the top 100 universities in the world) and "Leading Global Universities" (universities that can lead the nation to globalization). It was announced that ten universities would be selected as "Top Universities" and 20 would be awarded "Leading Global University" status. The successful applicants would be awarded grants of 500 million yen (about US$4.94 million) and 200–300 million yen (US$1.98 million–US$2.96 million), respectively. Sixteen universities applied to become "Top Universities" while 93 applied for "Leading Global Universities" status. From these, 13 and 24 proposals, respectively, were selected—a higher number than originally anticipated. This chapter focuses on the 24 successful applications in the "Leading Global Universities" category, and examines the ways in which internationalization is discussed. A closer look at the proposals that were awarded grants by MEXT is of particular interest, as it may enhance our understanding of what "good internationalization" means to the Japanese

208   *A. Inuzuka*

government and how Japanese people will be educated in internationalization in the future.

To conduct this analysis, I identify and critique themes related to internationalization, following Wander's (1983) ideological criticism. Wander suggests that rhetorical critics recognize and address their own subjectivity as well as "the influence of established interests" (p. 18). He consequently recommends that rhetorical criticism should be situated in its historical context. This approach allows me to examine Japan's internationalization, acknowledging the existence of "vested interests" while situating my analysis in its historical context. Consequently, I suggest a dialectic between nationalism and multiculturalism to extend the framework of the dialectical approach to intercultural communication (Martin & Nakayama, 1999, 2010). In doing so, I hope to provide implications for whiteness studies in non-Western countries as I unpack a potential internationalization bias towards Westernization.

Theoretical approaches: dialectics and whiteness

Martin and Nakayama (1999, 2010) argue for the importance of holding multiple contradictory ideas simultaneously in intercultural interaction to emphasize the complex and fluid nature of culture and communication. They suggest the following six dialectics: cultural–individual, personal/social-contextual, differences–similarities, static–dynamic, present–future/history–past, and privilege–disadvantage. For instance, in a cultural–individual dialectic, some of our behaviors are idiosyncratic (individual) whereas others are dictated by our cultural background. Similarly, in the case of a personal/social-contextual dialectic, while there are some aspects of communication that are relatively constant over various contexts, others are contextual. A differences–similarities dialectic recognizes the importance of both similarities and differences in intercultural communication. In the case of a static–dynamic dialectic, the ever-changing (dynamic) nature of culture is taken into consideration while acknowledging relatively stable (static) aspects of culture at the same time. A present–future/history–past dialectic illustrates the importance of both history and the present/future situation when studying intercultural communication. Finally, a privilege–disadvantage dialectic suggests that each of us carries various types of privilege and disadvantage. In proposing these dialectics, Martin and Nakayama (2010) assert that "[a]s a dialectical approach underscores the many relational aspects of cultures (both within and without), it can be powerful in understanding how gender, sexuality, race/ethnicity, age, religion and other cultural forces can help define and change cultures" (p. 75).

There have been many intercultural communication studies (e.g., Chen, 2002; Cargile, 2005; Eguchi, 2013; Martin & Nakayama, 2015) that utilize the dialogical approach. Responding to the call for more types of dialectical tensions to understand culture and communication (Martin & Nakayama, 2010), the present essay suggests a dialectic between nationalism and multiculturalism. Multiculturalism and multilingualism "aim to preserve and promote linguistic and

Internationalization discourse in Japan 209

cultural diversity where different languages and cultures can coexist harmoniously without having a single dominant language and culture" (Tsuda, 2010, p. 262). Multiculturalism, therefore, could be characterized as a harmonious egalitarian coexistence of multiple cultures in one society. While this has been a popular concept in many societies, opposing trends are just as prevalent. For instance, while, in the US, concepts like diversity and "melting pot" have traditionally had a positive connotation, California Proposition 187 (1994) prohibited illegal aliens, including their children, from using public services. Similarly, California Proposition 227 (1998), an English only initiative, eliminated bilingual classes from public schools. The popularity of Donald Trump which, to a considerable extent, is based on his aggressive stance towards immigrants and minorities is another example for such an opposing trend. Similarly, though the European Union has been supportive of minority rights, a tightening of immigration laws and increasingly xenophobic discourse in response to the refugee crisis caused by conflicts in the Middle East has recently been witnessed. In the case of Japan, multiculturalism, in the form of internationalization, where society is diversified by adopting foreign cultures and bringing in foreign nationals, has been a popular concept, especially in modern times. On the other hand, MEXT has also been interested in increasing patriotism and nationalism among Japanese school children.[3] It will be interesting to see how these two seemingly contradictory aspects play out in an educational setting. I will, therefore, attempt to trace and discuss the dialectic between nationalism and multiculturalism in the context of the successful "Leading Global Universities" applications.

In addition, whiteness in a non-Western context will be an important aspect of my analysis as Japan's internationalization process since the nineteenth century has really been a history of Westernization. An internationalization bias towards Westernization could serve as a starting point for a discussion of whiteness in non-Western countries. Whiteness studies were very popular from the late 1980s to the early 2000s among interdisciplinary scholars critiquing the "normative" and invisible nature of whiteness and white privileges (e.g., McIntosh, 1988; Frankenberg, 1993; Nakayama & Krizek, 1998; Warren, 2001). However, it seems that only a few studies have been conducted since the late 2000s possibly owing to the discourse of post-racial society.

Frankenberg (1993) defines whiteness as "a set of locations that are historically, socially, politically, and culturally produced and, moreover, are intrinsically linked to unfolding relations of domination" (p. 6). A number of scholars have argued for identifying the invisibility of whiteness as a way of challenging its "normative" nature (e.g., Frankenberg, 1993; Nakayama & Krizek, 1998; Wander, Martin, & Nakayama, 1998).

The universality of whiteness is, for obvious reasons, most notable in the West. However, because of the history of colonization and present Western hegemony, the dominance of whiteness can also be seen in non-Western societies. While most whiteness studies have been conducted in the West, a number of studies have been conducted in the non-West. Shome (1998) writes about whiteness/Eurocentrism/Anglocentrism in postcolonial India because whiteness

210   *A. Inuzuka*

"travels" to "other worlds" regardless of "whether it was the physical travel of white imperial bodies colonizing 'other worlds' or today's neocolonial travel of white cultural products—media, music, television products, academic texts, and Anglo fashions," maintained "by forces of imperialism and global capitalism" (p. 108). She argues that whiteness is more about *discursive practices* rather than actual skin color and, because of colonialism, "the global dominance of white imperial subjects and Eurocentric worldviews" are sustained (p. 108). Lee (1998) writes about gendered colorism in Taiwan—women with *Bai Pifu* [fair skin] are considered more beautiful and more privileged within the patriarchal system. Similarly, Fujimoto (2001) discusses Japan's *whitenization*—privileging white culture—while Toyosaki (2004) examines how Japanese students in the US assimilate into white culture, aided by Japan's white culture-centered internationalization efforts. The present essay aims to contribute to whiteness studies by examining the role of Western supremacy in the proposals that have been awarded grants to promote Japanese universities to become "Leading Global Universities." Revisiting the concept of "whiteness" from a more general point of view seems a worthwhile endeavor at a time when racial violence and unrest are on the rise in the US despite a discourse of "post-racial" society.

Internationalization in Japan

Since ancient times, Japan has related through trade and war with other Asian cultures, especially China and Korea, and has adopted some aspects of foreign cultures such as Chinese characters and Buddhism. In the sixteenth century, Japan started trading with some European nations, predominantly Spain and Portugal. In 1639, Japan closed its doors to trade with all foreign nations except Holland and China until the Meiji Restoration of 1868, the beginning of Japan's modernization. The Meiji Restoration marks the beginning of modern internationalization in Japan. Internationalization during the Meiji period (1868–1912) is known as Westernization, represented by the national policy "*Datsu-A Nyu-O*" [Leave Asia, Enter Europe]. During this period, many teachers from the West were employed at Japanese universities and high schools to teach a wide variety of subjects including arts, literature, Western languages, and sciences. At that time, Western teachers' salaries were three times higher than those of their Japanese colleagues (Tanabe, 1926). According to Fujimoto (2001), Japan's internationalization has been a *whitenization*; "the process of identifying with white Westerners and privileging white bodies" may be traced back to this period (p. 2).

Yukichi Fukuzawa (1835–1901), a prominent Japanese thinker and known advocate of Westernization, is generally credited with the authorship of *Datsuaron* [Discussions on Leaving Asia], a famous article about Westernization in which he urged Japan to "leave" Asia because "[these nations] were doomed to fall" (Zachmann, 2007, p. 17). Scholars such as Zachmann (2007) and Ge (2000) suggest that Fukuzawa was not blindly worshiping Western civilization while despising the rest of Asia, as widely believed. They picture him as a pragmatist

Internationalization discourse in Japan 211

who was well aware of the military power of Western countries and their technological advances.

Although Westernization was interrupted by a brief period of extreme nationalism during the 1930s and 1940s, Western influence, especially from the United States, became strong again during the U.S. led occupation following Japan's defeat in World War II. As globalization further intensified in the 1970s and 1980s, the need for internationalization was also widely recognized by the public in Japan.

Internationalization of school curricula has been an important aspect of wider societal internationalization in Japan. As mentioned earlier, Western teachers were employed to educate a young Japanese elite in Meiji Japan. In recent years, internationalization has become a potent public relations slogan used to attract potential students and more and more schools are making efforts to internationalize their universities. Consequently, a number of scholars have written about internationalization in the context of Japanese higher education.

Huang (2006) provides a generally positive assessment of internationalization efforts by Japanese universities after 1983, when Prime Minister Nakasone's cabinet announced plans for internationalization in higher education. These plans included an increase in the number of international students in Japanese universities. In the 1990s, as the trend towards globalization accelerated, the government started to place even more emphasis on internationalization in education with a focus on international economic competition. This resulted in efforts to popularize activities such as foreign language learning and short-term exchange programs for Japanese students. Internationalization efforts have been made both at private and national universities. Since the 1980s, the number of international students has increased dramatically reaching 109,508 in 2003 compared to only 1,168 in the 1980s (Huang, 2006, citing a study by MEXT, 2004). Many of these international students are from other Asian countries, mostly from China and South Korea. To increase the number of international students even further, universities are now increasingly offering classes taught in English. Also, many universities, especially those that are private, offer courses with international content such as international communication. Huang (2006) argues that although rapid internationalization has been achieved domestically, "there is a great deal to be desired in internationalization of university curricula across borders" (p. 115). He suggests some transnational degree/credit conferral systems in which two universities from different countries can accept credits and/or create a system in which students can earn degrees from both universities.

At the same time, Horie (2002) points out the problems with internationalization in Japanese higher education. She explicates the problem of discrimination against graduates from so-called "international schools" in Japan. Although the situation has improved somewhat as a result of changes in education policies in the 1990s, barriers still exist, especially for graduates from Asian international schools (such as Korean and Chinese schools) who wish to enter national universities that are under the more direct control of the Japanese education ministry.

212   A. Inuzuka

None of them accept diplomas from Asian international schools. Among approximately 500 public (prefectural and city) and private universities, only slightly more than 50 percent accept high school diplomas from Asian international schools. The Japanese government justifies this by the fact that international schools are, under Japanese laws, categorized as "miscellaneous" rather than regular schools. Yet, graduates from Western international schools do not face the same problem because they typically graduate with an International Baccalaureate or the German Arbitur, which gives them university access (Horie, 2002). Horie exposes the government's contradictory internationalization policy which, on one hand, aims to increase the number of international students coming to Japan, but, on the other hand, discriminates against foreign students, especially Asian students living in Japan.

Hashimoto (2000) discusses another problematic aspect of internationalization in Japanese higher education—MEXT's promotion of "Japaneseness." Based on her analysis of the policy text, "Japanese government policies in education, science and culture 1994—New directions in school education: Fostering strength for life," she argues that what the Japanese education ministry calls internationalization is actually "Japanization," an emphasis on the importance of respect for Japanese culture and traditions among school children. In her opinion the documents imply that "internationalization is a process of reconfiguring the Japaneseness of individual citizens who have a mission to be 'trusted' in the international community" so that the nation will be trusted in the international community (Hashimoto, 2000, p. 49).

Aspinall (2012) and Seargeant (2005) have written about internationalization in Japanese higher education, focusing on English language education. Although most Japanese people study English for six years in junior and senior high schools and many for at least two more years in college, surprisingly, the majority are unable to communicate in English. This problem has been addressed in the context of recent rapid globalization and its strong impetus on internationalization. For instance, Aspinall argues that although MEXT wants to improve Japanese students' abilities in communicative English in response to the threat of globalization—if Japanese people cannot communicate in English, Japan will fall behind in global economic competition—the ministry, at the same time, is concerned that the teaching of communicative English may undermine children's loyalty to Japan. Aspinall also identifies the dichotomous way of thinking among many Japanese (Japanese vs. non-Japanese) as a hindrance to the improvement of their communicative skills in English. He supports this idea by citing the popularity of "*Nihonjinron*" [discussions of the Japanese], a concept from the 1970s which celebrates the uniqueness of everything Japanese, while foreign countries are frequently viewed by Japanese society as dangerous places and presented as such in the media. As a result, many Japanese people tend to avoid interaction with foreigners.

In Japan, the English language is rarely utilized as a means of communication with foreigners despite its firm integration into society (Seargant, 2005). For instance, English has found a place in Japanese society through "its ornamental

Internationalization discourse in Japan   213

use" in popular culture (Seargant, 2005, p. 315). "Ornamental" English is written in the Roman alphabet and appears in a wide variety of locations including advertisements, clothing, and signs. Historically, Japan has been more interested in absorbing foreign cultures than in actually interacting with them. This attitude is reflected in the ways in which Japanese people travel abroad (e.g., traveling in exclusively Japanese groups with little interaction with others) or the popularity of foreign country theme parks in Japan. Moreover, intercultural interaction dimensions are not incorporated into internationalization policies in higher education in Japan (Whitsed & Volet, 2011). Whitsed and Volet (2011) examine some of the metaphors foreign English teachers use to describe their experiences in Japan, such as *uchi/soto* [inside/outside]—i.e., they are not encouraged and permitted to be fully integrated into Japanese university systems. They conclude that the lack of integration of foreign English teachers is a missed opportunity for increasing intercultural interaction dimensions, and, consequently, the internationalization of Japanese universities.

Overall, internationalization has been an important policy in Japanese education as well as for society as a whole. Japanese universities have made efforts to internationalize their schools by recruiting international students and sending Japanese students overseas with support and assistance from the Japanese government (MEXT). However, a fear of falling behind in an increasingly competitive world market rather than a true appreciation of cultural diversity may have been the primary motivator. While there have been some successes, problems have been highlighted such as discrimination against Asian students residing in Japan (Horie, 2002) or the emphasis on "Japaneseness" (Hashimoto, 2000). English language education, especially improving English communication skills among Japanese students, has become an important issue in internationalization in Japanese higher education. Keeping these characteristics of Japan's internationalization in society and in higher education in mind, I now turn to my analysis.

Analysis

I examined the 24 successful applications in the "Leading Global Universities" category in respect of how internationalization is discussed in these proposals.[4] I show, first, that a dialectic between nationalism and multiculturalism is at work in the internationalization discourse and, second, that signs of Western supremacy can be observed in many of the submissions. Universities were required to address specific topics such as:

- the number of faculty and staff members who are foreign nationals or Japanese citizens who have studied, taught, or conducted research abroad and strategies to increase these numbers;
- the number of female faculty and staff members anticipated in the future;
- the numbers of international students and Japanese students who have studied abroad and strategies to increase the numbers of exchange students (both foreign and Japanese);

214   A. Inuzuka

- the number of classes taught in foreign languages in general, and in English in particular, and anticipated goals for the future;
- the number of programs in which students can graduate only with foreign language credits and goals for the future.

In addition, issues such as Japanese language instruction for international students, Japanese students' foreign language ability, internationalization of education systems—e.g., incorporation of course numbering and grade point averages (GPAs), English syllabi—and openness of universities to internationalization (flexibility in the academic year, utilization of the International Baccalaureate and the degree to which information is disseminated in foreign languages) had to be addressed. Changes in university governance such as incorporation of a tenure track system and hiring of employees with international experience, as well as those in education, such as utilization of external exams—e.g., the TOEFL (Test of English as a Foreign Language)[5]—in place of entrance examinations, were also important topics in the proposals.

The selection of topics shows that MEXT's standards of internationalization are consistent with its previous policy of increasing the number of international students and Japanese students who study abroad. It also underscores the traditional centrality of English as a foreign language with an emphasis on both improving Japanese students' English skills and attracting more international students. There are other criteria that overlap with these two central themes: an increase in foreign professors and staff members and in Japanese nationals who have studied or worked abroad; the incorporation of tenure track systems to, possibly, attract foreign faculty members; and the incorporation of more flexible systems that would allow students to study abroad more easily and attract more international students (e.g., the quarter system), instead of the whole year term system that is presently adopted by most Japanese universities.

Not surprisingly, most of the 24 submissions responded in a similar fashion to these rather narrow questions. They all discussed how many international students they had and how many more they were planning to attract in the next ten years. Similarly, they all listed how many of their Japanese students had studied abroad and how many more there will be in the future. Most of them stated that they were planning to increase the number of English syllabi and to incorporate the quarter system.

Increasing the number of international students, faculty, and staff members and the number of Japanese students, faculty, and staff who have studied or worked abroad should contribute toward Japan's multiculturalism by diversifying the population and increasing the number of individuals who have a more diverse perspective. There is, however, a promise to bolster nationalism to be observed in many of the proposals. The promotion of "Japaneseness," of Japanese identity or culture, can also be seen in some of the proposals—an important concept for MEXT as Hashimoto (2000) discussed.

The move toward nationalism is accomplished largely in two ways: first, by fostering positive Japanese identity among Japanese students; and, second, by

Internationalization discourse in Japan 215

promoting Japanese culture overseas. In the first category, one of the universities proposes to require all students to take classes in "International Japanese Studies," which is intended to educate students to be globally minded individuals. The classes will be taught in English by a foreign instructor and will "help students understand the meaning of studying abroad and promote international understanding" (my translation). This is elaborated under the subheading: "Three types of foreign faculty members who will be hired in the new general education department." The first of these is:

> Faculty members who teach Japanese culture and diverse cultures—those who specialize in Japanese culture and comparative cultures and who will teach Japanese culture and diverse cultures in International Japanese Studies. By having foreign instructors teach Japanese culture in foreign languages, we can deepen the interest in Japanese culture among Japanese students.
>
> (My translation)

Having positive aspects of Japanese culture relayed to Japanese students by foreign instructors might boost their national pride because Japanese instructors might be considered biased, whereas praise from a foreigner is perceived as an "objective assessment."

Another university proposes to ingrain Japanese identity in Japanese students by promoting experiential learning in traditional craft studios in Kyoto. For instance, the proposal states:

> Since 2014, our university has been requiring all students to take classes in the traditional culture of Kyoto and in advanced technology to foster a creative spirit grounded in the history and tradition of Kyoto and Japanese identity. In addition, for this [super global] project, we are proposing to create more classes in problem-solving in communities and to deal with topics such as traditional culture and crafts and we will offer graduate classes in liberal arts in which Japanese culture is relativized.
>
> (My translation)

The university is considering teaching Japanese students traditional Japanese arts as an important component of their internationalized education. Interestingly, "relativizing Japanese culture," a multiculturalist concept, appears together with the more nationalistic expression, "grounded in Japanese identity." The above quote alone embodies a dialectic between nationalism and multiculturalism.

A common theme among these applications is that universities are proposing to teach traditional Japanese culture to their students to foster a strong "Japanese identity."[6] At the same time, they discuss an increase in the number of classes taught in English and in the number of Japanese students sent abroad. It is possible that these universities are trying to dispel MEXT's concerns that Japanese students may lose their loyalty to Japan if they learn communicative English

216   A. Inuzuka

(Aspinall, 2012). Presumably, students who are well grounded in their own culture are less likely to be influenced by foreign cultures. Instilling a positive Japanese identity in addition to teaching students communicative English and sending them overseas might be perceived as a protective measure by the education ministry.

In the second category, promoting Japanese culture overseas, a few universities propose to launch a program in which Japanese students who are planning to study abroad can be trained to introduce Japan and Japanese culture in English. By educating Japanese students to present Japanese culture in a positive light, the universities may intend to foster "trust" in the Japanese in international communities (Hashimoto, 2000). Another approach in this category is for the university to mention its Japanese studies/language program—one university prides itself on its Japanese Cultural Studies Institute as a place where scholars both inside and outside Japan collaborate to conduct research in Japan studies.

The Japanese education ministry has a known (and sometimes controversial) history of furthering patriotism and nationalism among schoolchildren (Takashima, 1994; "Aikoku," 2006). It is therefore not surprising that universities are trying to appeal to this orientation within MEXT. The strategy some universities express in their proposals is somewhat similar to the Japanese government's "Cool Japan" campaign and the popular TV show, *Cool Japan, Hakkutsu! Kakkoii Nippon* [Cool Japan, Discover Cool Japan!]. The "Cool Japan" campaign was initiated in 2010 to market Japanese culture overseas, focusing especially on contemporary Japanese popular culture such as anime and video games. The TV program, *Cool Japan*, has been broadcast on national television since 2006.[7] On the show, several foreigners living in Japan are invited as panelists to discuss which aspects of Japan and Japanese culture are "cool." The approach taken by universities in the second category follows the government led "Cool Japan" campaign by intending to market Japanese culture overseas, while the approach taken by one of the universities under the first category (encouraging positive Japanese identity among Japanese students) follows the *Cool Japan* TV show in reinforcing the positive image of Japanese culture by having "impartial" foreigners praise Japanese culture. The fact that the phrase "Cool Japan" is actually used in another university's proposal suggests that the applicants were aware of the well-known campaign and TV show:

> In this program [study abroad program for international students], international students can not only improve their Japanese language abilities, but they can also learn various aspects of Japan from traditional culture to more contemporary content, so-called "cool Japan," together with field experiences outside of the classroom.
>
> (My translation)

Since both the "Cool Japan" campaign and the TV show have links with the government the similarities found in some of the proposals are probably not purely coincidental.

Internationalization discourse in Japan 217

Some ideas in the proposals focus on the West, especially the US. This is consistent with tendencies in Japan's modern internationalization efforts. The centrality of the English language is one characteristic theme while proposed changes to match American style education systems are another (e.g., the tenure track system, the quarter system, GPAs). The incorporation of the International Baccalaureate, an international diploma that was originally created in Geneva, Switzerland, is another example. Internationalization with respect to other Asian countries does not receive very much attention.

Western supremacy reveals itself most prominently in the form of the centrality of the English language. Most of the proposals answered questions about "foreign languages" only with respect to the English language. For instance, there were questions regarding the number of classes taught in foreign languages (and, in this section, there was a sub-question asking about the number of classes taught in English), the number of programs that allow students to graduate with classes only taught in foreign languages, and the number of students who have competence in foreign languages. Most universities answered these questions only with regard to English, i.e., how many classes are taught in English and how many programs allow students to graduate with credits only in English, including plans to increase those numbers (some of the schools do, however, offer classes taught in other foreign languages). In reply to questions about the foreign language skills of Japanese students and staff members, most applicants cited English language tests such as the TOEFL or TOEIC (Test of English for International Communication). There were, however, a few universities that used tests for German, French, and Italian as well as English and another university that cited foreign languages such as German, French, Chinese, Korean, and Spanish in addition to English.

Most universities propose to increase the number of English classes and programs and improve Japanese students' English abilities. For instance, one university proposes to offer communicative English classes not only to their regular, full-time students but also to non-traditional, part-time students and students from their associated schools (pre-school to high school). Of course, this is not surprising, considering the status of English as a de facto "international language" and the fact that English is the only foreign language widely taught in Japan. In addition, it is a well-known and widely discussed phenomenon that Japan's higher education system produces graduates who cannot communicate in English. However, together with the comparative omission of non-Western languages/cultures, this still reflects Japan's Western-centered concept of internationalization. As Tsuda (2010) and Pillar (2011) argue, the hegemony of the English language in the world needs to be critically examined.

I found it interesting that in some of the proposals more non-Western nations were mentioned than I initially expected, especially by universities that are not traditionally known for their foreign language education. For instance, one proposal emphasized their partnerships with schools in non-Western countries such as Mexico, Mongolia, India, Vietnam, and China. Also, four of the 24 proposals

218   A. Inuzuka

had "Asia" in their titles or key words. In contrast, proposals from universities that have been well known for their foreign language education tended to focus more on Western nations. Those proposals mostly discussed their partnerships with schools in the US and Europe. Perhaps the universities with a long history of foreign language education had already established partnerships with Western schools before some of the newly developing nations in the non-West became more visible. Schools that have only just started to internationalize may be more aware of the potential value of partnerships with schools in newly developing nations of the non-West. Alternatively, it might be easier to form connections with these universities because non-Western schools are regarded as "less prestigious" and they might also face difficulties creating connections with Western universities. Nonetheless, considering the overall emphasis placed on the English language, Western degrees (e.g., the International Baccalaureate) and characteristics of the American higher education system (e.g., the quarter system, the tenure track system, GPA), there is a clear hierarchy to be observed—Western countries, especially English speaking countries, are at the top and non-Western countries are at the bottom.

Interestingly, in some of the more Asia-centered proposals, Western supremacy was implicitly communicated by valuing degrees from Western countries or comparing their universities to Western standards. For instance, one of the universities focused on Asia with additional plans to develop exchange programs with African nations. Over 80 percent of its students are international students with a majority coming from other Asian countries such as Indonesia, Sri Lanka, and Myanmar. Yet, the institution is still compared with Europe and the United States. Pointing out that students are required to live in dorms where they can engage in international interaction, it is stated that this is "rare even in higher education institutions in Europe and the United States." The proposal mentions that the institution's Master of Business Administration (MBA) program is highly ranked by the British *Economist* magazine. Also, it is cited as a bonus that most faculty members have degrees from universities in Europe and the United States. Similarly, the main focus of another university is Asia as their proposal title indicates: "Global diamonds: Aiming to become the hub university in Asia where global leaders gather" (my translation). Yet, we find information on its links with University of California, Los Angeles (UCLA) for its exchange program much more frequently than mentions of its offices in Malaysia, Thailand, and India. While there is an outward focus on Asia, Europe and the United States are still placed above Asian countries when it comes to education/internationalization standards.

Conclusion

In this chapter, I have attempted to examine 24 proposals that have been awarded grants from MEXT to enable their universities to become "Leading Global Universities." The emphasis behind the questions asked by MEXT is consistent with what has been reported by scholars of internationalization in Japanese

Internationalization discourse in Japan 219

higher education: a focus on the West and the centrality of the English language. Considering the proposals mostly discuss an intention to increase the number of classes taught in English as well as the number of programs in which students can graduate in English only, it is evident that Western international students are predominantly targeted and valued. Consistent with the fact that foreign Asian students residing in Japan are discriminated against in the admission process, other Asian nations are mostly overlooked in these internationalization proposals.

According to scholars such as McIntosh (1988), Frankenberg (1993), and Nakayama and Krizek (1998), whiteness is invisible and universal. In the case of Japan's internationalization discourse, whiteness invisibly manifests itself in the dominance of the English language. The importance of improving one's English is so naturalized and internalized that people do not question the hegemony of the English language that forces non-English speakers to learn English and results in non-English speakers being despised (Tsuda, 2010). By increasing the number of classes taught in English and programs that allow students to graduate in English only, the proposals will make the English language even more powerful and omnipresent in higher education. The unquestioned adoption of Western systems such as the International Baccalaureate, a quarter system, or tenure track systems may also illustrate the invisibility of whiteness. Together, such developments could be interpreted to suggest that Japan's higher education system will be adapted to enforce the hegemony of the English language and Western culture—with potentially far reaching consequences for Japanese society.

The weak emphasis on non-Western nations in these proposals resonates with Wander's "third persona" (1984). In discussing his ideological criticism, Wander talks about "audiences rejected or negated through the speech and/or the speaking situation" (p. 209) or the third persona:

> But "being negated" includes not only being alienated through language— the "it" that is the summation of all that you and I are told to avoid becoming, but also being negated in history, a being whose presence, though relevant to what is said, is negated through silence. The moral significance of being negated through what is and what is not said reveals itself in all its anguish and confusion in context, in the world of affairs wherein certain individuals and groups are, through law, tradition, or prejudice, denied rights accorded to being commended or, measured against an ideal, to human beings.
>
> (Wander, 1984, p. 210)

Through Western-centered internationalization in Japan's higher education, non-Westerners, especially other Asians (considering a history of discrimination against them), have been negated in some of the proposals through silence while in others they are placed below the West as they are measured against an "ideal" Western standard.

220   *A. Inuzuka*

While multiculturalism, despite a strong emphasis on the West, can be observed in the proposals, nationalistic ideals are also promoted. Multiculturalism, as defined by Tsuda (2010), promotes cultural diversity to the point where multiple cultures can coexist harmoniously in an egalitarian manner. This is a concept that does not sit well with internationalization as it has historically been practiced in Japan, which could be characterized as a process of assimilation rather than coexistence. Internationalization in Japan is a national project, a patriotic endeavor. It is a means to an end, designed to strengthen the Japanese nation. The "Super Global" proposals are certainly promoting multiculturalism on the surface. However, a closer examination reveals that a dominant language (English) and a dominant culture (Western culture) are considerably favored over non-Western cultures. This could be seen as a pragmatic bias fostered by the Japanese government: an attempt to acquire features that are desirable and advantageous in a global economic contest that has been historically dominated by Western countries. The aim cannot simply be undiscriminating Westernization as this would threaten the traditional, governmentally sanctioned values of Japanese culture. This conflict is offset by the theme of nationalism in many of the proposals: for instance, fostering patriotism and nationalism among Japanese students by having foreign instructors teach positive aspects of Japanese culture, or training students to promote Japanese culture in English before sending them abroad. The result is a dialectic between multiculturalism and nationalism, a conflict between homogenization and heterogeneity, in these proposals.

The aspects of Japanese internationalization promoted in the proposals examined may be symptomatic of a society that, as a whole, is not very supportive of the ideals of multiculturalism. This can be observed in various discriminatory incidents against other Asians despite the popularity of the notion of internationalization. Non-Westerners, especially other Asians, are discriminated against, negated and placed below Westerners while a positive Japanese identity is promoted. Internationalization and multiculturalism in Japan do not have as much in common as I would have expected. Japan's history of internationalization was an imperially inspired Westernization. In my view, this past, compounded by a history of racism and discrimination against other Asians, has had a profound effect on what is intuitively understood as internationalization in Japan today. The parallels between Japan's historic cultural assimilation and today's concepts of internationalization are, at the same time, troubling and intriguing. If a shift toward a more egalitarian society is one of the desired effects of establishing "Super Global Universities," these aspects of Japanese internationalization will need to be more critically examined and challenged.

Notes

1 This chapter was funded by a Japan Studies Small Grant from the Asian Studies Center at the University of Pittsburgh and a Hewlett International Grant from the University Center for International Studies at the University of Pittsburgh. The manuscript was presented at the 2016 International Communication Association annual convention. I would like to thank the University of Pittsburgh for funding this project and Thomas Fuchs for his support and invaluable comments on the manuscript.
2 On March 8, 2014, at Saitama Stadium, the home stadium of the Urawa Reds, a "Japanese only" banner was mounted by fans over an entrance and it was not removed until the game was over. Consequently, on March 13, the team was obliged to play its next home game in an empty stadium.
3 In 2006, a new education law was put in place with the aim of incorporating patriotism and nationalism in the school curriculum ("Aikoku," 2006). Takashima (1994) has also argued that MEXT suppresses negative portrayals of Japanese society and history in school textbooks.
4 The proposals were obtained from the homepage of Nihon Gakujutsu Shinkokai [Japan Society for the Promotion of Science], an organization linked to MEXT (www.jsps.go. jp/j-sgu/h26_kekka_saitaku.html).
5 TOEFL is a standardized test used to assess the English language abilities of non-native speakers when they apply for universities in English speaking countries.
6 The term "Japanese identity" is not defined in any of the proposals. It seems to imply an understanding and a deep appreciation of traditional Japanese culture.
7 The program has been broadcast outside Japan as well since 2007.

References

"Aikoku" hyoka to tomadoi. (2006, December 16). *Asahi Shimbun*, p. 2.

Aspinall, R. W. (2012). International education policy in Japan in an age of globalization and risk. Leiden: Brill.

Cargile. A. C. (2005). Describing culture dialectically. In W. J. Starosta & G.-M. Chen (Eds.), *Taking stock in intercultural communication: Where to now?: International and intercultural communication annual* (Vol. 28, pp. 99–123). Washington, DC: National Communication Association.

Chen, L. (2002). Communication in intercultural relationships. In W. B. Gudykunst & B. Mody (Eds.), *Handbook of international and intercultural communication* (pp. 241–257). Thousand Oaks, CA: Sage.

Eguchi, S. (2013). Revisiting Asiacentricity: Toward thinking dialectically about Asian American identities and negotiation. *Howard Journal of Communication, 24*(1), 95–115.

Frankenberg, R. (1993). *White women, race matters: The social construction of whiteness*. Minneapolis, MN: University of Minnesota Press.

Fujimoto, E. (2001). Japanese-ness, whiteness, and the "other" in Japan's internationalization. In M. J. Collier (Ed.), *Transforming communication about culture: Critical new directions* (pp. 1–24). Thousand Oaks, CA: Sage.

Ge, S. (2000). How does Asian mean? (Part I). *Inter-Asia Cultural Studies, 1*(1), 13–47.

Hashimoto, K. (2000). "Internationalisation" is 'Japanisation: Japan's foreign language education and national identity. *Journal of Intercultural Studies, 21*(1), 39–51.

Horie, M. (2002). The internationalization of higher education in Japan in the 1990s: A reconsideration. *Higher Education, 43*, 65–84.

Huang, F. (2006). Internationalization of university curricula in Japan: Major policies and practice since the 1980s. *Journal of Studies in International Education, 10*(2), 102–118.

222   A. Inuzuka

Lee, W. (1998). One whiteness veils three uglinesses: From border-crossing to a womanist interrogation of gendered colorism. In T. K. Nakayama & J. N. Martin (Eds.), *Whiteness: The communication of social identity* (pp. 279–298). Thousand Oaks, CA: Sage.

Martin, J. N., & Nakayama, T. K. (1999). Thinking dialectically about culture and communication. *Communication Theory, 9*, 1–25.

Martin, J. N., & Nakayama, T. K. (2010). Intercultural communication and dialectic revisited. In T. K. Nakayama & R. T. Halualani (Eds.), *The handbook of critical intercultural communication* (pp. 59–83). Chichester, UK: Wiley-Blackwell.

Martin, J. N., & Nakayama, T. K. (2015). Reconsidering intercultural (communication) competence in the workplace: A dialectical approach. *Language and Intercultural Communication, 15*(1), 13–28.

McIntosh, P. (1988). *White privilege and male privilege: A personal account of coming to see correspondences through work in women's studies* (Paper No. 189). Wellesley, MA: Wellesley College, Center for Research on Women.

Nakayama, T. K., & Krizek, R. L. (1998). Whiteness as a strategic rhetoric. In T. K. Nakayama & J. N. Martin (Eds.), *Whiteness: The communication of social identity* (pp. 87–106). Thousand Oaks, CA: Sage.

Piller, I. (2011). *Intercultural communication: A critical introduction.* Edinburgh: Edinburgh University Press.

Seargeant, P. (2005). Globalisation and reconfigured English in Japan. *World Englishes, 24*(3), 309–319.

Shome, R. (1998). Whiteness and the politics of location: Postcolonial reflections. In T. K. Nakayama & J. N. Martin (Eds.), *Whiteness: The communication of social identity* (pp. 107–128). Thousand Oaks, CA: Sage.

Steyn, M. (1998). White identity in context: A personal narrative. In T. K. Nakayama & J. N. Martin (Eds.), *Whiteness: The communication of social identity* (pp. 264–278). Thousand Oaks, CA: Sage.

Sun, Ge. (2000). How does Asia mean? (Part I) (S.-L. Hui & K. Lau, Trans.). *Inter-Asia Cultural Studies, 1*(1), 13–46.

Takashima, N. (1994). *Kyokasho ha ko kakinaosareta!* [Textbooks have been revised this way!]. Tokyo: Kodansha.

Tanabe, R. (1926). *Koizumi Yakumo Zenshu* [Writings of Koizumi Yakumo]. Tokyo: Daiichi Shobo Kanko.

Toyosaki, S. (2004). Ethnography of cross-cultural communication: Japanese international students' accounts of US-American culture and communication. *Journal of Intercultural Communication Research, 33*(3), 159–175.

Tsuda, Y. (2010). Speaking against the hegemony of English: Problems, ideologies, and solutions. In T. K. Nakayama & R. T. Halualani (Eds.), *The handbook of critical intercultural communication* (pp. 248–269). Chichester, UK: Wiley-Blackwell.

Wander, P. C. (1983). The ideological turn in modern criticism. *Central States Speech Journal, 34*, 1–18.

Wander, P. C. (1984). The third persona: An ideological turn in rhetorical theory. *Central States Speech Journal, 35*, 197–216.

Wander, P. C., Martin, J. N., & Nakayama, T. K. (1998). Whiteness and beyond: Sociohistorical foundations of whiteness and contemporary challenges. In T. K. Nakayama & J. N. Martin (Eds.), *Whiteness: The communication of social identity* (pp. 13–26). Thousand Oaks, CA: Sage.

Warren, J. T. (2001). Doing whiteness: On the performative dimensions of race in the classroom. *Communication Education, 50*, 91–109.

Whitsed, C., & Volet, S. (2011). Fostering the intercultural dimensions of internationalization in higher education: Metaphors and challenges in the Japanese context. *Journal of Studies in International Education, 15*(2), 146–170.

Zachmann, U. M. (2007). Blowing up a double portrait in black and white: The concept of Asia in the writings of Fukuzawa Yukichi and Okakura Tenshin. *Positions, 15*(2), 345–368.

14 "I never wanted to be famous"

Pushes and pulls of Whiteness through the eyes of foreign English language teachers in Japan

Nathaniel Simmons and Yea-Wen Chen

Globalizing forces have driven communication scholars to be more reflexive about cultural assumptions that underlie theory, practice, and research (e.g., Ganesh, Zoller, & Cheney, 2005; Nakayama & Martin, 1999). From the lens of globalization, "culture" is considered *de-territorialized* as people and their cultural practices are uprooted from one geographical location and transplanted to another (Appadurai, 1996; Shome & Hegde, 2002; Sorrells, 2010). Such uprooting, or "transplanting," means that sojourners, migrants, refugees, tourists, and business people from various places are interacting more rapidly than before. Simultaneously, individualized experiences of globalization vary due to differences in power relations and access to resources. Not surprisingly, colonialism and Western domination continue to define intercultural relations. Such inequalities reproduce hegemonic structures and binds (Collier, 2009). However, a gap exists in the literature in terms of how globalization influences intercultural dyads within the workplace, particularly among foreign workers such as (White) English language teachers (ELTs) in Japan.

English education in Japan

Besides English education, ELTs play a role in Japanese education in increasing internationalization (McConnell, 2000). Native English speakers are seen as an important, tangible symbol in language education programs that seek to promote internationalization through intercultural interactions (Breckenridge & Erling, 2011). Kubota (2002) argued that ELTs do not serve English educational purposes but, rather, promote internationalization—or international understanding. Due to their role in encouraging and fostering globalization, ELTs in Japan serve as a prime example for exploring ideologies that enable and constrain intercultural communication (McConnell, 2000; Simmons, 2012, 2014, 2016). Japan's Ministry of Education, Culture, Sports, Science, and Technology (MEXT) delivers standardized curricula for primary and secondary education which (re) enforces the role of English as a global language (Seargeant, 2011). This has not only led individuals and institutions to show an interest in English (McVeigh, 2002), but has also resulted in the continuous recruitment of foreign, "native-speaking" (*sic*) English language teachers by various private and government organizations. The plethora of global English teaching jobs for native-speakers attests to the existence of a global English ideology (Root, 2009). Native English speakers are viewed as the "best resource" for learning (Root, 2009, p. 59), despite the overabundance of qualified non-native English language teachers and teaching materials that are available. ELTs are not required to have any knowledge of Japan—or teaching experience—prior to moving to Japan. Importing iconic symbols (such as ELTs) that are not culturally literate could result in difficult intercultural interactions. ELTs are seemingly open and willing to acclimate sensitively to Japanese culture (Breckenridge & Erling, 2011), but given their seemingly public role and prominent position in Japanese education, it is important to understand how ELTs and their Japanese co-workers (JCWs) negotiate their intercultural relationships.

Globalizing Whiteness within Japan

Whiteness can be understood as a socially constructed positionality and as normative cultural practices/discourses in which Whites experience structural and racial privileges that are unnamed and unmarked (Frankenburg, 1993). Whiteness scholarship, which emerged from critical race studies (Kennedy, Middleton, & Ratcliffe, 2005), offers novel ways of talking about and conceptualizing power, inequity, and privilege (Wray, 2006). Nakayama and Krizek's (1995) seminal work theorizes Whiteness as "strategic rhetoric" that upholds White superiority and domination while rendering Whiteness invisible. Of particular relevance to this study, Allen (2001) and Leonardo (2002) have argued that White racial and structural privileges transcend the boundaries of nation states and that White supremacy is a globalized phenomenon. However, few studies have examined how Whites experience themselves (i.e., via their privileges) in a global context, such as within a non-English speaking country. At the same time, researching Whiteness faces unique challenges as it presents the danger of (re) centering Whiteness as the normalized position from which to view all intercultural communication interactions (Nakayama & Martin, 2007). Therefore, intercultural relationships between ELTs and JCWs are a rich site for examining how White privilege plays out relationally.

English language education in Japan is underpinned with racial constructions of difference (Rivers & Ross, 2013). Most Japanese students maintain the belief that "standard English" should be taught by European-looking native speakers of English (Bailey, 2007; Fujita, 2009; Kobayashi, 2010, 2011). This attests to the fact that "power relationships that structure social life do not stop at the classroom door" (Brown, Cervero, & Johnson-Bailey, 2000, p. 273). Many Japanese students perceive intercultural communication narrowly as contacts with White, native (American) English speakers (Kobayashi, 2011). This continues to be reinforced throughout Japan when English language education bodies seek to attract students and clients by hiring White teachers (Bailey, 2007). Rivers (2013) argues that the English language education system in Japan maintains a "masquerade of smiley [foreign] faces and perpetual pleasantness decorating the veneer of 'native-speaker' English teaching" (Rivers, 2013, p. 75). The English language education system in Japan promotes a false view of reality. These findings highlight the dominance of Whiteness throughout the English education system in Japan and support the thesis of globalized White supremacy (Allen, 2001; Leonardo, 2002). Thus, as part of a larger study that seeks to understand relationships between ELTs and JCWs, this study addresses how ELTs experience being White and a teacher in Japan and what ideologies enable and constrain ELTs' discourses.

Data was collected[1] in Japan from May to September 2013 by one of the chapter authors while he was working as an ELT. He had worked as an ELT previously (2007–2009) and used his contacts as an initial starting group to solicit participants for this study. ELT and Japanese participants were obtained utilizing a snowball technique. The study was advertised as seeking to learn more about communication between ELTs and JCWs. Having gained Institutional Review Board (IRB) approval and informed consent, and as part of a larger project on ELT and JCW privacy management (Simmons, in press), the chapter author used in-depth interviews to uncover participants' first-person stories and accounts. Past ELT-focused research has highlighted the utility of retrospective interview techniques (Komisarof, 2001, 2006; Simmons, 2012, 2016). Interviews ranged from 30 minutes to three hours, and the transcribed interviews yielded 490 single-spaced pages. For analysis, we employed critical discourse analysis (CDA). Guided by the lens of Whiteness, this study employed CDA to analyze cultural ideals and ideologies embedded in discourses by ELTs in Japan. Specifically, we followed Chen, Simmons, and Kang's (2015) use of van Dijk's approach to CDA to focus on frequent and repeated ideals and interrogate dominant ideology/ies present across ELTs' discourses as they relate to Whiteness.

ELTs, Whiteness, and cultural ideology

Japan has a history of resisting outside influences (Becker, 1936), which led to a period of isolation from foreign influences. However, in the summer of 1853 American ships sailed into Edo Bay and forcefully "invaded" Japan demanding economic trade (Beasley, 1995; Jansen, 2000). These events led to a political and economic restructuring of Japan referred to as the Meiji Restoration which is credited with "modernizing" the country and, thus, its birth as a major, global economic player (Beasley, 1995; Jansen, 2000). Since Japan has not always opened its doors to foreigners and is "suspicious" of ethnic Japanese (Brody, 2002), it has long been referred to as a xenophobic nation (Jung, 2004). Japan's xenophobia is not, however, a thing of the past. In fact, xenophobic discourses in Japan have increased online since the early 2000s (Yamaguchi, 2013). In today's age of globalization and English hegemony, nations are forced to accept the superiority of English in order to survive and compete internationally (Pac, 2012).

In his book, *The Idea of English in Japan*, Seargeant (2011) offers a critical reading of English language teaching in Japan. He claims that English has not

"*I never wanted to be famous*" 227

been imposed on Japanese citizens who have passively accepted it, but has been appropriated, resisted, and even ignored by Japanese people. Being excluded or ostracized by groups threatens an individual's need for self-esteem, belonging-ness, control, and a meaningful existence (Baumeister & Leary, 1995; Williams, 2001).

Consciously or subconsciously, ELTs are active participants in and carriers of English-only ideology/superiority. As the literal "face" of "true" (*sic*) English language education in Japan, their very presence and daily actions at work con-tinue to reinforce English hegemony and superiority. Understanding how English hegemony and xenophobia are at play can provide insights into why English lan-guage teachers might bear the brunt of this exclusion due to them being the literal "face" of English education.

On being culturally White and/or Western in Japan

We found that many ELTs reported feeling like a "celebrity" due to their race and/or Western upbringing. More precisely, White ELTs felt this "spotlight" was due to their racial/ethnic identities. Such discussions revealed that privi-leged White identity position, or the lack thereof, influenced their experiences as celebrities, and, ultimately, foreigners in Japan. For example, Samantha, a Caucasian female, co-hosted an English news item on television for her local community. Samantha's discussion of her role revealed her awareness of white privilege. When discussing her celebritized position, she said, "I never wanted to be famous." She explained how she felt after living in Japan for three years:

> I am much better at handling all the attention now than I was when I first arrived, and it was something I went home after my first year and I was like, "Why isn't anyone staring at me?" Because I fit back in America, and I enjoyed fitting back in.

Being a (White) foreigner was a new experience for Samantha that led her to stand out and to receive attention for being White. Samantha became accus-tomed to attention in Japan and noted the lack of it while in her home country (U.S.). Samantha commented that she "enjoyed fitting back in" which is another way of saying that she was the norm in her home country and no longer a minority or cultural outsider.

Katie discussed her role as an "entertainer" at work due to her white skin. She described her role of teaching adults as "kind of like being an entertainer." She explained:

> With adults, you're [ELTs] kinda like an entertainer. I'm a boring white girl, look at me. I have blue eyes and pretty skin, like, you know, [laughter]. It's a little unhealthy, I guess. Yeah, [I] actually had old people that would be like, "Your skin is so white."

228   *N. Simmons and Y-W. Chen*

As Katie told this story she rubbed her arm back and forth. She said, "They [students] would like caress my pale, soft, white, skin." She explained that it made her feel, "uncomfortable, just that they were so amazed by it." Katie's discussion of her role as an entertainer reveals that part of Katie's experience involved using her white skin as a focal point. This may be unintentional from Katie's perspective, but her use of "boring white girl" indicates that she was accustomed to taking her Whiteness for granted. She describes her students' fascination with her pale, white skin as "unhealthy," which suggests slight recognition, or discomfort, with her racial identity taking center stage at work. Although uncomfortable for Katie, this example illustrates her struggle with White privilege.

Similarly, Sara explained that non-Japanese in Japan are racialized and assumed to speak English. She said, "There probably isn't a white person in Japan or non-Japanese person in Japan who hasn't been used at some point by some random stranger for an English lesson." Sara described how her White body led Japanese people to perceive her as an English speaker and a desirable person to approach. She explicitly demarcated the racial line between Japanese and non-Japanese people as if the boundary was clear-cut. She explained that one's race often leads to the perception that foreigners teach, or are able to teach, English; this renders White bodies attractive and desirable. Also, Sara's comments evidence the linkage between Whiteness and Englishness. For Sara, being a (White) foreigner is a large part of her identity. Her white identity leads Japanese people to believe she is an English-speaker. She said:

> It's like the Britney Spears effect; you might not be on tour or on stage, but you're kind of an ambassador. So, you are always aware of how you're being perceived. So, I don't think you can really switch off the alien feeling. It kind of follows you around.

The "Britney Spears effect" refers to the idea that even though she might not be performing (i.e., teaching English), her celebrity status followed her around in her day-to-day life because of her social positioning and racial identity that rendered her unable to "blend in." What is less emphasized by Sara is the cultural symbolism of "Britney Spears" as the quintessential beauty standard of being blonde-haired, White, and female.

Performing the (White) celebrity role

For many ELTs, being white also implicated expectations to perform, behave, and be treated like a celebrity. For instance, White ELTs reported feeling like a celebrity when performing certain actions such as signing autographs, being on television programs, or meeting "fans." For example, Daniel, a white man, said that he felt like a celebrity because he gave students autographs. He said, "There was definitely that celebrity persona.... I signed at least 300 or 400 kids' notebooks every day." Daniel continued, "Every time I went to the school, they would ask me for signatures and it would be the whole class would line up and

"I never wanted to be famous" 229

I'd sign their notebooks." This became a ritual he would perform in each of his classrooms that served as participation encouragement and acted as a reward for speaking English. Daniel spoke about his performance at school as a way in which he performed his celebrity role. He described himself as a "Disneyland character" and said that performing his Disney character role helped him meet classroom expectations. He explained:

> If you went to Disneyland and Mickey Mouse is just sitting on a sofa and eating a sandwich and didn't want to talk to anyone, you would be somewhat disappointed. But if I am going to the school I have to be larger-than-life (or extra energetic), that is one of the reasons I'm there.

Here Daniel compares himself with Mickey Mouse—an imaginative character that captivates the fantasy life of both children and adults. The idea of Mickey Mouse sitting on a couch stands out, and it also seems odd. Daniel knows that, as a foreigner, he stands out within his workplace as an exotic individual who maintains agency, but also has constraints. He believes that he was hired to come to Japan to perform this larger-than-life, extra energetic, friendly character role, even though it is not necessarily him.

Brent, a white ELT, referred to his role as being an "ELT clown" whose job was to entertain students. Brent explained that, as part of this role, students were encouraged by his JCWs to ask him questions. He said: "They [students] were encouraged [in asking questions] by [Japanese] teachers. That this is the ELT clown who's been brought in to perform for them [students]. Not human. They aren't a real person. They are just here to entertain us." Brent defines his role as one in which he is an entertainer of students. His use of being "brought in to perform" for students hints at a perception that he is an imported entertainer. He views his role as a cultural commodity that has been imported to satisfy and entertain Japanese children. He did not, however, necessarily find this role upsetting; Brent did not consider the body politics of constructing some foreigners as desirable entertainers but not others. Laughing, he explained, "To a certain extent, I was willing to sacrifice some of my privacy for their education." Brent was able to educate Japanese children about different cultures from a culturally commodified and celebritized role. He viewed being willing to "sacrifice" his privacy for Japanese entertainment (i.e., answering any question Japanese co-workers or students asked him) as a way in which to educate.

In addition to providing autographs and performing entertainment roles for students or co-workers, some ELTs reported taking part in local television programs. Kelly, a half Japanese ELT, explained, "They [the local TV station] found out that I could speak [Japanese] and they got really excited. And were like, 'We can do a series where we follow you around'." Within this series, they recorded both a personal interview she had done with the mayor and her classroom teaching. She said, "They broadcasted that at least five times." I asked Kelly how it felt being on TV. She said, "I would rather not think about it.

I never wanted to watch it." She added, "That kind of is why I feel like everyone in the town knows who I am, whereas I don't know who they are. And they know a lot about me, because it's like personal." She said that the television interviewers asked her questions such as: "Where are you from? What's your race? How old are you? What do your parents do? What do you think about teaching?" This spotlight brings a lot of attention. She explained, "I meet people even if I'm walking on the streets, and sometimes they talk to me. It's like, 'Oh, I know you. You are Kelly'." This outside attention influenced Kelly's relationships with co-workers. She said, "They're [co-workers] always saying how I'm a celebrity." In fact, they jokingly tease her. She continued, "They call me a famous person and stuff like that ... it's hard, I don't want to toot my own horn." Kelly perceives the local TV coverage, fans meeting her on the street, and co-worker teasing as attention that puts her in the spotlight and in a position in which she is paraded as ideal.

The very action of meeting individuals who were excited to see and/or meet ELTs led to celebrity-like feelings. Edward, a White man, said he "absolutely" felt like a celebrity, an analogy actually used during his training to describe his role at work.

> It was crazy, like, day one I was walking up the hill to school and there were gangs of teenage girls hanging out of the windows screaming, and I will never forget. It was just absolute carnage. Literally, be like f**king Justin Bieber or something.

Edward experienced feeling like a celebrity at work due to his treatment by students. The screams of teenage girl students echoed, in his mind, what celebrities like Bieber experience in concert halls and public appearances. Being greeted by screaming "fans" led Edward to his spotlight performance in the workplace. ELT celebritized positionality was not only influenced by the performance of certain actions and one's racial identity, but by an institutionalized ideology that ELTs are not real teachers.

Ideological construction of "not a real teacher"

Discourses of whiteness and celebritization position ELTs in ambivalent roles as teachers and in awkward relationships with their JCWs as stereotypes clash between teacher and celebrity. There is an unspoken misconception that "celebrity" ELTs make "bad" or "unlikely" teachers. In other words, ELTs are perceived to be more suited as "celebrities" than teachers, which suggests that this ideology also functions to privilege ELTs. Nearly two-thirds of all ELTs in this study reported feeling that they were not a "real teacher." All the ELTs within this study were familiar with this expression, thus demonstrating its dominance within ELT participants' experiences and culture. The construction of ELTs as not real teachers functions to both marginalize and privilege them in interactions with students and co-workers.

"*I never wanted to be famous*" 231

For instance, Joshua said, "I didn't feel like a real teacher, but I felt like kind of almost a pinch hitter [substitute] a lot of times for the teachers themselves." Joshua described his workplace pinch hitter role as "one person from the rosters to be at bat every time the pitcher would be up because the pitcher is not a very good hitter … he [the pinch hitter] just comes into substitute for a person." Joshua claimed to be an English "pinch hitter" to substitute for the perceived poor levels of English of his Japanese team teachers. Joshua's comment suggests a preference for native English speakers and their superiority in the context of English language education in Japan. Since native European-looking teachers are preferred by Japanese ELT employers (Kobayashi, 2011), Joshua, as a white man, was an imported pinch hitter to fill in for perceived Japanese English-speaking inferiority. Joshua's comment reflected many ELTs' shared insight as to why they didn't feel like a "real teacher" in juxtaposition to what real teachers do.

Many ELTs defined a "real teacher" as someone who did "actual" work that could be measured in some way such as creating lesson plans. Cindy said, "The [where] schools we [ELTs] feel like a real teacher are also the ones we're going to put in your best effort, so it is in their [JCWs] interest, I think, to include you in things." Cindy's comments reveal that not only did she consider her work ethic to be influenced by her perception as to whether she is a "real teacher," but being excluded from lesson planning and more traditional Japanese teacher roles and duties also influenced her perception of the role. ELTs seem to adopt the "real teacher" ideology as a management strategy to cope with dissatisfaction from seemingly meaningless work. For instance, Daniel said, "A real teacher is someone who uses their skills and knowledge to help, but I guess I've never done that." In fact, it was during class preparation processes that Daniel reported feeling like a real teacher. He explained:

I definitely didn't feel like a real teacher; after all, I felt more like I was in Disneyland or something. Everything was just crazy and over-the-top…. And at the time, I felt sometimes like a real teacher, closest to the real teacher, when I was out of the school when I prepared.

Daniel's perception of being in "Disneyland" indicates being located in a magical, fake world constructed to be something it is not. Such a comment speaks deeply to Daniel's perception about his positionality within the workplace. For Daniel, the actions experienced in his "Disneyland" workplace were perceived to be exaggerated, which led him to believe his reality was fake or non-typical compared with Japanese colleagues' work. For example, since his workplace expectations were only met while preparing for courses, it was only then that Daniel felt like a real teacher. In juxtaposition to the belief that real teachers do stuff, ELTs' discourses reflect the fact that they experience themselves as not real teachers.

ELTs experience of feeling not like a "real teacher" stem from a system of cultural exclusion prevalent throughout the English language education system in Japan. In this context, excluding ELTs from fuller instructional involvement—consciously or subconsciously—is reminiscent of xenophobic practices and speaks to a "subtle" resistance to English-only ideological practices.

Discussion(s)

Before concluding this chapter, we reflect that who we are influences our unique perspectives and interpretations. As a White, American, former ELT, I (the first author) have been there in my previous experience in the Japan Exchange and Teaching (JET) Programme and was there throughout the data collection period. As I reflect upon my interview experience, the moments we shared—be it workplace trials, frustrations, and joys—I realized that this study is not just about their story, it is *our* story. I, personally, feel a great responsibility to truthfully represent the participants' experiences.

As a non-white former English teacher in Taiwan, I (the second author) occupy more of an outsider than an insider position. I am extremely sympathetic to the situations in which ELTs and JCWs are placed, particularly the challenges facing non-native English educators and foreign workers. I relate to the positions that many JCWs are in as a cultural host in Taiwan. Many of the ELTs' experiences reminded me of those of my foreign/White friends in Taiwan. I am committed to honoring stories of intercultural relationship building as humanely as possible.

The ideological construction of ELTs as "not *real* teachers" is rooted in both English hegemony and xenophobia which eroticize and exclude ELTs from productive workplace relationships with JCWs. On the one hand, ELTs are known as "Assistant Language Teachers." This label led ELTs to feel that they lacked authority, had nothing to do at work, and resulted in some taking on non-teaching roles at work in order to achieve some kind of meaningful work. Such practices led ELTs to feel as if they did not have a "real job" and, therefore, were not "real teachers." On the other hand, many ELTs were perceived, treated, and positioned as celebrities based on their status as (Western/European) foreigners. Such a placement not only commodified ELTs, but placed them in a "special" social position of exclusion.

The hesitation to allow ELTs to take charge of English language education within Japanese classrooms, let alone English education curricula, denotes a reluctance that speaks to a fear of Western imperialism and xenophobia. Hu and McKay (2012) explain that English in Japan is recognized as important for trade, globalization, and Westernization but, at the same time, is perceived to threaten Japanese identity, culture, and traditions. Such thinking puts ELTs in a position in which their presence is both a blessing and a curse. ELTs may be welcome and/or unwelcome guests within their workplaces due to differing perceptions of their role in Japanese society. This construction suggests ambivalence towards ELTs and English language education in Japan.

Ambivalence towards ELTs and English language education in Japan may reinforce Japanese identity. Hashimoto (2007) argues that "English is adopted

"I never wanted to be famous" 233

only as a tool so that the values and traditions embedded in the Japanese culture will be retained, and cultural independence will be ensured" (p. 27). Constructing ELTs as guests enables JCWs, and particularly team teachers, to instill a sense of "Japanessness" into their students by contrasting Japan with the "other" or, in this case, "the West" (Kobayashi, 2013; Yoshino, 2002). Reinforcing this perspective, Kobayashi (2013) argues that Japan's English language education system is very successful at (re)producing monolingual Japanese "who willingly ascribe their poor English skills to their pure, genetic, innate Japaneseness" (p. 6). Maintaining ELTs as guests excludes them from occupying true teaching roles and working productively. Such ambivalence and avoidance may be the result of both ELTs and JCWs responding to feeling like unwilling "imposters" who experience estrangement and alienation from the self.

As Tafarodi, Shaughnessy, Lee, Leung, Ozaki, Morio, and Yamaguchi (2009) explain, interaction with cultural outsiders "may well be avoided because of ignorance of their background and social position, and the resulting lack of a relational frame for appropriate conduct" (p. 570). At the same time, xenophobia diminishes with education, time, and personal contact with foreigners (Nukaga, 2006). In Japan, cultural outsiders such as ELTs remain objects of interest. At the same time, Westerners such as U.S. Americans are more welcome than other foreigners. Doi (1981) suggests that cultural outsiders attract curiosity, excitement, suspicion, and/or fear in Japan. In other words, as guests ELTs experience exclusion due to xenophobia, but at the same time they remain objects of interest from a socially distant position.

Situated in the context of English language education in Japan, this study showcases White experiences outside of predominately White countries. As such, we not only highlight Whiteness in a non-U.S. context, but offer insights into how Whiteness intersects with English hegemony and globalization. Our finding of White, celebritized ELT positions suggests that White privilege exists even when Whites are minorities. What is important about this finding is that it demonstrates that Whiteness functions both to privilege and to marginalize white ELTs in Japan. In particular, this study reveals that Whiteness functions dialectically in the form of agency and constraint, or privileged and disadvantaged, within the context of globalization. This is highlighted by the ways in which ELTs experienced their workplace positionality. As teachers, ELTs were not "real teachers," but performed important "teacher-type" roles within the classroom, which led to role confusion from both the ELTs' and JCWs' perspectives.

Overall, ELTs in this study experienced themselves from a celebritized positionality that led them to experience the dialectic of agency and restraint. On the one hand, White ELTs maintained a dominant position due to Western imperialism and English hegemony, which provided them with a great deal of agency in terms of higher social status and access to resources so they could control certain aspects of their situation. On the other hand, ELTs experienced restraints as they were perceived as inadequate teachers who were allowed only limited choices and had to follow the lead of their JCWs. As native English speakers, ELTs were both privileged and treated as individuals with agency and constraint. As the "rightful and legitimate" English language speakers, ELTs were valued within their workplaces. Viewing ELTs as a cultural product puts ELTs in a spotlight in which they have to navigate their front and back stage personas. However, due to their celebritized position, which was exacerbated by Whiteness, they were unable to successfully manage their identities due to occupying the front stage and being in the spotlight for most of their time. In fact, some ELTs in our study reported that their apartment was their only safe back stage area.

Our findings illuminate how discourses of Whiteness, English hegemony, and celebritization put ELTs in ambivalent positions where they experience both agency and constraint. Our study also underscores the importance of examining Whiteness in a global context where Whites are racial/ethnic minorities. Further studies could refine our findings through a variety of qualitative and quantitative methods. Such refinement will only benefit English teaching communities across the world and offer the potential to enhance intercultural training and education. To assist in this endeavor, future research should continue to extend Whiteness theorizing in different countries and additional contexts. In particular, it would be interesting to explore how Whiteness influences students' experiences while learning English. Additionally, the agency–constraint dialectic should be explored in other intercultural contexts, such as privacy management and disclosure, as both areas might influence globalized workplace relationships.

Note

1 A total of 39 ELTs participated in this study: 21 females, 15 males, 1 transgender person, 1 queer-female, and 1 queer-male. They came from seven Western countries: U.S, U.K., Australia, Canada, New Zealand, Romania, and Portugal. Racially and ethnically, 28 identified as white/Caucasian; others identified as Filipino-American, Chinese, Japanese-Romanian-American, Okinawan-American, Vietnamese-French-American, Indian-American, African-American, and Asian-American. The average age of participants was 29.5; ages ranged from 23 to 45 years old. ELTs had worked in Japan for an average of 4.3 years, ranging from eight months to 25 years.

References

Allen, R. L. (2001). The globalization of white supremacy: Toward a critical discourse on the racialization of the world. *Educational Theory, 51*(4), 467–485. doi: 10.1111/j.1741-5446.2001.00467.x

Appadurai, A. (1996). *Modernity at large: Cultural dimensions of globalization*. Minneapolis, MN: University of Minnesota.

Bailey, K. (2007). Akogare, ideology, and "charisma man" mythology: Reflections on ethnographic research in English language schools in Japan. *Gender, Place and Culture, 14*(5), 585–608. doi: 10.1080/09663690701562438

Baumeister, R. F., & Leary, M. R. (1995). The need to belong: Desire for interpersonal attachments as a fundamental human motivation. *Psychological Bulletin, 117*, 497–529. doi: 10.1037/0033-2909.117.3.497

Beasley, W. G. (1995). *The rise of modern Japan: Political, economic and social change since 1850*. New York: St. Martin's Press.

"I never wanted to be famous" 235

Becker, H. (1936). Sociology in Japan. *American Sociological Review, 1*(3), 455–471.

Breckenridge, Y., & Erling, E. J. (2011). The native speaker English teacher and the politics of globalization in Japan. In P. Seargeant (Ed.), *English in Japan in the era of globalization* (pp. 80–100). London: Palgrave Macmillan.

Brody, B. T. (2002). *Opening the Doors: Immigration, Ethnicity, and Globalization in Japan.* New York: Routledge.

Brown, A. H., Cervero, R. M., & Johnson-Bailey, J. (2000). Making the invisible visible: Race, gender, and teaching in adult education. *Adult Education Quarterly, 50*(4), 273–288. doi:10.1177/074171360005000402

Buzzanell, P. M. (2001). Gendered practices in the contemporary workplace: A critique of what often constitutes front page news in the Wall Street Journal. *Management Communication Quarterly, 14*, 517–537.

Chen, Y.-W., Simmons, N., & Kang, D. (2015). "My family isn't racist—however…": Multiracial/multicultural Obama-ism as an ideological barrier to teaching intercultural communication. *Journal of International and Intercultural Communication, 8*(2), 167–186. doi:10.1080/17513057.2015.1025331

Clair, R. P. (1996). The political nature of the colloquialism, "a real job": Implications for organizational socialization. *Communication Monographs, 63*, 249–267. doi: 10.1080/03637759609376392

Collier, M. J. (2009). Contextual negotiation of cultural identifications and relationships: Interview discourse with Palestinian, Israeli, and Palestinian/Israeli young women in a U.S. peace-building program. *Journal of International and Intercultural Communication, 2*(4), 344–368. doi: 10.1080/17513050903177292

Doi, T. (1981). *The anatomy of dependence* (J. Bester, Trans., Rev. ed.). Tokyo: Kodansha.

Frankenburg, R. (1993). *White women, race matters: The social construction of whiteness.* Minneapolis, MN: University of Minnesota Press.

Fujita, Y. (2009). *Cultural migrants from Japan: Youth, media, and migration in New York and London.* Lanham, MD: Lexington Books.

Ganesh, S., Zoller, H., & Cheney, G. (2005). Transforming resistance, broadening our boundaries: Critical organizational communication meets globalization from below. *Communication Monographs, 72*(2), 169–191. doi: 10.1080/03637750500111872

Hashimoto, K. (2007). Japan's language policy and the "lost decade." In A. B. Tsui & J. W. Tollefson (Eds.), *Language policy, culture, and identity in Asian contexts* (pp. 25–36). Mahwah, NJ: Lawrence Erlbaum Associates.

Imahori, T. T., & Cupach, W. R. (2005). Identity management theory: Facework in intercultural relationships. In W. B. Gudykunst (Ed.), *Theorizing about intercultural communication.* (pp. 195–210). Thousand Oaks, CA: Sage.

Jansen, M. B. (2000). *The making of modern Japan.* Cambridge, MA: Harvard University Press.

Jung, Y. H. (2004). Can Japan become "a society attractive for immigrants?" Identity, gender and nation-states under globalization in East Asia. *International Journal of Japanese Sociology, 13*, 53–68. doi: 10.1111/j.1475-6781.2004.00053.x

Kennedy, T. M., Middleton, J. I., & Ratcliffe, K. (2005). Whiteness studies. *Rhetoric Review, 24*(4), 359–402. doi: 10.1207/s15327981rr2404_1

Kobayashi, Y. (2010). Discriminatory attitudes toward intercultural communication in domestic and overseas contexts. *Higher Education, 59*(3), 323–333. doi: 10.1007/s10734-009-9250-9

Kobayashi, Y. (2011). Expanding-circle students learning "standard English" in the outer-circle Asia. *Journal of Multilingual and Multicultural Development, 32*(3), 235–248. doi: 10.1080/01434632.2010.536239

Kobayashi, Y. (2013). Global English capital and the domestic economy: The case of Japan from the 1970s to early 2012. *Journal of multilingual and multicultural development, 34*, 1–13. doi: 10.1080/01434632.2012.712134

Komisarof, A. M. (2001). Different ways of belonging: American Jet Program participants' perceptions of Japanese membership norms. *Human Communication, 4*, 11–30.

Komisarof, A. M. (2006). Facilitating positive acculturation outcomes amongst American sojourners teaching in Japanese schools. *Human Communication, 9*, 37–55.

Kubota, R. (2002). The impact of globalization on language teaching in Japan. In D. Block & D. Cameron (Eds.), *Globalization and language teaching* (pp. 13–28). London: Routledge.

Leonardo, Z. (2002). The souls of white folk: Critical pedagogy, whiteness studies, and globalization discourse. *Race, Ethnicity and Education, 5*(1), 29–50. doi: 10.1080/13613320120117180

McConnell, D. L. (2000). *Importing diversity: Inside Japan's JET program.* Berkeley, CA: University of California Press.

McVeigh, B. (2002). *Japanese higher education as myth.* Armonk, NY: M. E. Sharpe.

Nakayama, T. K., & Krizek, R. L. (1995). Whiteness: A strategic rhetoric. *Quarterly Journal of Speech, 81*, 291–309.

Nakayama, T. K., & Martin, J. N. (Eds.). (1999). *Whiteness: The communication of social identity.* Thousand Oaks, CA: Sage.

Nakayama, T. K., & Martin, J. N. (2007). The "white problem" in intercultural communication research and pedagogy. In L. M. Cooks & J. S. Simpson (Eds.), *Whiteness, pedagogy, performance: Dis/placing race* (pp. 111–137). Lanham, MD: Lexington Books.

Nukaga, M. (2006). Xenophobia and the effects of education: Determinants of Japanese attitudes toward acceptance of foreigners. *Japanese general social surveys, 5*, 191–202. Retrieved November 24, 2016, from http://jgss.daishodai.ac.jp/research/monographs/jgssm5/jgssm5_15.pdf.

Pac, T. (2012). The English-Only movement in the US and the world in the twenty-first century. *Perspectives on Global Development and Technology, 11*(1), 192–210. doi: 10.1163/156914912X620833

Rivers, D. J. (2013). Institutionalized native-speakerism: Voices of dissent and acts of resistance. In S. A. Houghton & D. J. Rivers (Eds.), *Native-speakerism in Japan: Intergroup dynamics in foreign language education* (pp. 75–91). Bristol, UK: Multilingual Matters.

Rivers, D. J., & Ross, A. S. (2013). Idealized English teachers: The implicit influence of race in Japan. *Journal of Language, Identity & Education, 12*(5), 321–339. doi: 10.1080/15348458.2013.835575

Root, E. (2009). "I'm just a foreign teacher doing my job": Ways in which discursive constructions mask an ideology of English in South Korea. *NIDA Journal of Language and Communication, 14*(14), 57–80.

Seargeant, P. (Ed.). (2011). *English in Japan in the era of globalization.* London: Palgrave Macmillan.

Shome, R., & Hegde, R. S. (2002). Culture, communication and the challenge of globalization. *Critical Studies in Media Communication, 19*(2), 172–189. doi: 10.1080/07393180216560

Simmons, N. (2012). The tales of *gaijin*: Health privacy perspectives of foreign English teachers in Japan. *Kaleidoscope: A Graduate Journal of Qualitative Communication Research, 11*, 17–38.

Simmons, N. (2014). My "big" blue health secret: My experience with privacy, or lack thereof, in Japan. *Health Communication, 29*(6), 634–636. doi:10.1080/10410236.2013 .786013

Simmons, N. (2016). (De-)legitimizing medical professional discourses: Evaluations from foreign English teachers in Japan. *Language & Intercultural Communication, 16*(2), 1–18. doi:10.1080/14708477.2015.1113984

Simmons, N. (in press). Cultural discourses of privacy: Interrogating globalized workplace relationships in Japan. *Journal of International and Intercultural Communication.*

Sorrells, K. (2010). Re-imagining intercultural communication in the context of globalization. In T. K. Nakayama & R. T. Halualani (Eds.), *The handbook of critical intercultural communication* (pp. 171–189). Chichester, UK: Wiley-Blackwell.

Tafarodi, R. W., Shaughnessy, S. C., Lee, W. W., Leung, D. Y., Ozaki, Y., Morio, H., & Yamaguchi, S. (2009). Disregard for outsiders: A cultural comparison. *Journal of Cross-Cultural Psychology, 40*(4), 567–583. doi: 10.1177/0022022109335182

Tsetsura, K. (2011). Is public relations a real job? How female practitioners construct the profession. *Journal of Public Relations Research, 23*, 1–23. doi: 10.1080/1062726X.1020.504763

Twenge, J. M., Baumeister, R. F., DeWall, C. N., Ciarocco, N. J., & Bartels, J. M. (2007). Social exclusion decreases prosocial behavior. *Journal of Personality and Social Psychology, 92*, 56–66. doi: 10.1037/0022-3514.92.1.56

Williams, K. D. (2001). *Ostracism: The power of silence.* New York: Guilford Press.

Wray, M. (2006). *Not quite white: White trash and the boundaries of whiteness.* Durham, NC: Duke University Press.

Yamaguchi, T. (2013). Xenophobia in action: Ultranationalism, hate Speech, and the internet in Japan. *Radical History Review, 117*, 98–118. doi: 10.1215/01636545-2210617

Yoshino, K. (2002). English and nationalism in Japan: The role of the intercultural communication industry. In S. Wilson (Ed.), *Nation and nationalism in Japan* (pp. 135–145. London: Routledge Curzon.

Index

affective labor 28–30, 33, 35–8
affective politics 38; of female desire 28; of the feminine 18, 37; of humor and comedy 29
Ahmed, S. 30, 95, 147
Aikoku 216, 221n3
Akan Keisatsu TV show 34
Alexander, B.K. 73, 87–8
Allen, R.L. 225–6
Allison, A. 58
An Jung-geun 123–4
Anderson, B. 27, 178
anti-Korean 114–15; book 118; comments 108–10; demonstrations 123; discourses 111, 120; movements and revisionism 118, 120; net rightists 125; rallies 114, 126; resentment in Japan 117; revisionism 119; sentiment 116–17; wave 119
Arioka, T. 177–8, 180–3
Aspinall, R.W. 212, 216
autoethnographic reflection 18, 73, 83
autoethnography 75–6, 130; queer 74–6
avatars 29, 184

Bailey, K. 225
Bakhtin, M.M. 2, 130
Beasley, W.G. 226
Becker, H.S. 146, 152, 226
Befu, H. 10–11, 13
Bernstein, A. 184
Bleach in Color (popular anime) 18, 87–8, 90, 96; universe 94–5
blue-collar ikumen fathers 62; single women 65
Boylorn, R.M. 73, 75
Breckenridge, Y. 224–5
Burgess, C. 167, 178
bushido (chivalry) 183

Butler, J. 3, 35, 52, 77, 130

Cabinet Office 27, 199
Calafell, B.M. 74–5, 94, 96
carnivorous women 29, 35
Charlebois, J. 18, 58
Chávez, K.R. 74–5, 81, 88
Chen, K.-H. 104, 116
Chen, L. 147, 208
Chen, Y.-W. 20, 226
cherry blossoms 92, 177–8, 180–3, 185; historicization of 19, 184, 186; *see also Someiyoshino*
Chongsindae munje 117
cisgendered male 75, 138
cissexual 78, 82; Asian men 81
citizenship 92, 139; law 170
Cohen, S. 145, 149–50
Collier, M.J. 4, 224
color 210; characters 95; gendered colorism 210; LGBT people 75; male color 80; men of 93; people (gay and lesbian, queer, women) 88; queer of color 18, 87–90; women of 88, 93–4
comfort women 116, 118
community 5, 129–30, 168, 196; building 75; development 161; global 154; international 9, 195, 212; Korean minority Zainichi 114–15, 166; local 64, 227; mixi 160, 164–5; national 15, 146; new-half 77; online 171; organic movement 191, 197–8; policy 200; seken 64
Connell, R.W. 56–9, 67
Conquergood, D. 4, 16
constructions 87; alternative gender 90, 96; gay Asian 82; of gender and sexuality 18, 87–8; male same-sex desire 80; of organic agriculture 193; Orient image

Index 239

135; racial differences 225; of sexual differences 78
constructions of identity 88, 91, 136; Asian US-American 136; cultural and ethnic 147; LGBT 74; national 19
cross-dressing 76, 80; male-to-female (MTF) 77; sex industry worker 14
cyberspace 29

Dale, P.N. 178, 184
Darling-Wolf, F. 15, 74, 96, 146
Dasgupta, R. 55–60
Democratic Party of Japan (DPJ) 201n4
Denoon, D. 1, 13–14
disability 13
disidentifications 75, 88, 90–4, 147
Donahue, R.T. 5, 12, 14–15, 131, 135, 147

earthquake 149, 154; Great Kantō 6, 124–6
Eder, K. 195, 198
education 17, 199, 229; American style systems 217; of children 134; cultural 132; department 215; English language 212–13, 224–5, 227, 231–3; ethnic 7; foreign language 217–18; intercultural 234; internationalization 20, 207, 211, 213–15; Japanese 9, 12, 213, 224–5; Japanese ministry 207, 211–12, 216, 224; law 221n3; policies 211–12; primary and secondary 224; for women 64; see also higher education
education system 7, 9, 177; American higher 218; English language in Japan 225–6, 231, 233; Japanese higher 217, 219
educational 209; internationalization 224; movements and programs 20; strengthening of Japan 6; system 6; training 3
Eguchi, S. 1, 10, 15, 18, 28, 74, 88–9, 96, 136, 146, 208
Ellis, C. 130
Eng, D.L. 74, 88, 95
English language teachers (ELTs) 224–34, 234n1
Eriko, Y. 102, 109
ethnic 79, 123; cross-ethnic cooperation 119; cultural revival 186; diversity 89; education 7; group 9; identities 86–7, 138, 146–8, 161–2, 164, 227; Japanese 226; Korean 114–15, 121–2, 124–6; minorities 13, 163–5, 167–8, 234; purity 132, 137
exclusion 19, 126, 146–7, 154, 163, 166–8,

170–1, 227, 232–3; cultural 231; Korean 122, 124
exclusionary 126; discourse 115; projects 155
exclusive 4, 116, 183, 195; international trade agreements 131; national/cultural boundaries 139

Facebook 30, 159, 168, 172n5
Fairclough, N. 190, 201n2
female caregiver 34, 61, 65–6
female singleness 41, 43–5, 51; non-traditional representations 47; representations 18; traditional construction 42
feminine affective labor 28, 37–8; affective politics 18; Asian men homogenized as 81–2; beauty 92; gender of parenting 60; normative behaviors 35; performance 93, 95; power 48; pursuit of happiness 43; realm of the home 67; the feminine 18, 28, 37–8, 43, 67; unfeminine 64
Frankenberg, R. 209, 219
Fujimoto, E. 6, 11, 210
Fujioka, N. 119, 124–5
Fujita, K. 197
futei senjin 114–15, 124–6

Gannon, M.J. 78–9
gay (gei) 1, 74, 146, 172n9; of color 88; discrimination 148–9; identities 81; men 73; people on television 153; Western/ U.S.American 15, 81–2
Gebser, J. 179, 185
gender 3, 13, 16–17, 30, 65; discourses 55, 57; expression of 45, 52; gender-ambiguous 79; gender-neutral 58, 73; ideologies 32, 62; inequalities 37, 55, 66–7; male-queer 82; norms 29, 31, 33; performance 14–15, 29, 38, 87–8, 90, 94–6; registered 77; relations 18, 31, 33, 37, 55–6, 64–7; stereotypes 31, 33, 95; traditional hierarchy 29, 37
gender construction 93; alternative 90, 96; female 42, 52
gendered 92; aesthetic 73; challenge 64; cisgendered male 75; colorism in Taiwan 210; constructs 89; homogenization 77; identity constructions 91; knowledge 74–5; labor 59; obligations 30; parenting 60; performance 18; politics 28, 37; privilege 65; stereotypes 90; style of speech 80

240　*Index*

gender identities 28–9, 38, 78, 90, 92, 95; disorder (GID) 38n1
gender roles 18, 27, 35–6, 42, 53, 61, 64, 107; practices 66, 74, 83; unorthodox division of labor 61
Gilbert, J.R. 31–3, 38
Goode, E. 145, 151
Gotei 13 93–5
Graburn, N. 4, 6–11, 13–16, 131–2
Great Kantō Earthquake 6, 124–6
Greenbaum, A. 28, 30
Guthman, J. 191

Haglund, E. 7, 131
Hall, E.T. 12
Hallyu 104, 114, 120
Halualani, R.T. 4, 178–80, 186
Hambleton, A. 8, 13, 15–16, 132, 147
Han, C.W. 81–2
hannichi (anti-Japan) 19, 116, 119–22, 124, 126; *kenkan* 117–18; narratives 125; nationalism 121
Hardt, M. 28, 30
Hasegawa, K. 194, 200
Hashimoto, K. 212–14, 216, 232
Hayashi, C. 177–8, 183
hegemonic masculinity 55–60, 62–4, 82; cultivation of 65–6; reformulation of 67
herbivorous men 29, 35, 58
heterogeneity 2–3, 16–17, 107, 137, 155, 220
heteronormative 78, 80; environment 31; femininity and masculinity 29; gender roles 18; happiness 36; Japanese masculinity 77; marriage 14, 38, 41; masculine workplace 89
heteropatriarchal 16, 78, 80; gender relations 37; imaginary 77; needs of the culture industry 83
heterosexuality 75, 77
heterosexuality–homosexuality 77
Hidaka, T. 55–6, 59, 89
higher education 11; American 218; English language 219; internationalization 207, 211–13, 218–19; Japanese 217; U.S. 28
Higuchi 115, 118, 122
Hiratsuka, A. 177, 181
historical revisionism 115, 118, 121–2, 125
Holman Jones, S. 74, 76
homogeneity 2–3, 11–12, 17, 107, 137; of Japan 4–6, 8–9, 14, 16, 19, 89, 95, 148, 178
homogenization 5, 11, 16, 19, 190, 220;

competing 6; cultural 18, 108, 111; gendered and sexualized 77; of Japan 101, 105–7, 112, 132; of Japan and Korea 109, 111; by organic agriculture movement 192, 198; process of economic globalization 191
homogenized 9, 18, 77–8, 81, 83, 101, 107, 110–11, 131, 155, 200
homosexuality 77, 80
Horie, M. 211–13
Horiuchi, T. 146–7
Hu, K. 102–4, 232
Huang, F. 211
Huang, S. 101–4, 106, 108
Hudson, M.J. 1, 178
hybridism 19, 137; strategic 102, 129, 138–40; theoretical cross-fertilization with Orientalism 130
hybridity 86, 137, 179
hyperfeminine performance 95; hyper-feminized 14; hyper-femininity 37

identity co-optation 109–11
ikumen (caregiving fathers) 55, 58, 60–3, 66–7; strong 61–2; weak 66
imagined boundary 166; of Japan 19
immigration 1, 13; law 11, 139, 209
Immigration Control and Refuge Certification Act 11
inclusion 19, 146, 166; discourses 167–8, 170; of gender performances 95; in Japanese national identity 148; Korean 124; national 126; politics of 163, 171
inclusive 4, 17, 116, 119, 125, 200; gender 73
inclusiveness 17–19, 121
intercultural communication 86, 208, 224; critical 4, 74, 111, 178, 180; critical scholars 146, 171; interactions 225; queer 74; research projects 12; scholars 140
Internet 86, 120, 159, 165; anonymous discussion boards 115; enabled mobile phones 160, 162; Japanese 166; menu-driven sites 162; users and activists 125
interpassive 18, 30; consumption 31–4, 36
interpassivity 28–30, 33, 35–6
Ishihara, S. 19, 74, 145–55
Ishii-Kuntz, M. 60, 62
Itagaki, R. 115–16, 118, 121, 124
Iwabuchi, K. 13, 15–16, 20, 86, 96, 101–4, 108–10, 129, 137, 150

J-pop (Japanese popular culture) 101, 104,

107–8, 112, 112n1; icon 103; pushes and pulls of 111; in Taiwan 18, 102, 105–6, 109

J-pop and K-pop 101–2, 105–6; consumption of 108–9; cultural images represented 111; pushes and pulls 18, 111

Jansen, M.B. 226

Japanese female comedians 18, 28, 30–3, 38

Japanese male-queer 74; bars 82; cultures 79–80; femininity 18, 77, 82–3

Japanese Ministry of Education, Culture, Sports, Science, and Technology (MEXT) 207, 209, 211–13, 215–16, 218, 221n3, 221n4, 224; standards of internationalization 214

Japanese Society for History Textbook Reform 119–20, 124

Japanese youth 11; xenophobic nationalism 119

Japan's internationalization 1, 4, 7–8, 11–13, 16–17, 19–20, 129–32, 134, 137, 140, 207–10, 217, 220; in education 211–14, 218–19, 224; *see also kokusaika*

Japan–U.S. relations 89

JOAA (Japan Organic Agriculture Association) 192–4, 196–8, 200

Johnson, E.P. 74–5, 88

Jones, S.H. 74, 76, 130

josei dorama (female dramas) 18, 42–3, 45, 52

K-pop (Korean popular culture) 108–9, 112; cultural images represented 111; pushes and pulls of 111; in Taiwan 101–2, 104–6

Kadokawa 151

Kanemitsu, D. 145, 150–2

Kang, L.H. 89

Kase, H. 118

Kawano, S. 57, 62, 64–5, 67

kenkan (hating Korea) 19, 114–20, 122–4, 126

Kimura, A.H. 199, 201

Kinefuchi, E. 89, 96, 179

Kobayashi, Y. 225, 231, 233

kokusaika (internationalization) 7, 9, 12–13, 15, 19, 131–2, 139–40

Korean 1, 117, 126; anticolonial 123; comfort women 116, 118; culture 101, 108–9, 112, 114, 120, 122; government 106; independence movement 124;

language 217; language schools 166; malcontents 114–15, 123–4; Peninsula 1, 184; people 125; pro- and anti-Korean comments 108–11, 114; people 115–16, 118–19, 122; schools 211; subversives (*futei senjin*) 114; wave 103–4, 110–11, 120; *Zainichi* minority 114–15, 121, 166

Kraidy, M.M. 137

Kramer, E.M. 178–9

Kudo, M. 45, 124–5

Lee, W. 4, 74–5, 210, 233

Leonardo, Z. 225–6

Leung, L.Y.M. 102, 104

Levine, L. 152

LGBT (lesbian-gay-bisexual-transgender) people 77; of color 75; identities 74; promotion of equal rights 74

LGBTQ (lesbian-gay-bisexual-transgender-queer) people 1, 14–15, 172n9

Liberal Democratic Party (LDP) 200, 201n4

loser dogs 14

Lu, A.S. 86–7, 90

Ma, S.-M. 129–30, 135–6, 140

Macdonald, G. 1–2, 8, 12–14, 17, 132

Macfie, A.L. 129

Maeda, E. 14, 42, 48, 52

male breadwinner 55, 65–7

male-queer 82; bars 82; cultures 79–80; femininity 18, 77, 82–3

manga (comic books) 19, 29, 101–3, 106, 165; fans and creators of 146; government restrictions 145, 150–1; *Kenkanryu* 115, 119–22; moral panic 19, 148–9, 152; publishers 153; series 44, 87; sexually explicit content 154; social shaming fans 153

Maree, C. 14, 73, 80

marginalization 14, 122; marginalizing Others 3

marginalized 74–5, 88; cultural groups 16; groups 32, 147, 153, 172n9; identities 41; Others 16, 96; positionalities 90; subjectivities 28

marriage 32, 42–5, 48–51, 57, 63, 65; declining rates 37, 64; desire for 35, 37–8; heteronormative duty 14, 38, 41; institutionalized 52; lack of 36, 66; patriarchal institution 33, 36–7; practical 50–1, 53

242 *Index*

Martin, J.N. 2–4, 191, 208–9, 224–5
Martinez, D.P. 10, 134
massacre of Koreans 6, 124–5
Masugata, T. 192, 197
Matsuko Deluxe 18, 73–4, 76, 78, 83
McConnell, D.L. 224
McCormack, G. 1, 5–6, 12–14, 118, 131
McIntosh, P. 209, 219
Mecha Mecha Iketeru 32, 34
Melucci, A. 201n1
menu-driven 168; demographic
    information 167; Internet sites 162; mixi
    163, 172n9
Messerschmidt, J.W. 55–6, 59–60, 65–7
Mickunas, A. 179–80, 185–6
Min, Y.S. 29
Ministry of Internal Affairs and
    Communications 13, 172n5
Mitsuhashi, J. 14, 77
mixi (Japanese social network site) 19,
    159–71, 172n2, 172n5, 172n9; friends
    162, 165; interface 159–60, 162–4,
    166–7, 170–1
Mizukoshi, K. 60–1
Moon, D.G. 4, 146
Morean, B. 178
Morris-Suzuki, T. 1, 115, 126
Muhr, S.L. 30
multiculturalism 4, 11, 14, 16, 20, 208–9,
    213–15; backlash against 120; cosmetic
    126; promoting 220
Muñoz, J.E. 74–6, 83, 88, 91–2, 147

Nakamura, A. 13, 162, 167–8
Nakano, L.Y. 64–5, 67
Nakatani, A. 58, 60
Nakayama, T.K. 2–4, 89, 146, 178–80,
    186, 191, 208–9, 219, 224–5
National Institute of Population and Social
    Security Research 13, 27
Nemoto, K. 46–7, 52, 57, 64–6
new-half (Mr Lady) 77, 81; *see also*
    okama
Nihei, C. 29, 35
Nitobe, I. 183, 186n2
Nogawa, M. 115, 117
non-governmental organizations (NGOs) 11
non-heteronormative 15; sexualities 14;
    sexual minoritarians 75
non-Western 102; countries 208–9,
    217–18; cultures 220; nations 219;
    subordination 82; world 9, 132

Ogawa, K. 178, 182–4

OgawaM. 115, 117, 185
Oguma, E. 10, 27, 114
Ohnuki-Tierney, E. 15, 177–9, 181–4,
    186
okama 77–8, 80, 82–3
Okano, K. 1, 7, 9, 14, 17, 131
Okubo Kayoko 30–1, 35, 37; Okubo
    Kayoko no Moteru Tekunikku 35
onē-kei 79; *kotoba* (queeny language)
    76–7; talent 18, 73–4, 76–7, 79, 82–3
Onishi, N. 6, 104, 108, 119, 131
organic agriculture 193, 196, 198, 200;
    community 191; development 194;
    discourse 19; initiatives 195; movement
    190–2; Organic Law 197; organization
    192; standardization 195, 197; *Zenyukyo*
    initiative 201n5; *see also* JOAA
oriental 16, 135, 137
Orientalism 16, 82, 95, 130, 135–7,
    139–40; global 129; self-Orientalism 96;
    US American 19
Othering 18, 130, 134–5, 139, 153
Otherness 17–19
Others/Other 28–30, 77–8, 129, 135, 166;
    cissexual Asian men 81; cultural 11–13,
    19, 107–8; excluded 146, 148, 154;
    external/internal 147–9; marginalized 3,
    16; oppressed 17; outside social norms
    152; silent 137
Otmazgin, N. 102–3, 108–9
Otsuki, T. 115, 120

patriarchal 33, 37; dominance 95;
    ideologies 27; institution of marriage
    36; Japanese society 28; order of the
    Gotei 13 94–5; social norms 18; society
    94; system 210; *see also*
    heteropatriarchal
Pensoneau-Conway, S.L. 130
performance 3, 17, 59, 83; comedic 33, 35,
    37; cultural 86, 91, 136; of
    disidentification 93; interpassive
    consumption of desire and purity 32;
    LGBT 74; of Orientalism 81; queered
    18; of queerness 74, 78, 80–1; of
    salaryman masculinity 89; at school
    229; of social conformity 79; stand-up
    comedy 30; in the workplace 230
performance of femininity 18, 28, 31, 36,
    38, 95; hyper 73; male-queer 77
performance of gender 29, 38, 87, 90,
    94–6; homogeneous 14; non-
    heteronormative 15
performance of identity 92;

hypermasculine 93; intersectional 75, 87; Japanese 88, 90; national 129, 132
postcolonial 115; India 209; Japan 19, 74; Korean identity 119, 122; *Zainichi* Korean 114
professional women 55, 64, 66
pushes and pulls 1; of J-pop and K-pop 18, 101, 105, 111, 131

queer 234n1; autoethnography 74–6; cissexual Japanese subjectivity 82; cultural representations of men 77; cultures 81; futurity 91–2, 94; intercultural communication 74; Japanese men 15; LGBTQ population 172n9; male talent 79–80; performance 80–1; relational ambiguity 90; relational dynamics 96; theory 75–6, 88, 147; visibility 73; worldlessness 83
queer of color 18; critique 87–8, 90; theory 88–9
queered performances 18
queerness 17–18, 78–9, 83, 88, 147; discriminations and prejudices 80; Japanese male 74
queers 75, 80; male 77

racial 90, 163; constructions 2, 225; discrimination 147–8; diversity 95; identities 161–2, 164, 168, 227–8, 230, 234n1; inter-racial citizens 13; minorities 89, 164–5, 167–8, 234; otherness 94; post-racial society 209–10; privileges 225; purity 132; threat to national homogeneity 148; violence 210
racialized 93, 228; bodies 92; explicit rejection 122; gender stereotypes 95; identity constructions 91; knowledge of gender 74–5; Other 28
representations of female singleness 18; non-traditional 47
revisionism 115, 118, 121–2; anti-Korean 119–20; early post-Cold War 119; neo-revisionism 125
revisionist 119, 124; history 120, 123; narratives 118, 125; nationalists 123
Rivers, D.J. 225–6
Roberts, G. 57, 63, 66
Root, E. 225
Rosenberger, N. 43, 47–8, 51–3, 64
Ruh, B. 151
Ryang, S. 6, 8, 124
Ryoo, W. 103–4

Said, E.W. 16, 81, 95, 129, 135, 137, 178
Sakamoto, R. 115, 120–1
Sakurai, M. 114, 125–6
salaryman masculinity 56–60, 62, 89
same-sex 82; cultures 81; desire 14, 78, 80
Sanchanta, M. 150, 153
Sato, T. 177–8, 180–1
Satsuka, S. 10, 132, 137
Schilling, M. 8, 132
Schrag, C.O. 3, 130
Seargeant, P. 212, 224, 226
Sekimoto, S. 10, 18, 147, 179
sengyô shufu (professional full-time housewife) 55, 57, 64
sexuality 13–14, 16–18, 35, 37, 74, 78, 83, 87–8, 95, 164–5, 168, 170, 208
Shibuichi, D. 115, 118
Shim, D. 103–4, 106
Shirahata, Y. 181
Shome, R. 4, 209, 224
Simmons, N. 20, 224, 226
single life 18, 44–5
single women 32, 43, 47, 53, 55, 63–4, 66–7; career-focused 52; loser dogs 14; white-collar or blue-collar 65
SNS (social network site) 159–61, 165, 168–9, 171, 172n2
Someiyoshino 177–8, 180–1, 185–6
Sorrells, K. 171–2, 179, 186, 224
South Korea 102–5, 109–11, 114–17, 120; anticolonial resistance 123; international students 211; *see also* Korea
South Korean 116, 120–1; critics of Japan 123; newspaper reports 117; politics and society 118; *see also* South Korean
Statistics Bureau, Ministry of Internal Affairs and Communications 13
stigmatized 14, 41, 75; unmarried women 18, 32
Straubhaar, J.D. 102, 109
Suganuma, K. 1, 8, 10, 15, 74, 81–2, 132
Sugimoto, Y. 64, 178
Sunderland, J. 57, 65–6

Tabeta, M. 192
Tachibanaki, T. 57, 60
Tajima, R. 89
Takashima, N. 216, 221n3
Tanaka, A. 116–17
Tanaka, H. 199
Tanaka, S. 90, 96
teikei 194, 197–8, 201; farmers 199; groups 196; non-teikei consumer movements 198

244 *Index*

terrorist 123–4
terrorists 122–3, 125; *see also futei senjin*
TOEFL (Test of English as a Foreign Language) 214, 217, 221n5
TOEIC (Test of English for International Communication) 217
Tokyo international anime fair 153–4
Tourism Bureau of Taiwan 103
Toyosaki, S. 6, 10–11, 17, 19, 28, 78–9, 89, 96, 111, 129–30, 133, 210
Traditional Japanese poetry: An anthology 186n1
transgender 74, 78, 234n1; cross-dressing performance 77
transsexual 29, 78
Trent, J.W. 14
Tsuda, Y. 28, 209, 217, 219–20
Twitter 159

U.S. (United States) 10, 73–5, 79, 111; American products 103; Americans 233; anime 87; armed forces 164; comedy 31; consumption 96; cultural products 47; dominance in Japanese politics 200; fans 86; gay imperialism 81–2; higher education 28; imports 8; Japan–U.S. relations 89; media 93; occupation 164, 211; otaku 87, 89; perceptions of Japanese 88; social network services (Facebook) 159, 169; State Department 145; viewers 92

Wander, P.C. 208–9, 219
Warren, J.T. 3, 36, 209
Washington, M. 89, 93
Watanabe, M. 148, 184–5
white-collar 63; executive transnational business masculinity 56; professional

women 55; salaryman 62, 89; salarywomen 66; single women 65
whiteness 2, 20, 111, 208, 210, 228, 230, 233–4; dominance of 209, 226; functions of 75; invisibility of 209, 219, 225; power 134; scholarship 225
Whitsed, C. 213
Wilson, S. 8–9, 132, 135
women 66; blue-collar 65; career-focused 52; loser dogs 14; professional 55, 64, 66; single 32, 43, 47, 53, 55, 63–4, 66–7; unmarried, stigmatized 18, 32; white-collar 66

xenophobia 115, 117, 119, 124, 226–7, 232–3
xenophobic 121, 209; group 126; nation 226; nationalism 114, 119; nationalist movements 115; political movements 125; practices 232; revisionism 122

Yamada, Y. 177–8, 182
Yamaguchi, T. 115, 118, 226
Yamano, S. 115, 119, 121–2
Yasuda, K. 115, 125–6, 193–4
Yasuda, S. 193–4
Yep, G.A. 2, 4, 74
Yoshino, K. 15–16, 167, 170, 233

Zachmann, U.M. 210
Zainichi Korean minority 1, 9, 114–15, 121, 126, 163, 166, 171
Zainichi Tokken o Yurusanai Shimin no Kai see Zaitokukai
Zaitokukai (Citizens's Association against Privileges for Resident Foreigners) 114–15, 122–3, 125
Zenyukyo initiative 197, 201n5
Žižek, S. 28–30